Hardest Times
The Trauma of Long Term Unemployment

Thomas J. Cottle

Westport, Connecticut
London

Cottle, Thomas J.
  Hardest times : the trauma of long term unemployment / Thomas J. Cottle.
    p. cm.
  Includes bibliographical references (p.) and index.
  ISBN 0-275-96984-3 (alk. paper)
  1. Unemployed—United States—Psychology—Case studies. 2. Hard-core unemployed—
United States—Psychology—Case studies. 3. Unemployed—United States—Interviews. 4.
Hard-core unemployed—United States—Interviews. I. Title.
HD5708.C68 2001
331.13'7'019—dc21   00-032373

British Library Cataloguing in Publication Data is available.

Library of Congress Catalog Card Number: 00-032373
ISBN: 0-275-96984-3

First published in 2001

Praeger Publishers, 88 Post Road West, Westport, CT 06881
An imprint of Greenwood Publishing Group, Inc.
www.praeger.com

Printed in the United States of America

The paper in this book complies with the
Permanent Paper Standard issued by the National
Information Standards Organization (Z39.48-1984).

10 9 8 7 6 5 4 3 2 1

For Luke Thomas Hinz, Nicole Kate Hinz,
Anna Carey Hinz, and those who might follow.

Contents

Preface

About ten years ago, I received a phone call late in the evening. It was from a woman, who along with her husband and me, had enjoyed many conversations about a host of matters, not the least of which was his unemployment history, at the time in its third year. Unlike many families I have come to know doing research on unemployment, Alfred and Bernice Syre, people in their fifties, spoke openly and forthrightly about their lives. They had no problem conversing about Alfred's unemployment and his bladder illness, which both alleged had been caused by his not working. They spoke as well of Bernice's good fortune in the labor market, so some of their stories contained silver linings.

There wasn't a thing I couldn't ask the Syres, and not a subject, moreover, that Alfred himself did not broach. If I wished to explore physical symptoms, mood swings, fantasies, sexual behavior, or the lack of it more likely, this was the couple to ask. It always appeared that Alfred and Bernice had made a successful adjustment to Alfred's inability to regain regular employment. His spirits rose and fell, but he always claimed to be optimistic; something good, he insisted, would eventually come his way. More important, he appeared reasonably content with the adjustments he had made in his life. If Bernice were to continue as the family's breadwinner, then so be it. They would be all right.

Then came the telephone call on a freezing January night. Bernice, screaming hysterically into the phone, finally had to give way and allow her sister to explain that Alfred had driven his car into an abutment. A driver with an excellent record, Alfred's death surely could have been considered an accident, but none of the Syres' friends could conclude anything other than that he had killed himself. The death had come without warning, without the slightest hint that he was depressed. When she got back on the phone, Bernice, barely able to calm herself, said she was convinced that Alfred had given up from the despair of being unemployed.

It was the first time Bernice had ever spoken in this manner. She honestly believed Alfred had "moved beyond it." He had never lied to her, and she always had been on target when reading his emotions. Besides, she said, apologizing for awakening me, "How could this unemployment thing keep eating away at him? It's already more than two and half years!" But we both knew it had. We both believed not working had taken bites out of Alfred's intestine and bladder. All three of us, perhaps, had denied the toll unemployment had taken on him. Beneath the occasional good cheer and expressed optimism, Alfred was a broken man. If nothing else, his illness revealed that much. Neither Bernice nor I spoke for long minutes. Then, suddenly, I heard her cry out for her husband, and the phone went dead.

It was during the weeks following the funeral of Alfred Harris Syre, a ceremony attended by hundreds of mourners, that I made plans to focus on long-term unemployed men and women, people out of work for longer than six months, the term officially demarcating what is called "very long-term unemployment," or the period following the cessation of unemployment insurance compensation. Alfred and Bernice Syre's history consequent to Alfred's layoff from a midwestern corporation that had closed its only New England factory, reminded me that the stories of these men and women rarely get told. In most instances, no one but their families and closest friends know the stories, or care to hear them. For six months following the loss of a job, a person stays on the welfare rolls, and thus remains as part of the country's official unemployment statistics. After six months of being out of work, with benefits terminated, the person may no longer believe that he or she is even a statistic, and in fact, he or she isn't.

Unemployment stories touched me for another reason. Many years ago when I was very young and just beginning to understand what my own father, a physician, did for a living, I came to believe that if one's work didn't deal somehow with life-and-death issues, it couldn't be considered all that important. Childish, of course, I imagine that more than a few doctors' children develop this opinion that mothers or fathers get paid for saving lives.

Not all social science enterprises, obviously, focus on life-and-death issues, nor should they. Yet unemployment appears to have a different quality of life-and-death import to it. Unless one confronts it directly, it is difficult to observe how powerfully it hits a man or woman, and how it can take a person to the brink, and then shove him or her over. For many people, long-term unemployment truly constitutes the hardest times.

There is, of course, mystery to unemployment stories, which no one told better than James Agree and Walker Evans in *Let us All Now Praise Famous Men*. No one knows for certain how a particular man or woman will respond to being fired, they themselves cannot predict with certainty how they will react. No one can say, moreover, how stripping a person from his or her job begins to affect the person's body or mind. Why, for example, would unemployment make people contemplate suicide, or cause them to run away from their spouses and children? Watching cases of unemployed workers unfold, one often imagines one is witnessing a person's spirit being shredded. Jack Blum, a thirty-eight-year-old man who is introduced in chapter 7, once remarked, "I'm alive but I'm not living. I'm going nowhere so fast you can't even see me move. But I'm moving. To nowhere."

I have focused attention in this volume on stories of men out of work. This focus should not be interpreted, however, as a disinterest in the stories of long-term unemployed women and the profound meanings unemployment has for them as well. If work is a central feature in the development of a man's identity and sense of personal satisfaction, a theme explored later on, then it is for women as well, but this exploration is reserved for another volume.

In the following chapters, none of the stories has been dramatically contrived and all events have been recorded as accurately as possible. From the outset, the families understood their roles in this research and acknowledged that should I witness some scene, I may well include it in the final account if it seems relevant and appropriate. These moments, along with all the other material appearing in the book, are approved for publication by the families.

Throughout the years, I have assisted the unemployed in landing jobs, any jobs they believe will pull them out of what they deem their dangerous circumstances. I have worked as well to locate support groups and when appropriate psychological counseling. In some cases, we have met with some success. The following chapters include accounts, however, of efforts with workers undertaken over years, which, to say the least, have proved profoundly discouraging.

The present state of the social sciences is such that in undertaking research, one must, I think, be especially careful to select areas of inquiry that have intellectual substance and merit, and at the same time relevance to the well-being of women and men. The promise of the social sciences always has been the investigation of crucial aspects of the human condition, both contemporary and historical, in an effort to inform a society and, ideally, to enhance the members of that society. If the stories collected in this book are successful, they should not only inform, they should remind us that life and death are the foundations of the humanistic inquiry. They should help us as well to understand and appreciate the society and culture that we ourselves construct, perpetuate, and hold in our minds, and make us wonder whether we have done all that we can for ourselves and for one another.

In this context, Billy Librandt, a sixty-year-old laborer out of work for more than three years, once remarked:

> You keep asking whether I'm sick of talking about being unemployed. Well, sometimes I am and sometimes I'm not. Sometimes I think I'm getting adjusted to the whole thing, which bothers me no end. But then you come along and I sort of have to "unadjust," if you know what I mean. You make me think about it. It's painful, but it's something I gotta do. I can't sit still. I gotta fight it.

> But now, if you could pull a few strings, I think I could also get myself adjusted to working again too. Fact is, if you could do that for me, or put me in touch with someone who might help, I think I could tell you a couple of things I never told anyone about these last years. Set me up. It doesn't have to be a great deal, and I'll feel more like a man on his feet, which will make it easier for me to sound, you know, not so strong, but not all that bad. I don't mean this as a bribe, it's no deal I'm cooking up here. I'd just like to be a man again, and let you see the devil in me, knowing I wouldn't be less in anyone's eyes, yours or mine. Well, I guess especially mine.

In the end, whatever the conditions of conducting research on such a delicate matter as unemployment, one personal thought remains: I hope that my friendships with the families matter to them. I know that on more than one occasion I intruded on people generous enough to speak with me during their hardest times. I hope that the opportunity to speak about whatever they wished, and tell whatever stories they needed to tell, may have proved helpful to these men, women, and children. I pray that in some of the lives with whom I made contact, our conversations might have made a bit of difference, both in practical and spiritual terms. Like the culture itself, I know that at times I failed some of these men and their families. I hope they may forgive me or, in those certain cases where there will be no further conversations and no further stories, forgave me.

Acknowledgments

There are quite a few people to be thanked for their invaluable contributions to this project and ultimately the publication of this volume. First, is a group of scholars at Boston University, notably my colleagues in the Special Education Department: Professors Arthur Beane, Leroy Clinton, Donna Lehr, Rose Ray, Kathleen Vaughan, the late Frank Garfunkel, and above all Gerald Fain. In addition, Deans Edwin J. Delattre, Joan Dee, and Boyd Dewey, and Professors Allan Gaynor, Roselmina Indrisano, Bruce Fraser, Victor Kestenbaum, Mary Shann, and David Steiner have all been terribly helpful and generous. Finally, there are my many students, people devoting their lives to the well-being of children and families, and willing to undertake the study that this work requires.

Professors Sara Lawrence Lightfoot, Robert Coles, Robert Melson, Gerald Platt, Jan Dizard, Oliver Holmes, and Robert Weiss are not only wonderful friends, they happen to be wonderful readers offering superb counsel. In this same regard, I want to thank Anne and Richard Rosenfeld, David and Judy Lahm, Anne and Martin Peretz, Salvador and Patricia Minuchin, Paul Strudler, and Brigitte Cazalis and Joseph Collins.

At the press, Suzanne I. Staszak-Silva is the sort of editor every writer treasures. She is as efficient as she is encouraging, as thoughtful as she is supportive.

Finally there are two sets of families. First, my own, which all of us agree has Kay eternally at the center. Our children, Claudia, Tony, Jason, and Sonya, have now been joined by three grandchildren, Luke Thomas, and Nicole Kate, and Anne Carey. My parents and Kay's parents are no longer alive, but they remain with all of us, always.

Second, there are the families of the men whose words appear in this book, as well as those families with whom I have spoken whose stories will remain for another volume. How does one ever thank these people, properly communicate condolences, adequately befriend them? It goes without saying that there is no book without them, and that my own life, as is the case with most all researchers undertaking this sort of enterprise, is defined in great measure by them. I always use the same words as I close this part of the acknowledgments: I just hope they approve.

I'm a monster. And I'm good for nothing. You have to be a worn out old alcoholic like Pásha in order to think I'm still worth something. God, how I hate myself. I hate myself with a passion. I hate the sound of my voice, my footsteps, my hands, these clothes, the things I keep thinking . . . Funny, isn't it? And depressing. Less than a year ago I still felt fine. I was strong, I was full of energy, I worked hard, I could do anything with these hands . . . I could talk . . . I could cry when I saw others suffering; I got upset and angry at the presence of evil. I knew what inspiration meant; I knew the joy and poetry of those long, quiet nights when you sit working, or sit and let dreams crowd your brain. I had faith; I could look straight into the future as if into my own mother's eyes . . . And now— oh, my God. I'm worn out, I've lost my faith, I spend days and nights doing nothing. My hands and feet, my brain, they're no longer part of me. . . . I have no future; nothing moves me; my soul sinks at the thought of tomorrow . . . I'm a complete coward. I'm ashamed, I'm so ashamed! . . What's the matter with me? What is this bottomless pit I'm hurling myself into? What's the matter with my nerves? . . . I lose my temper, I yell, I don't recognize myself . . .

—From Ivánov by Anton Chekov

Introduction

Work could cure almost anything, I believed then and I believe now.
— Ernest Hemingway, "A Moveable Feast"

I've never worked and I can't imagine not working.
— College student

Simon Weil, the twentieth-century theologian, once said, "The only real question to be asked of another is 'What are you going through?'"
— Cited in Judith Handelsman, *Growing Myself*. New York: Dutton, 1996

Telling about things is the one way we learn to live with them, and those of us who don't tell or talk about our own stories are the ones who have trouble grappling.
— Lois Lowry, *The Boston Sunday Globe*, December 20, 1998, p. 11.

NARRATIVES OF UNEMPLOYMENT

This book is about men who no longer work, not because they don't need to, not because they don't wish to, nor because they are unable to, but because they cannot find gainful employment. Men out of work for more than six months, which means they no longer receive insurance benefits or compensation, are labeled by the government as long-term unemployed. After losing their jobs, many of these men have spent months, if not years, seeking re-employment, but now some have given up their hunt for jobs and any hope of ever finding work, despite their desperate need for money. Most labor investigations, as William Julius Wilson pointed out, consider these people to be out of the labor force.[1]

It goes without saying, as the writings of Robert Heilbroner, Jeremy Rifkin, and Marie Jahoda[2] make plain, that unemployment has profound economic implications for a man and his family. The recent writings of Wilson, Rifkin, Summers, and Hacker attest to this point.[3] In the popular press as well, one repeatedly hears of unemployed families selling their belongings and homes, or being suffocated in the bureaucratic mazes of welfare, employment, and insurance offices. Although it is often said that we never appreciate something until we lose it, the men whose stories fill this book knew full well how important their jobs were long before they lost them.

The story of long-term unemployment begins with the inability to gain re-employment, an inability to reconnect with the job market, the focus of Mark Granovetter's important research aptly titled *Getting a Job*.[4] It involves a host of other significant matters as well. A person's sense of worth is called into question, political and religious attitudes as well as feelings about one's country come to be reassessed. Unemployment makes one redefine one's sense of masculinity or femininity. It raises issues of shame, guilt, and esteem, just as it affects one's physical and mental health.[5] It turns people against their spouses, parents, children, and neighbors. In many instances it turns a person against him- or herself.[6] In the most perplexing manner, it demands that people devise new philosophies of living that either justify their struggle to survive or terminate their life. It is not melodramatic to state that the effect on many long-term unemployed people is so wounding, they are forced not merely to seek alternative sources of income but alternative ways of living. And, after months or years without being able to find any work, some will decide to end their lives.

Presently, 4.5 percent of the U. S. labor force is without work, this in comparison to an unemployment rate of 7.8 percent only five years ago. Compare these numbers with the 11.8 unemployment rate in Germany, the 12.5 unemployment rate in France, and the 13.1 rate in Belgium.[7] In states like Massachusetts, the unemployment rate has fallen over the last years to some 3.5 percent, a full 1 percent below the national rate. In fact, unemployment rates are lower than they have been in twenty-five years. Across the board, some of the employment figures coming out of the Current Population Survey of the Bureau of Labor Statistics, are rather remarkable, especially given recent historical trends.[8]

Approximately 131 million Americans were working in the autumn of 1999, which represents an increase of almost 30 million workers in just fifteen years.[9] Almost everywhere one looks, new businesses have started up and, older ones have expanded. The computer industry alone has seen a doubling in the number of jobs in barely a decade. Similarly, since the mid-1980s, America has witnessed almost a tripling of jobs in health care industries. In October 1999, nonfarm payroll employment rose by 310,000. In the previous month it had risen by only 41,000.[10] Economists point to at least three reasons for these encouraging numbers: First, the Federal Reserve Board has managed to keep interest rates down without causing an increase in inflation; indeed we are learning that unemployment rates can go down without causing serious increases in inflation.[11] Second, the deregulation of hidebound industries has produced more jobs. Finally, the Clinton administration in particular opened a host of new markets throughout the globe. And dare one even mention what has happened over the last few years on Wall Street?

Now some of the discouraging news regarding the labor market, of the sort that Joel Blau and Kathryn Marie Dudley described.[12] To begin, although in historical terms these aforementioned numbers and rates may seem low, they are likely to be underestimations. Almost all official employment and unemployment figures are derived from so-called Household Surveys, which means that researchers actually go to people's homes or more likely telephone them. It is easy to see where the poorer the neighborhood, the more likely estimations of unemployment will be inaccurate. Similarly, one wonders whether people out of work in so-called middle-class and affluent communities will admit to being out of work or give a full accounting of their employment status to strangers conducting surveys over the telephone.[13]

Although they seem low, the unemployment figures point to millions of people out of work. As sociologist Kai Erikson observed, there is good reason to believe that unemployment is on the rise, along with "an increase in jobs with poor pay, low benefits, and dim prospects."[14] Confirming this observation is a 1998 Christmas time report on workers who had been laid off or furloughed:

> [R]oughly 600,00 American workers have been furloughed in 1998, which some labor analysts say will set a layoff record for this decade. It is a record that is being aided mainly by bad economies overseas, and partly by the end of a taboo against trimming payrolls just when people are trimming their trees.[15]

In October 1999, around six million Americans were officially listed as being unemployed. This figure normally is composed of so-called job losers, job leavers, and people who have completed temporary employment. Adult men, adult women, and Whites generally all revealed a 3.5 unemployment rate during that month. Teenagers, in contrast, showed a rate of almost 14 percent, whereas African-Americans were listed as having a rate of 8.3 percent, and Hispanics 6.4.[16] Now comes an additional 1.2 million out-of-work persons who, according to the Bureau of Labor Statistics are labeled *marginally attached to the labor force* inasmuch as they wanted jobs, had actually searched for jobs during the prior year, but were not counted as officially being unemployed because, for one reason or another, they reported that they had ceased hunting for employment during the four weeks prior to the survey. Of this group of so-called marginal workers, almost 300,000 were officially designated as *discouraged workers*. Believing there were no jobs to be had, they had declined searching for employment. These are the so-called hidden unemployed, workers who may never again seek re-employment, workers whom André Gorz was right perhaps to call the "non-class of non-workers."[17] Gone from the unemployment lines and employment agencies, most likely no longer receiving unemployment benefits, most of these people disappear from all government lists. In fact, many of them seem to disappear off the face of the earth. They are the ones properly described as enduring the hardest times.

Yet another confirmation of the discouraging aspect of an otherwise bright employment picture comes from recent research on the nature of life of families moving off welfare presumably into jobs. Elijah Anderson's work in Philadelphia suggests that the city has lost more than 100,000 jobs since the mid-1980s, and in particular, the manufacturing sector has dropped by more than 50 percent.[18] Similarly, *Boston Globe* columnist Derrick Jackson noted that no state is more aggressive in getting people off welfare than Wisconsin, and indeed a host of people are finding jobs, albeit some of them low paying. Then again, Jackson pointed out, even with a high percentage of people working, Wisconsin still showed an unemployment rate among former welfare recipients of 38 percent! In reaction to this statistic, he wrote: "It is amazing in an America that is supposedly in the midst of a boom, that 4 out of 10 people in a given group are unemployed and this is hailed as a major social victory."[19]

Still other reasons exist for asserting that the number of unemployed workers may be significantly higher than present labor statistics would suggest. For one thing, there are scores of people who, knowing the jeopardy in which they are placed by announcing they are unemployed, simply lie about their present work status. Second, as Jackson noted, millions of people no longer listed as being on welfare are not yet working, although these people, too, are frequently not counted among the unemployed. Third, as Lester Thurow reminded us, America houses populations of legal (not to mention illegal) immigrants and Native Americans who have learned that "nothing good happens by telling anyone that you are unemployed."[20] Keep in mind that in the United States, only about one-third of those workers listed as officially unemployed receive unemployment insurance. Quite likely, many of the other two thirds remain unaccounted for in official unemployment statistics, and no one knows for certain whether these workers are properly categorized as *discouraged*.[21]

The men whose voices are heard in this book were chosen from a sample of people from all walks of life, an apt phrase. They have been selected because each of their stories points up significant social and psychological issues faced by long-term unemployed workers. Yet there is an aspect to many of their stories that readers will find extreme; in fact, social scientists refer to accounts of this sort as *extreme case sampling*.[22] Not surprisingly, many of the stories do not reach happy endings, but this is not atypical of the stories of long-term unemployment. Merely to find these men and stay in contact with them for long periods of time is a task unto itself, one that government agencies having to conduct monthly household surveys, rarely can afford to undertake. To hear the stories of men being out of work for years hardly uplifts the listener but reminds him or her, nonetheless, that the human body and spirit are often extraordinarily resilient as a common phrase puts it. Still, bodies and spirits do break, particularly when the assailant is long-term joblessness.

Albeit small, the sample in this work also reflects several aspects of the impact of long-term unemployment, as I examine combinations of historical, familial, psychological, and social factors, and the ways in which the experience of unemployment insinuates itself into the fabric of a particular life. Many long-term unemployed workers have been hospitalized for organic and psychological illness. Some have battered their wives or children, some presently are in jail, some have children serving prison sentences, and some have committed homicide and suicide. They live in rural as well as urban areas of the Northeast. Several of the men were once well off, others have known nothing in their lives but poverty, and still others may properly be classified as working or middle class. They are as young as thirteen, as old as seventy seven. Most were born in the United States, a few immigrated to this country. Some were formally educated through college and, in several instances beyond college. Some of the men have completed no more than eight years of grade school. They represent the major religions, the major trades, and seemingly every point on the political spectrum.

Because of the frequency with which labor statistics are reported in newspapers and on television, it is only natural that many people might tend to think of unemployed people *as* statistics. And although in the following pages the reader will find even more references to various labor statistics, it should be stressed that as essential as these figures may be to understanding the scope of employment and unemployment, they cannot tell the complete story of the affect of long-term unemployment on a person or his or her family. To learn about this effect, and perhaps equally important, to feel it vicariously, we must listen to the stories of the unemployed as well as their spouses, parents, children, and friends. And we must honor these accounts of the *experience* of long-term unemployment in the same way that traditionally we have honored hard-earned statistics on unemployment.[23]

The focus in this inquiry is the single human being. The term used in describing this research is *life study*. Simply put, the life study is a personal portrait of a person in his or her own words, it is the person's (version of the) story one seeks to learn. "Stories set the inner life into motion," Estes wrote, "and this is particularly important where the inner life is frightened, wedged, or cornered."[24] Pulley adds that "stories are basic to our humanity. We are our stories. They literally organize our memory and determine our behavior. Stories also feed our imagination and in doing so, they form the fabric of our soul."[25] Our interest, therefore, is not so much in collecting utterances that reflect or illustrate particular attitudes or opinions as it is in presenting a personal narrative, an approach, among other virtues, allowing people to reveal the effects of social and economic factors on the most private and personal aspects of their lives. In collecting these narratives, we are tapping into what John Kotre called the autobiographical memory system.[26] But again, the focus remains on what the person him- or herself deems significant; it is their story, their account of long-term unemployment. In the process of developing these narratives, we learn how people have experienced the world of working and not working, and what meanings they have attributed to the experiences they choose to recount or recall. A more detailed discussion of the research employed in this work is offered later in the chapter.[27]

Without question, the human personality is always in a state of evolution and maturation. In addition, large-scale social, economic, religious, cultural and historical phenomena affect the development of personality. This means that people's accounts of the ways their lives have unfolded also will change over time, and their narratives accordingly, reflecting their evolving inter-pretations of events and perceptions, and of course experiences, being out for work for several years. A study of long-term unemployed men is undertaken in these pages not only so that we may examine major social, economic, and political issues but so that we may better know the fundamental meanings of working, and especially not working, and how these phenomena influence people's perceptions of themselves and their worlds.

All people have their work stories, just as millions of people in the United States, even in a period of unprecedented prosperity, have their out-of-work stories. As Wallace Peterson reminded us, there have always been people going through the hardest times,[28] just as there are always those who genuinely feel, in John Kenneth Galbraith's words, that they are living in a culture of contentment.[29] Each of these stories is unique; each involves accounts of employment and unemployment, on the one hand, and the human spirit, personal worth, the inclusion and acceptance of cit-izens in a society, and the sense of human contribution to the present and to history, on the other. In examining the physical and emotional effects of unemployment, we touch on people's definitions of self, feelings of worth, sense of personal and family evolution, the connections they create between themselves and their cultures, and most assuredly their attitudes toward living and dying.

Only a few of us will become actively engaged in the business of find-ing satisfactory employment for the long-term unemployed,[30] much less immerse ourselves in designing wholly new patterns and forms of work for the future.[31] Yet in listening to the accounts of long-term unemployed men, we learn about the living process of unemployment, how it is that people feel about working, and not working, and how working and not working ultimately begin to define a man's identity.[32] The narratives of the long-term unemployed enlighten us, enhancing our understanding of our own work, our own selves, as well as the culture and civilization in which we evolve partly because of our own work, or the absence of it. The accounts reveal, furthermore, what happens to people who don't work for long periods of time and come to exhibit a form of bereavement, the result perhaps, of the experience of chronic trauma.

Some of us may feel discomfort reading accounts of discouraged workers, where happy endings are exceptions rather than the rule. Some of us may prefer to read fictional accounts of unemployed workers where we have a chance to "protect" ourselves, as it were, with the knowledge that it is, after all, "only" fiction. This means, however, that at some level, we too, dread the possibility of unemployment, which, for the long-term unemployed has become an everyday reality. The reader should be assured that the men whose stories appear in this book and whose names have been changed to safeguard their identities, do not represent fictional cases. All of them, surely, would have preferred a happier endings to their stories, but not all of them were able to achieve them.

At this moment in history, unemployment rates appear to be holding steady, which means that the quality of life and the spirit of these certain Americans will soon begin to plummet. If one spends time with long-term unemployed men, one inevitably hears discussions of employment figures, demographics, and debates on insurance compensation programs. But what one hears more frequently, and what remains the focus of this book, is the day-by-day anguish of living without a job, coupled with the recognition that tomorrow offers little promise of improvement.

THE ROLE OF WORK IN DEVELOPMENT

If one thinks about conversations one has had with children, one surely recalls asking them, or stifling the impulse to ask them, what they plan to be when they grow up. It becomes almost a comical scene, adults asking children of four or five what sort of career they've been contemplating over these past months, but we ask the question all the same.

The fact that the question even arises in discussions with children indicates how important work is to us. No matter how humane we try to sound, no matter how assiduously we commit ourselves to thinking of people in wholly personal terms, we nonetheless define them and ourselves in the context of work. The question to the child is hardly absurd. When the child responds, I want to be a fireman, or policeman, we are supportive. These are expected answers, appropriate for the child's age, we assure ourselves. More importantly, the child is thinking about his or her future and career. Indeed, this is one of the reasons we ask the question in the first place: namely, to encourage the child to contemplate this quintessential adult endeavor. In a word, we are socializing the child, preparing him or her for the future, a future in great measure defined in terms of work. At the very least, our question encourages the child to appreciate the importance of the role of work and career in this future.

Now consider the scene of people at a social gathering. Perhaps a trifle uncomfortable, perhaps wishing we were home with a good book, we do our best to befriend a stranger. Inevitably, we ask or hear that question: "And what do you do?" It's the traditional conversation ice breaker, the inquiry everybody seems to expect. In recent times, there has been talk of whether or not one should ask this question. Yet if we don't, we are accused of assuming that the other person doesn't work or doesn't define him- or herself in terms of work. Is it merely the conventional masculine perspective to ask this question? And why do we still question whether a full-time mother should not be properly considered as a full-time worker?

Whatever the answers to these questions, it is clear that our jobs and careers remain critically important in our assessments of others and ourselves. Work very well may remain the means and ends of ultimate gratification, just as it can be the central feature of human oppression.[33] Furthermore, we tend to evaluate the success of a society and its culture in terms of an established standard of full employment. For men especially, work may be the central cord of life, at least during the years between ages twenty and sixty. Men do change, as Daniel Levinson's research on the male life cycle indicates, with many of them becoming less ambitious and more person-oriented over time.[34] Yet in those early decades of development, almost everything men experience leads them toward considerations of jobs and career. When they reach the end of high school or college, their families only naturally wish to know "what they have planned," a euphemistic phrase, surely, for work and profession. When they date, women wish to know what these men "do for a living," a rather intriguing phrase inasmuch as it permanently links work with being alive. When a man asks a woman to marry him, she and her family almost invariably consider his present work situation so that they may calculate what we still call his "prospects." And as the years pass, a woman, now in the role of wife, may well measure her own happiness in terms of the progress her husband has made in his work, this, of course, being judged by financial reward as well as his position in the community, which also tends to be associated with work and career. Work, in Fourier's words, makes the man.

Levinson's research should not lead us to believe that work no longer sits at the core of a man's life as he reaches his sixth, seventh, and eighth decades as well. How many men, after all, speak of their lives ending when they look ahead to forced retirements? For that matter, how many men look forward to the time when they no longer *have* to work, assuming, of course, that they have amassed a sufficient amount of money?[35] So men do change as they age, soften, most likely, in some of their attitudes and perspectives, but their appraisals of the role work plays in the emergence of their ever-changing identities and world views appear to remain relatively constant.[36]

Curiously, a man's job is so essential to his identity and self-conception, one almost never thinks about it. As the expression has it, it goes without saying.[37] The little boy grows up knowing at some point he will have a job like his daddy or mommy. Someday, when school is completed, he will go off to work and return home for dinner, just like daddy or mommy. He knows this as surely as he knows that someday he will be big and tall like his father, like all men, all of whom go off to work, or, at any rate, are supposed to.

If only from observation, the little boy will learn as well that men who stay home doing little in those realms the society defines as work are not held in high esteem. People wonder about them, disparage or avoid them, and never hold them up to the child as models of successful maleness and masculinity. It is expected that a boy will make something of his life, which, according to long-standing tradition, he will do exclusively by working. In most homes, moreover, the little boy receives the message that he must make a name for himself, which in part implies doing better than his father, a directive tied to the sort of employment he will be able to obtain and maintain. These matters, too, are launched when adults ask the child that fateful question: What are you going to do when you grow up?

Although most of these points must seem obvious, they are meant to illustrate how seemingly natural and inevitable the world of working is to most men. It is for this reason, this natural, seemingly inbred assumption of having a job, that makes the reality of unemployment so drastic and. as is argued later, traumatic for men.[38] There can be no preparation for unemployment; it overtakes the entire being of a man. Quite literally, he runs the risk of collapsing at the news that he has lost his job or from the experience of not working for years. It is not merely that a man assumes he will work until retirement. Nor is it true that he fails to tremble when he hears about factories closing, impending layoffs, or a corporate merger that will necessitate downsizing.[39] Rather, he believes that no matter what the personal exigencies confronting him, or the national statistics on unemployment reported in the media even in times of economic prosperity, no matter what the talk in the bars or the car pools, he will be able to keep his job.

In a way, the sentiment toward work resembles many men's attitudes toward death. All too many believe that they are, somehow, the chosen ones, the ones immune to failure and tragedy. Although psychologists teach that the way in which people respond to difficult moments are critical features of personality and character, that it is not what happens to us but how we react to what happens, one might argue that even those men who speak regularly and openly about unemployment hopefully maintain a belief that this one disaster, anyway, will pass them by.

Some would call this attitude one of denial inasmuch as it represents an unconscious decision not to recognize real or prospective danger. At the time of this writing, Americans are witnessing a fairly optimistic employment scene nationally, although there seem to be some tremors in the employment statistics in New England, where the research for this volume was conducted.[40] Whatever the ebb and flow of unemployment statistics, however, there are always men and women hurting from a recent job loss or long-term unemployment. Despite the optimistic figures cited earlier, one third of all U. S. households experienced job loss over the last couple of decades.[41] Every day, small businesses go under even as new ones emerge, individuals and corporations file for bankruptcy in record numbers, and large corporations announce major quarterly losses and threaten to lay off thousands of workers or perhaps merge with other companies and furlough workers in order to maintain or increase profits.[42] The American Management Association found that slightly less than 30 percent of companies they surveyed reported downsizing in the year 1994–1995.[43] Alongside the almost daily reports of initial public offerings (IPOs) producing wealth for thousands of Americans are the announcements of yet another massive worker layoff somewhere. Business pages are filled with stories of contrasts between massive unemployment and equally massive executive salaries. They contain as well accounts of men who once earned six-figure salaries standing in unemployment lines alongside people who might have been in their employ as recently as two months earlier. Where unemployment hasn't yet hit, the threat of it may well be in the air.[44] When we pass homeless people in the streets or witness accounts of them on television, we may ruminate on their plight or the possibility of their being mentally ill—even though the rate of mental illness among the homeless tends to be exaggerated. Too often, however, we fail to think about the fact that steady jobs providing calculable incomes would take these people off the streets and make it possible for them to live so-called normal and productive lives. It is striking to note the shear number of accounts of the homeless that fail to mention unemployment. But sleeping on the streets today, and seeking shelter tonight in the limited sanctuaries provided them, are thousands of men and women who know well from personal experience the impact of long-term unemployment.[45]

Even during these days, almost a decade after the Persian Gulf War, newspapers carry stories of former military reservists who returned home following their obligations in the Gulf only to discover they had lost their jobs. Some resumed work in family-owned businesses that were barely kept afloat by their wives and parents, many of whom came out of retirement to lend assistance. So even in a so-called robust economy, a six-month absence of a soldier employee might have been enough to push these small businesses over the edge.

RATES OF UNEMPLOYMENT

Essentially, four all-too-familiar factors account for job loss in America. First, all companies now experience extraordinary pressure to show profits, and layoffs frequently are used as a means of accomplishing just this. Second, increasingly, machines have replaced people not only in menial, repetitive functions, but in highly complex and delicate functions once thought to be forever the province of human hands and brains.[46] Third, a growing number of nations offers the possibility of equal production for lower costs, and hence the loss of U. S. jobs. Fourth, companies have cottoned to the idea of contracting increasingly more jobs, thereby reducing costs and number of employees, and especially younger ones.[47] It is estimated that about one sixth of all workers under the age of thirty-five will engage in "temp jobs." Never before has the term *part timers* been so popular. Most important, whether it is called downsizing, lay-offs, or firings, job insecurity is felt in almost every occupation in the country; almost no one is immune. As *The New York Times* reported,[48] income and layoffs, even in times of great prosperity, rise together, the former no longer precluding the latter. "The problem now," Richard Stevenson wrote, "is that growth and unemployment are straining against the limits of what even the new economy would permit."[49]

Fundamental definitions of unemployment may come as a surprise to some people. Whereas intuitively one might think that long-term unemployment refers to being out of work for years, the fact is that three months and six months, respectively, represent the cutoff dates used by federal and state governments as well as insurance companies to categorize people as long-term and very long-term unemployed. In one respect, these durations may not appear prolonged. Yet in the case of unemployment, they not only feel as long as several lifetimes, they often demarcate a period of time beyond which no steady employment will ever again be found, or sought. Studies indicate, moreover, that following this period of time, it is difficult for the worker to find a job as satisfying or as well paying as the one he lost.

Equally important, and something America does not like to make public, beyond six months—usually the termination of the period of benefit payments—established organizations and appropriate governmental agencies begin to lose track of unemployed workers.[50] As noted earlier, just as they fall off employment agency inventories, so, too, do they appear to fall off the ends of the earth, sometimes in their own minds, sometimes, as is observed here, in the most literal of ways.

Almost everyone knows of someone who has lost a job. During the 1990s one in twenty workers lost his or her job. Equally striking, one in ten Americans report that job loss ignited a serious crisis in their families. Granted, U. S. companies have produced a net increase of 30 million jobs since the 1980s but this figure should not conceal two significant facts. First, if one factors in inflation rates, Americans by and large earn less than they did two decades ago.[51] College-educated workers earn approximately 9 percent less than their counterparts of twenty years ago, whereas noncollege-educated people make approximately 25 percent less. Not so incidentally, in the last decade, CEO salaries on average have risen 480 percent.

The second point concerns the matter of a replacement job typically not paying as much as and offering even less security than the original job.

U. S. Labor Department figures indicate that only one third of laid-off workers can expect to receive a replacement salary equal to their original salary. Confirming this fact, research indicates that replacement salaries in the 1980s yielded an average income drop of about $60. In the 1990s, this drop has increased to $85.[52]

According to A. H. Raskin, on average, 2.5 million heads of families in America, male and female alike, have been out of work for more than fifteen weeks.[53] Surprisingly, no one seems to know precisely what all of the long-term unemployed people are doing, and that includes the National Commission for Manpower Policy, which remains one of the best sources of information on unemployment.[54] A government study undertaken years ago indicated that approximately 25 percent of long-term unemployed people gave up looking for jobs after one year of having their unemployment benefits expire. Contrary to popular belief, fewer than 10 percent of the long-term unemployed had turned to welfare by this time, something that is no longer possible, and fewer than 25 percent had applied for food stamps. In borrowing money, an almost inevitable course of action, White workers hold a distinct advantage over African-Americans,[55] just as men hold an advantage over women. On the heels of these data, White families reported a spouse with some job far more frequently than any other group in the country.

With the average duration of unemployment in America listed as 15.8 weeks, it is important to note that the federal government estimates the number of discouraged workers (people who have given up hope of finding employment) at somewhere around one million.[56] And let us keep in mind these are not people living with physical disabilities, nor are they what some insensitively have labeled *psychologically handicapped*. Nor are they necessarily people who tend to drift in and out of the labor market, thereby causing minor or seasonal fluctuations in employment statistics. These are people perfectly willing and more than qualified to work, but who, believing there are no more employment opportunities for them, have quit looking for jobs.[57]

In scanning the writings on unemployment, one discovers researchers relying heavily on statistics to tell the unemployment story. In fact, and this is the point, over time, unemployment essentially has become for many an essentially statistical story. Read any newspaper account of unemployment and you will encounter reams of numbers. The state numbers are lower or higher than the national average. The male rate compares favorably or unfavorably with the female rate. The Hispanic rate is higher than the White rate but lower than the African American rate. And always, the teenage rate is higher than the adult rate.[58]

As valuable as unemployment numbers may be, the reader should be aware that unemployment figures can tell misleading stories, not that anyone purposely falsifies them. To begin, unemployment statistics are not necessarily perfectly accurate, but merely the best estimates researchers can produce over regular monthly intervals, given their primary methodology of the Household Survey. Authors like Herbert J. Gans suggest the actual number of jobless people may be twice the official number reported by the government.[59] Important to remember in this context is first, that very long-term unemployed workers are not counted among official labor statistics, and second, certain employment statistics may include people working as little as one hour per day! It is axiomatic to state that unemployment figures represent an underestimation of the problem inasmuch as they typically are based on the number of people drawing unemployment insurance. No insurance means no listing on the official unemployment rolls.

The implication of this statistical imprecision is twofold: First, allocations of federal funds for insurance and job training programs are predicated on these numbers despite the existence of inaccuracies. Second, a state or a region's general economic health (or lack of it) often is calculated on the basis of these same statistics.[60]

Another statistical point to consider is that given the variables constituting the unemployment equation, as for example the number of people actively seeking work, the number of people finding work, the number of people being laid off or quitting work during a particular month, it is possible for the unemployment number we read in newspapers to drop when the raw number of people unemployed that month has actually risen![61] Said differently, because the country's workforce increases monthly, even if the percentage of unemployed workers remains unchanged, the actual number of people out of work may have risen slightly.

Further complicating the statistical picture of unemployment, is a series of demographic distinctions that must be thrown into the mix, as for example, rural and urban employment rates, large city and small town rates, college-educated and noncollege educated population employment rates, and even seasonal comparisons, because the summer normally reveals a higher number of people entering the workforce, many of whom are teenagers who well may be counted as unemployed when they resume their studies.

Unemployment statistics may be broken down to reveal precisely who is out of work at a given time, although it is important to note that no one under the age of sixteen appears in official unemployment statistics, as presumably they are in school, even if they're not, which includes thousands of young people. Needless to say, at any given time, many young people are out of school, and large numbers of them are hunting for work.[62] Similarly, people over the age of sixty-five are omitted from official statistics even though many of them consider themselves unemployed and not retired. The reason for this is obvious, as sixty-five represents the traditional retirement age. Still, many elderly people, continuing to feel resentment for having been forced to retire, experience some of the same problems as other long-term unemployed workers, and most definitely would describe themselves being out of work if anyone included them in a survey.

When the available figures are broken down by race, gender, and age, it is discovered that unemployment generally, runs high among men aged twenty-five to fifty-four, but highest among young people aged sixteen to nineteen, and within this group, higher still among African Americans, something social scientists like Nicholas Lemann and Michael Katz have explored in more historical terms as well.[63] In 1997, White youth revealed an unemployment rate of 15.5 percent, whereas Black youth showed a rate of almost 35 percent. In the 1980s and early 1990s, significant differences between male and female unemployment rates tended to disappear. Both rates presently hover around 5.5 percent. Almost 10 percent of women who head households are out of work (a figure standing in sharp contrast to married men's rate of 3.4 percent), as are 8 percent of full-time workers generally. Statistics indicate that the number of women entering the workforce increases numerically and proportionally each year. But it is important to recognize that although women show gains in the shear number of jobs they obtain, status within the job market is more difficult to acquire. Although the median income of women has continued to increase over the years, the proverbial glass ceiling persists in most fields, and women continue to be disproportionately represented in lower-paying occupations like clerical work.

More recently, high school graduates and dropouts diagnosed with some form of learning, or behavioral, disorder have caught the attention of researchers on employment. Although the employment histories of these young people commence on a relatively good note, there appears to be a rather rapid decline. More specifically, a study conducted in the early 1990s revealed that about 72 percent of students with emotional and behavioral disorders had jobs by the time they left school. Within two years, however, this figure had dropped to 45 percent.[64]

In terms of occupation, blue-collar workers, operatives, and nonfarm laborers normally reveal the highest unemployment rates. If one examines unemployment data in terms of industries, the construction worker and the agriculture wage and salary worker show the highest unemployment rates, followed by those in heavy manufacturing and the durable goods industries, as well as many in the craft industries.[65] Recently, business managers and administrators as well have found themselves unable to reposition themselves in the marketplace, typically experiencing long periods of unemployment. Although shifts occur among industries showing the lowest unemployment rates, aerospace, energy-related industries, and high technology and computer businesses, until recently, represented the realms of safest employment.[66]

Adding to the portrait of long-term unemployed Americans, the government in the mid-1970s, listed some 500,000 unemployed veterans of the Vietnam War, with the highest rates found among those people in the twenty to twenty-four and thirty to thirty-four age brackets. African American veterans showed higher unemployment rates than White veterans. In percentage terms, these rates followed closely the unemployment rates of men without military service. As a side note, it may be recalled that under President Carter's administration, despite strenuous efforts to reduce unemployment among veterans, the number of men out of work dropped only slightly; it is estimated that fewer than 20,000 men found work through government assistance programs.[67]

The demographic characteristics of the unemployed were detailed years ago in a book edited by Joseph Becker.[68] Although the book was published in 1965, the salient characteristics of the unemployed outlined then essentially hold true today. Predictably, unemployment is greatest in people over forty-five years of age, but significantly, re-employment is more unlikely to occur in people of this age bracket. Nonskilled and semi-skilled laborers, and particularly African American, Hispanic, and young laborers, consistently prove to be among the groups exhibiting the highest unemployment rates. According to reports published by the National Urban

League, the unemployment figures for African Americans consistently stand at more than twice the figure for Whites.[69]

Generally speaking, the more formally educated a person (a statistic based on the number of years in school), the less likely he or she is to be unemployed. However, and this may surprise some people, if and when unemployed, the more formally educated person will remain without a job for the same duration as the less formally educated person. Further confirmation that the occupational safety net once provided by a college education has disintegrated is the finding that in the last decade, college graduates age fifty and older reveal twice the number of layoffs as their counterparts in the 1980s.

It goes without saying that economic fluctuations play a significant role in determining unemployment rates, but the story is not as neat and clean as one might imagine given the expected fluctuations and seasonal adjustments. Older men, for example, seem to be hit harder than others in the workforce during economic recessions, which typically take their greatest toll on blue-collar workers and non-White workers.[70] Historically, women normally were positioned in occupations where long-term unemployment was lowest, although this pattern seems to have shifted over the last decade or so.

One also can trace regions of the country as well as areas of any particular state where long-term unemployment rates are highest and correspondingly, insurance benefits lowest. Becker and his associates found the most chronically depressed areas to be located in Massachusetts, which traditionally has relied on labor-intensive industries, Pennsylvania, West Virginia, and Puerto Rico. In contrast, one may point to the large number of unemployed people living in middle and upper middle-class communities. Needless to say, the poor have it the worst. The numbers continue to be unsettling, with one in five children presently growing up in poverty.[71] But the fate of poor families must not obscure the destructive quality of unemployment among more affluent families as well.[72] That these people rarely speak publicly about their circumstances should not lead anyone to believe that the face of unemployment is never seen by these families.

In truth, no one seems able to get an accurate fix on the unemployment rates among affluent workers. Some data, however, have become available. Paula Leventman, for example, reported that, in the early 1970s, 20 percent of America's technical professionals, a group that includes scientists, engineers, and data analysts, were out of work.[73] According to

Leventman, many of these professionals never got hooked back into jobs after their initial layoffs. Indeed, of the approximately one hundred men she interviewed in 1971, 80 percent still had not secured full-time jobs when she interviewed them again four years later. In the meantime, many had found work on contract jobs, but the contracts offered neither job security nor benefits. In a word, unemployment, although virulent among poor and working-class families, is no stranger to middle and upper middle-class homes, and particularly when the wage earners in those homes are fifty years and older.

THE IMPACT OF UNEMPLOYMENT

Anyone researching families observes early on that along with the death or abandonment of a family member, unemployment is the most powerful experience families ever have to sustain. As Robert Weiss observed: "For those who lose their jobs after having been with their firms for years, who may have difficulty in finding new jobs, and who feel that they have lost not only their work but their place in the world, the experience can be devastating."[74] Families often use the words *assault* and *attack* to describe what they experience during their years of unemployment. And let us bear in mind that as family systems theory rightly suggests,[75] a problem, long-term unemployment in this case, for one member of the family becomes a problem for all members of the family.[76] Many people actually liken unemployment to an illness, and among these people are, of course, the long-term unemployed themselves.

It is well known that when unemployment hits the main breadwinner, the spouse and children feel the repercussions within days. Research indicates that within two weeks of a man being laid off, medical and psychological problems begin to emerge among family members.[77] Indeed, any variety of physical illness may set in within days of a man losing his job. Insomnia, upset stomachs, ear and nasal infections, and all sorts of flu symptoms are reported almost at once and may strike any member of the family. Then there are the achy joints, back pains, and severe headaches felt by people, including children, who never have been sick a day in their lives. Bowel and bladder functions are disturbed, people may begin to eat almost compulsively, or conversely, lose interest in food altogether even to the point of dropping as much as fifteen pounds in a single week. In some instances where unemployment is found, family members require hospitalization for malnutrition. Over time, one notes a rise in the number of automobile accidents and infant mortality rates, and all of this may be traced to unemployment, or again, merely the news of impending layoffs.

Then there is the matter of psychological disturbances and outright mental illness[78] that may be detected in any family member as a function of a father or mother being out of work for long periods of time. As Ann Crittenden wrote: "For many individuals, apparently, hard times mean not only meatless meals and foreclosed mortgages, but also self doubt, depression, alcoholism, sexual problems, marital discord, and even psychosomatic illness."[79]

Compulsive behavior, the sudden onset of agoraphobia and other phobic expressions, depression of the sort that is barely controlled by medication, and all varieties of agitation, boredom, restlessness, and anger are observed in families. Anxiety, as several studies indicate, is commonly found to be increased in families where the breadwinner is experiencing involuntary unemployment.[80] Interestingly, too, and a theme that is repeatedly found in the following accounts, financial hardship typically is associated with a lack of social assertiveness.[81] Sexual behavior may be affected, including a rise in reported rates of impotence and infertility. Sleeping pills and tranquilizers come to be used in increased if not excessive amounts, and tobacco and alcohol abuse are common.[82] As Ed Zegler, a man who watched closely the decline of an unemployed neighbor and his wife, once noted, "I always say, the more the job rates go down, the more the number of bars goes up."[83] Similarly, Raymond Claymore, a fifty-year-old out-of-work executive remarked: "If there is an emotion or illness known to man, you will know it full face when you lose your job. And that includes cancer!"

Research conducted by Dr. Harvey Brenner of Johns Hopkins University indicated that in New York State, admissions to hospitals of psychiatric patients over a period of 127 years increased markedly with each significant national economic decline and consequent rise in unemployment.[84] Brenner's findings later were confirmed by studies undertaken in New Jersey and California. Intriguingly, Brenner also discovered that physical symptoms tend to emerge merely on hearing news of impending unemployment.

Specifically, Brenner was able to document how a sustained 1 percent yearly rise in unemployment significantly increased (statistically, that is) what he called "social stress indicators" such as suicide, homicide, mental hospital and prison admissions, cirrhosis of the liver, cardiovascular and kidney disease, and general mortality.[85] According to Brenner's figures, 26,440 cardiovascular and renal deaths could be attributed directly to the rise in unemployment during the year 1977. Similarly, 1,540 suicides and 5,520 mental hospitalizations also could be traced to the same rise in unemployment. There is little reason to believe that these same findings would not hold true today. Brenner also noted that despite the enormous rates in these various phenomena, the numbers hardly strike anyone as being elevated. They stand out perhaps because presumably these sorts of hospitalizations and suicides are avoidable.

There is no telling when and to what degree the relationships among family members begin to unravel, often to such a powerful extent they will never again resume normalcy.[86] Nor do we know how many cases of unemployment, or the threat of it, have led to separations or divorces, although it is fascinating to learn that many long-term unemployed workers actually remain in marriages they themselves describe as dead ends rather than seek a separation or a divorce. A common finding among married men is that although they may well value their families more than anything else in the world, they nonetheless find it difficult if not impossible to act as adequate fathers and husbands when they are without work.[87] Thirty-nine-year-old Stephanie Malzone once remarked that "unemployment does the same thing to a couple that losing a child does: It wrecks the bond once and forever." She knew both experiences, for her husband, unemployed for fifteen months, left her soon after their son Gene died of pulmonary complications during his second week of life. The couple had been married fourteen years. To some extent, empirical research supports Mrs. Malzone's observations. Admittedly, not all wives of unemployed workers walk out on their husbands. Nor do all unemployed men walk out on their families or file for divorce. Still, a great many do, or believe they should, as is seen in later chapters.

Unemployment does something else to a man. In assaulting his capacity to deal with stress and stripping away his pride, his self-definition,[88] his sense of personal power, and his belief in his ability to control outcomes, not the least of which is his own personal destiny, long-term unemployment may lead to aggressive, antisocial, and outright violent behavior such as wife and child battering, armed robbery, and murder. A study conducted years ago at the Boston University School of Medicine suggested that in areas of cities where unemployment runs high (and in some neighborhoods it may reach 75 percent), death occurs most frequently. Appropriately, the Boston University researchers called these areas "death zones."[89]

It is not melodramatic to use words like *despair, desperation, exasperation, confusion, powerlessness,* and *impotency* when seeking to capture the worlds of the long-term unemployed. There is also the shock and hurt of the experience. No matter how one receives the news, no matter how much lead time or advance warnings are given, people describe a shock rippling across their bodies and spirits. Almost all long-term unemployed men speak of this. So, too, do their wives.[90] Many use the words *trauma* and *traumatic* to describe their reactions, by which they mean deep wound coupled with a lack of preparation. Families recognize that their sense of trauma continues for as long as the man remains unemployed. It is, in other words, chronic, everyday trauma. And although the children in these families may not use these words nor fully comprehend the psychological repercussions of unemployment, surely they feel the impact of the trauma. In fact, research supports their describing the experience of long-term unemployment as traumatic, as studies reveal an association between unemployment and mortality occurring within one year.

It is assumed, as Halle suggested,[91] that a man will have a job. If he loses his job, it is assumed he will have obtained another one before his unemployment insurance benefits run out.[92] For many men it works just this way, but not in all cases. Stories of men remaining out of work for years are not often told. Well, that's not completely true. They are told, but not all that many people hear them. Journalists seek to get the stories of unemployed workers into the pages of newspapers, but in the main, accounts of unemployment and government debates on the phenomenon are drafted in statistical terms. There is, however, a certain variety of newspaper account that the reader surely has seen on more than one occasion, although it is not clear that all readers will notice the one word, "unemployed," that unobtrusively sits somewhere in the news item, usually within the first or second sentence. Here are some examples:

"Cambridge, Massachusetts-John F. Krohn Jr., an unemployed engineer, was found guilty yesterday of killing his cousin and wounding her daughter as they sat in the Littleton kitchen of Krohn's mother last year."[93]

"John Polinchak, 32, pleaded not guilty yesterday at Brockton District Court to a variety of charges, including two counts of assault and battery with a dangerous weapon—a car—after allegedly stealing two vehicles

Saturday, leading police on two low-speed chases and forcing civilian vehicles off the road. Polichak, who is unemployed, allegedly stole a Chevrolet Chevette early Saturday . . ."[94]

"Battle Creek, Michigan—An unemployed factory worker was jailed yesterday and charged with the attempted abduction of a safety patrol girl and of three other youngsters he allegedly attempted to coax into his car."[95]

"Boston police last night were seeking a man recently fired from his job at the *Boston Herald* for questioning in connection with the execution-style slaying of a pressman at the newspaper plant on Monday night."[96]

"Miami, Florida—'My daddy' . . . whispered 6-year-old Claudia Rivera, weeping as she stood in her front yard while paramedics and detectives moved about her. 'He shot my brother and killed my mama. He shot her once. She was bleeding. My daddy ran away' . . . Her father has no job, she said. Her mother worked at a downtown shopping center."[97]

One recognizes the familiar ring of these accounts and similar ones of significant drug disorders, alcoholism, criminal activity, homelessness, and, alas, murder and suicide as well. An unemployed man can become a quietly desperate and lonely man.[98] He probably has given serious thought to what he might do in the event of losing his job and not catching on again in the labor market, although when he mentions unemployment to other men, they most likely counsel him not to think in dire terms. Do your work well and diligently, he will be told—and most of us believe this—and you will be rewarded by holding onto your job. But it doesn't always work this way for men living through the hardest times. Sadly, some of the men whose stories are heard in this book chose to act on their desperate and lonely feelings.

WORK AS THE CENTER OF LIFE

Years ago on a Cambridge, Massachusetts, basketball court, I encountered a boy of nine whose father, I later would learn, had left the family and never returned. Apparently, after months of being unable to land a job, *any* job, as his wife emphasized on numerous occasions, he threw in the towel and disappeared. Twenty-five years later, his family still has not learned of his whereabouts or fate. The boy from the basketball court, now a man of thirty-four years of age, continues to believe his father is alive and someday will return to the family, if only to see how he, Johnnie Nobles, Junior, turned out. "When you name your son with your own name," Johnnie said one evening, "you have a special interest in him. I know. I got one myself, John the third."

No plan to "study" unemployment ever struck me in those early days. In fact, the idea didn't draw life for years, even though my research regularly took me into areas where unemployment ran high. It is ironic, actually, that one chooses communities because of social characteristics directly traceable to high unemployment rates like crime, poverty, lack of adequate child care, and inadequate medical facilities, but may not explicitly examine the experience of unemployment directly, but at one level this is understandable.

From early on, as was the case with Johnnie Nobles' family, one learns that long-term unemployment is not something people readily speak about. Although it may be the most obvious feature of a family's existence, it isn't discussed until the researcher is convinced that the person, idle for years, will not be offended or threatened by exploring this one particular story. Even then, one feels profoundly uncomfortable asking questions like, "What does it feel like not to have a job?" and "Does it ever seem as though you may never work again?" as inane and insensitive as they sound (and I confess to asking these questions). In many instances in the course of doing research, it is evident that a man and his family feel that inquiries about unemployment are off limits, and so a researcher honors a family's wishes even though everyone can see how unemployment is eating away at the family.

If I heard the word *cancer* used once to describe the feelings of being unemployed, I heard it a thousand times. Still, I never felt cancer to be the appropriate analogy, at least not cancer in the early stages of the disease when one can't see physical changes and a patient actually reports feeling perfectly well. With unemployment there is no way one cannot see profound transformations in the person and his family. And as for feeling fine, that feeling vanished sometime around the notification that a job might be permanently lost. Besides, unlike some forms of cancer, there is a cure for long-term unemployment.

To appreciate the felt sense of a man being out of work for long periods of time while at the same time believing he will never work again, we must briefly consider the meanings of working generally, although we return to this topic in the last chapter.

There is almost no study in the social sciences in which work is not placed at the center of a man's life.[99] Indeed, as the writing of David Roediger and Philip Foner suggest, much of the history of America is a history of human labor, as well as the failure to obtain it.[100] It is a cliché to suggest that a man is what he does. Wives and children are important, many will say the *most* important concerns of their lives, but one doesn't always hear that sentiment in the homes of long-term unemployed workers. Rather, their lives pivot around their jobs, or lack of jobs. Research only confirms this point.

That a man's work is central to his belief in his personal as well as social stability was documented by George Orwell in his book *The Road to Wigan Pier*,[101] then again by Adriano Tilgher in a work published in 1930, and still later by Herbert Applebaum.[102] Tilgher noted that a sense of optimism and a belief that one had a voice in his own destiny were intimately bound up with the reality of steady work. Take his job away and a man lost any sense that he could make things good for himself or his family. In the words of a wife of an unemployed worker: "Take the job away and a man loses his soul." And too, losing a job means losing one's psychological and physical health.[103]

Similar themes were echoed twenty-five years later in 1955 in a classic study undertaken by Ely Chinoy not of the unemployed, actually, but of employed automobile workers.[104] Given their circumstances, Chinoy's automobile workers, who labored daily in barely tolerable conditions, hardly imagined they had reached the promised land, much less fulfilled the American dream. Most of them, however, expressed the desire that ideal work conditions be established for their children. Accordingly, they took special steps to teach their sons and daughters, although mainly their sons, to dream the dreams of this country, aspire to white-collar jobs, and recognize that employment would always be the centerpiece of their lives as contributing and loyal citizens.

This notion of the American dream, the ideal of millions of people who began arriving in this country around the turn of the century, hinged essentially on the reality of work. Although some still imagine that immigrants rushed to the United States dreaming of streets allegedly lined with gold, it is clear they came because America offered the opportunities for a better life, which, of course, was made possible by stable work.[105] With diminished chances in their native countries to earn decent livings, immigrants rushed to America believing that no matter what the new country offered, it had to be better than what they and their parents had experienced. Yet invariably, work stood as the centerpiece, the quintessential ingredient in the concepts of prospect and hope. Why come at all if the reward was to be unemployed?

Behind the American dream was an almost religious calling: One reaches the great rewards of heaven itself through hard work.[106] Busy hands, after all, were said to be happy hands. Social institutions taught this, as did the church. Work hard, remain loyal and responsible to family, use your head and your hands wisely, stay strong, and you not only will succeed on this earth, but you will be awarded a treasured place in heaven as well. Need one even mention what the church said about idleness and its link with the devil! But the American dream contained another theme as well, the theme of control of one's destiny. If the worker in the factory had little or no say in the operations of the plant—and before the organization of unions he essentially had none—his labors would at least take him to the promised land, so in this sense destiny remained in his own hands and not in the hands of the devil.

If religions and families smiled on the hard-working employee, then the good citizen inevitably was defined as the good consumer, which implied that he was also a good earner. Conspicuous (or inconspicuous) consumption, after all, lay at the heart of America's economic machinery. One not only subsisted, one found a bit of extra money to purchase those items that made one's family happy. The formula for success loomed abundantly evident: Be competent in your work and willing to spend your earnings.

The theme, actually, has barely changed: The good citizen contributes to his community and country and in America tends to save rather little relative to his counterparts in Germany and Japan. He contributes his competence, his time, his services, his money. The foundation of all four contributions of course is steady work, it's not really all that complicated. America values charity and the notion of contributing; a man finds both difficult if not impossible without a job. A critical quality of the good citizen, moreover, is his personal stability, but this, too, may rest on the premise that he keep his job.[107] In the most fundamental of terms, as Katherine Newman wrote, people with jobs "are more inclined to develop precisely the values politicians and frustrated taxpayers want them to have: family values, responsibility, prudence."[108]

THE STRESS OF UNEMPLOYMENT

Critics recently have pointed to the phenomenon of the extreme work habits omnipresent in Western society, and, as Juliet Schor suggested, the end of leisure as we presently know it.[109] We have even coined the term *workaholic* as a way of highlighting some people's possibly obsessive and psychologically self-destructive (over) involvement with work. It well may seem, as Alan McLean suggested, that although the great madness of life has to do with adjusting to certain work organizations and demands, the choice for most people between this brand of madness and the hurt of long-term unemployment is all too easily made.[110]

Granted, the process of living is permeated by biological, psychological, and sociological stresses. It is hardly surprising, therefore, to learn that in contemporary America, the concept and reality of stress continually move closer to the center of health concerns, medical industries, and even definitions of the spirit.[111] At all levels, the human organism constantly is having to cope with stressful environments, many of them, sad to say, people made. This notion holds as true at the level of the cell as it does at the level of the whole person.

Among the many sociologically rooted areas of stress is the quest for status and position, two more products of steady work, good wages, and viable if not satisfying job conditions.[112] When a man loses his job, as is seen repeatedly in the forthcoming chapters, he loses face, status, position, income, and whatever economic security (or hope for it) he may have amassed. Peter Rosenbloom, an unemployed man in his mid-fifties, said it best: "When you lose your work, you lose the works!"

Let us be clear about one thing. The case of long-term unemployed workers represents the worst-case scenario, truly it is for these men the hardest times. Granted, we know of stories of men surviving the hardship of not working and recognizing they probably will never work again. Still, there are some readers who will contend that the cases portrayed in this volume are extreme and unrepresentative, somehow, of the long-term unemployed worker. Some surely will find this reflection by Kenneth Hawkins on his father to be excessive: "If my father would have had a job all his life, he'd be alive this minute. Wasn't his strength that gave way. His *job* gave way, and that took his strength. Killed my mother too."

If the men portrayed in the following chapters seem to behave "abnormally," if they sound more like psychiatric patients than so-called normal, healthy men who "merely" have experienced long-term unemployment, then consider the numerous studies indicating an almost immediate decline in the mental health of men when they lose their jobs and cannot gain re-employment. Given materials we have considered, one begins to question the observation of Harvard Medical School psychiatrist Joan Zilbach: "Blue collar workers have always felt a certain vulnerability, so they can take the loss of a job better."[113] The observation of Ed Zegler, a so-called blue-collar worker, may prove more accurate: "You don't live without a job and get by too long, emotionally I mean. It'll take the best out of any person."

Examining the lives of men experiencing the sorts of situations confronted as well by some of the men heard in this book, sociologist Arthur Kornhauser found that high-skilled blue-collar workers revealed higher mental health scores than nonskilled workers.[114] Lower mental health scores were found among people with lower-paying jobs and jobs that were perceived by the worker to be dull and repetitive. Working these jobs led to feelings of listlessness, alienation, withdrawal, passivity, escapism, pessimism, and hopelessness. This, of course, could be predicted. More interesting, however, was Kornhauser's discovery that it was not a man's wage that predicted his mental health score as much as it was the conditions in which he worked. If a worker is interested in what he or she is doing, his or her mental health is likely to be relatively good. Frustration, the curtailment of aspirations, the persistent feeling that one is a failure, and the general shrinking of life goals are found to result more from unhappiness in work than from low wages.[115] Given this finding, imagine what happens to a man when his job, even one performed in dreadful conditions, is taken from him and he is unable to find new employment.

In this same context, one might consider the results of a survey of more than 1,500 members of the American Psychological Association (APA).[116] When asked to list the major threats to mental health, 30 percent of these mental health professionals reported the decline of the nuclear family. In second place, at 20 percent, was unemployment, followed by drug abuse (18 percent) and alcohol abuse (14 percent). Reacting to the findings, several psychologists celebrated the fact that at last people were willing to examine root causes of illness rather than mere symptoms. Not surprisingly, the findings tended to confirm what many psychologists long had been observing in their clinical practices.

On the surface, the APA survey makes sense, even to researchers who may associate mental stress more with unemployment, or the threat of it than with the decline of the nuclear family. Although numerous factors must be enlisted to explain the decline of the traditional nuclear family, let it be said that long-term unemployment surely is one of them. Granted, people get divorced because they no longer can get along together. But thousands of people who, under different situations might stay together, often find they cannot rise above the palpable horror of long-term unemployment. In a word, the causative factor in the present research is unemployment. Give a man a steady job with reasonable conditions and wage, and importantly, good prospects for future employment, and you have the makings overnight of a better husband and father. Hardly credentialed professional psychologists, unemployed men would testify to this fact.

As for confirming the notion that mental illness relates first and foremost to the decline of the nuclear family as adjudged by numerous clinical practices, let it be said that relatively few long-term unemployed persons ever consult psychiatrists, psychologists, or social workers for long stretches of time, if at all. They may well consult professional mental health providers during the period in which they continue to receive benefits, but rarely afterward. Even if they felt it would do them good, they simply cannot afford it. The worlds of psychiatry and psychology, moreover, often are seen as offering little help generally, for they do not stand, perhaps, in the best position to evaluate relationships between unemployment and psychological symptomatology. As Dr. Peter L. Brill, himself a psychiatrist, once remarked, "many psychiatrists spend a good part of their lives buried in offices away from real-life situations."[117] Still, psychiatry and psychology remain potentially valuable resources for men and women going through the sorts of experiences associated with long-term unemployment. Undoubtedly there are thousands of unemployed workers in the world like George Wilkinson who commented:

> I could write a book on what unemployment does to people, how it eats them up worse than cancer. I can feel myself forgetting everything I've done for the last thirty years. If it wasn't terrifying,

it could be interesting. I have to laugh. I never thought of seeing a psychiatrist, not that I couldn't benefit from it. I wasn't that kind of personality. Now I want it, I need it, and we can't afford it. It's a shame. I'd be a beautiful specimen.

If, as some might allege, most people would not react as several of the men in this book have to the stressful reality of long-term unemployment—and recall that we know relatively little about men out of work for more than six months, much less two or three years—then consider the findings of the following research.

In studies carried out for more than fifteen years, Erdman Palmore found that the best predictor of longevity was work satisfaction.[118] This finding should now sound familiar. The next best predictor, not so incidentally, was a person's overall sense of his or her happiness. Consider now the meanings of these results: If you want to live long, love *what* you do, not *with whom* you may do it. Think, too, of how a man might change his attitudes toward living, and dying, after years of not being able to find work. As we are about to discover, this may be the quintessential feature of the entire research.

Surprised, perhaps, by the results, and wondering whether these same effects would emerge as well in the lives of younger workers, Palmore confirmed his findings in a follow-up study, which was further replicated in research undertaken in Italy.[119] In fact, many researchers have noted correlations between workers reporting job dissatisfaction, high risks in job conditions, occupational stress, continual changes in employment, and, of course, lack of jobs, on the one hand, and heart disease and high blood pressure, on the other.[120]

Confirmation of Palmore's work came as well from a survey of working conditions conducted at the University of Michigan in the late 1970s. When asked to rank the most important aspects of work, 1,500 people listed as their top five choices: interesting work, sufficient help and equipment to get the job done, sufficient information to get the job done, sufficient authority to get the job done, and good pay. Notice that good pay is in fifth place. Notice too, that all five answers assume that one *has* a job. One assumes that attitudes of this sort have not changed substantially since the Michigan research was reported. Darrell Sifford for one, believes the findings to still hold true: "Here's something that will shake your eyeteeth," he wrote. "Evidence is accumulating to suggest that the number one predictor of a long, healthy life is not your heredity, not your diet, not your exercise, but . . . your job."[121]

THE LIFE STUDY

About twenty five years ago, I undertook a form of research many now call *life study* or, Sara Lawrence-Lightfoot and Jessica Hoffman Davis' term, *portraiture*.[122] It is the intent of life study researchers to "work their ways" into people"s lives for the purpose of eventually retelling the stories of those willing to "sit for portraits." To be sure, we interview people, although given the highly personal nature of the work, we rarely think of it as interviewing. One prefers to think of the work not as questions and responses, but as simple conversations, or storytelling.[123] In a word, some of us working on life studies have come to believe that perhaps all we are are the stories we tell. We are, in other words, as much *Homo Fabulans* as *Homo Sapiens*.[124]

With the help of the subject of the portrait, we attempt to sketch out some of the significant issues of a person's life and, importantly, rely on the person's own words. How do we determine the so-called significant issues? Truth be told, we likely come on the issues as conversations evolve and friendships develop. The material, as it were, reveals itself to us over time, although clearly in many cases we know before meeting family members what some of the significant issues of their lives will be. It isn't difficult, after all, to know when one enters urban housing projects that one is going to hear stories of poverty, problematic schools, physical hardship, inadequate medical care, unemployment, and battles with bureaucracies. Still, one must be careful to guard against prejudices and preconceptions. In housing projects, for example, one also hears accounts of physical and spiritual strength, mercy and forgiveness, generosity, humor, and even joy, words that we tend not to associate with people living in these particular circumstances.[125]

Life study research is nothing more and nothing less than the collection of people's accounts of their own experiences. In offering and listening to these accounts, we employ a mode of thought psychologists like Jerome Bruner call *narrative* thinking.[126] In this mode, we strive to give meaning to experience, be it ours or someone else's. We hunt for what we consider to be the truths of these experiences, but not in ways that would allow us to scientifically test or verify them. In the daily leading of our lives, after all, we are storytellers, not scientists.

In the narrative mode, moreover, we become implicated in the thinking, feeling, and "knowing" of experience and essentially grow to appreciate the nature of the conscious world of the person to whom we are attending, and hence we begin to understand how the storyteller gives meaning to his or her experience. Equally significant, as Donald Polkinghorne noted, the narrative enables people "to construe what they are and where they are headed."[127] Their story, in other words, enlightens *them* as much as it does us. But there is another aspect captured as well in these words of Edwin Delattre: "A compassionate person is one who tries to understand how things look and feel to others. To be just in daily life, we must try to grasp the point of view of others, because their perception is an irreplaceable element in the overall facts."[128]

Life study inquiries fall under the broad umbrella of qualitative research. Eisner for example, as reviewed by Authur Beane, listed six fundamental criteria of qualitative research, five of which are directly relevant to the life study.[129] First, the work is field-centered; we go into the world of those we study and explore it as much as we explore the individual life. Second, as Beane wrote, "the self is used as an instrument."[130] That is, life study research essentially is an exploration of the self by the self. Third, qualitative research "uses expressive language"[131] and as often as possible brings into the text the actual voice of the person under study. Fourth, and following upon the preceding criterion, we pay strict attention to what people say because their stories serve as *examples* of a particular phenomenon, in this case unemployment, not because the stories necessarily *describe* something. Simply put, the storyteller is just that, he or she is not *per se* an (anthropological) informant; the storyteller and the account, therefore, are essentially one and the same. Fifth, qualitative research draws its credibility through the coherence of the story, that is, the insight brought to the story by the storyteller, and the way the person explores him- or herself (really his self or her self) through the story.

Eisner's sixth criterion involves the interpretive character, again, in Beane's words, "that attempts to explain *why* something took place."[132] Surely relevant to life study research, the notion of interpretation requires a brief discussion.

When we allege that we are the stories we tell, we mean only that each of us is constantly attempting to describe and make sense of the effect upon us of external events and internal sensations. Thus, when we ask people to describe how they feel about or perceive an experience like long-term unemployment, we are collecting information through their spoken accounts, their narratives. All of our recollections of the past, perceptions of the here-and-now, and expectations of what the future might look like, as Polkinghorne reminds us, are contained in these stories. So if we wish to know about these recollections, perceptions and expectations, we need only ask the people kind enough to sit for our portraits so that they and we together may discover their interpretations of these experiences. The reader should keep in mind that we are not listening as therapists, for we have not been invited to treat people for some expressed problem or disorder. We merely are attending to people as they describe and give meaning to their experiences through narrative accounts.[133]

If, as the writer V. S. Naipaul asserts, the good novel enlightens us and evokes something in us as well, then the same can be said of the life study. But there is something more: When stories are offered freely, the (subjective) interpretation, in a sense, already is contained within the account. Notice here the play on the word *account*. The interpretation, in other words, is part and parcel of the telling.[134] Again from Polkinghorne: "narratives exhibit an explanation instead of demonstrating it."[135]

The great story, moreover, ties people together. It may even serve as part of one's kinship structure, sense of community, and culture as well. Indeed, the role of the story looms essential in defining the nature of culture. Consider in this regard Clifford Geertz's definition of culture as "an historically transmitted pattern of meanings embodied in symbols, a system of inherited conceptions expressed in symbolic form by means of which men communicate, perpetuate and develop their knowledge about and attitudes toward life.[136] In undertaking life study research, one repeatedly recognizes that storytelling becomes the foundation of the communal attachments one develops with the storyteller.[137] Despite clear-cut differences in our appearances, backgrounds, cultures, and importantly for the present work, employment circumstances, the exchange of stories draws us together.

To repeat, the life study finds its origin in the act of bearing witness or testimony.[138] It emerges as a collection of portraits in which one relies heavily on recounting the words of storytellers. Emphasizing subjective analyses of the material, the technique depends in great measure on selecting and ordering pieces of conversations so that a coherent and representative product is achieved.[139] It is our purpose in this work for people to hear the stories as we have heard them.

From the beginning, the people with whom I meet learn of my intentions of possibly writing about them, for I cannot assure them that a written product will eventuate. We agree only that if I choose to write something, they must grant me permission to publish it. If they object to portions of the account, we negotiate a settlement, as it were. If they outright refuse permission, then the research project concludes, but not the friendship. That is, under normal circumstances this is how the arrangement transpires. In several instances in the present work there were some exceptions to this unwritten contract that none of us could have foreseen. In those cases, survivors read the various drafts.

It should be clear why so-called in-depth profiles preclude the possibility of studying great numbers of people. Yet large samples are neither the point nor a major drawback of this brand of research. The point, rather, is to locate people whose lives enlighten us and affect our sensibilities about the experience of unemployment, as well as its impact on families.

Having provided a sense of the way the research unfolds, let me offer a glimpse of what it looks like in everyday practice.

Research on long-term unemployment begins with a host of leads for recruiting families. There are, for example, formal and informal organizations such as churches, hospital staffs, personnel and welfare agencies, employment and social work offices, law courts, employers and educators, although all of these people must be careful to protect the confidentiality of those with whom they work. Still, by hanging around long enough in these various venues, one is able to meet all the men and women one would ever require in undertaking research on unemployment. One person introduces you to the next, and in time a small network of new friends has been established.

During the first meetings with families there is, predictably, some confusion over just what it is I intend to do. Their initial questions are perfectly logical: "What will I do with the material?" "Whom would it interest?" "Will I be speaking with others about these same issues?" "What if certain members of our family choose not to speak with you?" I assure them that is fine, even expected. "Will we be granted anonymity?" Most assuredly yes. "How long will the work take?" I cannot say for certain. "When do we start?" In a sense, we already have.

Interestingly, family members of unemployed people typically asked nary a question of me and wondered aloud surprisingly little about my purposes. They acted almost like patients so assaulted by doctors that one more person could hardly cause them additional pain. Rarely did any of them raise the matter of possible revenues. When I brought up this subject they waved it away with words and gestures. Money generated from research meant one thing to them; charity, and they would have none of it.

As noted, the work is predicated on conversations that may take place for any length of time, a few minutes on the telephone, to several hours during any one of the home visits. Some of the material contained in the book was collected within the first hours or days of meeting someone, other material did not surface until after I had known a family for several years. When we are not visiting face to face, we keep in touch by phone and mail, (although for economic reasons, some families are obliged to live without telephones). The reader should understand that our conversations are not restricted to the topic of unemployment. While the families know at once of my purpose, I have visited with people for weeks speaking very little, if at all, about unemployment. In these moments we are merely friends passing the time of day, shooting the breeze call it what you wish.

In life study research, we enter the home or community of a particular family, hang around, make our observations, and record what we see and hear.[140] There is no interview schedule, no time limit established. The conversations go on and on with no one knowing in advance what material will be utilized in any fashion. We go back again and again, and in this returning, in the course of regularly being there, we develop friendships. If nothing more, the families trust in the fact that the researcher will return.

A word about the recording of stories. If a tape recorder can conveniently be used, I will employ one, although frankly I prefer to take notes and then recreate the conversation after it was completed. The presence of the tape recorder, as small and inconspicuous as the modern machines may be, still interferes in the natural flow of conversation and the normal drama of people being together. Sitting across a table from one another, sipping our tea, the little dictaphone I employ often works well enough, although it never actually encourages people to speak openly. But when taking a walk or accompanying someone as they buy their groceries or pick up clothes from the cleaners, I find that the tape recorder becomes an incongruous and cumbersome item.

The typical recording scenario calls for taking notes as inconspicuously as possible, and then dictating my thoughts and recollections of the conversations into my machine. The longer one waits to do this, obviously, the more one's memory recedes. But the reader should recall that before reaching the public, all this written material is read by the people themselves and checked for accuracy of content and, normally, tone and style of speech as well. If I am remiss, it is in the capturing of the music of a person's voice or verbal style.[142] I find I get the lyrics fine; it's the music that suffers.

One last item regarding life study research derives in part from people's awareness of television news. It is often difficult to convince families that I am not on the lookout for an unforgettable quote or a poignant story. One is always collecting material, noting it down, filing it away. For when people are permitted to speak about what genuinely matters to them, the eloquent, even poetic remarks will come forth. In the case of long-term unemployed men, there are thousands more stories that could be told.

ONE FINAL CONCERN

Stated precisely, at the core of a man's sense of personal satisfaction, happiness, and overall quality of mental and physical health is his job, along with his attitudes toward it, which in turn shape his attitudes toward himself and the world. Take his job away and whether or not it sounds melodramatic, you are beginning to destroy this man, for long-term unemployment does kill. It kills bodies, minds, and spirits. As a Boston psychiatrist once remarked, when you withhold a person's humanity, you begin to see the shriveling of their souls. The sad truth is that I didn't know all of this at the beginning of the research because I never saw the bodies, nor had I heard long-term unemployed men describe their circumstances and the state of their minds. Obviously, they held back a great deal in the early months of our conversations, even as they offered intimate moments of their lives. Still, as most of the stories in this book reveal, they could not withhold anything too long. The impact of their pain gradually came to be heard, as, for example, in the words of Bill Leominster: "Maybe I tried to get those feelings to come out, maybe I didn't try hard enough, but there's nothing there. I'm pulling the blood out right this minute . . . If I had a feeling in there somewhere, it would have come out now, wouldn't it?"

Expressions like this raise a difficult question, one that readers may already have considered. Might it be that research itself brings forth pain from men who previously had been able to control it? Does the mere act of asking men to become introspective about unemployment cause them to feel the power of their disillusionment, as Leventman suggested in her study of unemployed scientists and technologists?[143] Would some of the men have been better off *not* speaking to anyone about their situations, lest they withdraw into despair? Given the substantial evidence reported by the psychologist Martha Straus[144] for why it is that traumatized children dislike speaking about their painful experiences, one wonders why it would be any different for adults. Perhaps a bit of life force is generated in the silence of the unemployed, and possibly in their denials of pain as well. Maybe obliging men to focus on the issue of long-term unemployment causes them to feel they are being closed in on, trapped like animals. Perhaps one does better leaving well enough alone. Perhaps I should have left *them* well enough alone.

Many days driving home I thought about these questions. Of course I regularly inquired of the families whether my visits were doing more harm than good. All of them assured me that the visits could only be beneficial, but I have never stopped wondering. Naturally, had the families confirmed my concerns, I would have at once stopped working with the men. It is not a pleasant feeling to know that someone close to you has gone away and never again appeared, as was the case with Ken Hawkins and some of the other men. Inevitably in these situations, one wonders. "what could I have done? What clues did I miss? What paths had I not taken?"

Yet, never did any of the wives of these men inquire about any of this. They knew from the start what I learned early in the research: Without jobs, there was no telling what would happen to their husbands. They must have seen in my face that I was not always fully convinced by their words; there might have been that one additional thing I could have done to find work for a particular man. Come to think of it, perhaps this feeling of self-reproach was what I always imagined I would see in *their* faces. Originally, I believed it was their intense displeasure with their husbands. On second thought, perhaps it was themselves they had grown to dislike; and, to think, long-term unemployment may have been the cause of this sentiment as well.

Even worse, all of them, the men and the women and probably the children too, knew that time was running out, and something was going to break, one way or another. Either a job would be found, or something drastic would occur; it was a palpable feeling in so many of these homes. One could not visit with these men and women and not imagine that a time bomb was ticking in this home, and clearly the timer was set off when the man's last, and final, job was lost.

NOTES

1. See William J. Wilson, *When Work Disappears: The World of the Urban Poor* (New York: Knopf, 1996.)

2. Robert Heilbroner, *The Making of Economic Society* (Englewood Cliffs, NJ: Prentice Hall, 1980); Jeremy Rifkin, *The End of Work* (New York: Jeremy P. Tarcher/Putnam Books, 1995); and Marie Jahoda, *Employment and Unemployment: A Social Psychological Analysis* (New York: Cambridge University Press, 1982); and "Work, Employment and Unemployment: Values, Theories and Approaches in Social Research." *American Psychologist 36* (1981): 184–91.

3. See William J. Wilson, *op. cit.*, as well as his *The Truly Disadvantaged: The Inner City, the Underclass, and Public Policy* (Chicago: University of Chicago Press, 1987); Jeremy Rifkin, *The End of Work: The Decline of the Global Labor Force and the Dawn of the Post-Market Era*, *op. cit.*; and Lawrence Summers, *Understanding Unemployment* (Cambridge, MA: MIT Press, 1990). See also Allison Zippay, *From Middle Income to Poor: Downward Mobility Among Displaced Steel Workers* (New York: Praeger, 1991); and A. Hacker, *Money: Who Has How Much and Why* (New York: Scribner, 1997).

4. Mark Granovetter, *Getting a Job* (Chicago: University of Chicago Press, 1995). On this point see as well D. E. Sanger and S. Lohr, "A Search for Answers to Avoid the Layoffs," *New York Times*, 9 March, 1996, p. 11; and J. B. Judis, "The Jobless Recovery" *The New Republic*, 15 March 1993, pp. 20–23.

5. On this point see P. B. Warr, "Job Loss, Unemployment and Psychological Well Being," in V. Allen and E. van de Vliert, Eds., *Role Transitions* (New York: Plenum), 1984, 263–85; S. P. McKenna and D. M. Fryer, "Perceived Health During Lay-Off and Early Unemployment," *Occupational Health 36* (1984): 201–06.

6. On this point see Marie Jahoda, *Employment and Unemployment: A Social Psychological Analysis* (New York: Cambridge University Press, 1982).

7. See James K. Glassman, "Lonely Unemployment Line." *U. S. News & World Report*, 22 December 1997, p.36.

8. The reader is advised to explore the following web site for constantly updated employment and unemployment figures: cpsinfo@bls.gov.

9. See Lawrence Mishel, John Schmitt, and Jared Bernstein, *The State of Working America* (Armonk, NY: ME Sharpe, 1993).

10. Government labor statistics indicate that approximately 6 percent of the U.S. labor force holds more than one job, a figure representing some 8 million people.

11. On this point, see E. J. Dionne, Jr., "Proof Arrives that Low Unemployment Doesn't Have to Mean Inflation." *The Boston Globe*, 8 June 1999, A15.

12. Joel Blau, *Illusions of Prosperity: America's Working Families in an Age of Economic Insecurity* (New York: Oxford University Press, 1999); and Kathryn Marie Dudley, *The End of the Line: Lost Jobs, New Lives in Post Industrial America* (Chicago: University of Chicago Press, 1997). On this point, see as well J. E. Schwarz and T. J. Volgy, *The Forgotten Americans* (New York: Norton, 1992); and T. R. Swartz and K. Maas, Eds., *America's Working Poor* (South Bend, IN: University of Notre Dame Press, 1995).

13. On this point, see S. Caminiti, "What Happens to Laid-Off Managers," *Fortune*, 13 June 1994, pp. 68–70; "From Coast to Coast, from Affluent to Poor, Poll Shows Anxiety Over Jobs," *New York Times*, 11 March 1994, A1; "Strong Employment Gains Spur Inflation Worries," *Washington Post*, 7 May 1994, A1; "When Will the Layoffs End?" *Fortune*, 20 September 1993, 40; "Family Struggles to Make Do After Fall from Middle Class," *New York Times*, 11 March 1994, A1; "Not Home Alone: Jobless Male Managers Proliferate in Suburbs, Causing Subtle Malaise," *Wall Street Journal*, 20 September 1993, A1; "College Class of '93 Learns Hard Lesson: Career Prospects are Worst in Decades," *Wall Street Journal*, 20 May 1993, B1.

14. In Kai Erikson and Steven Peter Vallas, *The Nature of Work* (New Haven: Yale University Press, 1990).

15. See Mark Fritz, "Steelworkers say Clinton's Campaign Promises have Rusted," *The Boston Globe*, Friday, 25 December 1998, A21.

16. These figures were reported in The Employment Situation News Release of the Bureau of Labor Statistics, Friday, 5 November 1999. Internet address: http://stats.bls.gov/newsrels.htm.

17. André Gorz, *Farewell to the Working Class: An Essay on Post-Industrial Socialism* (Boston: South End Press, 1982).

18. Elijah Anderson, *Code of the Street: Decency, Violence and the Moral Life of the Inner City* (New York: Norton, 1999).

19. Derrick Z. Jackson, "Creating, Not Curbing, Poverty," *The Boston Globe*, 20 January 1999, A15. See also R. Hernandez, "Most Dropped from Welfare Don't Get Jobs," *New York Times*, 23 March 1998, A1. In a simi-

lar vein, see the earlier study of Gregory Pappas, *The Magic City: Unemployment in a Working Class Community* (Ithaca: Cornell University Press, 1989).

20. Lester C. Thurow, "Jobless Figures Deceptive," *The Boston Globe*, 20 April 1999, C4.

21. On this point, see Terry F. Buss and F. Stevens Redburn, *Hidden Unemployment: Discouraged Workers and Public Policy* (New York: Praeger: 1988).

22. On this point see J. York-Barr, T. Schultz, M. B. Doyle, R. Kronberg, and S. Crossett, "Inclusive Schooling in St. Cloud: Perspectives on the Process and People," *Remedial and Special Education* 17 (1996): 92–105. This study is cited in Helen Roy, "Inclusion: Voices from the Inside," (Unpublished manuscript, Boston University, 1998), 35.

23. See the collection of essays published by the *New York Times*, *The Downsizing of America* (New York: Times Book, 1996).

24. C. P. Estes, *Women Who Run with the Wolves: Myths and Stories of the Wild Woman Archtype* (New York: Ballantine Books, 1992). Cited in Mary Lynn Pulley, *Losing Your Job—Reclaiming Your Soul* (San Francisco: Jossey-Bass, 1997).

25. Pulley, *Losing Your Job—Reclaiming Your Soul, op. cit.*, 6.

26. John Kotre, *White Gloves: How We Create Ourselves Through Memory* (New York: The Free Press, 1995).

27. The reader is also directed to Thomas J. Cottle, *At Peril: Stories of Injustice* (Amherst: University of Massachusetts Press, in press 2001). See especially the Afterword.

28. Wallace Peterson, *Silent Depression: The Fate of the American Dream* (New York: Norton, 1994). On this point, see as well, "Job Losses Don't Let Up Even as Hard Times Ease," *New York Times*, 22 March 1994, D5; "The American Dream: Fired Up and Melted Down," *The Washington Post*, 12 April 1992, A1; and L. Mead, *The New Politics of Poverty: The Non-Working Poor in America* (New York: Basic Books, 1981).

29. John Kenneth Galbraith, *The Culture of Contentment* (Boston: Houghton Mifflin, 1992).

30. On this point, see William Bridges, *Job-Shift: How to Prosper in a WorkPlace Without Jobs* (Reading, MA: Addison-Welsey, 1994); Cliff Hakim, *When You Lose Your Job: Laid Off, Fired, Early Retired* (San Francisco: Berrett-Koehler, 1993); Mary Lynn Pulley, *Losing Your Job, Reclaiming Your Soul: Stories of Resilience, Renewal and Hope* (San Francisco:

Jossey-Bass, 1997); and Anita Doreen Diggs, *Barrier-Breaking Resumes and Interviews: Jumping the Hurdle of Unemployment and Getting a Job* (New York: Times Books, 1999).

31. See Benjamin Kline Hunnicutt, *Kellogg's Six-Hour Day* (Philadelphia: Temple University Press, 1996); and Stanley Aronowitz, *The Jobless Future: Science-Tech and the Dogma of Work* (Minneapolis: University of Minnesota Press, 1994.)

32. There is no better description of unemployment and the formation of identity than that by E. Liebow, *Tally's Corner* (Boston: Little, Brown, 1967).

33. On this point, see Keith Thomas, Ed., *The Oxford Book of Work* (New York: Oxford University Press, 1999).

34. Daniel Levinson, *Seasons of A Man's Life* (New York: Knopf, 1978).

35. On this point, see "The Great Male Cop-Out from The Work Ethic," *Business Week*, 14 November 1977, 156ff.

36. See Mirra Komarovsky, *Unemployed Man and His Family* (New York: Octagon, 1970).

37. On this point, see John Hayes, *Understanding the Unemployed: The Psychological Effects of Unemployment* (New York: Methuen, 1981).

38. See Donald W. Tiffany et al., *Unemployed: A Social Psychological Portrait* (New York: Prentice Hall, 1971).

39. On this point, see S. Westin, "The Structure of a Factory Closure: Individual Responses to Job Loss and Unemployment in a Ten-Year Controlled Follow-Up Study," *Social Science and Medicine 31* (1990): 1301–11; and S.H. Applebaum, R. Simpson, and B. T. Shapiro, "The Tough Test of Downsizing," *Organizational Dynamics 16* (1987): 68–79.

40. On 8 March 1991, the federal government put the national unemployment rate at 6.5 percent. In Massachusetts, the rate climbed to 9.3 percent, the highest rate of all the industrial states on this one date, with the exception of Michigan.

41. Cited in *New York Times*, 3 March 1996, 26. Cited in Robert S. Weiss, "Responding to the Mental Health Implications of Downsizing" (Unpublished manuscript, 11 May 1996, 1).

42. On this point, see Charles Craypo and Bruce Nissen, Eds., *Grand Designs: The Impact of Corporate Strategies on Workers, Unions, and Communities* (Ithaca, New York: ILR Press, 1993). See also Bruce Nissen, *Case Studies of Labor-Community Coalitions Confronting Plant Closings* (Albany: State University of New York, 1995).

43. American Management Association, *1995 AMA Survey: Corporate Downsizing, Job Elimination, and Job Creation* (New York: American Management Association, 1996). Cited in Weiss, *op. cit.*, 1.

44. On this point, see Renee Loth, "A Jobless Pool That's Different," *The Boston Globe*, 24 March 1991, A17; and Guy Halverson, "Professionals Join Ranks of Nation's Unemployed," *Christian Science Monitor*, 28 March 1991, 1.

45. Although the present research does not focus directly on the homeless, some of the men with whom I spoke in gathering material for this book now are numbered among them.

46. See Rifkin, *op. cit.*; and "Businesses Prefer Buying Equipment to Hiring New Staff," *The Wall Street Journal*, Sept. 3 1993.

47. See "The Disposable Employee is Becoming a Fact of Life," *Business Week*, 15 December 1986, 52.

48. Louis Uchitelle and N. R. Kleinfield, "On the Battlefields of Business, Millions of Casualties," *New York Times*, 3 March 1996, 1ff.

49. Richard W. Stevenson, "For the Jobless Rate, the Forecast Is Hazy" *New York Times*, Sunday, 21 November 1999.

50. Presently, the state of Massachusetts is negotiating for a thirty-week period to be reduced to twenty-six while a federal program pays benefits up to thirty-nine weeks. Reported in *The Boston Herald*, 8 March 1991, 29.

51. David Moberg, "Most Young Workers Have Missed Out on the Boom," *The Boston Globe*, 16 October 1999, A21. These data were collected by Peter D. Hart Research for the AFL–CIO.

52. Cited in Louis Uchitelle and N. R. Kleinfield, *op. cit.*, 27.

53. "Long Term Jobless Are Hidden, Suffering," *New York Times*, 10 October 1976, IV, 4.

54. See Leonard A. Lecht, *Manpower Needs for National Goals in the 1970s* (New York: Praeger, 1969).

55. On this point, see J. H. Braddock, II, and J. M. McPartland, "How Minorities Continue to be Excluded from Equal Employment Opportunities: Research on Labor Market and Institutional Barriers," *Journal of Social Issues 43* (1987): 5–39.

56. In March 1991, Massachusetts reported that more than 115,000 workers had exhausted their thirty-week unemployment benefits. That figure marked an increase of 66 percent over the previous year. More to the point of this discussion, at that same time, the Massachusetts Department

of Employment and Training announced that 60 percent of unemployed workers were still out of work thirteen weeks beyond the expiration of unemployment benefits. These figures were reported in *The Boston Globe*, 14 March 1991.

57. Some economists refer to the phenomenon of the discouraged worker as *structural unemployment*. The term is meant to highlight those persons out of work despite fluctuations in economic cycles. In fact, because structural unemployment exists in boom-and-bust economic periods alike, some economists suggest that this most intractable form of unemployment should be able to be solved even in periods of high inflation. On this and related points, see Robert M. Solow, John B. Taylor, with an introduction by Benjamin M. Friedman, *Inflation, Unemployment, and Monetary Policy* (Cambridge, MA: MIT Press, 1998); and David Gowland, *Money, Inflation and Unemployment: The Role of Money in the Economy* (New York: St. Martin's Press, 1992).

58. "Youth Joblessness Is at Record High in New York City," *New York Times*, 4 June 1993, Metro Section.

59. In "Planning for Work Sharing: The Promise and Problems of Egalitarian Work Time Reduction," in Erikson and Vallas, eds., *op. cit.*, 259.

60. To counteract this statistical underestimation, some have suggested that discouraged workers should be deemed unemployed only if they met the following criteria: They were shown to be available for work, had given evidence that they had sought employment over the previous six months, but had not sought employment over the previous four weeks.

61. On this point, see Marc Fried, *The World of the Urban Working Class* (Cambridge, MA: Harvard University Press, 1973).

62. See Thomas J. Cottle, *Barred From School* (Washington: New Republic Book Co., 1976); and Katherine Newman, *No Shame in My Game* (New York: Knopf, 1999).

63. Nicholas Lemann, *The Promised Land: The Great Black Migration and How it Changed America* (New York: Vintage Books, 1992); and Michael Katz, Ed.), *The Underclass Debate: Views from History* (Princeton, NJ: Princeton University Press, 1993).

64. Cited in *How Are They Doing? National Longitudinal Study of Special Education Students and Youths with Disabilities* (Menlo Park, CA: SRI International, 1991).

65. See Michael Podgursky, "Sources of Secular Increases in the Unemployment Rate," *Monthly Labor Review*, July 1984, 1969–82.

66. See James Hildreth, "Stark Facts of Recession: A Bad Dream for Workers," *Philadelphia Bulletin*, 5 June 1980.

67. On this point, see Frank Greve, "Vietnam Vets—Lost Generation," *The Boston Globe*, 20 November 1977, 49ff.

68. See *In Aid Of The Unemployed* (Baltimore: Johns Hopkins Press, 1965).

69. On this point, see William Julius Wilson, *op. cit.*; and Douglas C. Glasgow, *The Black Underclass: Poverty, Unemployment, and the Entrapment of Ghetto Youth* (San Francisco: Jossey Bass, 1980).

70. On this point, see B. Mallinckrodt and B. R. Fretz, "Social Support and the Impact of Job Loss on Older Professionals," *Journal of Counseling Psychology 35* (1988): 281–86.

71. See Cynthia Croddon-Tower, *Exploring Child Welfare* (Boston: Allyn & Bacon, 1998); and C. Jencks and P. E. Peterson, Eds., *The Urban Underclass* (Washington, DC: Brookings Institution, 1991).

72. On this point, see P. Voydanoff and B. W. Donnelly, Eds., *Families and Economic Distress: Coping Strategies and Social Policy* (Beverly Hills, CA: Sage Publications, 1988).

73. See Paula G. Leventman, *Professionals Out Of Work* (New York: The Free Press, 1981); and "Nonrational Foundations of Professional Rationality: Employment Instability Among Scientists and Technologists." (Sociological Symposium, Summer 1976), 83–112.

74. Robert S. Weiss, *Responding to the Mental Health Implications of Downsizing, op. cit.*, 2.

75. See Salvador Minuchin, *Family Kaleidoscope* (Cambridge, MA: Harvard University Press, 1984); and Patricia Minuchin, Jorge Colapinto, and Salvador Minuchin, *Working with Families of the Poor* (New York: The Guilford Press, 1998).

76. On this point, see Richard H. Price, "Psychosocial Impact of Job Loss on Individuals and Families," *Current Directions in Psychological Science 1* (1992): 9–11.

77. See Komarovsky, *op. cit.*

78. On this point, see V. L. Hamilton, C. L. Broman, W. S. Hoffman, and D. S. Renner, "Hard Times and Vulnerable People: Initial Effects of Plant Closing on Autoworkers' Mental Health," *Journal of Health and Social Behavior 31* (1990): 123–40. On a similar theme, see M. Jahoda, "Economic Recession and Mental Health: Some Conceptual Issues," *Journal of Social Issues 4* (1988): 13–23.

79. Ann Crittenden, "U.S. Scientists Report Effect of Economy on Mental Health," *International Herald Tribune 21* April 1977, 4.

80. See, for example, Richard H. Price, "Psychosocial Impact of Job Loss on Individuals and Families," *Current Directions in Psychological Science 1* (1992): 9–11; and R. C. Kessler, J. B. Turner, and J. S. House, "Unemployment and Health in a Community Sample," *Journal of Health and Social Behavior 58* (1987): 51–59.

81. See Richard Price, *op. cit.*

82. See Robert Karasek and Tores Theorell, *Healthy Work* (New York: Basic Books, 1990, especially chapter 10).

83. See Thomas J. Cottle, *At Peril: Stories of Injustice* (Amherst, MA: The University of Massachusetts Press, in press).

84. M. Harvey Brenner, *Mental Illness and the Economy* (Cambridge: Harvard University Press, 1973). See also his "Importance of the Economy to the Nation's Health," in L. Eisenberg and A. Kleinman, Eds., *The Relevance of Social Science for Medicine* (New York: Reidel, 1980), 371–95; S. V. Kasl, "Strategies of Research on Economic Instability and Health," *Psychological Medicine 12* (1982): 637–49; S. Kasl and C. Cooper, Eds., *Stress and Health: Issues in Research Methodology* (New York: Wiley, 1987); M. W. Linn, R. Sandifer, and S. Stein, "Effects of Unemployment on Mental and Physical Health," *American Journal of Public Health 75* (1985): 502–06; R. L. Payne, P. B. Warr, and J. Hartley, "Social Class and Psychological Ill-Health During Unemployment," *Sociology of Health and Illness 6* (1984): 152–74; and R. C. Kessler, J. B. Turner, and J. S. House, "Intervening Processes in the Relationship Between Unemployment and Health," *Psychological Medicine 17* (1987): 949–61.

85. M. H. Brenner, "Relation of Economic Change to Swedish Health and Social Well-Being," *Social Science Medicine 25* (1987): 183–95.

86. Some research also indicates that the stress of long-term unemployment relates to the health of the fetus and later to the infant. Mentioned in Crittenden, *op. cit.* See also Marion Wells, "Job Loss Can Be a Health Hazard," *Labor News*, 31 October 1980, 8.

87. This point is elaborated by Robert Weiss in *Staying the Course: The Emotional and Social Lives of Men Who Do Well at Work* (New York: The Free Press, 1990).

88. On this point, see J. R. P. French, R. D. Caplan, and R. Van Harrison, *The Mechanisms of Job Stress and Strain* (New York: Wiley, 1982).

89. On a related point, see Gerald F. Seib, "Recessions Cause Death Rates to Rise, As Pressures of Coping Take Hold." *The Wall Street Journal*, 25 August 1980, 13.

90. On this point, see M. Dew, E. J. Bromet, and L. Penkower, "Mental Health Effects of Job Loss in Women," *Psychological Medicine 22* (1992): 751–64.

91. D. Halle, *America's Working Man* (Chicago: University of Chicago Press, 1984.)

92. The actual unemployment benefit varies from state to state. Massachusetts, for example, pays $272 per week to the unemployed person, with an additional $25 for each of his or her dependents.

93. *The Boston Globe*, 19 September 1990.

94. *The Boston Globe*, 12 March 1991.

95. *The Boston Globe*, 26 April 1979.

96. *The Boston Globe*, 11 September 1990.

97. *The Boston Globe*, 7 April 1980.

98. On this point, see Clark Moustakas, *Loneliness* (New York: Prentice Hall, 1961); and Robert Weiss, *Loneliness: The Experience of Emotional and Social Isolation* (Cambridge, MA: MIT Press, 1975).

99. For those wishing to know more about the general aspects of life study research, see Ronald Fraser, *Work: Twenty Personal Accounts* (London: Penguin, 1968, 1969, two volumes); and H. L. Beales, "Memoirs of the Unemployed" in H. L. Beales and R. S. Lambert, Eds., (London: EP Publishing, 1973).

100. David Roediger and Philip Foner, *Our Own Time: A History of American Labor and the Working Day* (Westport, CT: Greenwood Press, 1989).

101. George Orwell, *The Road to Wigan Pier*, Foreword by Victor Gollancz (New York: Harcourt, Brace, Jovanovich, 1958, 1972).

102. Herbert Applebaum, *The American Work Ethic and the Changing Work Force: An Historical Perspective* (Westport, CT: Quorum Books, 1998); and A. Tilgher, *Work: What It Has Meant To Men Thorough The Ages* (New York: Harcourt Brace, 1930).

103. On the subject of physical health, I received a letter years ago from a man living in Jacksonville, Florida. He was interested in knowing whether the re-emergence of his muscular sclerosis possibly could be related to the fact that he had been demoted and lost much of his salary. At the end of his letter he wrote: "A former supervisor told me that when he

was there, the working conditions described were worse than when he was a prisoner of the Germans in WWII." In more general terms, see "Job Seeking, Reemployment, and Mental Health: A Randomized Field Experiment in Coping with 'Job Loss,'" *Journal of Applied Psychology* 75 (October 1989): 759–69.

104. See Ely Chinoy, *Automobile Workers and the American Dream* (Garden City, NY: Doubleday, 1955).

105. On this point, see Oscar Handlin, *The Uprooted* (Boston: Little, Brown, 1951); and Stephen Thernstrom, "Urbanization, Migration, and Social Mobility in Late Nineteenth-Century America," in Barton J. Bernstein, Ed.., *Towards A New Past: Dissenting Essays in American History* (New York: Pantheon, 1968): 158–75. See also, John A. Garraty, *Unemployment in History: Economic Thought and Public Policy* (New York: Harper and Row, 1978); and Kai Erikson and Steven Peter Vallas, Eds., *The Nature of Work.* (New Haven, CT: Yale University Press, 1990).

106. Applebaum, *op. cit.*

107. On this point, see Robert Dubin, "Work and Non-Work: Institutional Perspectives." in M. D. Dunnette, Ed., *Work and Non-Work in the Year 2001* (Monterey, CA: Brooks-Cole, 1973).

108. Katherine Newman, *No Shame in My Game, op. cit.*, 119.

109. J. Schor, *The Overworked American: The Unexpected Decline of Leisure* (New York: Basic Books, 1991). On this point, see also Philip E. Slater, *The Pursuit of Loneliness* (Boston: Beacon Press, 1970).

110. See his *Mental Health and Work Organizations* (Indianapolis: Rand McNally, 1970).

111. On this point see R. S. Lazarus, *Psychological Stress and the Coping Process* (New York: McGraw-Hill, 1966).

112. See, for example, T. S. Langner and S. T. Michael, *Life Stress and Mental Health* (New York: The Free Press, 1963); and S. Levine and N. Scotch, *Social Stress* (Chicago: Aldine, 1971).

113. Quoted in Mitchell C. Lynch, "As Recession Deepens, White-Collar Workers Join the Jobless Ranks," *The Wall Street Journal*, 7 December 1981, 1.

114. See his *Mental Health and the Industrial Worker* (New York: Wiley, 1965).

115. On this point, see *Work in America*, Report of Special Task Force to the Secretary of Health, Education and Welfare (Cambridge, MA: MIT Press, 1971).

116. Reported in *USA Today*, 19 March 1991.

117. Quoted in Darrell Sifford, "The Right Job: A Life Saver," *The Boston Globe*, 25 March 1980, B1ff.

118. E. Palmore, "Physical, Mental and Social Factors in Predicting Longevity," *Gerontology* 9 (1969).

119. E. Palmore, "Predicting Longevity: A Follow-Up Controlling for Age," *Gerontology*, Winter (1969): 247–250; and M. Mariotti, "Working Conditions and Manner of Aging" (International Center of Social Gerontology, Paris, 1971).

120. See, for example, J. French and R. Caplan, "Psychological Factors in Coronary Heart Disease," *Industrial Medicine* 39 (September 1970); J. French, "The Social Environment and Mental Health," *Journal of Social Issues* 19 (1963): 39–56; S. V. Kasl and S. Cobb, 1982. Visibility of Stress Effects Among Men Experiencing Job Loss. In L. Goldberger & S. Breznitz, Eds., Handbook of Stress: Theoretical and Clinical Aspects (New York: Free Press): 445–65; A. Pepitone, "Self, Social Environment and Stress," in M. H. Appley and D. Trumbull, Eds., *Psychological Stress* (New York: Appleton Century Crofts, 1967); and S. M. Sales, "Organizational Roles as a Risk Factor in Coronary Heart Disease," *Administrative Science Quarterly 14* (1969).

121. Darrell Sifford, "The Right Job: A Life Saver," *op. cit.*

122. See Sara Lawrence-Lightfoot and Jessica Hoffman Davis, *The Art and Science of Portraiture* (San Francisco: Jossey Bass, 1997).

123. For those wishing to know more about the general aspects of life study research, see Ronald Fraser, *Work: Twenty Personal Accounts* (London: Penguin, 1968, 1969, two volumes); H. L. Beales, "Memoirs of the Unemployed," in H. L. Beales and R. S. Lambert (London: EP Publishing, 1973); Thomas J. Cottle, *Drawing Life: Portraits of Adults and Children* (unpublished manuscript, 1998); R. E. Stake, *The Art of Case Study Research* (Thousand Oaks, CA: Sage Publications, 1995); and H. S. Becker, "Problems of Inference and Proof in Participant Observation," *American Sociological Review 23* (1958): 652–60.

124. On this point, see, for example, George S. Howard, "Culture Tales: A Narrative Approach to Thinking, Cross-Cultural Psychology, and Psychotherapy," *American Psychologist* 46 (March 1991): 187–97.

125. Thomas J. Cottle, "Witness of Joy," *Daedalus 122* (1993): 123–50.

126. See Jerome Bruner, *Actual Minds, Possible Worlds* (Cambridge, MA: Harvard Press University, 1986. See also D. P. Polkinghorne, *Narrative Psychology*. Albany: SUNY Press, 1988.

127. Polkinghorne, *op. cit.*, 14. Much of the discussion in this section has been influenced by Polkinghorne's work, along with the work of Kenneth J. Gergen. See, for example, "The Social Constructionist Movement in Modern Psychology," *American Psychologist 40* (1985): 266–275.

128. Edwin J. Delattre, *Character and Cops—Ethics in Policing* (Washington, DC: American Enterprise Institute for Public Policy Research, 155). Cited in Thomas W. Nolan, *Character Education for Police Officers: Station House as Moral Milieu.* (unpublished manuscript, Boston University, 1999).

129. See E. Eisner, *The Enlightened Eye* (New York: MacMillan Publishing Co., 1991). See also Arthur Beane, *The Supervision of Student Teachers: An emphasis on self-reflection* (Unpublished manuscript, Boston University).

130. Beane, *ibid.* 32.

131. Beane, *ibid.* 32.

132. Beane, *ibid.* 32.

133. For examples of this point, see Charles Keil, *Urban Blues* (Chicago: University of Chicago Press, 1966); Todd Gitlin and Nanci Hollander, *Uptown: Poor Whites in Chicago* (New York: Harper Colophon, 1970); and Piri Thomas, *Down These Mean Streets* (New York: Knopf, 1967).

134. On this point, see William Earle, *The Autobiographical Consciousness* (Chicago: Quadrangle Books, 1972).

135. Donald E. Polkinghorne, *op. cit.*

136. Clifford Geertz, *The Interpretation of Cultures* (New York: Basic Books, 1973). Cited in Timothy Kunzier *Revealing the Mystic Cipher* (unpublished manuscript, Boston University, 1998).

137. See David Bakan, *The Duality of Human Existence* (Chicago: Rand McNally, 1966).

138. Interestingly, in the Hasidic tradition, it is said that the only way to determine the truth of a story is by noting whether it contains testimony from *true* witnesses.

139. On this point, see Sara Lawrence-Lightfoot, *Balm in Gilead* (Reading, MA: Addison Wesley, 1989).

140. On this point, see, for example, Oscar Lewis, *Five Families* (New York: Basic Books, 1959).

141. For a discussion of this point, see Thomas J. Cottle, *Private Lives and Public Accounts* (Amherst: University of Massachusetts Press, 1977).

142. See Paula Goldman Leventman, "Nonrational Foundations of Professional Rationality: Employment Instability Among Scientists and Technologists," *Sociological Symposium 16* (1976): 103.

143. Martha Straus, *No Talk Therapy* (New York: Norton, 1999).

Chapter 1

Mr. Housewife U. S. A.: Kenneth Hawkins

My father would have had a job all his life, he'd be alive this minute. Wasn't his strength that gave way. His job gave way and that took his strength away.

If one had to summarize the story of Ken Hawkins, a good place to start is with the concept of health. It goes without saying that we wish good health for people, and in the present context, hope as well that their employment conditions enhance their health, both physical and mental.

For some men, however, the concept of health has to be extended to include performing certain roles delineated by the society, and taught, normally, by one's parents. One such role is that of living life as a self-sufficient person, dependent on few, and known to one's family and friends as dependable. Another role is that of competitor, successful player in the marketplace. Yet another role is that of family provider, family protector, person of strength in all meanings of that word. Indeed, despite an assortment of cultural transformations, in the mind of a man like Ken Hawkins, society continues to make perfectly clear the nature of the roles men and women are meant to perform. The real man, for this kindly giant, knows his limitations, stays healthy, continues working, provides for his family, and takes pride in the fact that his efforts establish a foundation for their happiness.

For quite a few years, society's plan was followed to the letter, until physical illness limited the activities of this man and created a profound transformation not only for him, but for his family as well. No longer able to protect and provide for his family as he believed men were meant to do, no longer able to feel comfortable living as a man, given society's definitions of maleness and masculinity, no longer able to do the physical chores his work demanded, Ken Hawkins was left weakened and, well, heartbroken. Some men, after all, are destroyed by working too much, some by working too little, and some, like Ken, by working hard at what they ultimately must have decided was the wrong thing.

On May 18, Ken Hawkins and his wife threw a party. Ken was celebrating a significant anniversary, one year out of work. His friends found it hard to believe that so much time had elapsed. "A year gets shorter and shorter the older you get," he told them. "But no sadness tonight; tonight is celebration."

It was a celebration too. The moment people arrived, Betty and Ken brought out food. First trays of sandwiches and a cheese dip, then salad and fruit. "Where'd you get the strawberries?" someone asked. "Ken found them," Betty answered proudly. Ken turned away. The women in the room seemed amused by Ken's ingenuity and what they called "all his hidden talents." The men said little. As they had suspected, the evening was shaping up to be somewhat peculiar. One man thought he might laugh. He pretended to choke.

"How can you be choking on *that*?" Ken asked, coming to his rescue. "We haven't even brought out the stuff *I've* made." The remark cleared the air; no one could deny they weren't interested in how the Hawkins had arranged their lives over the last year. Everyone knew that Ken and Betty were the most talked about people in Flintborough. Mention of their name brought expressions of concern and bewilderment, as well as quips about the Hawkins' "new lifestyle." "How are Mrs. and Mrs. Hawkins?" someone would inevitably ask. "Haven't seen her *or* her around much recently." Some of those most amused by the family's transformation were actually guests in the Hawkins' house that May evening of the anniversary celebration.

The story of Ken Hawkins was hardly unique. Ken himself was quick to say that thousands of men were in his same position. A husky child, he had grown up to be a very strong but rather heavy-set man. He played football in high school until poor grades meant he had to stop. Knowing only too well his intellectual aptitude, he left school early in his senior year and found a job working construction. Singletary Construction was delighted to find a strong young man, especially in the autumn. They were known to hire young men during the summer and assign them physically punishing jobs with low wages, but in September, when the boys returned to school, the cheap labor market dried up. Ken couldn't have applied at a better time. He spoke to Phil Singletary on a Monday and started work the next morning.

It was a good thing too that the negotiations went fast because William Hawkins was incensed by his son quitting school. He even contemplated ordering Ken to move out of the house. If he wasn't a student, he should join the army. His wife convinced him it would help nothing to send Ken away. Besides, the boy had offered to give most of his earnings to his parents.

If it was foolish to throw the boy out of his home, it was also fruitless for Anne Hawkins to argue with her son when he offered her his salary. There was nothing to hide: Ever since William's heart trouble was detected, the family had little money. They lived with the burden of unpaid medical bills, the fear that their rent would be raised, and of course rising prices. Anne Hawkins was not an especially strong woman. While occasionally she took in sewing, the work brought in only small amounts of money. What her son offered was nothing short of a miracle. Reluctantly, William consented to let Ken remain at home.

From the time he became ill, William Hawkins had known that only Ken's working could ease the family's economic pressures. Still, he hoped Ken would complete school. "One never knows what opportunities come up when a man is educated," he told his son a million times. While his wish would not come true, he had to admit he was surprised by the salary Singletary Construction had offered. "Where were all those nice unions in my day?" he laughed with Ken, who had been prepared to accept any salary Mr. Singletary offered.

Although Ken Hawkins had known the job required union membership, he had no idea of the benefits. When Mr. Singletary announced the terms of employment, Ken recalls responding, "You got me!"

"I had you the second you came in this office."

"You're absolutely right, sir," Ken had replied with some penitence.

"Glad to have you," his new boss said, sticking out his hand. "And for Christsakes don't call me Sir. We don't even call my old man sir. Work hard and you'll get a raise in six months. Unless of course you can't use the money." He winked at Ken.

"I can use it all right. My parents get a big chunk."

"What you do with it is none of my business. Way I look at it, it all goes back to the government one way or another. Either they get you in taxes or inflation, or you spend the money somewhere. What you going to do about the army?"

"Go when they call me." Ken remembered telling him, once again reminded of the one issue that scared him more than anything else.

The excitement with the new job and the family's delight with the first pay checks made the Hawkins family forget about the army, although it was inevitable the army would contact Ken. Did he have to notify them that he had dropped out of school? Would his new status place him high on the list of men to be drafted? "When they want you, they'll call you," his mother said. "Besides, it'd be unfair if the army took you when you're now the provider in this family." Ken saw that the remark had hurt his father. It was one of the few times he could remember his mother commenting on her husband's failure to earn a living. But it was true that Ken had assumed the major financial responsibilities for the family.

For several months the Hawkins family lived better than they had in quite a while. Ken came home exhausted, but every other Thursday afternoon the pay check arrived and his mother went out shopping with renewed excitement. She had begun buying foods she had only looked at for the last years. The meals at the Hawkins home were once again first rate. Anne was hunting for recipes in newspapers and teaching Ken how to cook. Sunday morning was his time to make breakfast, which meant omelets. His father always snickered when Ken brought his specially prepared dishes to the table, but one mouthful was enough to silence everybody. Omelets and chocolate cake, his mother teased him, those were his specialties; Ken merely laughed. The smell of good food reminded them all of how difficult the years of William's unemployment had been. There was talk now of the family moving to a larger apartment, and there was the possibility of Ken finding his own apartment.

After a year at Singletary, Ken Hawkins heard from the army. The notification indicated that he had violated the law by not advising his draft board when he left school. Furthermore, he was to report for a physical examination, which he did. He told no one the reason for his absence from work. The day ended with Ken convinced he would be inducted. Yet surprisingly, he was deferred for medical reasons. The army doctors had discovered a heart problem, presumably one of a congenital nature, a condition that had never before been detected. Relieved, Ken told everyone he had been deferred because he was the sole support of his family; he chose to reveal the medical problem to no one. If Singletary heard about it, they might fire him, and construction jobs were becoming increasingly difficult to come by.

Without the army hanging over his head and his position at Singletary seemingly secure, the years passed easily, except that his parents were becoming increasingly ill. Ken noted drastic reductions in their energy. He may have lied about the reason for his army deferment, but no one could have doubted now that he was the sole support of his family, even if some people felt it unusual that at twenty four he continued to live at home.

Anne Hawkins died when her son was twenty-six. With money he had saved, Ken had purchased two funeral plots. Both his parents said they wanted to be cremated. Who would visit their graves anyway? they asked him. But he knew the idea of cremation was distasteful to them; they only wished to save their son some money. Ken bought plots at St. Mary's cemetery. His parents were pleased, but he assured them they weren't going to die for a long, long time. They all knew it was just talk. Anne predicted on the first of the year that she wouldn't see the spring. She died in April. She was fifty-three. Her husband immediately fell into a depression that Ken believed would bring him to his own end. But when the hot weather came, his spirits unexpectedly lifted. By the autumn he was his old self, exclaiming that his wife wouldn't have wanted to see him dragging around the house like an old man. "I'll tell you something else," he told Ken. "It's time you move out, get a wife, get on with your own life." Ken insisted there was no better place to live than with his father. Besides, because their expenses were so minimal, there was no reason not to take a vacation together, which they did. At fifty-eight, William Hawkins was gaining strength.

Then, in December, with no warning, William Hawkins collapsed in the little park near his apartment house and was rushed to the hospital. He was dead on arrival. The news of his death reached Ken, who was working at a construction site miles away. The men on the crew knew several things about Ken Hawkins. While he was overweight from the beer and cake he loved so well, he was never one to short-change his bosses or let the youngest man pick up the slack. He was a good man, even though it seemed peculiar for a man his age to live at home with his father. But what-ever the oddities, he would be devastated by his dad's death. When word of William Hawkins' death came to senior foreman Pepper Stevens, he didn't have the heart to tell Ken. He would have preferred to tell young Hawkins he had just lost his job.

Ken mourned his father's death as together they had mourned his mother's death. For several months, he was profoundly upset, although he lost only a few days at work. Phil Singletary insisted he take time off but Ken was unmoved. "I'm a big boy," he remembered telling his boss. "I belong here." Clearly, he feared for the security of his job, although there was nothing at Singletary Construction to suggest cutbacks or layoffs. The economy was in some trouble, and the building industry was among the first to feel the recession, but Singletary was holding up. Ken took two days off when his father died, then returned to his job set on meeting his responsibilities. The men on the crew expressed their sympathies, but they knew they were wasting their breath telling Ken Hawkins to slow down.

Within six months of his father's death, Ken rented a two-bedroom apartment. He was eager, he said, to start life all over again. He barely had his new home decorated when he met Betty Dercole. Those who saw them together knew it was only a matter of time before they would marry. The swanky bachelor headquarters Ken had imagined were not to be. Betty had no interest in living among the masses of young single people in the city. She preferred to find an apartment in one of the suburbs.

At twenty-nine, Ken Hawkins married and moved his young bride into a three-bedroom suburban apartment. Singletary moved Ken to a site two miles from his home. A year and a half later, the couple was fixing up one of the bedrooms with a crib and tiny chest of drawers. "It was too good to be true," Ken recalled. "If only my parents. . . . Hey, but what the hell. Some people's lives are like that. My mother would have gone out of her mind to have a grandchild. You know, I'd been with Singletary ten years. My dad and me, we were going to celebrate that anniversary together. I promised him I'd buy a bottle of French champagne. Twenty-five bucks a bottle. For once he didn't argue with me. It took him a lot of years, but he got over my leaving school. I agreed with him. I want my kid to finish. She goes all the way, too. Not like her old man. Tell you some-thing else: She's going to work. None of this men work and women stay home with the kids. Everybody has to know what it's like out there. Very few jobs women can't do."

"You know what my Dad worried about? He worried maybe his son was queer. He grew up with all the beliefs men in his generation were taught. How come his son lived at home? How come his son wasn't going out every night with some girl? But he was also brought up learning the meaning of work. Queer or not, if a man works, there's nothing else you say about him. He makes his money, he pays his bills, that makes him all man in anyone else's eyes. Even my old man's 'thing' that scared *me* all those years was that Singletary might lay me off. Then we'd have had a tough go. I suppose I could have managed, but then I'd have had to figure out how am I going to show this man I'm still a man when I don't work. Both my parents went to their graves thinking I was out of the draft because I supported them. They never knew a thing about the heart. I even began to forget it myself. Certainly wasn't going to tell the company. You want to be a man in my father's eyes, you proved you could work alongside any man and earn the respect of the men you work with. *And* bring home the check every two weeks.

"Funny the way people stop doubting you when you bring home the bacon. But something I've learned: bringing home the bacon matters a helluva lot more to men than women. I tell my wife I'm out of a job, she'd say, so, we'll find something. A man hears the news, he's beginning to wonder about you. He may know the job situation better than you, all these guys out of work in the country, hell, in the construction business alone they got thousands out of work. The guy may even be out of work himself, but he looks at you. You got to be queer. I don't know what the hell I'm talking about. Things stay like they are, I won't ever have to face that problem. Hell, my wife's talking about a second child, and you know what she's got planned then? *She's* going back to work herself. Jesus, we're going to be rolling in money. I may even buy my *own* construction company. Go into Philly and tell him I'm buying the joint. Jesus, wouldn't *that* be a laugh and a half. And my old man was worryin' 'cause I didn't finish that half-baked high school. Best thing I ever did. As short a life as they had, my working let my parents live just that much longer. For that reason alone I'll go to my grave thanking Phil Singletary. That job held three people up almost ten years. So maybe I won't buy the company, hate to put a good man like that out of business, although hell, he might like it. Never saw a man who hates to work as much as he does, and *he's* going to inherit the whole damn mess one of these days. His father must be pushing seventy-five and he comes into the office every day. Talk about what a job can do for a man.

There's a man never went to school, worked every day of his life since he's fifteen years old. Sure doesn't do it 'cause he needs the money, he needs the work. All right, so he doesn't do as much as someone younger. Or he's keeping his son from taking the big desk. He ain't hurting anybody, and he's probably doing his family the best thing he could do for them: he's keeping himself alive. My father would have had a job all his life, he'd be alive this minute. Wasn't his strength that gave way. His *job* gave way and that took his strength away. Killed my mother too. She was from the old school, didn't know how to live with unemployment. She didn't know what the hell to do with a man lying around the house all day, so messed up in his life he couldn't even get himself to watch television. Then she had me flopping in and out of school. She must have been worried sick wondering what in the name of God was going to happen to us. If I was worried about it myself, what did *she* think?

"That business of cooking together, I could see what it was about. She didn't have a husband; she was just nursing the man, so she turned me into a sort of husband. I knew what she was doing, although I always wondered if *she* knew. But she was brought up in the old school. Men worked, women stayed home in the kitchen and took care of the kids. What the hell were they supposed to do when their husbands didn't work I don't know. I don't think any of the women in her day were taught anything about that. You could see she resented my father for not working, for not eating, for not dying too, probably. So I was there and she played like I was the husband she was sending off to work every morning. He saw what was going on, but what the hell was he supposed to say about it? He never even got of bed before ten o'clock. Fact is, the earlier I went to work, the later he stayed in bed. He couldn't live without me working, or not working, and she couldn't stand him not working. I talk like I'm some expert on family relations. All I want to say is they did the best they could and I miss them both. No reason for either one of them to be gone. I blame *that* too on unemployment. That's what killed them. It wasn't going to get to me. But it ate the two of them up. I guess even my working didn't stop the old killer, though, did it?"

Betty Hawkins' blueprint for her family was working out perfectly. By twenty-five she had given birth to her second daughter, and was already making plans to return to her secretarial job. The return, however, came sooner than she had planned. A superb offer was made to her and after long deliberation with Ken she accepted the job. Jo-Anne was a year and a half old, her sister Julie eighteen months older. Ken wondered whether leaving small children was the best thing to do, but his protest was mild. He maintained his belief that women and men should work, and above all he wanted his wife to be happy. Then, too, how could anyone object to the money Betty would bring in? While her salary hardly matched his, it made the difference between renting a lovely apartment and purchasing their own home, which they did during the week of Julie's third birthday.

The house in Engleside, twenty miles from the city, could not have been more perfect. Four bedrooms meant that Betty's mother could visit regularly. The yard was more than ample for two children and the new kitchen so inviting Ken returned to cooking, although he couldn't prepare meals without thinking of his mother and how they laughed at the sight of omelets and chocolate cake.

According to Betty, the best part of her life was Ken, but that didn't mean she wouldn't leave time for her projects. She cooked, sewed, cleaned around the house, repaired appliances, tended to the children and, of course, had her own job with Burford Electronics. Still, there was always Ken to help her. Anticipating her moods, he either had dinner under way by the time she arrived home from work or greeted her at the door with the news that they were dining out.

"It's like Ken can look at me in the morning and know how I'm going to be feeling ten hours later. It's amazing, because he never discusses his own work, never complains about being tired, although you know he is because he can't stay awake past nine o'clock. They work him harder than he'll tell anybody, but he has this thing about being the hardest-working person they have. I've told him a million times, if they haven't fired you after all these years, what are you worried about? You know how many guys call in sick when all they are is hung over? This man is never hung over, never sick. He's the first to arrive, the last to leave. Ken told me Phil Singletary himself doesn't work that hard. But he keeps on pushing like they were still deciding whether to give him the job."

Ken knew all about his wife's concerns: "Yeah, I push myself. I don't adore work, but I got my reasons. When I was a kid I wanted to be the strongest guy around. Lot of kids, they called me 'fatty,' or 'the horse.' I didn't care 'cause when I'd go to fight 'em they'd back off damn quick, believe me. No one said nothing to me in high school 'cause I played football. I wasn't all that good. If I hadn't been so big they wouldn't have looked twice at me. Okay, God gave me big brawn and little brain. What are you supposed to do when you're built like that? You use the brawn. A genius uses his brains and can't even lift a pile of books. Me, I use the muscle. I went to Singletary that first time, he knew he wanted me the second he saw my size. You make the most out of what you have. That's the way I see it anyway. I got strong arms and strong legs. Working construction is what I'm suited for. You think I need someone to tell me it ain't the easiest way to make a buck? She says I'm pushing myself, believe me, I know why I'm doing it. I'll tell you sometime."

How to describe Ken Hawkins: He was a decent, straightforward man. He was reliable, dependable, kind, strong. And honest. His honesty could be observed in his ability to speak ingenuously about himself. When there was something he preferred not to reveal, he let it be known he was concealing something. That which he concealed most assiduously was his ill health. For the sake of his family and job, he never divulged the heart condition the army physicians had diagnosed. He must have known of the problem, the doctors had said, but Ken never asked his parents about it. A superficial heart examination required for a life insurance policy when he was twenty-nine revealed nothing, and for a time, his fears decreased. Perhaps the condition had disappeared. But another doctor noted the problem during a routine examination when Ken was thirty-two. Indeed, he was surprised that his patient never had complained of symptoms. Surely Ken had experienced shortness of breath now and again, or chest pains he might have attributed to indigestion. Ken smiled. He may have cut school, he told the doctor, but he hadn't missed a day of work. *That* had to prove something. "It proves you're either in better shape than I thought," the doctor replied "or you're lying!"

"Hey, Doc, if it helps your practice, I'll collapse on the floor, but between you, me, and the lamp post, I feel great. I ain't going to live forever, but I don't plan to turn out the light *this* young."

"Business must really be bad for these guys." Ken told me driving home from the doctor's office. "They can't stand the idea that you aren't getting sick like their instruments are predicting. *You* have to be wrong, it can't be them or their million dollar instruments. My mother always said doctors were the biggest waste of money in the world. The body takes care of itself. If *it* can't, nobody can. If my body can take care of my problem, then no matter what these doctors charge, you're going out. Hell, I don't see where these famous doctors' patients are doing all that well. I've been reading about their cure rates.

"You know why people get sick? Either they work too hard, or they don't work hard enough. Some people are in the wrong jobs. Other people are in the right ones, but they don't push themselves. They get job flabby. Like these men I work with, they don't mind the work, even though it gets more than a little boring. But if you push yourself you can always find a challenge. It's boring to put ten molds an hour into the box, so you push it up to twelve. The boss likes it, if you aren't rate busting, but it's for yourself. Phil is someone who underworks. His problem is he's where he is because of his old man. He doesn't mind what he does but he knows he didn't work for it. He's like a vice president riding somebody else's work. He's not going to quit, but he's not happy. What's the answer for a guy like that? Push it. Not so hard you end up in a hospital, but push it. People are built like cars. If you want to kill a car, just keep running it in city traffic at twenty-five mph, and that car will give you trouble every other month. What do they say about the heart? It's just a muscle, right? You use it a lot, you keep it in good shape. You don't use it, it gets flabby. You should see some of these old men we got working with us. They know exactly how to push themselves and when to relax. They know their bodies a helluva lot better than all these doctors with their multimillion-dollar EKG routines. You want to open the window a second, please?"

Opening the window for air, pausing at the top of a staircase, suddenly sitting quietly as though he had just gone into a trance; Betty had noticed the symptoms. But if she asked if he were in distress, the answer was always no. "Just felt a little warm there for a minute" or "Got to stop this three beers at lunch routine." The denials were absurd, although the men at work suspected nothing. Ken did not return to his doctor for the six-month visit, although he did promise to watch his diet more carefully.

If his health concerned him, the layoffs of men at Singletary troubled him more. The economic picture had darkened, the building industry was taking a hard blow. During the winter some of the older men were laid off, the summer brought cutbacks in the number of new employees. This should have told everyone the state of the business. If Phil Singletary was refusing the strongest and cheapest labor, what could the future hold for men like Ken Hawkins, even with their fifteen years of service?

Business at Singletary underwent major change when Phillip Singletary, Senior, died and his son took over. An easy-going, likable man, the younger Singletary was always loyal to his employees, but his main concern was the budget. As expenses for his company were running high, he immediately took two steps. First, he hunted out new contracts. Second, he slashed expenses, no matter how hard it hurt a worker or his family. If a twenty-year-old man could do better work than a man under company employ twenty-five years, the latter was laid off. Personal letters accompanied the notification, along with a statement of union benefits, unemployment insurance, and a promise that if the economy improved, old employees would be the first to be rehired. The first group of layoffs was announced three days after Phil Singletary became president.

Ken saw the writing on the wall weeks before the letter arrived. He had expected that Phil would write something personal, but the letter was identical to those received by the other men. At thirty-three, Ken Hawkins was unemployed. It was very lucky, he said, that Betty had decided to work at Burford, where they were also laying off men. In fact, with his insurance money and her job, there was no reason why their lives would have to change, for the while anyway. It wouldn't be all that bad, and certainly not as grave as the situation one heard described on television.

"Jesus," Ken would say, "to hear those people, you'd think we just lost World War III! Bitching and moaning. You hear these guys, they're angry with *everybody*, from the government to the grocer, walking around with chips on their shoulders the size of rocks. They make it seem like the whole goddamn world decided to make it rotten just for *them*. They forget about all those people in India and South America who've starved all their lives. And what about people after an earthquake? Jesus, the luckiest thing that could happen to some of those people there is to get swallowed up in the earth. Nobody's saying being out of work is easy. But it isn't the end of the world. Most people make the best of a horrible situation, they find ways to survive. Hell, I'll bet these guys you see on the talk shows, moaning about not working, I'll bet they had a job offer the next morning. Some rich guy, you know, feels a little guilty and calls up the station. That's why those people go on, probably.

"I'll make it. Hey, listen, a little vacation isn't bad. I can use the rest, get to know my kids. I'm going to start looking after Jo-Anne. I'll do more of the shopping, it won't kill me. And I'll clean inside the house instead of outside. And I'll cook. So what's the difference? I'll tell you something. This women's movement, I used to think it was just a lot of rich ladies barking out their own personal gripes. But they got a lot going for them. Where's it say men clean only outside? Or that men can't cook and change diapers? You have a custom and suddenly it's like a law. A man *can't* wash the kitchen floor. A woman *can't* take out the garbage. Where the hell's that written? All right, I'm uncomfortable sending my wife off to work every day, I'm a product of my culture. I don't do this from my own choosing. I want to work, outside my home, I mean. But if I'm unemployed, I'm unemployed.

"Tell you something I don't like. I don't like the fact that I work twelve, fourteen hours around the house, and I mean doing everything from washing the bathroom to making the meanest Jello you ever tasted, and they tell me I'm out of work. *I'm* out of work? They must be kidding. Construction work was never this bad. You don't get a break doing *this* stuff, you know. I'm going all the time, like a real honest-to-God housewife. I clean up one closet 'cause I don't have nothing better to do and all of a sudden I get it in me to clean *all* the closets. Then I get to looking at the clothes and choosing which ones need cleaning. Then I have to take them to the cleaners, all my wife's sweaters and skirts. I swear to God I'm becoming a housewife. Mabel Hawkins. You think I used to care what my kids ate? My wife said drink the milk, I said it to sort of back her up. Now when I say it, baby, I mean it. *I'm* the one who'll have to pour it back into the bottle and wash the glass, and I want that milk drunk. I shopped for the food, I prepared the food, I *served* the food, so you'll eat it, goddamn it, or I'll ram it down your throat! Or worse, I'll cry if you don't want it. Even the lousy breakfast cereal. You're going to eat it whether you like it or not, even though these kids would be a helluva lot better off *not* eating that stuff. The only good thing in them is that *we* made the effort to give it to 'em. I tell you, man, I'm becoming Mr. Housewife, U.S.A.

"Hey, I don't mind it. Lots of guys will say, women got it easy. Sit home all day with nothing to do, watching television, makes me buy her a color set, you know. Nothing to do? There is nothing harder to do than be a housewife! I don't know how they do it. I can't do it and I got to be stronger than most women. I'll never understand how my mother did it. When she didn't have *me* to take care of she had my father, which has got to be the hardest job 'cause he acted like a baby. Jo-Anne shits all over the place ten minutes after I've got her cleaned up, I'm going to be pissed, sure, but it isn't *her* fault; I can live with that. But nursing someone your age, Holy Jesus, that has to take the prize as the number one worst job in the world.

"I can be going all day with the kids, being Mr. Housewife U.S.A., then Betty will come home. I'll have supper going, little macaroni and cheese.

She never complains. But then maybe she'll say, she won't be thinking about it, but she'll say, what do we have that's cold to drink? I'm thinking, what do we have that's cold to drink, and she's not thinking about what she said. You get up off your big fat can and you look in that little box we call a refrigerator and you just reach in there with your little hand and you take what you like all by your little self because I was the one who went shopping and figured out what we need, and can afford, and I'll be goddamned if I'm going to *wait* on you! *That's* when you begin to see what the housewife's life is like. It just seems natural that one person has to wait on another, but let me tell you, there's nothing natural about it. But you can see why it is. The society says there's only one kind of work. You must leave your home to do work in the morning, and you must travel to your *place* of work, and travel home just before dinner. And you do it five days a week, and it must be Monday through Friday, and you must not have more than two or three weeks vacation a year, and you must get paid, *then* what you do is called work. Being a housewife doesn't count. You don't leave home, you don't get vacations, you don't get paid. So it doesn't count for work. What the hell, call it whatever you want, it's all I got going these days. When the insurance runs out I better have a job, and I mean a job that *everybody* calls a job. When they change the society I'll make different plans, but until then I'm from the old school: Men leave in the morning and come back at night with a pay check in their hand. Makes me old fashioned? Then I'm old fashioned.

"Am I angry about all this? Of course I'm angry. I don't *want* to be doing this. I don't get looks in the store? I don't get remarks thrown at me by neighbors? You see a guy give me a wave in the car, you know damn well he's telling his wife, 'What's with Hawkins? When did he stop being a man?' Okay, so the neighbors talk, what am I supposed to do? Tell my wife she shouldn't work so that I can save a little self-respect? We can't use the money? You better believe we can use the money she's bringing in. Let's face it: She's living with a big fat overweight cripple. A *housewife* cripple to boot. You want to call it by what it is, *that's* what it is. So I get angry, but who do I get angry at? The government? Phil? These systems that make up the labor markets are too complex for anybody to come along and say, 'I'm going to point my finger at this guy or that guy and say *he's* the reason I'm out of work!' All that matters is I'm out of work. Want an honest feeling about it? All right, here's the word that comes out: heartbroken. And that word isn't one I'd use every day. I guess that's sort of a play on words too, heartbroken. I mean, it is if that doctor's machines were right. Heartbroken, my ass!"

Play on words or not, the coronary attack the doctor had predicted for Ken Hawkins struck nine months after he was laid off from work. It began with a small attack in the afternoon followed by a more serious one that evening. The doctors' examinations indicated prior blood vessel damage. Sometime in the past, Ken had had an attack that either he ignored or never felt. The doctors were surprised that he had not complained of shortness of breath or chest pains. Ironically, during the period of unemployment, he had been taking excellent care of himself. He had lost weight, was drinking less, and often slept when Jo-Anne took her afternoon naps. "Why then," Betty asked the doctor, "should it come now?" "It happens a lot with men out of work and people who've just retired," came the answer. "They don't push themselves hard enough for the body. There's a psychological side to these illnesses too. Who knows how the heart and mind are connected."

Ken was hospitalized for three weeks. When he returned home, he followed a strict diet and exercise regimen. An ideal patient, Ken followed every order to the letter. The doctor said, "walk two miles a day;" Ken marked off exactly two miles. The doctor prescribed a certain amount of grams of carbohydrates; Ken had Betty buy a precise scale, and he himself weighed the slices of food. The regimen worked; monthly examinations revealed excellent progress.

Pleased by the attention he had been shown by his doctors, Ken promised he would report all symptoms. After playing the role of housewife so long, he enjoyed being cared for. Even if Betty were not around the house during the day, he felt safe and protected. During the first weeks of his recuperation he thought little about work. His spirits were holding up remarkably well for a man whose financial position was growing steadily worse. The insurance he carried did not fully cover the hospital expenses, and property taxes were being raised 4 percent. This, coupled with the unceasing inflation, was forcing the Hawkins family into a difficult position. Still, whatever troubled Ken did not show in his behavior. He was a man with a single purpose: complete recovery. He studied all the actuarial figures pertaining to men suffering heart attacks, especially those whose attacks came before the age of forty.

It was almost a year since Ken Hawkins had been out of work. He told his wife he was well, and that his spirits were "up there" too. Betty was working at Burford; Ken was back tending to the house and children. He had a good excuse now for not seeking employment. As the labor market was still in precarious shape, why exert energy pursuing jobs that didn't exist. If things grew worse, he would sell the house. Betty disliked this plan but could not argue with it. The doctors had made it clear that her husband had been extremely ill. The prognosis for a thirty-three-year-old coronary patient, moreover, wasn't the brightest. He might be well for a long time, but his life would not be the same; they had to be prepared for the possibility of further illness. Still, the best thing for Ken was to find a job. He needed something to keep him busy.

"Can *you* find him a job?" Betty asked me smartly, for the first time showing resentment. My response was weak, something about promising I would make some calls. "Then he'll have to keep messing around in the kitchen, won't he, doctor?"

On the morning of the party celebrating Ken's one year out of work, the Hawkins family acted like any other family preparing for a party. Glasses were being washed, food prepared, chairs arranged. Betty and Ken worked easily together, each knowing the other's movement so well they hardly needed to speak. When one of the girls needed attention, a quick look was enough to communicate the next action.

Then Ken expressed a desire to take a walk. He hadn't put in his two miles that day. He asked permission of his wife; "What am I, a warden? You're in my way anyway." Betty joked.

"How do you like *that* for gratitude!" he mumbled. "And me with my dishpan hands, my career as a concert pianist and meat packer finished!"

"Don't overdo it," Betty called out solicitously.

Then he was outside in the bright chilly day, walking at a good pace as the doctor had advised. He looked up, turning his head back and forth as though examining the sky. "I tell the truth on cold days," he said.

"I'm not ever going to be well. And my chances of finding work get worse every day. If I keep going like this, I'm going to end up exactly like my father. I was taking a nap the other day, and suddenly I had this sight of my father, like he was alive and younger than I remembered him. I saw him as a big man, big like me, like it suddenly made sense why I was as big as I am. He must have been big when he was my age, but the unemployment and the doing nothing shrunk him. I'm going to look through my mother's old stuff and see if I can't find some photographs of him to prove it. That man got shrunk by his life. The bigger I got the smaller he got.

I'm already fifty-five pounds lighter than I was when I went to work, and that's not even twenty years. Imagine where that puts me when I'm fifty. I haven't measured my height, but I bet I've lost an inch. Give me fifteen years, I'll be down another couple of inches. All this came to me in a dream. I'm going to be small like him, shriveled up, a sick old man by the time I'm forty. Man, this being out of work has got to be a ball breaker. You can't even begin to imagine how it's going to affect you. I can see now what happened to my father. That man went down and nobody ever told me what the hell was the reason for it. I used to think, the best thing could happen to my old lady is for him to go. He's a pain in the ass and she deserves a few years of happiness, not having to nurse him and pick up after him. Let her have a little break before she dies.

"So then *she* goes first, and goddamn it if the old man doesn't start coming back. Fact is, he ended up a helluva lot better off two months after she died. I really resented it too. I said to myself, how do you like this, she's dead two months and the son of a bitch is getting better every day. I think I *hated* him for it. What the hell was he doing, celebrating the fact he lost his wife? She was the only person in the world who gave a damn for him. I brought in the money, but I never took care of him. Took me a while to get over his getting better.

"Now I see what happened. My getting ill tells the story. Not working destroyed that man, because not working meant he couldn't be a man. And if a man can't be a man, what the hell can he be? A baby. He couldn't be a husband or a father, so he became my mother's kid, and *I* became the father. And the more it went that way, the sicker he got. She dies, he becomes a widower, and that's better than being a child. This way at least he can be half a man again. I see it happening with me. I'm not a father, I'm not a husband, I'm not a bachelor, I'm not even a common laborer. I'm a kid, a sexless kid. I can't make it another six months like this. The hell with the neighbors and the idiots looking at me in the grocery store. I don't give a rat's ass for them. It's how it worked with my old man. I see now why he was sort of relieved to see my mother go. It meant he could be part of a man again. It doesn't have anything to do with not liking women. Fact is, that's what makes it worse. He loved my mother, like I love my wife. But you love people because of what they are and because of what *you* are. You want to call me nuts, call me nuts, but I can't love my wife enough no matter how great she is when I'm not really a husband. These guys out of work, you think they got other women on the side just to prove their still men? I doubt it. *I* never have. I look. I'm not dead. The trouble is the rotten nine-to-five routine we've invented and call work, *that* affects who you are, and how much you can love.

"You can hate yourself, see yourself as weak or bad, but you aren't going to love people like you should. Work tells you you're a man or a woman, and that affects the love situation too. My father wasn't glad she died. He was probably scared shitless about what would happen to him. All he had left in the world was me, and he never did believe that much in what I could do for him. But when she died, he realized how he kind of got something back. Maybe he didn't know what he was missing, but he must have when he got it back. So, I know now that's what I've lost and I'll never get it back. Okay, so a guy looks at me with my kids and thinks, well, if old Hawkins is a queer, at least he hides it pretty good. But I know it's *me* thinking all these thoughts. A few talk, sure, but most of 'em don't even see you. I'm telling you, I got two strikes against me: I have no job, and I'm sick. Good things can still happen. I ain't going to end up in prison, but no one can take away the strikes. And baby, you can foul 'em off for a while, but sooner or later you either get on, or the third one goes past you!"

The crowd at the party could not have enjoyed themselves more. Everyone expressed delight at how well Ken looked, and no one talked about his unemployment. Later that evening some of the men told their wives how badly they felt having joked about Ken being a housewife. He was holding up pretty damn well, they had to agree. And he was all man, despite being out of work, despite his illness and obvious sense of failure, despite the fact that he had to assume the role of mother and housewife. Unemployment made for an ugly picture, they said. Just to survive it, *and* have the heart attack, *and* be without his parents, *and* have the bills pile up. The hospital must have cost a pretty penny too, and how much longer was the insurance going to last? Was there even unemployment compensation after one year?

That is some terrific couple, they were still saying days later. To think that with what they're going through, they would throw a party and laugh in the face of their circumstances. How many of us have even asked them over for dinner? "A person should be ashamed of himself to gripe about anything after seeing what's going on in that home," is what they said, and they promised there would be no more treating the Hawkins family like the plague. The suffering people have the time, the money, the generosity, they said. It's the Hawkins families of the world who make the time. Down and out, they come up with the energy and the money. Strange how it works out. Well, it won't be repeated this year. If they think we're patronizing, they'll just have to tell us. But no more ignoring them. I'll tell you something else, one of the men said, there's no reason in the world we can't find that man a job. With all the contacts we have, there has to be a job for him.

The pledges were kept. The Hawkins' friends rallied around. It mattered a great deal to Betty, but it was hard to know exactly how Ken was taking the sudden change in his friends' behavior. The party had something to do with it, not that he and Betty had given the party for that reason. It was just always hard to know with them.

Six months after the party, a year and a half after he had been laid off from work, Ken Hawkins left home and never returned. He gave no warning, no explanation. His family has never received no word from him, or about him.

Chapter 2

You Work Nine to Five or You're Dead: George Wilkinson

Not working? I can't believe what it would be like. It'd be like not having your arms or legs. Lots of people live through being unemployed, but I'm not equipped for it.

As in all the accounts explored here, a host of themes emerges, a host of events shape the story of a man's experience of long-term unemployment. In the case of George Wilkinson, there is first the matter of his inability to express fully the range of emotions from sadness to guilt to anger, all ignited by being out of work. Quite possibly, the most overwhelming of the emotions experienced by this one man was shame. Only naturally, he looked to other parts of the world where success is commonplace, and smart people constantly prepare for the horrible circumstances that befall all families. When he grew particularly depressed, he had to admit that too many others just had it better than he; all the world could see this plainly.

For George Wilkinson, there was no reason to fail. Proper education, proper work ethics should have brought him success in work until the time of his retirement. Perhaps he trusted too much in his company, perhaps he trusted too much in the economy, perhaps he was never able to make the proper adjustments, the adaptations to unemployment, whatever they might be, although he would have uttered words like *adaptations* and *adjustments* with sarcasm.

In the end, in his own eyes, he just failed miserably as a man. That he could find all variety of reasons for failure but no justifications for it surely contributed to the rage he brought on himself. Whatever it was, he came to realize that he had become immobilized. He himself once remarked that working is breathing. So it comes as no surprise that not working would be associated with the cessation of breathing, the cessation of life. If the writings on long-term unemployment reveal anything, it is that some men remain unable to transcend the trauma of this ordeal.

Robert Wilkinson heard his father say the words, for he was meant to. He was fourteen and old enough, his parents insisted, to know the facts of his father's possible employment. There was no excitement in the house that afternoon. George Wilkinson had come home, changed jackets and shoes as he always did, for he argued that jackets wore longer if one changed them regularly and feet stay healthy by changing shoes. Then he washed his face and hands and descended the stairs. When he reached the kitchen, his wife, Ethel, handed him a piece of bread she had just pulled from the oven. A lacy layer of steam could be seen rising from it. Robert entered the kitchen and was given a piece as well, and Ethel watched the two men sample her work.

Light streamed into the kitchen making the tile floor seem even warmer than usual. There wasn't a sound, which was a good sign. When talk came too quickly it meant George and Robert were not enjoying the food.

"I'll have another piece," George said, winking at his son. "It's not half as bad as it looked. I don't think we'll get the usual ptomaine poisoning if we follow it up with a second piece." Ethel cut two more pieces and handed them out. There were no thank-yous.

"Now watch," Robert began, the bread still filling his mouth, "she's going to do it again. We get two little pieces and then off it goes to the freezer. Mother, do you know how many loaves of bread you've put into that freezer in the last two months alone?"

"About 10 million!" Ethel Wilkinson replied with a straight face,

Everyone laughed.

George took a deep breath. "I've lost my job," he said softly. "The whole division's going, one month, that's it. Maybe we could send out for food tonight."

Ethel never looked up. She carefully wrapped the remainder of the bread in tin foil. No emotion showed on her face. Robert looked at his mother who was acting as if she hadn't heard her husband's news.

"You don't have a job?" Robert asked. His voice trembled, and the color drained from his face as it did when he ran long distances. The look always terrified his mother, who insisted her son should never exert himself because he ended up looking tubercular. Ever since he was a baby he had seemed weak. George felt the boy's weakness resulted more from his mother's pampering than any physical problem. Now Robert looked, stricken, but for once his mother didn't notice him.

George was licking bread crumbs off his fingers. "There's no job, at least at Tech." George Wilkinson too seemed curiously sober about it all. Robert saw not a sign of worry on his father's face.

"What the hell is going on?" Robert suddenly blurted out. "How come nobody seems surprised by this? I mean, is this supposed to be a regular event around here?"

George Wilkinson responded quietly to his son's anxiety: "It's not as bad as it sounds. There are other jobs. If not here, then in another city. What do you say to moving to California if nothing turns up?"

Robert was hardly appeased. "I thought jobs were tight in electronics. Why if there isn't anything here would there be something in California, where everybody wants to live anyway?"

"Okay, if not California, maybe Ohio or Illinois. Or I'll tell you," George himself appeared surprised by how little the matter seemed to trouble him, "I'd like to explore southern states. Atlanta's supposed to be beautiful. Tell you another place, Houston, terrific opportunities in . . ."

"You know," Robert interrupted facetiously, "this is a little play. Daddy's lost his job but he doesn't' care because we're going to move to Georgia or Texas or Alabama or California. And dear old mother, she's so busy wrapping loaves of bread she hasn't even heard the news about her husband losing his job, the little tiny job he's held for sixteen years."

"Eighteen," George corrected his son flatly.

"So here we are, ladies and gentlemen, coming to you from the charming little kitchen of our happy suburban family about to enter the ranks of American poverty, and we ask you the million dollar question: Do we or do we not tell the little sister of the happy suburban family? I mean, do we call her up and say, hiya Judith, how's the old studying for exams going? Hope you're working hard and getting good grades. What's new here? Oh, nothing much. Same old stuff. Mom's baking her bread, Dad's lost his job. Oh, we might be moving but we haven't decided whether to tell you. Yessiree. You might come home for vacation, if you don't freak out from this news, and find someone else living in your bedroom. Want us to pack your wallpaper when we go?"

Ethel Wilkinson turned angrily toward her son: "Are you quite finished with your ridiculous melodrama?"

"About as through as you are finishing your bread."

"And what exactly do you have in mind you'd like to tell us without that sickening sarcasm of yours?"

"*My* sarcasm?" Robert shot back.

"Well, you seem to be the only one talking in here."

"You're damn right I'm the only one talking. This guy's lost his job but *he* doesn't have anything to say, and all *you're* interested in is freezing bread, so you'll have to excuse me if I'd like to know what's going on."

"Don't worry so much," George said firmly. "We're in no great emergency. There's severance pay, or whatever they call it. I don't even know, you know that. I don't know anything about this. It's never happened so close."

"I'd say it's fairly close now, wouldn't you, Dad?"

"Stop being facetious," Ethel warned her son.

"I'm not being facetious. I'm being honest. Someone here has to. You know what you're making me feel like? An alarm clock. I go off and you keep shutting me up. Don't *you* want to know anything about it, Mother? I mean, what happens if you can't make bread anymore? Hey, maybe you'll have to go to work for the first time."

George Wilkinson slammed his hand down on the table.

"That's enough, Robert," he shouted. "It's *my* problem, not yours, don't drag your mother into it."

Robert headed for the door, making certain his parents saw his total befuddlement. He was so preoccupied with what he later would call his performance, he didn't notice his mother crying.

The calmness that George Wilkinson hoped to convey seemed a natural response to the loss of his job. In his last month at his job, he did some of his best work, hoping to demonstrate his loyalty and talent to his colleagues, as well as potential employers. If he was feeling a strain, he hid it from everyone. Even Ethel knew little of what a layoff would mean to him. He rarely spoke to his co-workers about unemployment, although some of the men had already been laid off. A part of him wanted to seek solace in the misery of others, but he knew this to be childish. Besides, as everyone at the division agreed, the layoff was only temporary. Other jobs were available, and who was to say that Bilton Electronics wouldn't hire most of their men back? Joel Epstein, who was George's closest friend at work—although the two never met socially—constantly reminded George that at any minute Bilton could pick up a new contract and everybody would be back in business.

Joel Epstein was a good-natured man with a joke for every situation. When he was deep at work he hummed Broadway show tunes. George, who loved the music, would kid him: "You're humming, Mr. Epstein," and Joel would break out in song. It always brought a laugh to see Joel, his bald head with the little bit of shaggy hair on the sides covering his ears, his pipe, never lit, dropping out of his mouth, humming away. His favorite speech to George went: "You know, Wilkinson, I'll never understand two things in the world as long as I live. First, why does a good Jew like me have fixed in my mind the lyrics to Broadway shows written by Cole Porter? What is a Jew interested in how the Japanese are making circuit breakers and transistors doing walking around in the middle of a bunch of Christians singing Cole Porter? What's in my background that I'd ever *want* to know 'Begin the Beguine?' Second, I'd like to know why in God's name you changed your name from Wilensky, or Warshowsky? I'll bet it was Warshowsky, right? Be a man, George. Change it back."

George loved it. Joel had temperament, style. What a beautiful man he was, and what an engineer. How many times had they spoken of going into business together. "*Your* friends would hate you for being in partnership with a Jew," Joel would say. "*My* friends would hate me for being with a goy, and that would leave us the entire Western world as a client." And George would sing, barely able to keep from laughing, "*So then let them begin the Beguine, let them*, what the hell's the line?"

The two men would roar with laughter and pound each other on the arms and shoulders, but there was always something that stopped them from embracing. Once, when the desire to embrace was too obvious, Joel remarked, "The trouble with the two of us has nothing to do with the fact that we're of different backgrounds. The problem is we're engineers. Good job, good prospects, good money, but something happens to your personality. We're a different breed. I'll be very happy if my Danny comes to me someday and says, "You know what, Dad, I've been thinking about my future and everything's unclear except for one thing. I haven't got the slightest desire in the world to be an engineer. You guys are way too uptight.'"

George had felt the same things. He was pleased that Robert had maintained his childhood interests in law and journalism. There *was* something about engineering that stifled his feelings. It was miraculous that Ethel, who was so different, would tolerate his emotional quietness, even though they both recognized his desire to break out of his old ways, possibly even start a new career. A first-rate student all his life, George Wilkinson played with the idea of becoming a performer. Perhaps it wasn't too late at age forty-six to study acting. Or perhaps he could explore the television industry. The quiet inner world could awaken; it might not be dead, after all.

When it became clear George Wilkinson's layoff would not be temporary, he stopped at once toying with ideas of performing. There were no more dreams of *adult education*, a term he dreaded. He would remain an engineer; the inner world would remain silent, despite the trickles of emotion and the fact that he was slowly being consumed by shame, the very shame, his wife believed, that should rightly be felt by politicians who couldn't care less about men like her husband. They had their jobs so why should they worry, those shameless, selfish people with their miserable policies!

"For God's sake, George," she told him, "there are four diplomas hanging in your study. Look at this house, this community. Look at what we own. You can't feel shame. There's not a job in the world worth that. You say the word and we'll change our lifestyle. So maybe I'll have to work. So we'll both work. So we'll move to Georgia or Texas. Or we'll do the hardest thing of all: We'll stay right here with all these people looking at us and feeling sorry for us. I couldn't give a damn about any of them. I'm not going to underestimate the seriousness of this, but you didn't rob a bank, you know. You worked damn hard for that company. They could feel a little shame too. What about Joel? Are they laying him off too?"

As close as they were, George Wilkinson and Joel Epstein worked three weeks without speaking of Bilton's impending layoffs. Each had heard rumors of cutbacks, divisions closing, first line men being severed, but they also knew the company was not closing down, a certain number of people would be retained. Nobody knew for certain who was leaving, nobody was eager to speak about his or her position, even to best friends.

Ten days before he had to be out of his office, George went to see Joel. He had stayed late the night before trying to figure out why he hadn't confronted his friend at once. He had wanted to say, 'Joel, I'm fired, I wanted you to know.' What kept him from speaking to Joel was not only shame, but a feeling of being in competition with his friend, a feeling he had often pushed aside. What helped their friendship was the fact that their salaries, years of service, quality of contribution, popularity, were almost identical; there was no reason for competition. George never felt it during the early years of their friendship. It woke in him when Joel, some eight years before, walked into his office one evening as he was preparing to go home and handed him a letter. "Please advise" were Joel's only words. The letter contained a handsome offer from a firm not far from Bilton. The salary was higher than Joel was earning, but the job entailed administrative work, which George knew his friend despised. It was a good offer, but not for Joel Epstein. Yet something kept him from saying so. Instead, he went on about how people can always tolerate doing a little administration. Besides, how could anyone in his right mind turn down an extra $8,000 a year? Even if the job turned out to be horrible, George insisted, it could always be a stepping stone for other offers. Nobody sneers at advancement.

Joel Epstein had snatched back the letter. He folded it carefully and put it in his jacket pocket. "I knew the second I began negotiating with these people the job wasn't for me. You, you jerk, are too polite to tell me the truth. This is a job for a man with no imagination. They don't want an engineer, they want a paper pusher. Wilkinson, you're a good friend. Thanks for the help." Then suddenly, Joel was gone and George stood behind his desk dumbfounded. It hadn't been his response at all. Truth be told he *did* think it was a good deal and was jealous the offer hadn't come to him. If it had been the other way around, he would have walked into Joel's office and announced with modesty that he was leaving Bilton to take a new job. Joel would have been pleased by his advancement but sad to learn the two men would no longer be seeing each other. George would say he had been thinking about refusing the offer because his friendship with Joel was more important than any $8,000 salary increase. But Joel would say, "You're mad not to take it. If *you* don't *I* will." "Well, I am going to take it," George would have said, "but I'm going to miss the hell out of you." For once they would have embraced, and George's eyes would have become moist with tears.

When Joel Epstein showed him the letter, George's feelings of competition rose up to the point that he actually felt pain. He had never realized how much he kept inside, and how little of himself he really knew. As always, Joel was right: Engineers are a different breed. He had never guessed he could be so competitive with Joel. Knowing that his friend would never take the job made it easy for him to be effusive and encouraging.

"Don't torture yourself," Ethel had told him that evening. "Don't you think Jews are more competitive than anyone else? Maybe they have to be because they know they're not fully accepted in the country. Maybe Joel showed you the letter to let you know if he wanted to move up he could. Why did he even have to mention the letter? He didn't tell you about the job when he first started negotiating it. Right?" George had to agree this was so. "He never asked your opinion along the line. Should he pursue it, should he not pursue it." Again George Wilkinson found himself agreeing with his wife.

"He says you're his best friend, but just at work. You say he's your best friend maybe in the world. And yet the first time he comes to you with this matter is when he's assured of the job. He has it in his hand. Seems to me he's rubbing your nose in it, isn't he? I mean, how come he didn't tell you what he was doing all along? Because *he's* in competition with you just as much as you are with him. He doesn't want you to know what he's planning because if he doesn't get the job *he* goes down a few notches in *your* eyes. Right?"

Once more George Wilkinson agreed with his wife. Of course, there was competition in the division. They were highly trained men, reared to compete since their early years of school. The competitive aspect of friendships was always in evidence, even if no one spoke of it. Any new step a man took put him in a wholly new situation with his friends. The tiniest promise of success, an encouraging conversation with a powerful person could mean a significant transformation in the network of human relationships. One could preach all one liked about equality and sharing, brotherhood and fair play, but it was all hypocritical. Everyone knew there were only two or three openings in each of the outstanding universities and engineering institutions, and then two or three openings in the best seminars, and two or three openings in the best graduate schools, elite honor societies and prestigious jobs. One continued learning as an engineer, but one also continued competing, with people one liked as well as disliked.

Preston Cooper, known as the most detestable man on campus, frequently lectured George on competition when they were college sophomores. If Preston had a friend it was only because his father had a great deal of money, much of which flowed to his son, which meant that Preston's friends were taken to fancy restaurants and enjoyed weekend trips off campus. George remembered thinking that if Preston was admitted to college only because his father was a big shot, then it was the school that came out looking shabby. Besides, the people who should have objected to Preston's admittance were the deserving high school students never admitted to the best places. George recalled feeling sorry for Preston Cooper. He felt envious and competitive as well.

"You meet the highest standards the society can throw at you," George's father, a postal worker, always had taught his son. "You fool yourself into believing that when you get the highest mark in class you've really done something. There is only one standard and that's the highest standard in the society. You can earn $10,000 a year and tell yourself, well, I earn more money than 60 percent of the people in the country, but you mustn't deceive yourself. The real standard isn't $10,000, it's $1 million! Don't confuse standards of contentment with standards of achievement. An A on an examination is nice. But when you think about the really powerful, influential people in this country, people who work every day of their lives on an international level, people who speak six languages, know their way around fifty cities, then you know where you stand in the world.

"And one thing more," he would tell his oldest son, in whom he seemed to invest his entire future, a son who remembered every word practically verbatim. "You can mock rich people all you like. You can resent what they have and what their children are going to have. But you'll never know what this country is until you look at what the rich do. This country moves because of them. It may be held up by people like me, but that's all we do. It moves because of big people making big decisions with big money. We keep going, but *they* set the standards. If you ever get into places where you can hear what they're talking about, watch the way they operate. You may not approve of who they are, but if you want to change the country, *they're* the ones you have to influence."

George Wilkinson thought often of his father's words when he was in college. Preston Cooper, too, had spoken of the dog-eat-dog world of commerce and the fact that in that world nobody can be trusted. People don't like the Jews, Preston had said, because they're envious of the way they transact business. It's a competitive society, he said again and again, and in a competitive society you compete. Doing the work, he counseled, will earn people high paying jobs, but some people, no matter what their education and skill, will lose their jobs. One has to prepare for it; something horrible always happens.

George listened closely to this unpopular young man. Preston was absolutely right: George never thought of anything but school. He never looked beyond the present even to the nearest edge of the future. Prepare for horrible events? That idea never occurred to him. George knew the meaning of money and working hard to attain goals; his father had tutored well, but the prospect of losing a job had never occurred to him. People had jobs until retirement and that point was so far off it seemed foolish even to think on it.

George's model for work had always been his own father. Everyone said that George Wilkinson, Senior, had done extraordinarily well for a person who had started with little, but there was no reason why George, Junior, shouldn't do better. The elder Wilkinson made a good living and the family was committed to giving their children a rich education. They knew if a person wanted to progress, they went on in school no matter what the cost. In time all the investments were more than paid back.

By thirty-five, George Wilkinson, Junior, was an employee of Bilton Electronics, a worldwide corporation expanding at rates that made them a contender for the top ten firms of its kind. While George and Ethel told people they considered themselves middle class, they knew they were better off than that. "A man who earns $40,000 a year can call himself middle class 'till he's blue in the face," Joel Epstein always said. "But he's no more middle class than I'm in line to be the Pope. All right, George," he would joke, "go home to your upper-class house in your upper-class suburb and park that upper-class car in that upper-class garage of yours, have an upper-class dinner with your upper-class family and come back tomorrow with those goddamn middle-class clothes of yours. We're both a couple of phonies. We're both rich. This is it, man. This is the life. This is what we must have been working for all these years. The job, the home, the position, the status. Jesus, guys I know would blow their brains out to have a situation like we got here. And it's good as gold, my friend. You know when Bilton falls apart? When America slides into the Atlantic!"

Joel Epstein was as certain of his future bringing security as Preston Cooper, years before, had been certain that horrible events would someday strike the engineering profession. Both sentiments stuck in George's mind, yet he always felt he could never gain a proper perspective on the world. What kept him going was faith in the country, in Bilton, in the fact that well educated people who did it the right way don't end up in trouble, unless of course there's unforeseen tragedy, but that's why people had insurance policies. If something happened to him, the family would make out, for he was a responsible man. His papers were in order, his bills paid on time, his correspondence always up to date. He rarely procrastinated nor found excuses for not meeting commitments. It was the way his father had been, and the way he hoped his children would be. There was no alternative to being responsible, no excuse, when one had means, for not being successful. In a word, there was no reason for failure. "If one works steadily and honestly," he would tell Ethel, "the rewards come, and don't think for a minute that biweekly checks aren't rewards. All you have to do is look at people who don't even have the means to go on welfare, and you'll see what a reward that little checko is."

"I love you, darling," Ethel would respond, "but sometimes you're a little melodramatic, if you don't mind my saying so. You act like you don't deserve your money. You *do* work for it, you know, so why look at it as a reward? It's your earnings; that's exactly why they call it that. I'd have to say though, you are a little excessive on the issue of loyalty. I mean, in the privacy of your own house, you *could* complain about the work."

"I do complain," George would protest mildly.

"Listen," Ethel would tease him, "if politicians complained like you do, there'd be nothing to report on the evening news. You don't complain."

Ethel was right, of course. He did work hard and rarely complained. Nobody ever knew if he held any of the bitterness many people feel, even those who the world considers successful. Not too long, actually, before the notice of his layoff arrived, he remarked:

"I don't know myself, what I feel about my life. I don't think about it that much. Oh, I'll think about Friday afternoons a lot on Monday mornings, but just as often I'll think about Monday morning on Saturday night when I'm supposed to put work out of my mind. But most men are like that. When you get my age, you don't think much about work. You get tired, sure, but you don't ask yourself too many questions. Luckily, I like a lot of what I do. Things could be better, but what does that mean. I don't fill my head with thoughts like, be content; Wilkinson, millions of men would love to be where you are. I just do the work. I don't think about what my life would have been like had I become a doctor or a businessman. I can watch the pros play ball on television and never even think of what their life is like, even though it's a lot more glamorous than mine. It just seems like all of us are doing our work. I do mine at Bilton, this one does his on a football field. If you enjoy it, you have a leg up on a lot of people. If you don't, you do it anyway because you have a leg up on a lot of people, and because the alternative is unthinkable. Not working? I can't believe what it would be like. It'd be like not having your arms or legs. Lots of people live through being unemployed, but I'm not equipped for it.

"I'll tell you, as unpopular as Preston Cooper was, he was smart in ways that none of us could understand. He had a strange sort of wisdom about him. I always thought he knew more than he actually knew he knew, if that makes sense. That idea of preparing yourself everyday for the horrible things that could happen, it's not a bad idea. If nothing happens you go to bed feeling pleased. If something *does* happen, you're ready for it. Competing for jobs is something I know about; that was the hidden message of my training. But prepare for a situation when I couldn't find work, I'd die. I couldn't make it. I wouldn't even know how to go looking for a job. What do you do, stand in line at some office? Go fill out forms with people, some who haven't worked a day in their lives? There's only two worlds for me: Either you work in a normal everyday, nine-to-five job with a couple weeks' vacation, or you're dead! There's no in-between. I don't think about welfare offices or employment offices. I hear people talk about these things, but it's not anything that's going to happen to *me*. It doesn't happen. If it happens, I blow my brains out. I couldn't live with it. It's too destructive, not working. Too shameful.

"Working is breathing. It's something you don't think about, you just do it and it keeps you alive. When you stop, you die. I don't even believe in retirement. Nobody stops at sixty-five with nothing to do. That's why people die when they retire. How can they go on with nothing to do but think about the way things used to be? That's a part of life that scares me, that they turn you out to pasture and have people take care of you. Maybe that's the part of not working that would disturb me so much, that I'd be dependent on people for everything. I believe in the idea of the pay check as an earned reward. I can live with the idea of retirement benefits, but I've earned those. But not to work when your mind is alive and you want to work, when you're willing to put up with all the boring parts and disappointments which never seem to end? That's death.

"I had a friend when I was younger, a fellow named Blatty; I'm going back twenty years now. Met him in a cocktail lounge in Cleveland. There was some professional meeting going on there. Here's a guy I've never seen. I don't think there was a person we knew in common. Guy was in a wheel chair, paralyzed from the waist down. Paraplegic. Sweet man. But he drank like a fish. In two hours he put away fifteen big drinks. He was getting drunker and drunker and telling me all the time how he's a happy guy even though he's crying as he's getting drunk. Every five minutes I make a move to leave and he grabs my arm and orders another drink. So finally I tell him, "What are you trying to convince me you're so happy when you're here getting drunk?' I'll never forget it. Guy looked at me as if for one moment he was sober, and he says, and his eyes were actually clearing up, he says, 'I'm happy because I'm going to die.' So I said to him, 'What are you talking about?' I didn't know what to say, but he touched something inside me, maybe something I thought about but wouldn't let myself be conscious of. Anyway, he said, "I'm going to die and everybody thinks it's because I'm a cripple, but it's not. It's because I can't find work.' I'll never forget it, how he *lectured* me on the subject like he was some professor, on how it wasn't because he couldn't walk, but because he couldn't *work*.

"So I said to him, 'Just because you can't find work doesn't mean you're going to die. You don't die that easily.' That's one of Joel's favorite lines. I'll tell him, 'if I don't solve this problem in a week, I'll die.' And he'll say, 'You don't die that easily. Take it from a reformed undertaker, you don't die that easily.' Which is right. You cry from disappointments, from not living up to those standards. But you don't die that easily.

"Anyway, I told all this to this Blatty fellow. So what did he do? He opened up his coat and pointed to the breast pocket where there's a gun. A little black gun. Then he closed his coat. Then he put his drink on the table—all of this is going on in the middle of a cocktail lounge in one of those big hotels. Cocktail waitresses practically naked serving drinks, place is packed with people, all these engineers like me were there with name tags on our coats, and here's a man who I never met, showing me a gun, and then he proceeds to reach into his pocket and pull out a fistful of bullets. Not just a couple, a fistful! There they were in his fist, like little fish.

"I remember having two thoughts when I saw the bullets. First, I thought, I never realized bullets could be so small, or that his gun could be so small. It hardly seemed they could do any damage. How could a little bullet like that kill a person? If you wanted to commit suicide, you'd put the gun up to your temple and pull the trigger, but what if that bullet did-n't do the trick? What if this Jack Blatty pulled the trigger and it turned out he didn't kill himself? Then he's not only a paraplegic but his mind is destroyed and he doesn't have the capacity to decide whether he should keep living.

"Thought number two. I realized when he showed me the gun that he was serious. I could have taken the position he was joking, that it was a play for my sympathy, because what was the man doing in that cocktail lounge in the first place if he didn't have a job and was planning to take his life? But I felt he was serious about the whole business. The thought I had was, don't people in the horrible shape he was in—and he was a deeply dis-turbed individual—don't they hang out in dives? What's he doing in a swanky hotel? I don't run into these people, that's all I'm saying. You read obituaries but you don't know when people die suddenly if it's suicide; newspapers hide information like that. But Jack Blatty opened up some-thing in me. Just him sitting there with his eyes clear, and his drink in one hand and that fistful of bullets in the other, that awoke something. It awoke the idea that I *do* run into people who get so depressed from things like not having a job, or a future, that they'll quit living. More important, I knew by looking at him, that not only would I do the same thing if I were in his shoes, but somewhere in my mind I'd been thinking of suicide. Not like something coming in the normal course of events. It was the words of Jack Blatty meeting up with the words of Preston Cooper. I knew I'd never be able to deal with the event of being out of work. What it would do to me I'd never know, because I would do the same thing as Jack Blatty. All these thoughts I had sitting with the guy. On the spot, face to face with the man, this is what I was thinking.

"So something snapped in me. I thought of all the famous lines I could throw at him, like, 'You don't die so easily,' then I said, 'You drunk?' He didn't say a word. '*I* may be but I'm not sure,' I told him. Then I told him: 'I don't even want *them* to die. And if I don't want *them* to die, I surely don't want *you*, a man I've just met, to die. But I'll tell you this, and it's the most honest thing I've ever told anyone: If I were a prisoner in a wheel chair I'd hate it. But if I had a job I'd make out. But take away my job and tell me I wasn't going to have a job that made sense to me given all I'm trained for, I'd buy a gun and some bullets like you have, Mr. Blatty, and I'd put those bullets in the gun and pull the trigger. You wanted my response, that's my response. I can't be more honest with you.

"The man didn't move a muscle. He just looked at me, blank faced. That's the story. He finished his drink, said good-bye, I finished my drink, said good-bye. What he did, what he thought after that, I haven't the faintest idea. The old chance meeting, strangers in a bar, just like the movies. And all of a sudden, like they say, I wasn't so scared to die. It didn't seem so bad as it always did. I knew that in an hour, the next day, soon, the old fears would come back. You don't find magic in these episodes. But what did happen was that I knew a minute or two when I wasn't afraid of Cooper's most horrible thing happening. It would have been better had I made the preparations Preston warned me about thirty years ago, but at least I now had a few minutes I could remember when I wasn't afraid. I did make a pledge, however, that if things ever got horrible I'd put my life in order and contemplate the reasons for putting that pistol to my head. I don't mean I pledged to commit suicide. I only pledged that I'd never let myself reach the desperate point Blatty had reached. He was one desperate man. He had no legs and no soul. Maybe I'm a coward, or unprepared, but I wouldn't go another step without a soul. So I tucked that experience away in my mind, and it seems vivid still, like it happened yesterday. I must have wrapped it in dry ice, because it's like it's still alive."

George Wilkinson's job situation grew far worse than he ever imagined. For a brief spell, it appeared that Bilton Corp. would cancel the planned layoffs and retain him, but this turned out to be a rumor; the entire division was to be dissolved. Joel Epstein was in the same situation, but after two months of job hunting he landed a position with a midwest firm. It was not a great job, certainly nowhere as good as his old position at Bilton, but as Joel admitted, beggars can't be choosy. His departure deeply affected George. The old feeling of competing with Joel returned, but this time he felt he had lost.

There were job interviews, hours on the phone and hundreds of letters to be written. Every advertisement in the newspapers and trade magazines was read, the promising ones filed away in scrapbooks. He bought file cards and manila envelopes to hold and organize his correspondence. At one point, he convinced himself that his job actually consisted of searching for a job. He worked like a demon tracking down employment situations, telephoning, doing everything to latch onto a position, but nothing opened up.

As the family's money problems grew worse, George told Ethel he was leading the life he had seen portrayed in a million movies. The bills continued to arrive, their savings were gradually eaten up. Robert and Judith grew increasingly anxious; their parents were unable to convince them things would soon be resolved. Everyone felt a sense of doom hovering about their home. Once or twice a week a possibility for employment would arise. The position might seem degrading to George, but he would pursue it. "Sure I want it," he would shout excitedly into the phone. Ethel warned him about sounding like a beggar, but he could no longer control himself. Both of them saw the deterioration in his spirit.

"I'm deteriorating," he would tell her. "I feel it happening. It's almost interesting to watch. I'm watching myself deteriorate. I could write a book on what unemployment does to people, how it eats them up worse than any cancer. I can feel myself forgetting everything I've done for the last thirty years. If it weren't terrifying, it could be interesting. I have to laugh. I never thought of seeing a psychiatrist, not that I couldn't benefit from it. I wasn't that kind of personality. Now I want it, I need it, and we can't afford it. It's a shame. I'd be a beautiful specimen."

In fact, he began consulting a psychiatrist. After a few sessions he felt stronger, but then, without warning, he quit. He told Ethel, "If I can't afford it, I can't deserve it. It's all part of the cancer."

On a Thursday night in April, George Wilkinson shot himself in the head. He was found with a small black gun near one hand, a small pile of bullets on the floor near his head. He had bought the gun and bullets at a sporting store in a neighboring state, sixty miles from his home. The salesman remembered him requesting just enough bullets to make a fistful. The salesman recalls laughing. He had told George he sold bullets by the box, and that a box ought to make a generous fistful. When George left the store, the salesman advised, as was his habit with all first-time gun purchasers, "Don't do anything I wouldn't do." He remembers George saying, "That's exactly what I am going to do. I have no job. You know the feeling?"

Phil Canelli claims he thought of calling Mrs. Wilkinson, for he had a premonition that the troubled man to whom he had just sold a gun might be thinking of taking his life. It was the remark about being unemployed. Phil Canelli had heard of cases like this, the once-rich man without a job. But how could he, a perfect stranger, telephone a woman and say he had a hunch that her husband was thinking of committing suicide. Besides if *he* had a hunch, surely she would know; she was the one living with him, after all. Then again, if a man was thinking of committing suicide, why would he need a fistful of bullets. He must have had other things in mind. Tension release at a pistol range seemed a logical possibility, Phil Canelli reasoned. Sad, he remembered thinking, that the loss of a job would lead to suicide. But it was all idle speculation; he didn't know if this Wilkinson fellow planned to kill himself. How could he know what a man he had never seen had in mind? But he knew what unemployment could do to a person. Hadn't his mother's brother shot himself after two agonizing years of being out of work?

Chapter 3

They Want Me
to Be Invisible:
Peter Rosenbloom

You think there are clubs for unemployed people? And if there were, you think I'd join? I wouldn't be caught dead talking to people like me.

The history of immigration to the United States is replete with stories of people arriving in this country unable to speak the language, and yet, within short periods of time, settling into jobs, and homes, and living as contributing members of their new society, one that appeared to justify the title "land of opportunity." The act of relocating and in addition gaining employment is one that must create a sense of pride equal perhaps to the pride that one will forever safeguard for one's family, one's family name, and one's mother country.

All of this means, of course, that those immigrants who fail to find steady work and end up living on welfare lose any sense of pride they may have ever known. Their country surely cannot be happy about the destiny they have created, and their own family members may well exhibit disgruntlement, disapproval or outright humiliation over their lack of a position in society. To end up unemployed is to let everyone down: one's family as well as one's new country. It is, perhaps, to know a brand of shame that renders people not only helpless, but unable to let others even see them. So often we discover these people hiding from the gaze of family members as if their mere presence on the earth caused a humiliation for their entire family, their entire ethnic group.

Irrespective of the actual historical circumstances underlying long-term unemployment, the individual worker, now idle, must feel socially without status, personally empty, faceless, useless, and most assuredly disposable. The word he hears, the word he may even employ to describe himself, is *bum*. In his own mind, the word is apt, for he is an idler, a vagrant, a loafer, a dissolute or worthless person exactly as the dictionary states. All of these descriptions fit the life of Peter Rosenbloom, and come to be magnified by dint of his immigrant status and the stories of his father and brother who early on found the very success in America that continued to elude this man. Without work, indeed, work yielding a certain status, there would be no compassion, there would be no dignity, there would be no appreciation for his situation. There would be only shame and disgrace. In his own words, without work he would live as a stone, a stone that his own brother sought to discard.

Peter Rosenbloom tells anybody who will listen to him that if he had a choice, he wouldn't be Jewish. "What have I gotten from all these years of being Jewish? Someone knocks on your door and says, 'Tell me, you're Jewish? Because if you are I've got a present for you. You play the banjo, Rosenbloom? You don't, all right, so now you do. 'How's that? Play the banjo. Look, here's a banjo, play me a song. What do I have to do to find a job? Go on. Take the banjo, you'll find you can play it like an angel.'" Then Peter Rosenbloom looks away, embarrassed not only for his predicament, but that he should mock his predicament.

"The whole thing's not worth it. The whole thing stinks with a bad smell. I can't believe it's me sitting here, making fun of my life: The way I look, the way I sound, everything that's happening to me. Is this where I'm supposed to be? Is this what people had in mind for me at my age? I'm sixty-two years old. You know what it means to be sixty two years old? What do you think they think of me, my family? You think they look at me and they're admiring what they see in this face, or what I do with myself? Or maybe they think, 'Ah, he's old, what can you expect? Life's been hard on him.' You think that's what they think? You want to know what I think? I think I don't care what they think, because what I think is much worse than what they could ever think; I'm living it with myself. I'm living my life with myself, no matter who's here, there, anywhere. I'm the guy living here with me, so I don't need them to tell me what they think. You follow what I'm saying? Give an old man a chance to talk, he'll talk you right out of his house. Don't worry, I know exactly what I'm doing. A man is alive, he works. he's dead, he don't work. That's a formula. A man is alive and he don't work, he's not in the formula, he's not a man. Fifteen years now I'm not working. Fifteen years, not a single thing I can say I earned. Fifteen years of my family looking at me and saying to themselves, 'What is he, some kind of fish? Maybe he's a stone who sits around all day not doing anything. Heavy, ugly, a stone. You get out of him what you get out of a stone. You get blood out of a stone?' You don't work all these years, you're a stone. That's what they're thinking; that's what I'm thinking."

Peter Daniel Rosenbloom came to the United States from a small town near Budapest when he was sixteen years old. His father, mother, and brother were lucky, his father said. Not everybody gets the chance to go to America. Aaron Rosenbloom told his two sons that although the stories of American riches were exaggerated, there was some truth to them. Many immigrants had arrived penniless and within a few years were living in big houses, driving big cars, and having people look up to them. They were doubly successful, he said. They had proved themselves successful in a country that worships success, and they made it after starting out with nothing. America was like everyone described it, a land of opportunity. But that was all it was. Nobody gave out anything for free. The jobs were there, the work possibilities plentiful, but what a people did with these possibilities was their business. If you worked hard in America, it paid off. The serious problem, his son remembered him repeating often, was whether immigrants were big enough and strong enough to deal with being successful, or not being successful, because that could happen too. There was no bigger move a person could make than to leave his own country, to leave the people he had known all his life, learn a new language, and prove he could work as good as the next guy, if not better than him. They'll always be looking at you differently from how they look at their own, he had said. It will always be different.

Aaron Rosenbloom quickly found work in America. The wages were hardly generous, but he went to his grave telling his family that no one could see him as anything but a success. Although he never earned more than $12,000 a year, the fact was that the family lived in only one city, and in only two apartments. Anybody judging the Rosenblooms had to agree they were stable; how else could success be defined? Aaron Rosenbloom died when Peter was thirty-seven, his brother Marcus thirty-nine.

Sonia Rosenbloom, always a sickly woman, never recovered from the emptiness she felt on the passing of her husband. Nor did her uncertainty about the move to America help her to feel resolute about her future. Money wasn't a problem. The family wasn't rich, but Aaron had left her some funds through an insurance policy. Her sons afforded her pleasure, although she worried about both of them, especially Peter. His education was not what it should have been; like her, Peter never seemed to take to America. Marcus was like his father. If Marcus had regrets about leaving his native land when he was eighteen, he never exhibited them. He assumed the same spirit of challenge his father had embraced, and made a comfortable life for himself working in a leather company. That his wife's father had a few connections didn't hurt his career. Marcus Rosenbloom was the success his father required as proof that leaving Hungary was a wise decision. Every Sunday the elder Rosenblooms lunched with Marcus and his wife, Sarah. It became a ritual. Peter was always invited but he rarely attended. But no matter, the lunch visit only confirmed Marcus' unquestionable success. "It takes a generation to make a success," Sonia Rosenbloom heard her husband say every Sunday night. "Marcus is a success. Peter will come around too. Maybe not while I'm here to see it, but he'll come around. Some people just start slower than others. Maybe he was too young when he left. How could anyone know."

Peter Rosenbloom always felt closer to his mother than his father. The move to America was no small venture, nor was it an overwhelming experience. He would be all right, he told his mother whenever she asked if he was happy, which was often because she invariably saw in him signs of discontent. He was not faring well in America. Driving a taxi cab part-time, starting and stopping with school, not getting married, all were signs for the family that Peter was experiencing problems. He had few close friends, rarely went out; it even seemed strange to find him coming regularly to Friday night dinner, not that the Rosenblooms were religious people. It was nice that he came, for it meant a lot to his father, but his mother knew he had nothing better to do. Sonia worried about him, and the little he told her about his life made her worry more. There was no hiding the fact that mother and son shared many things, the most important being the realization that neither of them ever considered themselves Americans. "Your brother's Mr. America," Sonia would tell Peter, "but you belong in Europe. Maybe you should go back."

Peter would force himself to laugh at her words, but he knew there was wisdom in them. "I'm buying my own airplane right now, and as soon as I learn how to fly it or parachute from it, I'll go back to Hungary. I'll go to the president and I'll say, 'Mr. President, you're so good making peace with the Russians, how about maybe you could give me a job as your chauffeur or your private pilot. It wouldn't look so bad, a nice Jewish man from Budapest driving you around. You could set another example for the world.'"

Peter Rosenbloom knew perfectly well that his mother was never amused by his sarcasm. "What was right, maybe, for your father and your brother," she would reply, "doesn't have to be right for you."

"How many times I had those conversations with that sweet lady," Peter Rosenbloom remembers, thinking back over more than thirty years. "She knew, I knew. It was the work. She saw it all in my work. You come all the way from Budapest to drive a taxi? That's what my father had in his mind when he left, to see a son drive a taxi? And how long was that going to last? Everybody thinks, you got nothing else to do, *nu*, you'll drive a taxi. How bad can it be? You buy a map and everyday you get the paper before anybody else does so you can make conversation with the fares, how hard can it be. You think people ever wonder about a taxi driver? They figure they give him a big tip, how bad can things be for him. Look at the meter, $5 for a few minutes' work, how bad can it be? They worry, all these people, how little you keep? I don't want to talk about it. It's over. It's fifteen years since I did it. I'm on welfare, with a lot of other people, my parents are dead so they don't know, my brother Marcus thinks I'm a bum, and if his children aren't sure what they're supposed to think about me, he makes sure every night to tell them. 'You're wondering about your Uncle Peter, who, thank God, we don't have to see that much, let me tell you, he's a bum. Fifteen years he hasn't worked. So, what does that make him? A bum. You got a better name for it? A stone. You want to meet a stone, I'll invite your Uncle Peter for dinner some night. But if it's all right with you, I'll be out of town that night, because I'm ashamed to be in the same house with him. On the memory of my mother and my father, I'm ashamed to be in the same house with him.'

"You want to know about my brother Marcus? I'll tell you a story. Ten years ago he comes to me. Calls me up one night and tells me we have to talk. 'Such a mystery,' I told him. 'What are we going to do, invest a million dollars somewhere?' You should have heard him. 'We have to talk, we have to talk.' 'Okay, so come over and we'll talk.' 'I'm not coming by your home,' he says. '*Nu*' I tell him, 'I'll come to you.' 'No, you're not coming to me either.' 'What, I'm not good enough to come to you?' I wasn't either in his eyes. So wait, you'll hear the story. So we meet, just like he says, in this little restaurant. I know where it is. It's a perfect meeting place because it's a million miles from where both of us live. He's got it figured out perfect. No one in his neighborhood should see me with him, and he wouldn't be caught dead in my neighborhood. All right, so I don't argue. Why should I argue? How do I know what he wants? Maybe he wants a loan. Maybe he wants to cut into my $83.65.

"So the next thing I know we're sitting in this restaurant where he's never been and I've never been. What does he want? You're ready? 'Peter,' he tells me like he's the president of the United States, 'we've got a little problem.' I haven't worked then, it was five years, I couldn't get a job anywhere, and I tried. Like a dog I ran around looking. Like a dog. I'm not working, and I'm getting sicker in my body everyday, because it takes it out of you, not working. It takes it out of you, but he's telling me we've got a problem. Him in his big home, me without a job, and he's telling me, we've got a problem. *Nu*, what's the problem? 'You know my wife, Sarah?' he says. 'No, I don't know your wife, Sarah. Of course I know your wife, Sarah. What kind of question is that?' I'm thinking, know her, yes, like her, no! She's a *schnorer*. You know who Sarah Rosenbloom is? She's a person who ten minutes after you give her a $10,000 diamond ring she's fishing in your pants, maybe she can find a dollar bill. She'll even settle for a little loose change, maybe she'll buy some chocolates. 'Yeah, I'm acquainted with this woman you mention.' 'Don't be fresh,' he tells me. 'I'm not fresh, but what kind of question is that?' 'All right,' he says, 'so you don't know all her relations.' 'No, I don't know her side of the family,' which is the only side because it's ten years my parents are dead and I'm as good as dead in their eyes because I don't work, so who's on our side? All her people are both sides of the family. If they got married today, I'd be the only one on my side of the shul. I should say, my side of the aisle because Marcus doesn't know from shuls; he knows only from getting married in swanky hotels.

"So what does he want from me, my wise considerate brother with his mystery meeting in this tenth-class restaurant we're sitting in? You can guess. You can also guess that when we're done, which we're going to be in a very short time, that he's going to insist on paying the bill, all $2.50 of it. Marcus Rosenbloom, the rich Hungarian turned 100 percent American. Mr. Yank. 'So, Marcus, tell me, you're ashamed I don't work.' He knows I try all the time to find work, but facts are facts, I don't work, I collect welfare. It's a big shame. 'What should I do?' I ask him. Well, he says, he knows it's not my fault. Still it doesn't look so good to some people that he's got a brother who in his heyday was a taxi driver, in his heyday, and now, in his not so heyday is doing nothing, but sitting by himself all day long. 'You want to give me money?' I ask him. No. No money. 'You want I should tell people I'm president of a bank?' I already guessed what he wanted. He's going to give me money for transportation, an airplane ride, anywhere I want, but it just doesn't' look good on Sarah's side of the family for him to have a slob for a brother. Being out of work, *they've* decided, doesn't look good. It reflects on the family and affects the children. It makes everybody think someone's too shabby. How I feel about it, how *I'm* suffering inside and have nobody to talk to because after my mother died there was nobody, this they aren't interested in. Twenty million times my brother talked to me, always with one question. Not how are you feeling? Did you find something yet? When my mother was alive, he had another question: How's Mamma? Because after my father died he didn't have time for her because his wife, the great human being, when she wasn't fishing in his pockets, she was whispering in his ear that maybe they had enough with his mother. And anyway, Peter the bum could look out for his mother since they had in common the fact that they were both out of work. I'm sure it went that way. He wouldn't have turned his back on his mother unless his wife told him to.

"So here he is pushing me out of town. I can go anywhere I like. Like I won a prize on a television show, *they're* sending me out of the city. He's going to write to me, call me, help me get settled. But it will all be better, for him, not me. The shame is less with me gone. The farther away I go, the better it is for all of them. Marvelous, isn't it. I wasn't even surprised. That's the kind of person he was. I say it that way because as big a *schnorer* as *she* was, *he* has to be weak to let her put him up to that. So I told him, 'Go away? I wouldn't go away if you put me in a palace. I want to go away, I go away. What are you, the government extraditing me? What am I, a crook that's making trouble for people? I'm a sick man with a two-room apartment and a welfare check and I can't find work. I'll drive a taxi any time they want, any hour, any day, Saturday, Sunday, Christmas, *Pessach*, but they don't want me. What am I supposed to do, take them to court? Go away? Never. Not by your command, not by your wife's command, not from nobody.' But Marcus is waiting for me. He knows what I'm going to answer even before I'm answering. Maybe in the little goodness it would be nice to think he has, he wants me to say no. But I don't care *what* he thinks because he's not moving me out or anybody else. If he's so ashamed of me for being unemployed—or maybe he doesn't like the idea that I'm robbing the country with my welfare check or that I'll be richer than him some day on eighty five bucks—but if it bothers him so much and his wife, then let *them* move. Let *them* tell their children, 'We're so ashamed of that bum, that stone, we're moving. And you should always remember one thing: That man you used to call your uncle, he's not really your uncle. By pure chance he happens to have the same last name like you. Maybe by pure chance he happens to have the same parents as your father, but you shouldn't think that's important either. He's a stone!'

"So I give him my answer. So here he comes again at me. Maybe I could change my name. This is even a better idea, he says, because I could take back the name we had in Hungary. So again I have my answer waiting for him: 'You don't like the name, *you* change it.' Can you imagine all this happening just because I'm not working? The word of the century is unemployed. Rich, middle, poor, everybody's unemployed, or knows somebody who's unemployed. You always got people who don't want to work, but I'm talking now about when you *can't* find work. It's like people with false teeth. Sometimes you can tell right off, sometimes you don't know. They hide it. Just like unemployment. Are you going to be ashamed about it? How can you be ashamed? You prayed that your teeth would fall out? You asked somebody to knock them out of your head? It just happened. So you do the best you can. You don't announce, 'You want to see my dentures, I'll take them out so you can study them.' But you also don't throw people away because they have a serious problem. What do they think, these pocket pickers like my sister-in-law? That we *like* to go without work? What have they got in this country, 5 million people out of work? And we're supposed to like it? You don't like false teeth. You don't like being in public wondering when they're going to fall out in your soup. You don't like being all by yourself, and see them sitting there in a glass. People don't have to come around and have secret meetings in tenth-class restaurants to tell you you're not working. My good and wonderful brother, get your real teeth put back in your head or you'll have to fly in an airplane somewhere, just you, your teeth, and that last name of yours, which is the cause of all these problems, that and the fact that everybody in our family was able to get a job and hold it but you! How do you explain it? This is my brother speaking to me. Like I'm a little baby. How do you explain it? He wants to know.

"So how *do* I explain it? 'I don't work. If it's shameful to you, Marcus, then it's shameful to me ten thousand and ten. If it's hurting your reputation with your family, what's it doing to my heart? Can you explain *that* to me?' I asked him. 'I'm sure it hurts.' That's his answer. 'I'm sure it hurts.' Yeah, it hurts so much he wants me to change my name. What, I'll become Jake Epstein and it won't hurt no more? Or maybe I could become Ronald Reagan and they'll make me president. What is it with people like this? They believe only in money and magic. Change your name, fill the pockets with money and magic, you're a rich man. It doesn't work like that. If magic could have got me a job, any job, I'd have found that magic a long time ago.

"We were drinking coffee, my brother and me, each with a little pot of coffee. This is ten years ago. I told myself, don't tell him nothing more than you have to. He's like a boxer; he's looking for weaknesses. My own brother, huh? 'So you won't move, eh?' 'No, I'm not moving. You got a job for me, we'll talk. You don't want me to see your family because you're ashamed, that problem's settled: you'll never see me. What do they say? I'll never darken your door.' 'I should give you a job?' he says to me. Suddenly, *he's* angry like *I* was the one who wanted to send *him* away. I should have told him, Marcus, I'm ashamed of you for working when I don't have a job. You're a shame to an unemployed man. There he is behind his little pewter coffee pot shouting at me: 'I should give *you* a job? Chutzpah like this I've never heard in my life.' So, while he's looking like a boxer for my weakness, he's made his mistake, and I have *his* weakness.

"'Marcus, that you even say the word chutzpah is the biggest chutzpah you could ever know. So now I'll ask you'—and I'm telling you the pewter is making a noise by this time because who in my life did I have to speak to, much less fight with? Who spoke to me then, who speaks to me now? You think there are clubs for unemployed people? And if there were, you think I'd join? I wouldn't be caught dead talking to people like me. What are they going to tell me I don't already know? 'Marcus, I got a question for *you*: How come you stopped speaking Yiddish? How come when the few times you talked to your mother she spoke Yiddish, you answered in

English? Not even Hungarian. How come it was she who cried to me about you all those nights you didn't have time for her 'cause your debt was paid off to your father? What about *that*, Mr. Yankee America? How come *you're* ashamed of me and *I'm* ashamed of you *and* your work, a hundred hours a week of it for all I know?' What I wanted to tell him I couldn't. With a wife like his I'd work two hundred hours a week. Even if she took all my money it'd be better than sitting home with her or lying in bed watching her fish through my pockets. *Nu*, Sarah, don't forget to look in his vests. Men like my brother always have a little something tucked away in the vest. 'So, Marcus,' I'm telling him in the secret restaurant, 'don't *you* tell me about unemployment because I'll tell you something about life that's more important. I'll tell you about history, about forgetting where you came from, what your parents and grandparents were, my such a grownup brother. That's for number one. I'll tell you about being loyal to your family. Not just your wife and that group she calls her family who couldn't be so wonderful if they work so hard to yank you away from your own family. That's for number two. And for number three, what about a little dignity for the first, second and third temple? What do you think, Marcus, you could have a little respect for the people here and there who died or hid or felt terrible about being alive so that people like you could ask for secret meetings with people like me and plan ways to get rid of me?'

"Was I giving it to him, Marcus, the boy who beat me up so many times in my life I'm still black and blue? But he was listening. I'm still his brother. He knew who was talking to him, and he knew I was 100 percent right about everything. The history, the coming from Hungary, our father, our mother being sick and he came, what, three times a year ten miles, to look in on her. That's what I told him. 'You looked in like a doctor looks in, because if he spends too much time, if he talks a little with someone and makes them feel like a human being, he'll lose money. You looked in on her. She knew it. She knew you were too busy for her.' You know what our mother told me? For only one reason did she want me to get work: To make enough money to go back to Europe. Nothing about me being happy or feeling good, just take her home. She was never home here. Our father wanted to come so she came, but she didn't want to. You know what she told me, and all this I'm telling Mr. Successful. In fact, I was beginning to think, I'm living alone and have nobody to talk to, and this man's living in a family, it seems like there's ten thousand of them, and *he's* got nobody to talk to either. I told him, 'Your mother held on to one thing when she came here, Yiddish. She spoke Yiddish with our father and me. You remember on her death bed when you finally found ten minutes to make a visit? Yiddish. Always Yiddish. And you use the word *chutzpah* like you spoke it everyday. 'Marcus,' 'I told him, 'I haven't worked in five years and the chances of me ever finding work are lousy. You'll work 'til you drop which I hope won't be for a long, long time. But I got dignity, and you haven't. All you got is a job, but I know my place, my position, and I don't care what *anybody* says about unemployed people. I know the important things, all you know is the buck, nine to five, doing what everybody wants you to do no matter what *you* think about it. You shouldn't have quit on your mother so soon!'

"He comes back at me, because he's not dumb. 'What,' he's yelling at me, 'you *like* not working? You're *proud* that you don't work? You don't think I'm good at my job and a good family man?'

"'I *hate* that I don't work. What do you want me to tell you? I cry every night. Okay? You happy now? I'd beg on the streets in your neighborhood, *my* neighborhood if I thought it would do any good. I'd walk around in front of a bunch of children with my teeth in a glass if it made them laugh and I got paid for it. What are you telling me, I'm proud? I'm proud of nothing in my life! I wasn't so proud when I did drive the taxi. What was so great about *that*, I'd like to know? Everybody asking me questions like I was a professor. What do you think about the president doing this or doing that, or senator this one or that one? What's to be proud. I'm ashamed. You think I need a secret meeting with you like we were a couple of spies to remind me I'm sick from not being able to find work? You think it's good how I live, where I live, that I even live? Who knows me better than you? Who knows how I feel better than you, and you come here ready to shove me like baggage, into the first plane? You want to send me away, Marcus, all right, I've changed my mind, send me. Look at me. Everything worth owning is what you see. Put me on a plane right now, I don't need to pack anything. Not a tooth brush, nothing. You want to laugh, Marcus, here's one for you. I don't even own a suitcase; you got Mamma's. So go ahead and send me. America is getting rid of it's unemployed men, you're just doing your share. That's what people will say, so you don't have to worry. The problem of unemployment starts at home, you're doing your little bit to clean up the problem. Someone asks, what did you do for unemploy-ment in your company, Mr. Rosenbloom? *Nu*, you'll tell him, in the com-pany nothing, but I shipped my brother to the west coast. So now the east coast doesn't have to worry anymore, and the west coast won't sleep at night. Now *they* got the problem.'

"So there's my poor rich brother, the man I know in my heart isn't happy in Hungary, here, anywhere, 'cause he's just like me and is afraid to admit it even to himself, and he's crying and he's laughing. And I'm beginning to laugh and cry a little myself. 'Peter,' he says, 'tell me you have a good dentist?' I told him, 'Who needs a dentist, I need teeth. Is there any chance,' he asks me, 'that you could find work maybe in another part of the city? Maybe you should move some place new.' 'I look everyday,' I told him. 'Everyday. My job in life is to find a job.' 'You got friends?' he asks. 'You want the truth, Marcus? Only you.' 'You got me,' he says. I remember, he pushes the little pewter pot away and touches my hand. We're both crying. I felt a little proud, not so much that he loved me and how in all the world he's the only one I have, even with that pocket fisher of a wife he's got, but not so proud that I could forget that when I would leave him I'd still be a man without a job. *That* you don't forget. In the day, the night, it's always there.

"I'll tell you something I don't feel so proud about, something I never told my brother. I didn't go to temple for four years when I lost my job. *That* much ashamed I was. I couldn't sit there and go through the motions and make believe everything in my life was going so well. I still don't go to temple with a free conscience. I'm like a criminal, like I did something and I can't go into a place of worship pretending. I can't be there with the feeling I'm hiding something. It doesn't make sense, but that's how it is. but I couldn't tell my brother, which shows how sad it was between us, and what not working has done to me, *and* to him, *and* to his wife who spends all day on the telephone telling her family what a monster her husband has for a brother. First she kept him away from my mother, now it's me.

"Well, what can you do?" Peter Rosenbloom was standing up in the living room of his small apartment, looking about at the objects he had collected. He didn't seem particularly sad, he was merely looking. "Maybe that secret lunch with my brother was the highlight of the last ten years. That and a couple of funerals and that about takes care of my social life. Put it together with a little shame and a little, what do you even call that feeling, that what's the sense of going on, and that's my life. Nobody likes to see himself as a failure. You think people standing in front of a mirror and pointing a finger and saying, 'Morris, you're a bum.' Jewish, Gentile, who wants to see that in the mirror? Not from yourself, not from your brother, from nobody do you want to hear about what you are, unless they got good things to say. Move away, change my name, disappear, all right, so now I'm invisible; so they got jobs for invisible people like me? They *want* me to be invisible. I should go away and take the nothing I got with me. Then they got their memories. Oh, that Peter Rosenbloom, what a wonderful man he was. Didn't work for fifteen years but did it matter to anyone? Not in the slightest. Because even with the false teeth and the nothing apartment and the few hours he drove a taxi, which is below him; naturally, he was wonderful to his brother and his mother and father and his little nephew and niece. You hear them saying all this? I hear them every day of my life. So he didn't work, so who's fault was it that America fell apart and none of the Peter Rosenblooms could get a job for love nor money? Was it *his* fault? Not on your life. He was a beautiful man. Isn't that what they all say now, a beautiful man? No job, but beautiful.

"You want to know where all this leaves me? I'm a double bum. Bum number one because I'm not working like a good Jewish man, and bum number two because I'm not working in the right profession or the right business. You can be sure my sister-in-law thinks like that. Fellow walks up to her and says, 'How do you do, my job is to kill Jews like your husband and his brother.' 'Tell me,' she says, 'What you do, it's steady work that pays well? You go to college. What do you think, they'll teach anybody how to kill Jews?' '*Nu*,' she'd say. 'If you're working regular and you've finished with college, how bad a person can you be. Anyway, you can't be as bad as my brother-in-law. He's going to die before he finds a job.'

"She's not a Jew. And my brother isn't either. Should I tell you what they are? They're nothing. They're not us, they're not them, because they don't feel. She never did, and once he did, but she took care of that for good. Now they're made for each other. A match made in heaven between the two of them. They can't feel nothing, not the weather, nothing. You know what they should be doing? They should be helping me, making out like I'm wanted in their home. People around here do that for you, and none of them has a job or ten cents they can spare. They aren't even Jewish, 90 percent of them. There's very few of us around here, but all of us hold together, even if we don't say anything to anybody half the time. We have our jobs to do; it's only the Rosenblooms on the other side of the city, they can't see what we do. They should look a little closer one of these days, they'd see how we got first the job of trying to find a job. Then we got the job of surviving. They don't see that because it's too big for them, and we're too small for them. You want the truth? We're better without them, without their ideas about what we should do. We're perfectly fine without them. As far as they're concerned we're all without faces and names, and we got no feelings, no pride. If they want to feel like that, I say let them go ahead. Maybe they'll go to their graves without even wondering whether we're alive or dead. They want to judge a person on whether he's got a job, let them go right ahead. I wouldn't stop them if I had the power. I could care less about the whole lot of them. Fact is, I'm too busy these days to even think about them.

"You see what all this time without work does to a person? What's the word I want. It warps us? It makes us different from what we are. I don't think about my brother every day of my life? I don't think about his wife and his children? As much as I think she's the world's biggest nothing, the biggest thief in the country, I don't want to be invited by *her*, by her, not him, to dinner once in a while? Once a month maybe? I don't think what it would feel like to drive a car I own up to their home and carry in some flowers and a little bottle of wine and some little something for the children? I don't think about that? Or that they'd ask me about my job and I'd tell them, well, you know business, Marcus, and you know too, Sarah darling, because you talk to your husband, some days you make a dollar, some days you lose a dollar, but in the end we all make out all right. And they could see just by looking that I make out a lot more than just all right. I don't want the chance to take a drink of the wine I brought, give thanks that we're all healthy and the children are growing nice and let out a big sigh and say, *Nu*, things could be worse? I could be unemployed. And everybody would laugh. Even the children. I don't want that? That's *all* I want, all I've ever wanted, even with all the closeness of my mother. A man comes to the door right now and says, 'Rosenbloom, you can have it, just like you told it. The price? Give me your eyes.' 'I can sit at my brother's table, Sarah's table, with a suit, the presents, the wine, the whole deal, you'll give me that and a regular job, and I give you my eyesight?' 'That's the deal.' 'Take my eyes, ears, my hands, my feet. Take everything you want. It's yours.' *That's* how much I think about them on the other side of the city.'

"It could be funny, you know. It could be a wonderful comedy. It could be that like magic, this man, this Elijah walks in here and gives a look, like, what, Rosenbloom, all these years and all you got is two rooms, and makes his proposition about you give me your eyes and I'll give you the job and the suit and the wine and the flowers. It could be funny because it could end up that he gives me all he promised, and when he goes to collect from me, he finds he can't get a thing because after all these years of not working I don't have anything left to give him. Maybe somebody somewhere could find it funny. Who knows these days what makes a person laugh, a person with a job I mean."

Chapter 4

A One-in-a-Million Chance to Earn a Living: Ollie Sindon

My life has been wasted, and wasteful. Never was much of a kid, ain't much more as a man. I have a wife who wouldn't be as bad if I was working. Got a kid in jail who for sure wouldn't be there if I was working.

Although the temptation in these discussions is to place our focus on the unemployed worker, the fact is that his family can never be forgotten. Entire family systems are affected by long-term unemployment in ways that no one could ever have foreseen. We have already noted how physical illness is a common phenomenon in the family members of the long-term unemployed, and how crime rates rise as well among these people, and especially the men, the fathers and sons. It might be said, therefore, that unemployment causes people to act out, in the form of aggression, violence, crime, or perhaps act in, in the form of psychological and physical disorders that overwhelm the body and psyche. Either way, unemployment profoundly damages the protective capacities and membranes of the family's operating systems.

Ollie Sindon is a man of enormous pride, one his family feels as well, or did, anyway, when he enjoyed steady work. Born in this pride were the seeds of the respect his family maintained for him, or did anyway, when he had steady work. After months of idleness, however, his anger and moroseness overtook him to the point where he not only appeared absorbed in self-pity, but reduced to the level of a child, a son requiring protection and nurturance rather than a father providing protection and nurturance for his wife and children.

As Ollie felt the pain and humiliation of being out of work, his son David internalized his father's emotions and made his father's circumstances his own. Yet, whereas Ollie turned his anger and sense of failure inward, David exploded these emotions on the world, even as he battled to preserve what little respect he had for his father. In one moment he felt for his father's situation, the injustice, the hurt, the shame. In the next moment, however, he would scream his profound rage to the point of losing control altogether. The two could barely be together, they could barely allow themselves to look at one another so intense was their shame, so intense the pain of their feeling abandoned by each other.

In time, whatever admiration father and son might have shared seemed long vanished, and two men essentially were left to deal with their aloneness. Each felt their fright and their rage, each felt the fright and rage of the other man. With long-standing dreams of successes shattered, the two went on with their singular lives, utterly unable to find ways even to look at one another, much less offer one another a shred of hope.

When Davey Sindon was small, his mother would put him on her lap and sing, "Davey Sindon's gone to sea, leaving his father and his sister and me." No matter how often she did it, the little boy laughed and bounced up and down, trying to get her to repeat it. By the time he was five, he couldn't remember his mother Victoria ever singing to him. As for the song, Davey wasn't even certain what it meant. "Is Daddy a sailor?" he would ask his mother earnestly.

Like his older sister, Effie, Davey gave his mother great pleasure. She could be strict with them, but she never did anything that made her children question her love for them. Victoria's rule was constraint. She never left the children unattended, nor surprised them with sudden changes of mood. People wondered how she did it, in light of the difficulties involved in being married to Ollie Sindon. But Victoria always said, "It's easy to be a gentle boat when the sea is roaring. If the sea roars, boat doesn't have to do nothing but hold on to its course." Her friends would smile; Victoria had a way with words. She had a way of making the hard times seem easy, and survival, even during the most precarious moments, appear effortless. She also had that special capacity of keeping people from asking her pointed questions. All one had to do was walk past the Sindon house when Ollie was going through what Victoria called his "complaining lessons," and one knew her life tottered on the point of disaster.

The problem wasn't Ollie's mercurial temperament, his fiery responses to everything from politics to changes in the weather. The problem was his being out of work. It was the moroseness, anger and sickness caused by being turned down by employers, from being lied to, from having his few little hopes shattered. "They're bombing me out," he'd roar, if he wasn't weak from drinking. "Bombing me out with their promises and their bull shitting. I had it with those folks a long, long time ago. They hate Niggers 'til it just about kills them to have to look at us. Give us a job? Shit, they'd just as soon give what little they got to an animal 'fore they'd give us a look. Go in there with them White faces staring at me. Oh-oh, here comes another Nigger wanting to be lazy on another job. Close the door on him 'fore he gets in too far so's we can't throw him out. You got a family, Nigger? Holy shit, here's another family man out on the street. Hey, but what the hell, Niggers don't give no shit for their families. His old lady's probably doing it with some son of a bitch right now, so what's this guy care. *Do* you care, Nigger? You Goddamn right I care, 'cause I ain't working. You hear me? If I ain't working I ain't living. You hear me, man? I'm not living no more 'til you give me a job!"

Victoria would stare at him, and without raising her voice she would warn him: "You don't talk that way with me or I take these children and I leave. I am just as upset about your not working as you are, but I will not have everybody's life being spoiled by your problems. We live on what we have, what we'll get. But don't you go playing those plays of yours. I will not be your audience anymore." Then she would leave before he had a chance to speak, and by his own admission, he would be relieved that she had silenced him, for his complaining hurt him almost as much as his not working. Besides, jobs had turned up in the past, they would again in the future. "Just let the future come quick," he would whisper, following Victoria into the single bedroom in the apartment where the children slept. What a feeling to look down at the two of them asleep, breathing so slowly, the two of them so unaware of his problems and the miserable times the family might be facing.

Ollie Sindon wanted to share his agony at being unemployed with his children, despite their being too young to understand what it meant. He wanted them to say, "Daddy, you got the rawest deal any man on this earth ever got. But you'll see, if things don't turn out better, *we're* going to make it better for you. We're going to stay by you no matter what, even if it means we'll *never* get married or move away. But no matter what happens, we'll never see you as a failure. It's the country that's at fault, not you!" Ollie wanted so much to be happy. He saw his life as complicated, but he never gave up the idea that he could be satisfied. He was willing to settle for little, the only requirement being steady work until he was sixty-five. He dreamed of the day he would be too old to work and could say to his son, "Well sir, Davey, the load's all yours. From now on, *you* look after this family." The day dreams were plentiful, all of them with happy endings, but each one based on the idea of a man working forty hours a week and bringing home a pay check for his wife and children.

Victoria was the only one who knew of Ollie's fantasies. She teased him about them when she was certain his mood was strong enough to take the chiding: "For someone who spends as much time dreaming as you do, your dreams don't make us too rich, do they? If I was dreaming, I'd put us in a big house somewhere, but all you dream is working steady forty hours a week."

"That's all I see," he'd answer quietly.

"Maybe that's all any of us have the right to see. Well, maybe someday you should dream about working forty-*five* hours a week. Then we'd have a little bit extra."

"If I start dreaming big," Ollie would say, starting to laugh, "I'm going to dream about working steady *twenty* hours a week and still end up better than what I got right now."

"Bet you would too."

"You *know* I would. Then I'd add that I could see my boy working even less and getting even more. No. Let him work as long as I did, only let him come out of it a whole *helluva* lot better than I did."

Ollie Sindon's dreams never came true. His periods of unemployment were frequent. Although not a skilled laborer, no one could work harder. He quit only when the job was done, even if it meant coming home a few hours late. Victoria never liked to add to his burdens, but when he was working regularly, she wouldn't hesitate to ask about his long hours. "No one's asking you to work more than eight hours a day. You aren't that young that you can go on like a boy."

Ollie loved to hear her talk this way. He loved the feeling of being exhausted from a hard day of work, knowing that no one in the world could tell him he hadn't put in one amazing day. "I got pride," he'd say. "I may not love what I'm doing, but I'm working, and working is the act we're put on earth to do."

"Glad you told me," she'd wink at him, "'cause a person like myself's always happy to know why we *were* put on the earth. Now that I know it's because we get a chance to dig ditches for some rich White man, all of us can sleep better tonight."

"Don't you fool yourself, Victoria. Everyone gets his kind of gratification out of his work he can. Doctor gets his kind of gratification, butcher gets his kind, even an old woman like you gets her kind. Some folks use their heads, some folks used their hands, but it don't make no difference 'cause the world needs all of us to be doing our work. There is no world without people working. I'm digging holes for telephone poles. Wouldn't exactly call it the greatest job in the world, but if I don't do it I don't stay alive."

Victoria was happy when Ollie worked. Her children too, seemed healthier. And it was good knowing there was a little money to buy those special treats the family enjoyed. No one in the world loved steak like Ollie. It was there when he worked, it was never mentioned when he didn't.

By the time he was eleven, Davey Sindon knew all about his father's difficulties in finding and keeping jobs. He knew it was bad luck to say anything about a job his father might get. He also knew better than to ask where his father had gone on a particular day. Maybe Ollie had worked, maybe he hadn't, but one waited to see what he would say. Most days no one had to ask; it was evident he had not worked. His eyes and posture told the whole story. He might ask Davey if he wanted to throw a ball around. Davey would grab their mitts and be downstairs on the street in seconds. Ollie would follow minutes later, wearing his suit jacket, and they would throw the ball back and forth, Ollie's mind a million miles away. When Ollie was working, there was real excitement in the game, and Ollie would do a play-by-play description of their game.

"There's a ground ball in the hole," he'd shout out, rolling the beaten up old ball down the sidewalk. "Sindon over to his right, makes a great pick up and throws him out. What a play!"

"Do it again," Davey ordered his father.

"Ground ball to Sindon. He hasn't much time, Morgan can fly, but he throws him out. Get down lower, David. What, you afraid the ball's going to hit you in the face?" Davey had to admit he worried about the ball skipping off the concrete and hitting him squarely in the mouth. "Hey, listen," Ollie would say, "you want to be a major leaguer, you got to take the chances. It's just another job. Man digs holes there's the danger he could fall in one of them. Man digs for coal, there's a chance he can get caught in the collapse. You go for a grounder, someone leaves a little bitty stone out there, that ball's going to pop up right over your head. Got to have fast hands, fast hands."

"You play ball, Ollie, when you were a kid?" Davey would ask.

"Did I play ball when I was a kid?" Ollie would shout back in disbelief. Victoria would be watching from the window, barely able to hear them, and making certain little Effie didn't fall off the ledge. Ollie's deep voice rushed in through the window like thick smoke. "Who do you think taught Billy George Blatter everything he knows about baseball?"

"Billy George *who*?" would come Davey's little voice.

"You don't know Billy George Blatter?" Ollie would say with exaggerated incredulity.

"No. Who's Billy George whatever his name is?"

"Victoria," Ollie would shout up to his wife. "This boy of yours doesn't know who Billy George Blatter is."

"Then suppose you just tell my son who he is."

"Tell him yourself," he'd shout, laughing to the point his mitt would fall off his hand and he would drop the ball, which only irritated Davey that much more.

"How the hell should I know? Anyway, hurry up, the steak's almost ready."

"Steak!" Davey would scream, dashing upstairs and leaving Ollie to carry up the mitts and the ball. At dinner, Ollie would tell Davey that Billy George Blatter was a boy who went to church with him when he was little. Truthfully, he couldn't figure out why the name had come into his mind, except that Billy Blatter was the worst athlete in the neighborhood, maybe the worst in the state. Ollie even remembered hearing the boy's father say that Billy George was so bad at sports, he must have had White blood in him. The thought made Ollie Sindon laugh out loud.

His father's enjoyment with such foolish stories irritated Davey. "We ought to have steak every night," he would say.

The remark quieted everyone.

No one knew exactly what had happened to Ollie Sindon. Merely remembering the event was difficult enough. It was a Wednesday morning, a Wednesday morning when he was out of work. He awoke and found he couldn't get out of bed. Victoria told him to quit joking, but he insisted he couldn't move his left leg, he had lost all the sensation in it. Victoria was terrified. A police ambulance arrived and two attendants carried Ollie down the stairs. After several weeks, he recovered most of the feeling in the leg, although a small limp remained. While he tried to hide this slight disability from potential employers, the few job possibilities he had accumulated grew even thinner.

The minor stroke Ollie had suffered occurred when Davey was thirteen. Victoria took odd jobs—sewing, house cleaning, laundering—when she could find them. She disliked being away from her husband who had grown depressed after his illness. The little bit of energy he always had been able to draw on during the weeks of unemployment had vanished. He threatened suicide, went several days without speaking to anyone, and demanded that food be prepared for him when he knew there was no food in the house. When Victoria offered to go shopping for him he would yell at her for leaving him alone. What if he suddenly needed her? What if he fell, or suffered another stroke?

"Get someone else to go shopping for you and arrange your life to shop when Effie's here. And how come Davey isn't home at night? Just 'cause I'm not working don't mean he's supposed to be playing around all the time. What do you tell him? His father's a cripple? His father's a bum? That why he's not here. What is it with these kids that they get so damn disrespectful? Who they think they are anyway, acting like they're superior to everyone, wanting only this kind of food or wearing only that kind of clothes? I'd like to see them do a whole lot better what with the conditions I had facing me. Big time, that's all they want. Hell, I'll bet they sit around talking about me. 'My father don't work no more 'cause he's got a bum leg that keeps him home. Of course, even if he didn't have it he wouldn't work anyway 'cause he always had trouble. Probably didn't want to work neither. Never saw a man so lazy. Hell, he didn't even have time to play ball with me when he wasn't working. Told my mother, you're not supposed to work, then he didn't work himself. So what'd he expect, *us* to work? Laziest Nigger in the city, my father. Wasn't even a good ball player.' VICTORIA! Where the hell are you?"

"I'm here," Victoria would scream back. "I am goddamn sick myself with all your complaining. You've complained about one thing or another from the day practically we got married. What the hell is it now? You want to eat, I told you I'd go to the store. You want to talk, we'll sit here and talk. But if it's the feel-sorry-for-the-poor-old-man bit, I have had it up to here. You want to complain about how you're the only person in the world who's got problems, you go right ahead, but I ain't listening to it, and I'll be damned if I'm ready to tell my son he has to sit here at night with his father and listen to all the garbage that flies out of your mouth!" Ollie listened to his wife when she spoke to him. He felt increasingly sorry for himself. He fought her, but he listened to her, because, like her, he blamed himself for his troubles. Still, he fought her:

"You don't want to hear me talking, that's fine. Why don't you just take all your junk and get out of here. Take the children, empty out the kitchen, take all your friends for all I care. I'd be better off without them floating in here all the time asking me about this job or that job, or saying it don't look to me like you got any problem with your leg. Take 'em all. Or maybe you'd like *me* to leave. Why don't you go down to the five and dime and buy me a track suit and I'll *run* out of here. Give all of you the big laugh you want out of me. What the hell, you laugh at me behind my back, might as well do it in front of me. I sure would love to know just what it is you tell that boy about me.

"Well, son, your father's a big bust. Just another one of those dumb Niggers that didn't spend enough time in school so here he is a big failure. He tried. Even thought he'd be able to make it, but it didn't work out. Tell you, son, there's only one thing a man's supposed to do, and that's work. If he don't work, well, he just ain't a man. So you see, son, your old man ain't a man at all. He's just a dumb old NIGGER!"

"Shut up," Victoria would cry out. "Shut up or I *will* leave."

"Go on. Who the hell needs you around here anyway, all you do is mother people. Hell, you been mothering me like I was the boy's brother 'stead of his father."

"You act like you were his *baby* brother 'stead of his father. 'Bout time you started acting like his father."

"'Bout time you shut your face up."

"I don't see where just because you ain't working don't mean you can't take a fatherly interest in him."

"A fatherly interest in him," he would mock her. "You know something, Victoria, you're beginning to sound like some of those high class White folks you been working for. Maybe that's what you want too, since you *are* the man of the family. Ain't that it?

"What you want to eat?"

"I'm asking you a question," he would scream at her.

"What do you want me to say?"

"I want you to say that because I don't work I'm only his father by title. I carry the title, like I carry a card saying I got a right to work. Neither of them does no good. I'm a shit ass father and you know it. But I ain't making excuses to nobody. Don't care what happens to either of them, 'cause *I* come first, man. *I'm* the one. I don't have a job, there ain't no work in this country, bad leg or not, then I don't mess around with no children. That's *your* job. Don't give a damn about them. Don't need to see them, don't need to talk to them. Boy wants to talk with some man, let him find somebody at his school. Better yet, let him go find one of those bullshit Nigger ministers. You want real men with real jobs, men working their asses off for the community just for the love of God, then that's who he can go talk to. He can go in the church with all those other guys running around in there. 'Hey man, what you do?' 'I work for God, man.' 'Oh yeah? What you do for God, man?' 'I light candles and keep people from sinning.' 'Yeah, that right, man?' 'Yeah. Get money for it too, telling all the little children with fathers who don't work what to do.' 'Yeah, what is it you tell 'em to do?' 'I tell 'em how they got to have *compassion* for their poor old stumbling fathers. Poor old man sitting up there in his ridiculous little house watching the walls and waiting to die. Got to *advise* all those little children so's they see the light of God.' 'Hey, man, that's one helluva job you got there working for the church. I talk to those children myself, man.' 'Yeah? Ones with the unemployed fathers?' 'Sure, man. I talk to 'em just like you do.' 'That a fact? And what do *you* tell 'em?' 'I tell 'em if you're old enough to see your old man ain't working, and you're old enough to understand that when he don't work it means he ain't bringing home a fuckin' dime, then you're old enough to get away from that man as soon as you can 'cause he *ain't* no man. He *ain't* no father. He's nothing, man. And the sooner you forget the sight of him, the better off you're going to be. Don't hang around him if he ain't working. Man will just bring you down with him.'"

Victoria would close the door to the apartment and quietly start down the stairs. She would be weeping. Then Ollie's big voice would bellow from the living room. "Victoria, VICTORIA, you get back in here at once! You come back in this house in one minute or I won't be here when you get back! You can just say good-bye right now."

Victoria would go buy strawberry ice cream for him, even though the doctor said Ollie would feel better without starchy foods.

No matter how hard she tried, Victoria never convinced her husband that being out of work did not reflect on him as a man or father. But there was no assuring him. A job possibility would arise and his spirits lifted, but Victoria could see that he was scared now from the uncertainty and months of inactivity. There were days when the little bit of hope she wanted to hold on to seemed real enough, but no jobs ever lasted, and Ollie wasn't getting any younger. Indeed, he seemed to be aging more quickly than anyone she knew, with the exception of her son.

At fourteen, Davey was a strong young man, quiet, and filled with anger. He rarely let even his closest friends know what he was thinking and feeling. His father had lost touch with him, and his mother, he insisted, hadn't the slightest notion of who he was. A complex person with many talents, he dreamed of becoming many things. Yet in conversations that dwelled on his life, his father's unemployment inevitably played a significant role. It was like a fire that never went out. He himself could never say precisely what angered him: Was it widespread unemployment, or the mere fact that his father spent so much time out of work? He might start a tirade against America, its racism and poverty, but within minutes he was raging against his father, calling him weak and a quitter. He labeled his father the nice little Nigger in the company of White folks. The odds, he would always say, were so stacked against families like his, the only way to lead your life was to take the attitude that you had everything to win and nothing to lose, except the respect of a few people, like perhaps your own father.

Davey's manner troubled Victoria and infuriated Ollie.

"They're all fancy big shots," Ollie would growl when Davey went out on a Friday night. "Son of a bitch child looks down his nose at me, and there he is strutting around as if he was the goddamn tax collector. If he disapproves of me so much, let him get his own goddamn home. If he can do so much better without me, let's see him try. While he's at it, he can go show this great big world he thinks he's discovering to his sister. Then *she* can be a phony big shot too. Where'd he get all those clothes?"

Victoria held the same fears as her husband about where their son went and what he did. Her problem was to get Ollie to turn his attention from his own concerns to those of his son. Ollie himself said that his salvation lay in making certain his children wouldn't share the fate he had known. But something always prevented him from putting his own problems aside long enough to attend to his children. No matter how intensely he resolved to devote himself to Davey, his bitterness at being sickly and out of work kept him from carrying out his intentions.

"You know where that boy's going to end up, Victoria?" Ollie would mutter.

"I know exactly where he's going to end up. He's going to end up in jail. Won't be long now."

"Way you say it, makes it sound like that's what you want."

Victoria wouldn't bother to respond.

The thought that he might end up in jail had also crossed Davey's mind: "Could happen, man," he would say. "Steady work though, in jail, ain't it. I mean, you don't even have to go looking for it, or have some Mr. Nobody with a big stomach interview you or nothing. You walk in there and the man says, your job's working in the carpentry shop. They even pay you to work. Ain't much, but what the hell, working for peanuts is better than not working. You don't believe me, you just ask my old man. Man, has this country screwed *that* guy up. Down on his knees, I'll bet, more times than he'd ever admit, begging for people to give him a job. So what the hell if I am in jail. They give me the work, I'll blow out my time there.

"'Course my old man, he'd be angry. Love to see that man's face when the man comes and tell him, 'We got your boy locked up for ripping off a bank.' 'Son of a bitch kid,' he'd yell at my mother. 'Told you he was no good. Yeah, but tell me, Copper, how much the boy rip that bank off for? Couple thousand maybe?' 'Couple thousand, man? Shit. I may go into prison somewhere, if they catch me. But if I go I ain't going for no two thousand dollars. I go in for the kill. Six figures right up front man, or I don't even *talk* about the job.' You see my old man starting to smile. 'Is that a fact? Old Davey boy ripped 'em off for six figures? Son of a bitch kid didn't do so bad at that, even if he *is* in prison. Hell, time will come when they got to let him out. Say, tell me, Copper, they find out maybe he left a little money for his poor old Mom and Dad? Ain't worked in twenty years, man. Bet he left a little something for me.' 'Hell, he did, old man. Told me to tell you you played the good Nigger too long, man. You could have been in on anything you wanted.' Sitting in that chair of his, bitching all the time 'bout this and that to my *mother*, man, like she was the governor or something.

"You get a load of that guy, man, begging in the streets so's he got the whole community laughing at him, and he's putting it to my mother? What the hell he think she's ever going to do for *him*! She walked blocks, man, more streets than you could count, looking for the food he told her he wanted. You imagine that, man, sending that woman 'round the city shopping in just the stores *he* wants, buying him just the certain kind of ice cream he wants, 'cause you can't get the brand in stores 'round here? Son of a bitch worked, hell, no more than a few years all together since he was married, and he's pushing her 'round like he's some king. Should have seen him too when he got sick, you know with that leg of his. Doctor told my mother he was fine. He went around acting like they took his leg off. Made everybody treat him special like he was somebody famous. He's nothing man. He can't stand to face it, but he's nothing. You want to bullshit guys at the poolhall, let 'em think you ain't drawing welfare? That's okay, man. Nobody says you got to advertise your losses, you know what I'm saying. But he was acting like he was doing all right in his own home, front of me and my mother and my sister. Who's he think he's kidding?

"And another thing. All this time he ain't working, all he's thinking about is me. Half the time I think he's trying to figure out ways I won't end up like him. But the other half, man, I really think the son of a bitch was plotting how to have me end up in the same shit pile as him. I think it's killing him to see me successful when he failed so bad. There ain't no one talked so bad as he did. But don't think once he's paid any attention to my sister. I can't even remember him asking her what's she doing, like at school. And that kid is smart, man. She reads out loud to my mother sometime at night, I tell her to shut up 'cause I'm trying to sleep, but I'm only pretending 'cause I love to hear her read. My mother gets her all these adult books and she goes through them, zip zap zip. She remembers 'em too. I do too when I hear her reading them out loud. But you think my old man has once said, 'Hey, you know what, Effie, you're the best reader in this city. I'm proud of you, Effie. Good, Effie. Fuck you, Effie.' Don't say a word to her. Man's got no job so he thinks he's got the right to order us around. Nobody's told him you got to earn your place in the house. You don't just get it for free.

"Other thing he thinks about is how soon it's going to be 'fore I end up in the slammer. Shit, I got a mind to walk in on him one day and say, 'Listen here, I'm going to take a big load off your mind. I'm going to be in jail in less than a year, so now all you got to worry about is feeling sorry for yourself. But don't trouble yourself none, 'cause it wouldn't look right, your getting off your sweet ass trying to find a job somewhere so's your old lady might have a couple of nice days on the earth before she croaks. And while I'm in jail, why the hell don't you introduce yourself to the little skinny girl who lives in the same apartment as you. You named her after your own mother so you must have been interested in her once. 'Stead of sitting there trying to convince everybody you can't walk and that's why you don't go looking for a job, have her read out loud to you.' Shit, man, I'm not so sure my old man even knows how to read himself. Guess he must, I see him with the newspaper everyday. Don't do him a helluva lot of good though, does it. Maybe he don't know they print jobs in it. Probably all he's doing is choking himself to death on the comics.

"I don't know, sometimes I feel sorry for the man. Tell myself, hey, the world is tough, 'specially if you're Black. Lots of folks out of work. Nobody cares all that much about how many folks don't have jobs when it's just Black folks. People going around mumbling, Uppity Niggers won't work for five bucks an hour no more. Then all of a sudden, like, all these White folks, they start losing their jobs too, high paying guys too, lots of 'em. Then that's *all* you hear about: unemployment, unemployment. Ten years ago nobody said a word. Now everybody's bitching and moaning, you know what I'm saying. Who was looking out for my old man ten years ago? Nobody, man. They were out there on the streets looking for the cheapest labor they could find. Hell, they knew they could buy men like my father cheap, and man did they ever give 'em the shittiest jobs. They had my father standing waist high in shit, digging, and the son of a bitch came home proud of his work, telling my mother he did a good day's work. They paid him shit, man, for working in shit, and the man felt proud. I can't believe it, man. He used to come home, he'd be smelly like you couldn't imagine. Me and my sister couldn't stand how much he smelled. We had to get out of the house, man. My father and my mother pretended to be angry with us for walking out like that, but you could see they were only pretending. Everybody was happy then 'cause the man had work. I was happy too. I mean, I wasn't old enough to be ashamed of what he did for a living. What's your old man do, David? My old man stands ass high in shit and shovels it around, but he's happy 'cause he's got a steady job. Little kids ain't ashamed of their fathers. They don't know what being out of work is all about.

"But all that's different now, man. He never works. I ain't got a reason in the world why I should stay around the house. I might have thought he was pretty cute when I was small, but I don't see nothing cute about him now. It's my job to make sure my mother and Effie are going to be all right, 'cause he sure gave up on *that* job a long, long time ago. He'll push my mother around, man, about the slightest thing that bothers him. 'Hey, Victoria, how come my shirts ain't clean? Hey, Victoria, how come your son's always getting into trouble?' But she takes it. Maybe there's something wrong with her too, taking all his pushing her around. Hell, if I was her I'd tell her, 'Hey, look it here, man. You work for a living, get up off your ass one second of the day and I'll *think* about obeying some of your orders. But if you just sit there looking so goddamn mad at the world, I wouldn't go across this room to open the goddamn window for you.' She don't tell him nothing though, man. It's like he's got some special right to be out of work. It's like he's always telling her, lots of guys like him out of work. You can't argue with the man. Black folks are getting killed without a job. They'll take a Black man's job from him ten times faster than a White man's job, you know what I'm saying. You got a bunch of cats working on some big construction job and the word comes down to cut off some men, who you think they're going to cut first? They'll cut every Black man off that job unless the man is so well trained they can't get along without him. But there ain't a lot of specialized folks cause they don't train 'em until they've trained all the White guys they can find. Shit, jobs being what they are, you can be damn sure the man's going to turn his back on his own brothers if he can save his job.

"So who's my father got helping *him* out in the world, man? There ain't nobody, unless it's somebody watching him figuring out how he's going to take my old man's job, if he ever gets one. Man don't stand a chance. He's got a one in a million chance, man, just to earn a living. You imagine how that makes him feel? Man has to pull his body out of the bed every morning knowing he's got a one in a million chance to make his goddamn living, you know what I'm saying. It's no wonder he got sick like he did. This thing breaks your spirit; there's nothing left of the man. When I was small, you know, and he was working, that man was fun to have around. Man used to play ball with me, man was a stitch. He'd make it fun for me, 'cause it sure couldn't have been too much fun for him. Hell, I couldn't catch the damn thing, and half the time I had him running in the street or down some cellar stairs chasing after that ball. But he was a jive, man. Folks used to stand around and watch him. He knew everybody, man. After work, all the men would come down to watch my old man play ball, and all these little kids wanted to play with us. He knew I didn't want to play with 'em. He knew what I was thinking even without me saying a word. He'd tell 'em, 'this scene's just with me and my son. This here's our special after work baseball game.' Man, I felt fantastic. I'd think, son of a bitch, man has to be the greatest father alive.

"Hey, but you grow up, you learn what's happening in the world. You see your father sitting home all the time, bitching 'bout that, moaning 'bout that, and no matter what he says about how Black folks got it tough, I see him not working. Words are one thing, but what he does or doesn't do, that's a whole other thing. And the man ain't working. Just picking on my old lady, which means he's probably knocking hell out of her when me and Effie ain't there. But she don't say much. I used to think to myself, I'm going out to make money. I'll give 'em both all my money. You see me, ten years old looking for a job? Get me fifty, sixty thou a year and give it to my folks. Little kids and all their dreams, huh?

"I didn't know what to do with either one of my folks when it got bad. I said to myself, I'm either going to run away, or I swear to God I'm going to kill 'em both 'cause they're both crazy. I'm watching my mother, this is like two years ago, and she's not well, but I don't say nothing. What am I going to do about it anyway? I was waiting for my old man to do something, but he didn't move up off his ass far as I could tell. So one day I come home from school and I got to take a piss something terrible, man. So I run upstairs thinking for sure I'm going to do it in my pants and I like fly into the toilet, and there's my mother sitting there crying. She's surprised to see me, the tears are all *over* her face. I didn't have to piss no more. I mean, you see your mother and she's all by herself and she's crying. So I ask her 'What's wrong?' and she keeps saying, 'Nothing's wrong, nothing's wrong.' 'But you're crying.' 'That ain't nothing,' she says. 'I don't know why I was crying. Something in my eye.' You got something in your eye you ain't sitting in the bathroom looking like she looked. My father was sitting in the living room like he always did, he didn't even know she was in there, 'cause I went in there and asked him. He called her, you know, 'You crying,

Victoria?' and she comes out and she says 'No.' She don't have to tell me not to tell him no more. I can see plain as hell she don't want him to know nothing about nothing.

"Then nothing happens for a while. My mother's going 'round acting like everything's fine. Then about a month later I heard my aunt talking to my mother's best friend. They were outside on the sidewalk and I hid behind the door. My aunt is talking and she's telling Morane how my mother's sick and what the doctors have to do, which is to go, like, once a week and get an x-ray. I can't figure out what they're talking about 'cause I thought x-ray was like when you broke something. But this was something different. Anyway, I figured some of it out and Morane told me the rest later. My mother had cancer, maybe she still has it, and she was afraid to say nothing about it to my father 'cause he was too upset about his own life to hear any *more* bad news. You believe that woman acting like that? Shit, man, I get cancer and wonder if I'm going to die any minute, I'd go crying to anybody I could find, and the first person I'd cry to is my husband. He tells me not to moan 'cause he's got worse problems, I tell him to get the fuck out of this house and don't ever bring his Black ass back again!

"That woman hid that she was sick from him. He didn't know 'til after she was done going for those treatments. Then she had to keep going back to see if she was well. They can burn you up but good and it still grows back. I learned all this from one of my teachers. She said, 'You worried by all this, David?' I said 'No, what's to be worried about? She's only got it in one part of her body.' I didn't even know where she had it. When I found out I almost threw up. I mean, I never thought too much about how women are put together, then this teacher tells me how they did it and I imagined my mother lying there on this table and them putting this machine over her, man, and it doing whatever it does, and all I could think about was her sitting in the bathroom and not telling my father 'cause she was worried about *him* all the time. About *him*, 'cause he was always so down about not working. Shit, I'd have killed the motherfucker for acting like that with her being sick, you know what I'm saying. Never got her flowers or nothing, or helped her in the house. The both of them were just walking around pretending nothing was wrong. I couldn't believe it, man, and Effie didn't know nothing about none of it. Didn't even know my mother was sick, and I didn't know if she was better from all the treatment. Even my mother didn't know if Morane knew about what was going on, and she for sure didn't know what *I* knew. When I told my teacher, you know, not to say nothing to my folks, she goes, 'I didn't even know your father was alive. You never say nothing about him.' That was true too, 'cause most of the time at school I pretended like he was dead 'cause I never wanted no one asking about him.

"But the thing was, my Dad was upset by everything going on. He got scared about my mother same as I did. Then he got feeling sorry 'cause he'd been such a bad husband to her. That's all he could say for months. He was like a little kid. I didn't know whether to feel sorry for the man 'cause he had no job and his wife might be dying, or pissed off 'cause he was acting like a baby. You could love him or hate him practically in the same minute. Hell, I got so frustrated from seeing him acting like he did, I decided I'm getting out of that house as much as I can. I know my father real well, and I know what he was thinking. He was thinking, Dear Lord, let me find a job with my wife sick. I'll do *anything* but I need a job *now*. But he couldn't get nothing, man. So between him not working and my mother lying on that table with that x-ray machine burning her insides out, where a woman has her baby, you know what I'm saying, you can imagine how we was doing.

"Effie, though, she was doing fine. She'd come home and read all her books, and help my mother. You couldn't tell by looking at her she knew anything different from before. So one day I took her outside and I said to her, 'Effie, you got any idea what's going on in our house?' 'You mean Dad not working?' she goes. 'I say, that ain't new.' 'You mean about Mom and the x-ray treatments?' 'You know where she's getting them?' 'At the hospital,' she goes. 'Not in the hospital, man. Where in her body, you know, where they're working on her?' 'Yeah.' She knew. 'They're working on her uterus,' she said. 'On her *what*?' 'Don't worry about it none,' she goes, 'you ain't got one so you ain't going to get sick there.' And all that time I was walking 'round trying to make sure my kid sister don't know what's happening. So I ask her, 'How come you know so much?' So she says, 'cause I talked to the same teacher you did. She even gave me a book to read.' Effie's going to be all right, even though she's the daughter of a sick old mother and a father who's barely staying alive.

"Then there's me. I got the same parents and look at me. Kind of sad, I'd say, way I'm turning out. I'm sure it makes my parents sad too. I don't know what Effie thinks. She can't think much of me. Most of the time now I don't know whether to blame people for what's happening or just forget them or what. Talking with my old man don't help, 'cause no matter how good he sounds when he's talking, I just can't get up the respect for the man. Like, when he talks to me about being a man, it'd be a whole lot better if someone else was talking, you know what I'm saying, 'cause he ain't much of a man himself. I mean, I'm sitting there, and the man's telling me about working and making steady money and taking vacations, which is something we never did once in our life. I don't blame him for nothing, but what's he talking about living in the middle class scene for when he ain't worked, like, for years? There ain't nothing he's done that makes him so much of a man he can talk like that to me. Hell, it ain't nothing to be a father; it's the woman does all the work. My old man could have done a lot more than he did too, 'cause he didn't have nothing else to do with himself. Man just lies to me now. We both got all the time in the world on our hands. Neither one of us no better than the other."

David Sindon was fifteen years old when he knifed Jared Alexander in a street fight. Nobody knew what started the fracas, although both boys had been drinking. Apparently, Davey had cajoled a woman into buying liquor for a group of boys, then suddenly he and Jared were fighting. Jared produced a long knife and the boys wrestled around and fell over one another. Finally, a gurgling painful sob came from Jared, and he was lying doubled up in the street, a knife stuck in his abdomen. Blood was everywhere and the boys were terrified. At first, Davey thought of leaving Jared there, but some boy named Jamal insisted they had to call the police. Davey argued with him, but another boy already had run off to get help.

Davey was charged with manslaughter and put in jail to await trial. His parents were sickened with the news. They visited him every day, nervous and confused by the long wait before his trial. A court-appointed lawyer met with Davey three times in four months.

Victoria had not responded well to her radiation treatments and underwent surgery. The cancer had spread to her bowel, a section of which was removed. Her son cried when he heard the news of the operation. Effie came to the prison but Davey refused to see her. She was too good and too smart, he insisted, to get messed up by his troubles. She offered to read to him but he refused this too, even though he loved listening to her. Ignoring his request, she brought him magazines. Effie had landed a job with a neighborhood store and spent her money on little gifts for him and her mother, who was recuperating at home. Amazingly, Effie's schoolwork never faltered, despite so many of the family's burdens falling on her shoulders. "Effie's going to make it," Ollie said. "With her brother and her mother and me and every other problem in this world she has to face, the girl's going to make it."

Friends rallied around the Sindons. Everyday someone else was in the apartment preparing food, cleaning up, attending to Victoria and allowing Effie time to do her school assignments. Davey's friends washed windows and floors and went on errands for the Sindons. Gradually, Victoria's condition seemed to improve, but Ollie had become increasingly quiet and depressed. No one could convince him that what he called his collapse as a man hadn't brought down his entire family. He made arrangements to visit his son everyday. When Davey rejected him, he sat alone in the jail's waiting room, his eyes fixed on the door leading to the cells. When visiting hours ended, he rose and walked to the bus stop, and began the two-hour journey home.

In the year following Davey Sindon's trouble, Ollie lost forty pounds. Whereas once he had an enormous appetite, he now missed meals. He ate better on the evenings when his son met with him, but even these occasions failed to lift his spirit. He blamed himself for everything; Victoria's illness and Davey's jail sentence were his punishments.

"Going to starve myself," he said, "'til I find out about my son. It ain't going to be good with him no matter how it comes out, but it don't make no difference to the way I feel about myself. You take any human tragedy, and you'll find right from the get-go the person who's got to take the blame for it. You may not be able to put your finger on him, but he's there. I can go the rest of my life saying, bad economic times, that's why there weren't jobs. I can say, Black folks always have it the worst. But some Black men get work. Even if they have 20 percent unemployed, they still have 80 percent employed, and a lot of that 80 percent is Black, ain't they? So lots of men living right in this community may be in the same boat I am, but most of 'em ain't, they got work. There *is* someone to blame, and you don't need the police to find him.

"My life has been wasted, and wasteful. Never was much of a kid, ain't much more as a man. I have a wife who wouldn't be as bad if I was working. Got a kid in jail who for sure wouldn't be there if I was working. I got Effie too, bless her. Maybe I go on just for her, or maybe for all of 'em, I don't even know. I could quit. You got lots of folks in this country quitting where I'm going on, you know. Guys blowing their brains out when they lose their jobs. Rich ones, too, folks used to having everything they want and suddenly they got a whole new life. They see where it's at. You got lots of reasons to call it quits. Saddest thing to me is I don't even know how to go about thinking about all this. I never did much at school, quit going to church long, long time ago. When I do go I don't learn anything from it. I don't even know what I'm supposed to know about living and dying. Way it looks to me now is the whole point of living *is* dying. 'Cept I know there's one helluva lot more to living than that. I didn't think much of dying when I was working regular. Just took what come each day and let it go. Times got tough, things would just work themselves out, I'd say. Now I ain't got anything else *to* think about.

"Whole thing's a goddamn war. That enemy out there is beating the shit out of me, man, and I'm not up to taking it much longer, which is probably a lie, 'cause I been taking it this long I might just go on and on taking it. Man like me wants to yell out, 'It's somebody else's fault.' But it's my fault. I could have done so's it would have come out better. But now, I don't even know how to go about thinking this thing through. My boy don't want to talk to me, my wife's been sick, my daughter could go at any time, and I'm walking around wishing my mother was still on the earth so's she could fix everything. Now is that the way a man goes through his life, wishing his Mamma was here to take care of him? That's a beaten man talking. That's no winner coming at you. I got so much pain now, pain inside pain not a doctor in the world could fix. Take one pain away and I'd come up with a hundred more to take its place.

"Holy Jesus, give me a break, will you? Ain't it been long enough? You want to punish me, okay, but get it the hell over with already. What I need to take more pain for? I'll tell you why He gives me all that pain too. Because He knows I can take it. He knows I ain't about to jump out of no window or stick no gun down my throat. He's got an easy victim with me. Tells all His angels, look it down there at old man Sindon. Got a boy in jail, got a wife going to go back to the hospital one of these days, that's the boy you want to give your pain to. Man hasn't worked all these years, so he's got nothing to do with his time but take all your pain. So give it to him. I know that man down there, he'll take it, has no choice but to take it. We're going to give him the job he's been looking for all these years. We're going to give him the job of taking all this pain. You hear us, Ollie, we got a full-time job for you. You're going to be working day and night, seven days a week being a pain hauler. Don't make much money hauling pain, but it'll keep you out of trouble. Keep you from eating like you should and sleeping like you should. Just relax now, man, 'cause we got mountains of the stuff for you to haul, and you got the rest of your life to do it. What the hell, man, you ought to be in good shape for it too. You ain't been doing nothing to tire yourself out for the last ten years. You deserve it, man. This job is *marked* for you. Got your name on it. You're the only man who can do it, you pain hauler, you!"

Chapter 5

Never Dreamed
It Would Get This Bad:
Cyrus Mullen

I wanted to kill Cyrus' boss. Get a gun and shoot him. Then I wanted to go around the neighborhood shooting any man who held a job that Cyrus might take, and if the man's wife tried to stop me, I'd kill her too.

In many respects, the story of Cyrus Mullen encapsulates the essence of the long-term unemployed worker. In his words, Cyrus, in the best sense, was an uncomplicated man. Faithful, loyal, moral, he had for years known the rewards of putting in an honest day's work. From all reports, even as a boy he was an uncomplaining, kind, and rather shy person who minded his own business and expected little of the world. Entitlement was not a concept he ever embraced.

Modest to the point of self-deprecation, disciplined, and living his life with a pronounced sense of fairness, Cy Mullen would have considered himself perfectly content. Sure, he could have earned more money and probably, too, a bit more respect from the various corners of his business world, but he would have been the first person to express gratitude for what he had achieved.

Beneath the moral goodness of the man, however, was an anxiety, a palpable set of fears. The reality of aging always scared him, and death was an unthinkable moment. Despite all the virtuous qualities he displayed, he could never successfully hide the feeling of being unsettled, almost as if he were uncomfortable about something, not that he ever anticipated what would happen should unemployment ever assume a prominent role in his life. Indeed, there would have been no way he could have foreseen the physical deterioration of his body that accompanied the tenure of unemployment. Nor could he ever have foreseen what unemployment would do to his marriage, and more specifically, to his wife, Rosemary.

It is fair to say that in this instance, unemployment contributed profoundly to the dissolution of a man, a woman, and a marriage. Both husband and wife lived for months with disbelief that this one element of their lives could produce such damage. Or perhaps one should say that they could find no ways to counteract and protect themselves against the feelings of depression that overtook them, and the idea that they had been betrayed by the culture. Even in their understanding of one another, their utter appreciation of the other person's circumstances, they could not bring themselves to resurrect their union, nor for the moment, their individual integrity.

Cyrus Zachary Mullen despised his name. He despised his mother for suggesting the Cyrus, his grandmother for insisting on the Zachary, and his father for carrying on the name Mullen. Although his friends didn't seem to find the name objectionable, he always felt he was cursed with it. By the time he was fifteen it had become the most disagreeable thing about his life. That, and the unpleasant fact that he couldn't live forever.

His name and his death preoccupied him through adolescence and into adulthood and middle age. His conversations, and especially with girls when he was young, invariably turned to these two subjects. "A name's a name" they would say, and "aren't you a little young to be worried about dying, especially when there's nothing you can do about it?" Cyrus is a horrible name, he would argue, almost as horrible as the thought of death. Even at forty-three, a mature and attractive man with a full head of hair, he launched into his old war-horses minutes after meeting someone. "What do you think of the name Cyrus Zachary Mullen?" People answered as they always had: "It's not so bad." "It's the worst name, and good manners prevent you from telling me it's the worst, sounding name you've ever heard. You think much of dying? What a shame it is that people can't live forever? That the older they get, the worse it is for them, the faster time seems to pass for them? Tell the truth. You think about these things all that much? I think about it all the damn time. That's all I think about. That and how ugly my name is. Crazy isn't it? Wouldn't you say that anybody who thinks of nothing but his name and the lousy fact of life that people have to get old and die is crazy! I *am* crazy too. All the way gone around the bend crazy! But I didn't make myself crazy. And it isn't my name, and it wasn't even the idea of dying. It was that other thing. And I'll be very happy to talk about that lovely other thing anytime anybody wants me to."

Cyrus Mullen finished high school at seventeen and spent two years in the army. When he came out of the service he found a job working in a brick factory. After a year, he decided he wanted to become an insurance adjuster and so he took special courses and passed the qualifying examinations for the insurance business. By pure accident, he met a man who worked for an insurance company that happened to be looking for new employees. Within weeks Cyrus was hired by the company. He was twenty-three years old.

The job at Buccaneer Insurance turned out to be a better situation than even the optimistic descriptions had portrayed it. Most of his fellow workers were young, but that didn't please him as much as people's comments on his name. "Pretty bad, eh?" Cyrus would jump in prematurely. "I can change it if it's no good for the job." "Change it?" the staff members would practically shout with disbelief. "It's great! Tremendous for business. You just go to prospective clients and say my name is Cyrus Zachary Mullen and they'll forget every other insurance salesman they've ever heard of. You got a name that's going to make you an instant success!"

The prospect of his name actually helping him made the present seem good, the future better. Even his parents, who had always wanted him to go to college, had to admit that success had come to Cyrus rather early. By the time he was twenty-six, he had shifted jobs twice, both positions being with insurance companies. It was not uncommon, he learned, for people to move around in the business, the only problem being how to convince clients to shift companies with you. But Cyrus answered their questions in his characteristically ingenuous way. He told them there was no advantage in changing policies. The advice he had given them when he worked with another company was as sound now as it was then.

Clients went for this approach; they stayed loyal to the man with the unforgettable name. Cyrus had become a more than competent insurance salesman. He looked forward to meetings with prospective clients and enjoyed answering people's questions. He learned that one must be firm but friendly, and that people want as much information about insurance matters as he could provide. As he prepared to leave them he reached into his pocket and handed them his card. "I doubt very much," he would say, "that you'll forget my name. You'll lose my card, but this name ought to stick in your mind." The name stuck, clients called him, his business held steady, and his managers were constantly impressed by the way he was able to retain old clients. There was a special quality about this man, they said. He wasn't sophisticated and urbane like many of the men in his field. He was more like, well, wasn't his father a farmer or something?

Cyrus understood why people couldn't easily articulate his honest quality. He understood, too, his own situation, and he watched it closely. He had a job that took up at least fifty hours a week. Even after his marriage to Rosemary White and the birth of their two children, people had to understand the importance of his working long hours. The insurance business was competitive. If one wasted time, one lost potential accounts and fell behind the thousands of men and women coming up to take your job. "The insurance business," he would tell Rosemary, "is a simple affair. You bring in policies, you get a commission, the company makes money. No work, no commission, no job. No job, no pay, no food, no home."

It was Cyrus Mullen's earnestness that made people take him seriously. It showed itself clearly when he made his no-work-no-pay-no-food-no-home speech to his wife. No matter how upset Rosemary might be by his long hours away from her and the children, his rational attitude toward work and his discipline convinced her of the necessity of his working precisely as he did. Cyrus was not an aggressive or ambitious man. He had grown up with parents who always had enough because they worked hard. They weren't a family who knew luxury nor craved it. If living through the week required $200, then his father was content to earn $200. Charles Mullen told his family that, barring accidents and illness, he would provide the necessities. Any luxuries they wanted, they would have to get themselves. His wife supported this philosophy, and the Mullen sons grew up believing it to be the only sensible philosophy of work. It was the same philosophy Cyrus preached in his own home.

"No one ever needed to tell me anything about me. I know me better than all my teachers, all the bosses I've ever had. I'm not an educated man, I'm not even a particularly intelligent man. People see me as a sort of farm boy type. My father worked on the railroad as a brakeman, later he worked in the station office, my mother ran our house. I suppose I'm seen as a farmer type because I'm not complicated like many people you meet. Like, I'll talk to a professor or doctor about life insurance. Now, here's a man much more intelligent than I am. He has in front of him a bigger pile of books than I've read in my whole life. In the last year he's traveled in more places than I'll travel in my entire life. He has it all over me in every way and I'm trying to sell him a bit of security that I myself can barely afford and need more than he does. But make a decision? This man can't even figure out for himself where in his own living room he should sit when he talks to me. Next to that man I'm simple. He sees me as simple, and likes the fact that I'm not complicated, just a hard-working guy earning his living, and I like the fact that that's how he sees me. All I have is my wife, my children and my job. I work to make sure all of them are safe. I look simple to that man because I don't have much ambition. I think I used to, but when I passed forty I lost what little I had. Now all I care about is eating as much as I can and not gain weight. The problem is that the Cyrus in me wants to eat all the time but the Zachary part says no."

Cyrus Mullen laughs out loud. He places his hands on his belly. If there is worry in this man about getting older and dying, one does not detect it. One would have to say, this is a contented man.

"I *am* a contented man. I make no bones about that. You've got years like we've had in business and government, people are screaming with problems. And they've got real complaints. What can I say? I'm lucky; so far I've escaped the real problems. I have my health, I have a good marriage, healthy children, I have a good enough job, I'm a contented man. Maybe its bad luck to go around saying things are good, but I'm in no position to talk poor. I don't go without like the poor people of this country. I don't think a person has to brag, but when you don't have problems you don't have to go off and moan. All you do then is take the problems out of the homes of people who really do have problems.

"My dad taught me my philosophy of living. All of us sit at the dinner table. We all need to eat, we all need to drink, we all need a bed to sleep in. If you have enough for yourself, and you're not hungry, and your family's well enough to sit at that table, then you have no problems. People want more because they can't ever get enough, or because the next guy looks like he's got a little more. That's something I can't deal with. I make the same pitch to anybody buying life insurance. How much do I need? They ask. You tell me, I say. The more you buy, the better it is for me, but it may not be necessary for *you*, and that's who we're talking about. So they'll name some figure and if I think it's out of line I'll tell them. You don't need that much. You aren't Ted Turner, why make your widow Mrs. Ted Turner? Leave your family with enough, but don't kill yourself in the process. The future's plenty important, but without the present it doesn't mean a thing. People are killing themselves to make themselves happy; everybody's got a reason for being ambitious to where they'd kill the guy they share an office with if it would bring them a few extra dollars.

"I know what my parents meant when they taught me to know my place in the world. I won't kill anybody for a few bucks. I won't steal it from anybody either, even the potential client who's sitting there with millions. Why do it? Life's too short, and in the long run I don't benefit from taking any man's money unfairly, even the man who can afford to lose it. When the guy I share my office with is ready to kill me 'cause he wants to bite into my business, I got to make a change. I want my share and I got a right to say to that man, keep your grimy little fingers off my plate. 'Course there's a lot of difference between preaching that philosophy and acting on it, but I don't think you'd find too many people saying I've overreached. I think I've been pretty fair about the way I've conducted my business. Bitch and moan about my name all the time, and I'm still scared to death about getting older, but I've gone about living in a fair way. Put it this way: When I don't sleep at night, it's *not* because I'm fretting over something, it's due to good old-fashioned over-eating. So I'd say I'm a pretty simple guy with a complicated name. Ought to at least get rid of the Zachary. Imagine naming a baby Zachary? Can't imagine what got into my parents' mind. Maybe they needed something special, like, having a baby wasn't enough by itself."

It was hard for people to describe Cyrus Mullen. His colleagues at work, his relatives, everyone groped for the right words. They saw Cyrus as a man without the problems that aggravate most people. His own well-disciplined manner and workable philosophy of life carried him through life, but his sense of feeling content was hard earned. Some people were surprised by his successes. Those who remembered Cyrus as a boy never saw him as a creative type. They were quick to add, however, that the world would be in a horrible fix if everybody were creative. Someone had to handle life's menial jobs, like selling insurance. Nor did Cyrus strike them as being particularly industrious. His Aunt Alicia once told him he carried the two worst qualities of any student: He wasn't bright and his work habits were downright awful. There wasn't a way in the world, she said, that Cyrus could build a successful life for himself. The only chance for Cyrus was to get some rich young lady to fall in love with him. But that brought up another problem.

Throughout his adolescence, when most of his friends were going out with girls, Cyrus appeared shy. He had dates now and again, but nobody could imagine him comfortable in the presence of women. The idea that he would ever marry seemed unlikely. He was too reticent, too immature, nobody could define it precisely. To say the least, his parents, were delighted when, at twenty-seven, Cyrus announced his engagement to Rosemary White.

In retrospect, it was foolish for anyone to have worried about Cyrus. He made it through school without difficulty, and rarely got into trouble. He found steady work immediately after coming out of the army. And he married a very fine woman. What was it then, that caused people to predict hardships for this man?

"I know how they saw him from the minute he was old enough to walk," Rosemary Mullen could say with authority. "Nobody in his family was ambitious. But it wasn't that. It was a simple matter. Cyrus just never talked about himself, so pretty soon people began to think he didn't know anything, or feel anything. He still gives that impression. Would he get married? How could anyone tell? Did he ever say anything when they asked him about work or making money? Did he know who he was? All these things contributed to what people *think* is his simple way. Everything stayed inside him, his whole life, until it couldn't stay any longer. He knew people expected him to talk about himself, so he'd raise his two famous topics, his name and his fear of getting old. But they were cover-ups. He didn't even tell *me* that much about what was going on inside him. That's the way some people are, you know. He didn't talk about himself, so his parents and me too, I suppose, believed he was pretty simple about some things.

"So then what happens, after working every day for almost twenty years, he's out of work. It's eight months now. And now do you think anybody wants to talk to him? Of course not. Now they say, the trouble with him is he can't stop talking about himself, he's feeling too sorry for himself. Here's a man who never asked a single person to do a favor for him until he made everyone think he was simple, that he didn't have feelings, that he wouldn't get a job or get married or have children. First, people didn't respect him because he acts simple, now they don't respect him because he's cursed, out of work. They don't want to hear what he's feeling now. All they're interested in is, did he get a job? Well, he didn't, he didn't get anything, his job, his dignity, nothing. And I'm pretty damn sick of the whole bunch of them, and that includes his parents with their nice *simple* philosophy of life. Even *they* aren't so sure they want to know how he's doing. They want headlines: Job or no job? Money or no money? That's all. *He* wouldn't talk against them, but I sure don't have any reasons not to.

"The whole world makes me sick. This man has been destroyed. Maybe he *is* simple. Maybe he doesn't have the right words or all the psychological skills to figure it out, like all these geniuses like his Aunt Alicia. He needs a psychiatrist, she says. Take him to see a psychiatrist, she says. Take him to see a psychiatrist. She doesn't even care that much about talking with Cyrus. Take him to a hospital, get him pills to calm him down. Get him pills to pep him up. If you think he needs to go to a mental hospital so damn badly, *you* take him there, you old witch! He doesn't need a doctor. He needs a job. Anybody can see that.

"I don't understand what happens to people who say they love someone so much, or are concerned about him. Don't they think a forty-four year-old man with a wife and two children and a million debts has the *right* to be sad, depressed, angry, even crazy when all of a sudden the company he's been working for for ten years lays him off with no guarantee they'll take him back? That man had two weeks warning. Ten work days to clear out his office and settle with all his clients. You think his clients are going to worry about him? The hell they are, why should they! They get a notice saying their new insurance man is Mr. Somebody and from now on they won't be involved with Cyrus Mullen. What do they care. This man was never the strongest person in the world, but he was never sick either, and look at him now. He's lost weight, he's physically ill, he's psychologically ill. He's under enormous strain. You want to know about unemployment and what it does to people? Cyrus had good teeth. He had cavities like everybody else but he had good teeth. Do you know that since all this has happened he's had trouble with his teeth. His gums bleed now, they never did before. His teeth hurt him all day, they never hurt before. His stomach aches all the time, it never once gave him problems before. Now he gets up every day not knowing whether he's going to have constipation to where he sits in the bathroom and cries from pain, or whether he's going to have such horrible diarrhea he can't control it and has accidents. If anything, he eats less now than he every did, and still he can't get through a day without having some stomach disorder. It's from not working. The worry, the stewing in your own juices because nobody's interested in you, nobody has the time to listen to what's going on. They're either out of work themselves and maybe with no time for talking, or they're too ashamed or too ill to talk to anybody in the same boat with them. Or they're just too busy working. Sorry your husband's having problems. Good-bye!

"Forty-four years this man lifted, pulled, pushed, packed up cars when he went on trips, built things for his father, climbed roofs when they needed to be fixed. I saw him once pull a machine up a hill for a friend of his. I said to myself he's going to be in a hospital from pulling that machine. Not Cyrus. Not an ache, not a bruise. Back at work the next day like he was used to having physical exercise every day of his life. Now he doesn't work, he doesn't even ride in the car, and he's bent over with back pains, pains going down his back, his legs, down to his toes. From lifting. He hasn't done anything physical in over six months. He's lying around the house. His biggest effort nowadays is making a telephone call. So what's it from? Not working. It's from not being physically and psychologically strong enough to hold your own body up the way it's supposed to be.

"I could puke when I hear these politicians talking about America helping one country or sending aid and food to another country. Russia even, we help Russia. And here you have millions like Cyrus lying around, dying from a disease they could easily cure. These people should be ashamed of themselves. You work in this country and it's fine, the second they lay you off you go right into the garbage and nobody looks twice. And what are people doing about it? What are my children supposed to think? You think it's good for them watching their father change into something they don't even understand? They surely can't *like* him like this. I wonder whether they even recognize him anymore. What do they think when they see a man fall to pieces like he has? What does all of this do to them? You think they forget about it? I read an article about children of people who go into mental hospitals, not even for a long time, a month maybe. All of these kids suffered in one way or another from having a parent in a mental hospital. It affected them at the time it happened and it came back to trouble them later on. That's a month or two with a parent in a mental hospital. So how's it going to be with my children living with a man who's sick enough to be put away in a hospital? According to that, my children are already damaged. It's like they've already breathed in the fall-out of some bomb, the fall-out from unemployment. And they're sick from it.

"No president of the United States wants to admit he's done badly with unemployment. It'll kill him in any election and he knows it. So they lie, or they'll tell you what the unemployment story is in such a complicated way they can cover it over or make it seem like things are getting better when they're really getting worse. But that's not even so bad; the country's used to politicians lying. The bad part is that no matter how many people they say are out of work, the number of people directly affected is far more. People think if a man loses his job when he's thirty-five or forty-five that by magic a whole lot of jobs open up for him. They forget each day you can't get new work, the harder it gets. For men in their forties and fifties it's the worst. They're too old to take on strenuous jobs, and too old to where it pays a company to train them or send them back to college. But nobody takes into consideration what it does to wives and children. Maybe it's because there's no way of knowing how many millions upon millions are being crushed to death by this thing. I'll tell you about one person. I'll tell you what it did to me:

"Cyrus came home on a Monday morning and said his job was finished. He said the words, 'My job is gone.' I felt nothing. I didn't think I was fooling myself either. It wasn't my job, it was *his*. About two hours later I was bending over a table and suddenly I got a headache like someone had shot me. Had such blinding pain I don't even know how I managed not to fall over. Cyrus was there helping me. *He's* lost the job and *I* had the headache. All that night I cried. I lay on the bed fully dressed— he had to take off my shoes—and I cried. 'What are we going to do? What are we going to do?' It was Cyrus who had to calm me down. 'It's not so serious.' He was amazing. I was lying there with a towel on my head while he put the children to sleep. I was scared. It was like someone said in a few minutes an airplane is going to fly over and drop a bomb. It's going to kill some people but not everybody. So the problem is, do you stay where you are or do you run? I kept saying to him—I'd become a child–'Are you going to be able to get another job?' Of course he could only say, 'I don't know,' or, 'I'm sure I can.' But I kept pushing him. Finally, just before I fell asleep, I said to him, 'Tell me you're absolutely certain you'll be able to get a job.' 'How can I be sure?' he said. Naturally. How *could* he be sure? 'But you *must* know. You can't go on without a job.' 'All right,' he said. 'I know for a fact there are ten jobs where if I'm not the number one person in line, I can't be worse than two.' He said it just like that, in a very soothing way. He knew it was foolish, and I did too, but before I closed my eyes I wanted him to be certain. I wanted a final promise.

"The fright went away although the headaches didn't. They haven't until this day. They probably will when he gets a job, *if* he gets a job. I feel numb or angry. For some reason, the fright came when he said he'd lost his job; from then on I either walked around like a zombie, or I walked around feeling angrier and angrier. I'm sure the anger was connected to when I was a child and I'd get this special kind of anger when I couldn't get exactly what I wanted when I wanted it. And the more I couldn't have it, the more angry I got. Someone was saying no to me and nothing I could do would make them change their mind. But there's a difference between that kind of anger and when your husband isn't working and your life changes. You begin to think about what you're going to do in very real terms.

"I wanted to kill Cyrus' boss. Get a gun and shoot him. Then I wanted to go around the neighborhood shooting any man who held a job that Cyrus might take, and if the man's wife tried to stop me, I'd kill her too. Then I thought about marching in on some congressman or senator and holding him hostage until he got Cyrus a job. These were *my* thoughts, *me* who never thought of hitting a fly. I was furious with people who tried to show us sympathy, or give us advice. One night we went to have what I call the unemployment burger with some friends. That's when you go to the cheapest place in town and split french fries and eat the lousiest food in the world. We went with a couple in the exact same position as us. Peter Selbey hadn't worked by that time for maybe fourteen months. All of us in the same boat and they're telling us how they manage, how they budget, what they do, little tricks for saving money—everybody who's unemployed has tricks for saving money, but no one has tricks for saving face. You blame everybody in sight and rattle on about the president and his economic advisors, but no one has a way to save face. Anyway, we're there munching on our unemployment burgers and Terry Selbey's going on how life isn't so bad and how we have to stick together and all the rest of this garbage when I suddenly became furious. I threw down my food and started shouting in this loud voice: 'I'm not here to be lectured to. I don't need advice, I don't need people to patronize me. I'm not the one who's out of work. I'm not the one who's the failure. Five percent of men out of work, whatever it is, but what about the 95 percent who are doing well? How come we don't talk about *them*? Maybe Cyrus and Peter are just failures. Maybe they didn't do so great and that's why they were laid off. What about the men who get laid off and find work? *Their* wives are lucky.' I was really coming apart. Cyrus had to drag me out of the place. People were looking at us like we were mental cases. At least I was sane enough to go through that little routine when the children weren't there.

"But do you think I stopped with him when we got home? Oh, and we walked, not that it was so far, because we had just sold our car and the Selbey's had driven and I refused to get in the car with them. I didn't stop the whole way home. I was yelling and screaming like *I* was the bomb being dropped in the neighborhood. I blamed him for everything. I told him he was damn lucky to have worked the time he did, that he didn't deserve anything, that he wasn't that bright, that he wasn't even trying to get new jobs, that he was a goddamn horrible monster failure and I hated him. 'I hate you, I hate you with that stupid name of yours. You're a failure, the most horrible kind of failure there is because you never reached a time when you were successful. We've always lived on a shoestring. I never should have married you. My whole life's a mistake. *I'm* the failure for staying around. *You've* made me into a failure. You're ruining all of us and I despise you for it. I used to feel sorry for your not being able to find work, now I despise you for it!' Cyrus kept looking at me and nodding his head up and down, the patient father with the screaming child. He kept saying, 'I know, I know. You're right.' I hated him. The more he tried to calm me down, the more I realized how stupid and miserable I was being. I was the horrible monster. But he shouldn't have calmed me down. He should have screamed at me. If I screamed back he should have screamed louder and louder until he would have been the only one we could have heard. When I started hitting him he should have hit me back. I slapped him when I got my hand free once, right dead across the face, and all he did was nod, and keep mumbling, 'I know, I know.' He should have slugged me. I mean it. He should have knocked me out. I should have fallen down on the pavement right then and there. The more he didn't do anything, the more I thought, you weak, sissy, non-man nothing failure. You're nothing. You don't even have the energy or guts to shut up a miserable hysterical woman. You're *nothing*.'

"I'll tell you something else he should have done that I knew he never would, but he should have, that night or any night for God sake. He should have taken me somewhere, threw me down, slapped me if that was the only thing that would have quieted me, and made love to me. I mean pull off my clothes and *rape* me, if he had to. Anything to show me he wasn't scared, that he was alive, that he had some energy left. Something, some little bit of life. I mean it. I wanted to be roughed up that night and feel that he was really a man. But he was dead. I was going mad, and the devil in it all was the being unemployed. Maybe it's a good thing to be unemployed so you can find out what your marriage is like. Maybe it's all a wicked trick some-one plays on you. They want to know whether you're alive or dead, whether you're sane or off the deep end, whether you're still sexual or not. Okay, so now they know, so call the trick off. The devil's had a great laugh over Mr. and Mrs. Mullen. Now he can let us go back to normal life and let my husband go back to work."

Cyrus Mullen sits in the little room off the kitchen, most of his body hidden by a table with piles of books on it. He has a drink before him, his hair is neatly combed, his white shirt open at the neck, his fingers stained from smoking. No longer slightly overweight, he is now thin, the skin underneath his chin pulled tight to the jawbones, his cheeks drawn. Shades of purple surround his eyes and his brow quivers with almost every word he utters. Behind him are stacks of newspapers and magazines. In the cor-ner is a collection of letters and postcards that appear to be the accumula-tion of a lifetime. The room is not in disarray, merely busy. One wants to say it is a worried room. Cyrus Mullen's eyes are weary eyes. He barely looks up when he speaks. Knowing that he is a changed man, he is accus-tomed to helping people get used to his new appearance.

"I look like I just got out of prison, eh? Maybe I did. Whoops, better not feel sorry for myself. The books here say a person in my state mustn't feel sorry for himself." His hand pats a pile of books on mind control, per-sonality change, earning money while being at home, investment banking, finding jobs, astrology, guides to Canada, Mexico and South America. "I tried night school five months ago," he announces quietly. "Three nights a week, then two nights a week, then I dropped that too. I even had a col-lection of college brochures. Must have looked at material from fifty col-leges. That was a strange dream. Spent two weeks with some laborers I know. One of them's a steam fitter, another's a carpenter's foreman. They told me they'd help. Stupid. I can't learn trades like those. They got guys with twenty years experience on me, men who know *all* the trades, and they're not even barely thirty. It's wonderful being out of work. You get to travel. I got out books on Greece. Now I look at Canada. Nice in Canada. Supposed to be a wide-open place for jobs. Why not? Maybe I could go up there and sell insurance to all the kids who ran away from the draft thirty years ago. I'm sure they're all loaded with money they don't know what to do with. I'd have done the same as them. I'd do anything if it looked like a good proposition."

Cyrus' voice is weak, the pattern of speech has changed. It is slower than before, and the words come in quick rhythmic bursts. He is speaking almost in stanzas, as if he has begun to think in shorter durations.

"I'm sick now. Everybody knows. I fought it. The budgeting, the letter writing, the phone calling. Made every contact I could. I went through the name and telephone number of everybody I ever did business with. Called each one. 'Mr. Prince, Cyrus Mullen, 'member me? Sold you insurance when I was with Wilcott? Fine, and yourself? How's that little boy of yours. Billy, right? Do I remember? Yeah, Zachary, that's me. Yup, I'm still worrying about dying. You know of any jobs?' If I made one call I made a million. Had leads coming out of my ears. From one guy alone I got twenty names. I actually celebrated. The next day I was going to call twenty new people. Not one of them had anything. Some of them didn't even know the man who told me to call. Some of them were confused: 'Why'd he think we'd have openings? We're bailing out like everyone else.' So much for that celebration.

"There's only a certain number of no's you can hear before you crack. My number wasn't all that high. My wife's was even lower. She practically fell apart the first night. I went on a little longer. Your mind suffers. You have thoughts you never knew could come into a person's head; it's like you're dreaming in the middle of the day. Weird sensations like lying in the clouds, or falling out of airplanes, or watching a doctor operate on your own brain. Then your body goes. Doctors have you taking pills for everything. First you have diarrhea then you can't do it at all. Then you can't sleep, then *all* you do is sleep. I used to get relief by walking, but I've lost the energy for that. You keep looking in the mailbox as though something great was going to come to you: An invitation, a job, a letter saying my company wants me back. There are plenty of ideas, I'll tell you. Gee, Honey, I'm home all day, we can have sex whenever we like. Then that stops. I take the kids to school, I pick them up; I used to anyway. Everybody looking at me: 'You lose weight, Mullen?' 'What are you doing home from work so early?' 'Lady, I'm cutting work. I have millions of dollars lying around, so I gave up work. You want to have sex, lady?' 'Don't worry about him, Martha, he couldn't get it up with a crane.'

"I do two things in my life. First thing is I make tea. I boil the water. Very difficult. You don't want too much water because it takes too long to boil, you don't want too little water 'cause it scalds the bottom of the pot. Then you pour it into a mug, not a cup. Has to be a mug. Then a little sugar and lemon 'cause milk isn't good for you. That ends job one. Job two, clean up. First the mug. Shake it like mad to get all the water out 'cause it's cheating to dry it with a towel. Then the little spoon which you shake like a thermometer. Put it down next to the mug. Then you look at the clock. Hooray, ten minutes gone. Only four more hours and you can make yourself a sandwich. One little spoonful of jelly, one little spoonful of peanut butter. Don't cut the bread too thick, that would be wasting it and we're in no position to be wasting it. Then, what do we have to drink with our little sandwich? How 'bout some tea. Boil the water, make sure the mug is dry. I have a thing about pouring hot water into a mug with cold water in the bottom. The lunch is over and oh, don't forget, check the mail. Even though nothing's been delivered after ten thirty in the morning for fifty years, this could be the day. And the pills. A little ulcer pill, pop, a little gall bladder pill, pop, a little painkiller from a tooth extraction, pop, a little settling the nerves pill, pop. Almost tea time. Then in the afternoon I get to do the big thing: I get to take a little nappy, as if I could sleep. If I do sleep I get up just in time to get the afternoon paper. Wouldn't want to miss the stock quotations. My God, if you oversleep in this civilization you lose the financial chances of a lifetime. Have to contact my broker, not to mention my insurance salesman.

"Tea time. Yes, friends, Cyrus Zachary has gotten home from buying his afternoon newspaper which repeats the same stories he's already read this morning. But now he reads the paper with his afternoon tea. Afternoon tea's different from morning tea. Afternoon tea has two lemon squirts in it. Then the paper. Oh, check the mail. Somebody could have left something while you were out. Only takes four minutes to the news stand, but you never know. Maybe they slipped it under the back door too. Have to check there too. There's no way in the world anybody can get from outside to the backdoor but maybe a mailman or messenger wants to do it the hard way. Maybe right on the kitchen floor under my nose is a yellow telegram, they still have those? 'Dear Mr. Mullen. We are proud to announce that you have just been made president of our corporation.

'Course you'll have to start at the bottom and work your way up, but we think you can go from stock room boy to president in two days, unless you think this is unreasonable. Naturally this matter and your salary are open to negotiation. And we'll want to reimburse you for your year and four months out of work, wipe away all old wounds, as they say.' Then I get to drink more tea.

"It's very terrible sitting around doing nothing. I have no garden, no lawn to cut, nothing around the apartment needs fixing. One day I broke a vase so I could go get glue and fix it. I got the glue but it didn't hold. It's the loneliness and the endless boredom. You can always be a failure with a job. But when you go months with nothing to do, it drives you mad. It's like I'm being starved. I've lost any drive I've ever had. I don't know, really, if I could hold a job anymore. I might be too afraid they'd be testing me and take the job away the first time I made a mistake. I can't eat, or sleep, there's no love, no sex, no touching. And I was the guy who was afraid of dying. It doesn't seem so bad anymore. Neither does my name. But with all the horribleness, I still haven't convinced myself it's really happening. The other day I saw this car accident, nothing serious, and my mind is just on what I'm seeing. I start walking again and I'm feeling not bad. Then I say to myself, what the hell are you so excited about? Where are you going anyway? I'm like the car that had the accident. Maybe I should give up going to doctors and find a good car mechanic. That's a joke. But does old Mullen laugh? No, he doesn't laugh anymore. He wants to, but the laugh muscles don't work. Whoops, I'm feeling sorry for myself, and that's something the little head of the family isn't supposed to do. Not supposed to get under the weather from not working. Supposed to get just a little blue. Like the sky is a little blue. Otherwise I become a babbling idiot. Just a little blue. Like Russia's a little red. That's a joke too, but again the kid doesn't laugh, not because he's afraid to disturb the neighbors. The neighbors aren't home, they're at work. The kid doesn't laugh. It doesn't happen anymore. There's time for it. A good laugh could kill five minutes, that's 50 percent of tea time. There's no more laughing. No more running, no more easy bowel movements.

"Tell you something that still works. I am very proud to report I can urinate, which I do eight hundred times a day because of the tea. Fact, I like to urinate because I can do it and it won't take up valuable time or embarrass me while I'm talking to a client. I just say excuse me to the walls and my little tea mug and off I go to the toilet. I'm the little boy who just learned how to do it like the grownups. I am a little disappointed though. I thought when CBS or NBC heard about my going to the toilet so easily they'd want to interview me. Ladies and Gentlemen, the Olympic record for number of urinations in a single day was set today by an out of work insurance salesman named Cyrus Zachary Somebody or Other who went nine hundred and eighty one times without spilling a drop. The man reports he loves doing it because it makes the day pass quicker. Get it? *Pass* quicker? Mullen, you haven't lost your wit, just your mind, body and soul. But they haven't got your wit yet. Maybe if you keep running to the toilet eighty times a day they won't find you. Oh hell, they wouldn't find me if they were standing in front of me. I'm nowhere to be found. And if that's self-pity then screw it!

"So, what else is there to tell? My legs, arms, genitals, stomach, heart, liver, mind, brain, ears, eyes, don't work. *I* don't work. That about sums it up in a nutshell, which is about what I am. Nobody left, nobody I want to see. I don't have any secrets, even with all this privacy. I write no letters, get no letters, make no calls, get no calls. You know what I did once? I wrote a letter to the editor of the *Star-Tribune* just to see my name in print. I got scared one afternoon about something. It was like I couldn't be sure if I was really someone anymore. So I thought, how do you prove you really exist? So I wrote a letter to the paper. If they publish it, it means I really wrote it, sent it, they got it, read it, published it. When I see my name and I know what's in the letter without reading it, then I know I am. So I wrote about this man who was running for mayor; witty, witty letter. Even I, the devil's helper here, thought it was terrific. Did I mention that I was a poet for two weeks? I got some poetry books, then a couple of books on writing poetry and how you get them published. I figured, how hard can it be. In the first place, poems are short. In the next place, they don't have to make sense to anyone but the poet. So if they make sense to me, what else do I care. So I wrote poems about my life. Short ones, 'cause I don't do anything for more than three minutes. If I have to piss longer than that I quit. I don't know anything about poetry. I read some books and I wrote some poems. They were horrible, like everything else I've been doing with my life. So I gave that up too.

"I get tired talking about it, the routine, the wishing, the illness. But I'm stuck with one feeling: I never dreamed it would get this bad. Then I'll think, but it's not quite bad enough. It still has to get worse before I stop feeling guilty about it. It's still my fault in some way. It has to get worse before everything bad is burned away. If it really got bad, worse than where I could stand it, it would either all go away, or I'd die. There will be a settlement. I don't sit around hoping it will get worse. I just want it to be burned away. Strange, isn't it. But I was strange to begin with, what with a name like Cyrus Zachary. Okay, I've told it all. Or almost all."

No one of course tells it all. Neither Cyrus nor Rosemary Mullen did. No one in the family liked to talk about the reality of Cyrus's unemployment continuing. Neither Cyrus nor Rosemary spoke of their separation that occurred ten months after Cyrus lost his job. More than unemployment, the dissolution of their marriage was the taboo subject. Neither had found anyone else, neither mentioned divorce. They lived apart, reflecting on what had happened, dreading the future, and in their words, watching the light of hope go out. Merely enduring was their preoccupation for this moment in their lives, and so they felt it best to be apart from each other. Both saw the foolishness and the futility, but then again, everything else had become unnatural.

Chapter 6

Only One Thing In Life That Matters and That's Working Steady: Cleveland Wilkes; Jeremiah Kelser; and Eddie Harrington, Jr.

With a job you got life, without it, you're long since dead.

If one reviews the unemployment rates presented in the introduction, one recognizes at once that although prime-aged men, as they are called, between the ages of mid-twenties to mid-fifties account for a good portion of U. S. unemployment, the largest portion of unemployment is comprised of younger people. Some experts suggest that a good rule of thumb for determining youth unemployment is to simply double the national unemployment figure and take that number to represent White youth unemployment. Then take this number, double it again, and use this new number as an estimate of African American youth unemployment. According to this formula, if the national unemployment figure stands near 4 percent, White and African American youth unemployment should hover near 8 percent and 16 percent respectively.[1] In fact, the numbers may even be higher. It is also clear that for a certain population of Americans, the periodic or even long-term unemployment they know as teenagers will continue into their twenties, thirties, and beyond.[2]

Although the focus in this book is the issue of adult male unemployment, it is essential that we examine, in this one chapter, the experiences of some young men, if only to broaden our perspective on the problem of unemployment, and reveal in the process the value of job training programs aimed at these young men.[3]

The story of teen unemployment is all too familiar, and actually may receive more attention than adult unemployment.[4] Television programs showing young people selling drugs, gang violence, children in homeless shelters, and children just hanging on street corners, depict the reality of unemployment often without using the word or referring to the problem. Any scene of urban poverty necessarily is a scene of significant unemployment, which means youth unemployment as well. Any story of teenagers dropping out of high school—and in many cities the annual dropout rate is upwards of 35 percent—is a story of youth unemployment.[5] And then there are the isolated stories of plant closings and middle size and small town recessions, all of which, eventually, become still more of the background of youth unemployment.

There is another, often hidden aspect of youth unemployment, that being the work histories of students requiring special education. One study, for example, found that 50 percent of students graduating from special education programs not connected with regular classrooms were unemployed after being out of high school after only one year.[6] Even more compelling are data reported by Dianne Berkell, that as many as three quarters of the students with disabilities of one sort or another are found to be unemployed a year after their high school graduation. Additional students, moreover, were found to be underemployed.[7]

Differences between unemployed youngsters and adults are both numerous and obvious. They have to do with levels of need and maturity, educational and work histories and experience, marital status, living at home with a parent, or assuming the role of family provider. Youth unemployment also attracts the sort of comments one hears from teachers: Too many of these youngsters are seen as irresponsible, unreliable, unable to concentrate on assignments or learn new tasks quickly. The students seem preoccupied, moreover, with their emerging sense of manhood and independence. Quite possibly, Erik Erikson was correct when decades ago he wrote: "In general it is the inability to settle on an occupational identity which most disturbs young people. To keep themselves together they temporarily overidentify with the heroes of cliques and crowds to the point of an apparently complete loss of individuality."[8]

Whether or not these assertions are true, youth unemployment continues to be a major American problem, and statistically at least, a significant aspect of the U. S. unemployment fabric. Only logically, one wonders why the hundreds of millions of dollars in job training programs, of which the Comprehensive Employment and Training Act (CETA) is the most well known, have yielded relatively few success stories.[9] Everywhere in this country, devoted advocates of young people battle to procure funds with the single intention, as the common expression goes, of getting young people off the streets and into jobs. None of these community leader earns a great deal of money, and even less fame in this important endeavor, and all feel the frustration of a government that never has come forth with sufficient resources to combat this crucial problem.

If economic and sociological factors combine to make unemployment generally, a complicating phenomenon, then youth unemployment in particular adds another complex chapter to the story: namely, the young man himself. Clearly, the meaning of work to a young man is not the same as it is to someone twenty or thirty years his senior. The psychological context of the young man's story is distinct if only because his reading of the past, present, and future is different from that of an older worker. Yet, according to some of the people running job training programs, this is only a minor chapter of the story.

Dr. Samuel Huffman of Chicago's Manpower Demonstration Research Corporation, an organization that, in the 1980s, oversaw a five-year job training experiment, offered some rather discouraging words about the young worker:

> *You're talking about a hard-core, undereducated, undisciplined guy who has been drifting around. His economic needs might be met by working three days a week, so he won't come in the other two. Absenteeism is rampant. . . . He's not saving money for college. He's not looking to the future.*[10]

Young unemployed men who may or may not have finished high school—in many cities a diploma hardly guarantees anyone a job—often wage battles against middle-class rules and rituals in their hunt for work, as well as in their everyday experience at work. One such hurdle for which young men may or may not be prepared is the proverbial trudging through bureaucratic red tape. For some, the activity required from the moment one learns about a job to actually obtaining it, is beyond their psychological capacities. Many young people, furthermore, cannot reconcile their own work with the image of work they always imagined for themselves.[11] This is not what they were meant to do, they report to job training counselors. Many often cannot abide by the fact that they work menial jobs while being forced to wear jackets and ties in order to give the impression to the public that they are middle-class employees. And some, simply, cannot commute the distances required to work certain jobs.[12]

Finally, there is the matter of asserting independence and manhood.[13] A young man wishes to dress in a particular way, or wear an earring, or cut his hair in the fashion of the day, but the plant manager disallows these requests and in so doing undercuts the young man's sense of identity. The job is lost, the young man becomes bitter and discouraged, the manager is confident that sooner or later the job will be filled, for the labor pool of young people remains a bottomless pit.

The typical formula for the job training program, of which many have been tried, is familiar to students of the workforce and unemployment, not to mention millions of young workers as well. The name of the game is to reduce youth unemployment, thereby reducing the cost of welfare and what this country continues to call delinquency. If, in addition, work programs can stimulate businesses and rebuild a community's confidence in its schools and industries, the grand prize has been achieved.

For those running the programs, the job, in theory anyway, is equally straightforward. First, help people develop distinct and useable job skills. Second, if necessary, fill in the educational crevices and outright deficiencies by providing the young people with remedial reading and mathematical programs. Third, and now one begins to see how the project becomes a trifle complicated, motivate the young man or woman first, to graduate high school, and then commit himself or herself to finding and keeping a job.[14] Fourth, pay close attention and offer special care to each and every participant as they need *human* support just as they need *vocational* support.[15] Finally, one more fact to keep in mind: the job a young person presumably will find and keep probably will pay him or her minimum wage.

In thousands of schools across the country, dedicated men and women for decades have fought the battles of vocational curriculum and improving guidance and job placement services. They have sought to develop new systems for monitoring programs and better strategies for assessing these programs. They have worked out scores of details involving the safety of the equipment used in skill training and the efficiency of teachers and students. Government audits and program reports contain a veritable plethora of ideas and recommendations.[16] There is never a shortage of energy, resourcefulness, or commitment, and no one conceals the fact that the public school has been assigned the job of preparing young people for work. If youngsters go from school to jobs the school triumphs; if youth unemployment increases, public education is viewed as the cause of this, and hence is deemed a failure. As educator John Holt was fond of saying, the original purpose of compulsory education was to prepare people for work, that's why industry got behind the schools in the first place.

For decades, well-meaning job training programs, situated both inside and outside the school, have been proposed, funded, and established, and still there has been a steady rise in the rate of youth unemployment, and particularly among African American and Hispanic youth. Some experts claim that the problem of youth unemployment hasn't improved in fifty years, which is remarkable, in that the 1940s saw the birth of a host of federal legislation intended to significantly alter the state of jobs for the young.[17] None of these facts, however, would surprise people like Erik Butler, once the director of Boston's EEPA, Boston's Manpower Agency, who years ago remarked: "the government isn't sincere; they don't want to solve these problems. In their meager attempt they're dividing the people."[18]

In some respects, the stories of out-of-work teenagers should not be considered as grievous as those told by men reaching their forties. It is expected that some teenagers will drift from job to job, and rarely conceive of any position as permanent. Indeed, seasonal adjustments are constantly being made in unemployment statistics in part to accommodate these fluctuations. For a variety of developmental reasons, both psychological and sociological, an adolescent's attitude toward work is more casual than it will be when he reaches his twentieth or twenty-first birthday.[19] For these reasons, and because most employers prefer to hire people in their twenties rather than teenagers, some experts recommend that job training programs be devoted more intensely to people in their twenties. Teenagers, these experts claim, will not be damaged later in life by periods of unemployment.[20] Besides, even casual work allows an adolescent to develop an employment history, job skills, higher work standards, learn the requirements of various jobs, derive a fuller sense of employment options, and of course, earn money.

The facts surrounding the failure of various job training programs may surprise some Americans. Paul Osterman, for example, discovered that in finding employment, the high school graduate who does not go to college fares no better than his former classmate who dropped out of high school. Similarly, those students attending vocational schools have no better luck finding good and steady employment than those who enrolled in regular academic curricula. For the youngster entering the labor market for the first time, reading and mathematical skills may prove to be of greater value than job training. Finally, and something teenagers know all too well, many corporations prefer to underwrite their own job training and hence refuse to honor any training course previously completed by the young candidate. As Elijah Anderson succinctly puts it, many programs tend to fail because of "their inability to place participants in gainful occupations."[21]

If all of this sounds discouraging, then imagine what young people experience as they pound their neighborhood pavements in search of interesting work. Unlike the professionals who study their every action, these young people will fail to discover that youth unemployment is a structural phenomenon, that is, something built into the social economy of the job market.[22] The dilemma, some experts argue, is that teenagers in job training programs either take jobs in the public sector away from older workers, or find the make work assigned them repetitive and unappealing. However much a young man understands the problem, inevitably he will be blamed for his failure to find or keep a job, until eventually he himself will come to believe that unemployment is the result of personal failings. As Osterman observed, "If you look at the unemployment programs, they reinforce the idea that the kids are at fault."[23]

In practical terms, the young worker will learn that more than a job training program, he or she needs good old fashioned contacts. And if a man is young, poor and African American, he will learn that his contacts may be few and far between. It is not merely that he lacks academic competencies or job skills, although he may. More significantly, he has practically no one to lift him on to a potentially lifelong employment track. For this reason, he necessarily favors affirmative action programs if only because they tend to compensate for his lack of employment connections.

Borrowing Kenneth Keniston's phrase of years ago, the odds are stacked against a host of American families, and this means their children as well.[24] Being poor and African American means that they are vulnerable to a range of misconceptions and distrust, which only make finding jobs that much more difficult. The result of this living with the odds stacked against you, living with what Anderson called "the specter of distrust and discrimination," is that young workers, now on their way to becoming the discouraged worker of the sort we have met in previous chapters, "often become resigned to their outsider status, becoming unwilling or incapable of recognizing and seizing opportunity even when it does exist."[25] As we are about to see, all of these issues are found in the stories, however brief, of America's young workers.

I.

Just as one is unable to speak for all the conditions, circumstances, and problems facing young people, no one can distinguish *the* most pressing concern of the young. If I ever doubted this fact, more than twenty-five years of speaking with young people has settled the issue. Everyone has their problem, their hurdle, their one thing to get beyond. It takes the form of an examination, entrances to a club or college, a dental appointment, a time barrier to break in the 100-yard dash. One person cannot find the time to do his homework, another one earns straight As, plays on the school's tennis and field hockey teams, studies piano and flute, works on the weekends, babysits in the evenings and somehow manages to see every new movie and television show. Some young people have an ungodly amount of energy, some young people in this country have serious nutritional deficiencies, which make mere walking an onerous chore. And some sell crack cocaine.

Among a certain population of young people, where again individual needs, talents, and capacities surely vary, one problem too often comes to the fore: Unemployment continues to be among the major problems confronting the young. One of those people who has felt deeply the ill effects of this "disease" is Cleveland Wilkes from Providence, Rhode Island. The Wilkes family has never had much money. Both parents have known only too well what unemployment can do, not only to the person out of work, but to an entire family.

Let me briefly make one point about the following snippet of conversation with Cleveland. The reader will see at once just how powerfully and movingly this young man is able to speak about his search and need for work. But let no one think this is all the young man has on his mind. There is much more to his life that could be recounted, but with his consent, and advice, I have selected this one bit, for Cleveland Wilkes cares about the well-being of young people like himself, who have reached a desperate point in their lives.

"I don't go 'round talking about what young people can go do or not, ain't my business to care one way or the other. Folks like you gotta come up with those answers. What are the *big* problems facing kids like me? How the hell am I supposed to know? Hey, there *ain't* no kids like me; I'm one of a kind, my man, broke that mold they're always talking 'bout when my mother gave old Cleveland to the world.

"Take the kids 'round here. They ain't all alike. This one worries 'bout this, 'nother one, he'd like as much to bust the hell out of this place. I got a sister talking 'bout going to college. She may do it too, man, you can't never tell; I seen stranger things going on. Saw a man get knifed once. Person stuck him so many times doctor came and couldn't figure out which hole to stop 'em up with first. Tell you, man, the brother was lying on the street, wasn't an inch of him didn't have blood coming out of him. Bunch of brothers, we was watching the whole thing, ten feet away. I heard and saw most everything they did. Finally, you know, doctor told him, 'Hey listen to me, man, I don't know what to do for you first.' And I'm telling you, man, the brother is bleeding from all *over* the place. Doctor, he didn't know where to go. So the brother gets up and *walks* to the ambulance. I mean, he stands up, bleeding, man, like a *cow*, and he gets into that ambulance, and goddamn if all those people s'posed to help him ain't watching him do it, mouths like to drop open. I seen that. Strange things going on 'round here, I tell you. You seen what I seen, you don't get no surprise when your sister comes up to you and say, I think I may try on that college scene for size. Hey, girl, work out. Try it on. It's for you, too. Ain't so strange.

"Now, you 'member me telling you I seen all the strangest of the strangest sights? Whole world floats by 'round here. This here's the whole world only in miniature, like they call it. There ain't nothin' you can't see on these streets. See more in a month here than a life time where them rich folks live all protected from the big bad world, you know what I'm talking 'bout. I ain't saying it's so great over here. Ain't saying this would be my first choice for children growing up in this city. I'm only saying where we ain't rich with money we are rich, man, with things happening every second. Only thing we don't have is the thing we need the most of: jobs. Ain't got no jobs for us over here. Not a one, man, and I know too, 'cause I been looking for three years, and I ain't all that old. *Act* old, but I ain't old. *Seen* things old people seen, but I ain't old, least not today. Next week I may be old, next year for sure I am fixin' on being old if I don't find no work. They ain't got no work over here for young people. Rich kid, he's going to find jobs. Month here, month there. Kid don't need nothin', neither. Got his father handin' things to him on a silver platter. Over here, man, we *need* that work, but they got nothing for us.

"I'd take anything too, man, *anything* they got for me. That surprise you? Don't surprise me none. You sit in the middle of all this, this mess, like they call it, you ain't got no choice. Like they say, beggars can't be choosy. But I ain't about to go beggin', 'cept that seems like all I do, specially in the summer. Man, we go to these fat calves, sitting there in their offices, you know. 'Hey, mister, you got a job?' 'We'll call you. We'll call you.' They tell me that or they'll say, 'Got your name, Mr. Cleveland, on the top of my list.' I say to the dude, 'Hey, that's cool. You got the only list I ever heard of with my name right at the top. But if you're thinking 'bout me so special, how come you call me Mr. Cleveland when Cleveland's my *first* name?' Got me on top of his list, my ass! Turkey! Country got no use for me, folks 'round here neither. Ain't nobody care too much what happens to us. Tell us, ain't you boys got nothing better to do than stand 'round the street all day? What you find to talk about all these hours? And ain't you s'posed to be in school? Ain't you s'posed to be helping your mamma? Ain't you s'posed to be doing this or doing that? I tell 'em, 'Hey listen to me, Turkey. I ain't *s'posed* to be doing nothin' if I don't want to. You hear me? Ain't *s'posed* to be nowhere, helping *no* one. Can you appreciate what I'm saying to you? I don't take no orders from you just 'cause you're old and I look so *young* to you. You want to talk to babies so much, why don't you go down to that day-care center they got at the project and you can talk to all the little babies you want. But I ain't no baby filling my mind up with s'pose to's. What I am doing is looking for work, a job, employment, boy for hire, you got it, my man? Ain't s'posed to but I gotta. You got that? Folks wanna give me the money I need, I say, all right, come on over here and give it to me. But since no one's *s'posed* to do that, only way for me to go is go find that old employment road and follow it to the end.

"Now if you want to know what the *teenagers* over on this side of town are doing to pass the time of day, like you'll hear folks talkin', now you got it. We got so many folks here out of work it's enough to blow your mind.

Can't believe so many folks can't find nothing. I mean nothing at all, man. Not a drop. If jobs was water, man, you'd be standing in the middle of a bunch of dying men drowning. Young *and* old. That's the God's honest truth, too, man. We got folks dying from having no jobs. I can't even taste it no more and I ain't even old enough to vote. You better believe folks in government afraid to let me vote on them. I'd vote for 'em, too, man. All these bullshitters talking 'bout jobs. Ain't nobody's talk going to get me no paycheck. And you ain't heard me talking 'bout making lots of money, have you? You ain't heard me say nothin' 'bout how *much* I want to make, or *gotta* make, more like it. Like I told you, man, I'll take anything. If I can't do it I'll learn it. You don't have to pay me to learn it. Let me learn it and I'll come down and give you a day's work you ain't never gonna forget 'til you're old. That's the God's honest truth. I am *bored*, man. I can *hear* my brain rottin' it's been so long I ain't done nothin'. How they let this happen in a country like this, having all these kids, man, ain't no grownups, I'm talking 'bout all these kids walking 'round the streets, got their hands jammed down in their pockets, you can see 'round here all the time, head down, like their necks was bent in half? Where these kids gonna go? What they gonna do? Who's lookin' out for all them? What do folks think these kids gonna do when they go month after month, year after year without nothin' that even *smells* like a job? Not even no part time affair. Hell, they might get to the point to where they'll waste some kid working the cleaners. Waste the kid and take his job. Folks do it when they ain't got enough food, they'll start doing it for jobs, too. Ain't got no job, ain't got no food, you know what I'm saying.

"Don't want to think 'bout no welfare neither. I don't want nobody *giving* me nothing. I ain't no beggar. I'll work for it same as everyone else s'posed to do. It's gonna get bad 'round here, though, man, if things don't change. I mean, you can tell just from listening to the way I talk. Half the time I'm worryin' 'bout all those teenagers out there that you're so crazy 'bout, rest of the time, I ain't kidding you or *nobody*, I am looking out for number one. This here's the brother I'm looking out for. But I'll tell you the God's honest truth, little bit longer without no job and I ain't gonna be no number one no more. I ain't gonna *be*. You get what I'm trying to tell you? I ain't gonna last forever standin' in all their lines, puttin' down all this scribble stuff on their forms. That's 'bout the only job I *do* have these days, but it don't pay nothin' you can be damn sure. Don't pay me a livin' cent. You believe, man, and I'm only seventeen years old.

II.

The notion that children have only the barest sense of deprivation is quickly disconfirmed by a host of conversations with a great number of children. One might wish that systematic or even wholly idiosyncratic deprivations would escape the eye of the child, but the facts speak for themselves. Adults are just as adept at knowing when they have been taken in, or outrightly deprived.[26] Yet detection of deprivation is hardly the significant matter. More to the point, all too many forms of deprivation take their bite out of the child and influence the child's own assessments of him or herself, not to mention other people's assessments of the child. This last point, incidentally, should not be too quickly passed over. People are what they are, or what they think they are. Their self-assessments are in part a product of others' assessments of them, not to mention the culture in which they live.

We are speaking here not only of the psychological phenomenon known as the self-concept. We are speaking more generally, more philosophically, if you will. Our very self-knowledge is lodged in our cultural, societal, political, economic and linguistic patterns and styles.[27] At some level, we recognize these "other factors," yet the dynamics of that which we call our identity, fights against these "other factors." We would like, in other words, to be known as unique beings, products of nothing but our own efforts, initiative and capacities, our "possible selves," as Hazel Markus and Paula Nurius wrote.[28] No, let me amend this slightly: Young people seem to fight more strenuously, and at times rather dogmatically, against the idea of a sociological, cultural or political determinism. I am me, they contend, which means all my good parts combined with all the less good parts. Most significant, however, I am the sponsor of all the parts, indeed they constitute my singular identity, although I am not always certain what to do with the apparent discrepancies in my self-conceptions, just as I am concerned that I abide by the dictates of what E. Tory Higgens called "self-guides."[29]

Not mere words, the foregoing philosophy has surfaced in one form or another in myriad conversations with America's economically poor children. In the words of a thirteen-year-old African American boy from the Washington, DC, area: "I believe Black people are oppressed. I believe racism makes it hard for me to get to where I want to go. But in the end, like my Daddy says, the only thing going to hold me back from getting *anywhere* is me. And I believe that too!"

The speaker is Jeremiah Kelser, whose mother has been on welfare for as long as he can remember. Jeremiah speaks often of his father, but in truth he sees his father infrequently, less than a half dozen times a year, and unemployment remains the family's invisible but prominent theme. Jeremiah's older brother Lamar is one of his school's extraordinary athletes, his two younger sisters are known for their outstanding academic work. Although Jeremiah has never been in serious trouble, this slight, handsome boy, has always been his mother's greatest worry. Somehow, Millie Kelser just doesn't feel the boy has what it takes to "make out all right." Maybe too, she feels that although, in a broader sense, the whole family has known its share of deprivation, Jeremiah carries an additional burden. I must confess, although I admire Mrs. Kelser, and trust in her deep knowledge of her children, I have never seen anything in Jeremiah that would confirm her apprehension. Granted, I have heard all too often her arguments about the deprivations experienced by poor families and her belief that only the special child can escape the destiny shaped by these deprivations, but I remain unconvinced by her assessment of this one young man. Yet significantly, I have heard her assessments in the beliefs and attitudes of the boy himself:

"My mother thinks I'm not as good as my brother and sisters, which may be right. There's nothing I do as good as they do, sports and schoolwork, but I still don't think that means I can't do as well as they do. Let's face it, you can't grow up Black in this country and expect to make it as easily as all the rest of those folks. You're always going to be one step behind, least in their eyes. Even when you go do something extra good, folks look at you like maybe they're surprised you could do something sort of all right, you know what I'm saying? Even my mother, she feels that way every once in a while. She may not mean to, but that's what she makes me think she's thinking. Hell, I don't know for sure.

"Fact is, I don't know nothing for sure, 'cept if you work hard enough at something, chances are you gotta make out all right. Sure I have to go without lots of stuff other kids have, or all those products they advertise on television, half of them all they have 'em for is to remind you of what you don't have and what you're supposed to have if you want to call yourself a big success. But I can live with that. So I don't have this, or that, a big yard or lots of trees, or a new baseball mitt every year. I can make out. I can make out with what I got just being me, you know what I mean? I got the right number of eyes and ears and arms and legs, don't I? I got a brain that works, don't I? So what's the big deal! Maybe I got a little farther to go than a lot of these other folks, but in the long run all it depends on is little ol' me. Sure I come from what they call a deprived family. Fact is, that's all my mother talks about half the time, how we've been deprived this and deprived that. My father used to tell her she'd do better getting down to work on no matter what, 'stead of limping around the house complaining all the time about this and that. How many times you think folks have to hear all that before they have it stuck in their minds for good that, like, something's supposed to be the matter with them? You don't have to keep throwing out the same message everyday, you know.

"Trouble with my mother is that she believes I'm the only one who's going to fail. She thinks my brother's going to make it with sports, and my sisters with schoolwork. But then there's me, and she can't figure how I'll do it. I think she's got a big excuse all ready just in case. She'll tell folks, 'hey, what chance do you think kids like mine got? Growing up the way we did they got to be twice as good and twice as smart as anyone else. That's right. Got to be better than better! We're different from all these other folks. Nobody gives us a break. Nobody helps us. Nobody even believes we can make it even when we're right in the middle of making it.' My mother's got so many lines, you can't tell which way she's going.

"Way I see it, a person goes just as far as he can by himself. If you're a sixty-mile-an-hour man, you go sixty. If you're only a twenty, then you go twenty. No, it's true you got half the society trying to keep you going sixty. But what you going to do if they're trying to keep you from going sixty? You just work harder, push your engine so damn hard there's no way folks going to stomp on you, keep you from moving, you know what I'm saying? Now these other kids, if they worked as hard as I'll probably have to, they'd be going seventy and eighty miles per hour. But nobody works harder than I have to. If all you have to do is spit in the engine to turn it up to sixty, then all you're ever going to do is spit. No one makes it harder on himself. Things go smooth, you take it easy. Things go tough, you push harder. That's all you can do. That's all anybody can do. My mother, see, she's got herself believing I don't have a chance 'cause there's nothing I can do that comes real easy to me. Okay, that's fine. But just 'cause I got to work hard for it don't mean I ain't going to get it, no matter who wants to keep me from getting it. But she don't want to see it that way. She thinks 'cause of welfare and all these other programs that we're already out of it, or I am anyway. And I haven't even done nothing yet to make her think that way.

Nothing at all. I ain't in no trouble. I do my work in school like I'm supposed to. I ain't so happy about the way we have to live doing all the things we gotta do in order to keep getting what we get from the government, but she doesn't hear me complain. I don't say nothing to no one. I don't understand where she gets all her ideas. Living in a housing project ain't what you would call being a big time millionaire. But just 'cause you live in one doesn't mean you can't change things. Hey, I could become a millionaire myself and end up buying some great big house for all the rest of the people in my family, which means especially my mother. Could happen, you know. Just 'cause all these conditions you gotta grow up in are supposed to mean you sort of end up just where you started from doesn't mean it has to happen to everyone.

"'Course I'm not so sure I'm the one who's going to make it. I mean, I don't want to seem like I'm bragging. I ain't sure about nothing. I might do it, and I might not. Nobody knows for sure. You can't tell what's going to happen. My mother thinks you can, but you can't tell nothing! I could be higher than high tomorrow, or in two years, how's anybody going to know. I could be a bum too. I could be way up in one part of my life and just that far down in another part. That happens, too. Pushing eighty per one second, and stalled, man, 'til the motor burns out the next second. How you going to tell? How you going to know how anybody or anything's going to deprive you? And if I'm so *deprived*, like my mother always tells all of us we are, but especially me, then how come I know all about these things? How come I understand about life and she doesn't even know how I think about any of this stuff? If you're really deprived, like she tells me, then you wouldn't even know it. Fact that you know already means you're pushing twenty, maybe even thirty per. Has to, man!"

As I noted, this bit of conversation took place with Jeremiah Kelser when he was thirteen years old. That was seven years ago. Now, three months short of his twenty-first birthday, Jeremiah Kelser is in prison, serving a three- to-five year sentence for his role in the robbery of a grocery store. His mother says that any sort of reasonable employment during these years would have kept him out of trouble.

III.

It was not true, as many people believed, that Edward Harrington was out of work most of his life. He began working full time at seventeen without problems or mishaps. Every few years he changed jobs because he was dropped, or he saw an opportunity to improve his wages, or something else looked more interesting. By the time he turned thirty-five, he had worked in sugar processing, hardware, produce, steel, and trucking. But by forty-two, he was certain he would remain with the Hadley Coal Company until he retired. The job paid well enough, there was a chance for salary increases, and there seemed to be beneficial union representation. When Ed Harrington felt his job was secure, his spirits were high and his relationship with his wife, Gloria, was pleasant if not always affable.

It was said that Ed had women on the side. Surely he was a handsome enough man with a well-preserved body. Gloria thought she knew about the other women, although she could never prove anything. Yet deep down she felt she had no right to complain. Edward could have refused to marry her when she got pregnant with Anne-Marie. In most every case she knew of, the man left the woman to have her baby all by herself. Edward was different; he felt an obligation to Gloria.

Then suddenly, when he was in his early forties, Ed Harrington's job situation changed for the worse. Hadley Coal began laying off men temporarily. Ed was assured he would be among the first rehired because he had a consistently fine record. But being out of work for weeks at a time made him scared and irritable.

When the anxiety and frustration became too intense, he would go off somewhere to be with friends and drink. He did attempt to find new jobs, but after several hours in employment offices or waiting outside factories and warehouses, he would head for his favorite drinking haunts with his unemployed comrades. Soon, the afternoons in bars were expanded and he would disappear for several days at a time. He always returned home sober and freshly shaved, however, and begged his wife for forgiveness. She always granted it. After all, Edward *had* married her, so where possibly would a separation or divorce lead her? Anyway, Hadley Coal was hiring former employees, and everything seemed to be back to normal.

Eventually, the stretches of unemployment became more trying for the entire family, with fourteen-year-old Edward, Junior, appearing the most upset by the new pattern in the house. As far as young Eddie was concerned, his father seemed a good man who spent the better part of his life working and bringing home pay checks. Although he knew that many of his friends' fathers were out of work, he could not imagine his own father staying idle for more than a few days at a time. Before the layoffs, Eddie never had seen

his father drunk or engaged in bouts of fury. Unprepared for these transformations, he became terrified and angry. He would stalk into the room he
shared with his brother Peter and break things or rip the sheets off his bed.
Gloria tried to be sympathetic with her son but he would only fly into a
greater rage and run out of the house screaming.

Young Eddie could not have been more distant from the neighborhood
boys who seemed to find trouble no matter where they went. He wanted
no part of anybody, preferring to stay by himself:

"I'd tell myself, 'Okay, man. Get hold of yourself, don't let yourself go
all the way.' Stupid things like that. I couldn't understand my dad just walking out on us. I didn't think I was blaming him, because I didn't want to
blame him. He's not a bad guy or anything. I knew he had a lot of problems. I guess I was always a little afraid of him, more than a little when he's
been fired from his job—he never admitted to anyone that he was fired, but
he was. I was hoping he'd come and talk with me. But he'd just go off. I
told him lots of times I'd like to go with him where he goes, but he said I
had to stay around home 'cause I had school and stuff like that. Once he
said, even if I cut school or quit for good I could find better things to do
than go with him. I never told him nothing, but I was thinking that I'd
never do anything that'd amount to all that much even if I stayed in school.
I wasn't meant to become much of anything."

In time, the running away to be alone turned into running away and
being consumed with fear. It was as if Eddie, Junior dreaded the coming of
a momentous event, a calamity. One night, on an occasion when his father
had gone off, Eddie collected a huge pile of newspapers and placed it in a
dilapidated sandbox in his housing project's playground. Then he took
some of the papers, rolled them up, and dipped them into the gas tank of
a motorcycle. Making certain no one saw him, he set fire to the roll and
threw it on the pile. In minutes, huge flames rose up from the sandbox.
Fortunately, the fire was quickly put out and Eddie was never caught.

He repeated the action two weeks later. Something seemed to be pushing him to set fires, but he could not find a reason for this destructive
behavior. "I can't explain it," he would say later. "Sometimes things just
come into my head, so I have to do them. Like, I'll be sitting on my bed
and I won't be thinking anything special, but then suddenly I'm slamming
my fist into the wall, only I don't even know I'm doing it. And like, when
my hand hits the wall, that's like the first time I think about it. Maybe
there's another me inside the one everybody sees ordering me to do things.

"I think my problems are due to my parents, 'specially my father, although I hate to blame him. But like, when a kid like me grows up, he kind of expects his dad and mother to be certain ways. Like, first off, he expects them to be married or not married, right? Or take my folks, let them be separate, with the kids sort of knowing, over here's where your mother lives and over there's where your father lives. I mean, they got to make up their minds where they stand.

"The next thing kids got a right to expect is that their fathers or mothers got a job. In my case, I think it should be my father who has a job 'cause he ain't separated from us. When you see him hanging around the house doing nothing then he ought to explain it. 'Specially to me. I'm his son. And *he's* supposed to be training *me* for when I'm a man. But he doesn't trust us enough to tell us anything, I guess.

"My father's ashamed he's out of work. You can see it just the way he's like, afraid to look at us. He don't even want to be seen. He's hiding from us. He's like a little boy. He tells me all the time, 'You got to be a man. Don't let people beat you or get the best of you.' But he can't be that way himself. I'd tell him he shouldn't be ashamed if he gave me the chance. He ain't the first guy out of work around here, and he sure won't be the last. I just wish he'd give us the chance to talk about it with him so he wouldn't have to keep going away."

The lighting of fires went on for months until, finally, young Eddie Harrington was picked up by the police.

"You should have seen those cops, they couldn't wait to get their hands on me. They acted like I was the number one most wanted crook in the country. I couldn't believe it. Then, like at nine or ten o'clock this big fat cop comes in, guy had the reddest face I ever saw with all these pimples all over his nose. He comes in here and says, 'Okay let's have it.' So I started to tell him about the fire and he stops me. He says, 'First off, who's your father?' So I tell him. Then he says, 'What's your father do?' So I tell him, 'I don't know,' 'cause I don't, and he says I'm being fresh. So I tell him again my dad don't work. So the cop says, 'Call him on the phone,' and he gives me a quarter. So I tell him I don't have any idea where he is.

"The cop says, 'Call your home.' So I call home with his quarter. My sister Elaine says my father isn't around but she has a number where maybe I could get him. So I have to ask this cop with the nose for another quarter. I call this number Elaine gives me and this woman answers. So she says, 'Yeah, he's here, who are you?' So I say, 'Who the hell are *you?*' *That's* when

I found out about my old man, 'cause she put her hand over the phone, you know, thinking I couldn't hear.

"She goes, 'Hey, Harrington, put your pecker in your pants, there's a kid on the phone says he's your son.' Then I heard him say, 'How the hell did he find me here for Christsakes? Tell him you never heard of me.' So she gets back on the phone and says, 'I never heard of anyone named Harrington. You got the wrong number.' I was so surprised, I didn't know what the hell to tell her. I said, and I'm starting to cry now, 'Tell my father I never want to see him again, Tell him he's chicken shit.' The cop thought I was stalling, woman hung up in my face.

"But this cop with the nose, he was all right. He made me talk about my father. At first I didn't want to, then I thought, why not. I said I was ashamed of him and he was ashamed of himself 'cause he didn't have a job and he didn't have a place to go where people respected him, which I suppose was a lot like me too. He couldn't look at my mother so he found this other woman. He couldn't be a man with any of us. Like, he couldn't be a husband 'cause he didn't have any respect from my mother, 'cause she only respects men with lots of money. She told me that herself: 'I'll always love you. I'll always do that 'cause you're my own blood. But just 'cause I'm your mother don't mean I have to respect you. You got to earn that.' So when I asked her what I have to do before I earn it, she said: 'I'll probably never respect you. You ain't going to end up too much better than your father, and there isn't a soul who's going to respect *him*.'"

Eddie was detained in the precinct station eight and a half hours at the time of his first arrest. In the end, there was no formal charge, merely a severe warning that if there was a next time, the police would come down hard on him, even though he was only fourteen years old. On his way out of the station house that evening, he overheard a policeman say: "That Harrington kid? Kid's sharp as a buck. But sick in the mind. I'll predict right now that boy will be in here one day with a murder charge wrapped around his neck."

The words terrified Eddie because he had been thinking a great deal of killing. Almost every day he would fantasize murder. Sitting on the trolley he would see an elderly gentleman looking tired, depressed. He would imagine what the man's life was like, or feel sorry for the man and wish he could help him. Then he would imagine having a conversation with the man, and a whole scene would unfold. They would be traveling on the trolley. It would be night and only a few people would be riding in the car.

Eddie would strike up a conversation, letting the man first see his good-natured side.

"What do you say, dad, how's it going with you?"

"Not bad, son," the man would answer.

"But you look so glum. What you need is a good stiff drink or a night with a broad. Which is it?"

"Nah, that's not it," the man would protest, looking sheepish. "Can't get a job, that's all."

"Is *that* all it is? Eddie would ask. "Hell, we can always find a job."

"There ain't no jobs, son. I've tried. Been trying for years. Shoveling shit off the dock even, if they'd offer it to me. Got children to feed and a wife that still can stomach the sight of me. Got to find something or, I don't know what."

Then, as his hands began to perspire, and his breathing quickened, Eddie would imagine himself becoming crazed. He would see himself standing up in front of the man holding a large-link steel chain. He would yell at the passengers to get off and they would run away screaming. Then Eddie would begin to destroy the man. Starting with the man's legs, he would chain and whip him. With all his might he would swing the chain at the man's chest and hear the ribs crack and the man cry out in pain. Then he would fling the chain so that it would not only crash against the man's skull but wrap around it, splitting open the cheeks and bones around the eyes and ears. Blood would spurt out onto the seats and floor of the car. Eddie Harrington's heart would beat faster and faster. He would imagine laughing and crying, swearing and yelling all at once. He would feel gratified and fulfilled, guilty and ashamed. Always the man's broken body would fall over frontward, thumping on the dirty floor of the trolley car and landing against Eddie's own legs in a sickening hulk. Eddie would kick himself free and want to vomit or urinate on the man. He would say aloud:

"There you are, old man. Lucky you aren't my real father. Now you don't have nothing to be sad about. You don't have to get up every morning wondering, do I have a job today or don't I? Will my wife and kids like me because I do have a job or I don't have a job? Now you don't have to look nobody in the face again and let 'em see what sort of bum you really are. So long, old man."

When he wasn't having such fantasies, Eddie thought a lot about his father's last steady job with the Hadley Coal Company. His father had told his wife the job looked secure. Money was tight in the coal industry, but he had seniority in his department. Besides, he was a well liked employee. Even his co-worker Frankie Amano said that Harrington deserved to stay with Hadley more than any other man, and everybody knew Amano never complimented anyone, especially someone with whom he was competing for a job. Young Eddie had been with his father the day the two men talked. His father was proud to have him there overhearing the adults converse.

But most of the men despised Frankie Amano. They said he was so ruthless he'd kill his own children if it meant getting a job. "You'll see what happens when he talks to Trent," they warned. "Bill Trent got to be foreman 'cause he did anything anybody told him. He's as big a liar as Amano, only he don't have none of Amano's guts. Even your kid could scare the piss out of him."

Eddie remembered his father's bitterness toward Bill Trent, who had fired Ed Harrington for reasons that were never made clear to anyone. He remembered listening from his room when his father came home that afternoon and went into a rage, telling his mother how he was going to buy a gun:

"What the hell do I have to lose anymore? Might as well get a little bit of goddamn satisfaction out of my life. Ain't had a fuckin' shred of it in forty years. I'd only be doing everybody coming up behind me a favor if I got rid of that son of a bitch Amano. Trent will choke on his own shit. Miserable bastards! You work your goddamn ass off for years and what the hell does it bring? They screw you behind your back, in front of your eyes. What the hell they give a good goddamn about? They care if you work? Dog eat dog out there? My ass. It's man eat man, and those bastards always win. They'll win when I'm dead and buried, too.

"Christsakes, that son of a bitch Amano was bullshitting me in front of my kid. Frank Amano, baby, I know your kind. I can smell you out ten blocks away. You eat people and you spit 'em out to take care of yourself. You and Trent, who is the biggest bullshitter 'cause his real name's Grady, or O'Grady or something, and he's afraid some folks will steal his little job from him if they find out he's a mick. Christ, he'd pass as a goddamn Jew or Nigger in Blackface if he could save his job, or take someone else's from him.

"What the hell is anybody supposed to think when all they hear about is me losing my fuckin' job all the time? 'Hey, daddy, how come you ain't working and Frank Amano and Bill Trent are?' What do I say? 'Well, son, I'll tell you what the story is. You see, guys like Amano and Trent can be explained real simple. Say there was one job in the world and two people who might take it. They're one of the guys, see, and the guy competing for the job is their own son. Now mind you, their son is just a newborn baby still in the hospital. They still got him there in one of those cribs. Amano and Trent would go into that nursery and, thinking their boss just might give the job to this two-day-old kid lying there in his own piss and shit, would squeeze the kid to death. Then they'd go out, have a drink, and bring their goddamn wife a bunch of flowers and a big card that says 'Jesus Christ, hon, you know how bad I feel. I wanted that little fellow in there just as bad as you did.'"

Eddie, who had been curled up on his bed, heard his mother cry out to his father:

"Jesus Christ, you're mad. You're really sick. They've made you sick, or this job thing has, or something has, and I don't give a damn what it is. But you are *sick*. I forbid you to be near the kids when you're like this. Killing babies? What the hell's with you? Get out. GET OUT!"

Young Eddie heard a chair fall over and a noise that sounded like someone being hit. He was too terrified to open the door and see what his parents were doing. Suddenly, the door to his room flew open and his father was standing there.

"You hear?" his father asked calmly.

The boy merely nodded.

"Good. Might be the best education about life you'll ever get. You hear the part about choking babies?"

Eddie could not move. His mouth was dry and the palms of his hands were covered with perspiration.

"I'll tell you something else," his father said, "just to make certain you got it in your head for good. There's only one thing in life that matters, and that's working steady at whatever the hell you do. It ain't important whether you choose it or find it or stumble on it. All I know is you got to work. Every day. And you got to fight for every job as if they were trying to take away your arms. Don't believe nobody. Listen to nobody. The only thing that talks is the job. When you got it you got everything, when you lose it, you got nothing. They can throw every word in the goddamn dictionary at you and you still don't have nothing. You understand that?"

Still his son did not move.

"Get a job, then get yourself a gun. Keep it with you loaded, so the first guy that starts messing with you gets it right between the eyes. Let 'em take your wife, your home, your car, anything they like, but die before they take your job away, 'cause you're going to be like me, 'cause you're my blood. And you're going to die the same way I do. With a job you got life, without it, you're long since dead. You get what I'm saying?"

Eddie nodded.

"I'll be back. Look after your mother." Ed Harrington closed the door. His son heard the door to the outside close and his father slowly descending the steps.

Ed Harrington's speech to his son had been perfectly direct, and delivered with calmness and strength. He knew exactly what he had wanted to say, almost as if he had been waiting for just that moment. Yet, it was impossible to believe that he could have been as calm and straightforward when such heavy tears had flowed from his eyes. His son too had been crying.

Not long after his fifteenth birthday, Eddie Harrington, Jr., was arrested by the police for stealing money from a grocery store. At the police station he also was charged with setting fires on six different occasions. One of the fires had destroyed an old wooden building that had been condemned. As it happened, a little boy had perished in the fire. This meant that Eddie was charged with involuntary manslaughter. He remained in jail thirteen months awaiting trial. When his case finally was taken to court, the judge ruled that there was sufficient evidence to prove his role in the setting of two of the fires as well as the robbery. He was sentenced to prison for a term to run no less than one year, not more than three.

At the sentencing, the judge apologized to Gloria Harrington for the way the boy had been detained. Eddie stood motionless, looking tough, but beaten. Then the judge asked, "Is your father alive?" The boy thought for a conspicuously long time. Finally, he looked down and mumbled, "I don't know. But if he is, he wouldn't be here. He'd be out looking for a job!"

NOTES

1. On this point, see Richard R. Freeman and Harry J. Holzer, Eds., *The Black Youth Unemployment Crisis* (Chicago: University of Chicago Press, 1986.) For a comparative examination, see P. B. Warr, M. H. Banks, P. Ullah, "The Experience of Unemployment Among Black and White Urban Teenagers," *British Journal of Psychology* 76 (1985): 75–87.

2. On this point, see M. P. Jackson, *Youth Unemployment* (London: Croom Helm, 1985); A. Furnham, "Youth Unemployment: A Review of the Literature" *Journal of Adolescence 8* (1985): 109–124; P. R. Jackson, E. M. Stafford, M. H. Banks, and P. B. Warr, "Unemployment and Psychological Distress in Young People: The Moderating Role of Employment Commitment," *Journal of Applied Psychology 36* (1983): 525–535; P. B. Warr, P. R. Jackson and M. H. Banks, Duration of Unemployment and Psychological Well-Being in Young Men and Women" *Current Psychological Research 2* (1982): 207–214; and J. G. Bachman and P. M. O'Malley, "Self-Esteem in Young Men: A Longitudinal Analysis of the Impact of Educational and Occupational Attainment," *Journal of Personality and Social Psychology 35* (1977): 365–380.

3. On these points, see K. Borman and J. Reisman, Eds., *Becoming a Worker* (Norwood, NJ: Ablex, 1986). P. Osterman, *Getting Started* (Cambridge: MIT Press, 1980); E. Greenberger and L. Steinberg, *When Teenagers Work* (New York: Basic Books, 1986); D. C. Gottfredson, "Youth Employment, Crime and Schooling: A Longitudinal Study of a National Sample," *Developmental Psychology 21* (1985): 419–32; D. Stern and D. Eichorn, Eds., *Adolescence and Work* (Hillsdale, NJ: Lawrence Erlbaum, 1989); M. Fine, *Framing Dropouts* (Albany, NY: State University of New York Press, 1991); R. Polner, "Cuts Vex Young Workers," *New York Newsday*, 23 January, 1996, A5; and "Youth Suicide Said to Rise in Europe," *New York Times*, 11 June, 1996, A6.

4. See, for example, Edward Palmore, "The Perceptions and Attitudes of Some Urban, Unemployed Black Youth Regarding the Extrinsic/Intrinsic Utility of a World of Work, (Doctoral thesis, Boston University, 1981). For a more general discussion of the role of work in adolescent development, see Norman T. Feather, "Values in Adolescence," in Joseph Adelson, Ed., *Handbook of Adolescent Psychology* (New York: Wiley, 1980): 247–94.

5. Adding to the drop out problem is the inevitable waiting time between leaving school and registering for a job training program or obtaining a job. On related points, see R. M. Gurney, "Leaving School, Facing Unemployment, and Making Attributions about the Causes of Unemployment," *Journal of Vocational Behavior 18* (1981): 79–91.

6. See M. Wagner, "Youth and Disabilities During Transition: An Overview and Description of Findings from the National Longitudinal Transition Study," in J. Chadsey-Rusch, Ed., (Transition Institute at

Illinois: Project Director's Fourth Annual Meeting, Champaign: University of Illinois, 1989). This work is cited in Helen Roy, "Inclusion: Voices from Inside," (Doctoral dissertation proposal, Boston University, November, 1998).

7. See D. E. Berkell, "Working Toward Integration," *The Forum 17* (1991): 3. Cited in Helen Roy, *op. cit.,* 29.

8. Erik H. Erikson, *Identity, Youth and Crisis,* (New York: W. W. Norton, 1968).

9. See Katherine Newman, *No Shame in My Game* (New York: Knopf, 1999, especially chapter 9).

10. Cited in Jerry Crimmins, "Opening Job Door for Hard Core," *The Chicago Tribune,* 2 March 1980, 10.

11. See N. T. Feather and G. E. O'Brien, "Looking for Employment: An Expectancy-Valence Analysis of Job-Seeking Behavior Among Young People," *Journal of Occupational Psychology 78* (1987): 251–272; and E. M. Stafford, P. R. Jackson, and M.H. Banks, "Employment, Work Involvement, and Mental Health in Less Qualified Young People," *Journal of Occupational Psychology 53* (1980): 291–304.

12. Katherine Newman, *op. cit.*

13. On this point and for an excellent discussion of job training programs, see Elijah Anderson, "Racial Tension, Cultural Conflicts, and Problems of Employment Training Programs," in K. Erikson and S. P. Vallas, Eds., *The Nature of Work: Sociological Perspectives* (New Haven, CT: Yale University Press, 1990).

14. On these points, see Phyllis Coons' discussion of such a program, the Northeast Economic Action Research Corporation, in "Job Training Plans for Young People," *The Boston Globe,* 26 October, 1980, Metro Section. See also, M. Tiggemann and A. H. Winefield, "The Effects of Employment on the Mood, Self-Esteem, Locus of Control, and Depressive Affect of School-Leavers," *Journal of Occupational Psychology 57* (1984): 33–42.

15. As an example of such a program ideology, see "Dorchester Gets 3 New Programs for Out-of-School Youth," *Dorchester Community News,* January 1979.

16. See Muriel Cohen, "Job Training: A Boston Bust," *The Boston Globe,* 28 September, 1980, D1ff.

17. Readers should be aware of Glen H. Elder's remarkable account in *Children of the Great Depression* (Chicago: University of Chicago Press, 1978).

18. This citation is attributed to Erik Butler, director of Boston's EEPA, Boston's manpower agency. In *Bay State Banner*, 6 July 1978, 11.

19. On this point, see Robert Kegan, *The Evolving Self* (Cambridge, MA: Harvard University Press, 1982).

20. See Diane Dumanoski, "Youth Unemployment: Who's to Blame?," *The Boston Globe*, 11 January 1981, C2; and Paul Osterman, *Getting Started: The Youth Labor Market* (Cambridge, MA: MIT Press, 1980).

21. Anderson, *op. cit.*, 231.

22. On this point, see G. H. Elder and A. Caspi, "Economic Stress in Lives: Developmental Perspectives," *Journal of Social Issues 44* (1988): 25–45.

23. In Dumanoski, *op. cit.*

24. Kenneth Keniston, *All our Children: The American Family Under Pressure* (New York: Harcourt Brace Jovanovich, 1977).

25. Anderson, *op. cit.*, 231.

26. This point puts me in mind of the volume *The Belief in a Just World* by M. J. Lerner, (New York: Plenum Press, 1980). See also R. Folger, Ed., *The Sense of Injustice: Social Psychological Perspectives* (New York: Plenum Press, 1984).

27. On this point, especially as it relates to unemployment, see P. Kelvin and J. E. Jarrett, *Unemployment: Its Social Psychological Effects*, (Cambridge, MA: Cambridge University Press, 1985). See also M. Rosenberg, "The Self-Concept: Social Product and Social Force," in M. Rosenberg and R. H. Turner, Eds., *Social Psychology: Sociological Persepctives* (New York: Basic Books, 1981).

28. H. Markus and P. Nurius. "Possible Selves," *American Psychologist 41* (1986): 954–969.

29. On the point of discrepancies, see E. T. Higgens, "Self-Discrepancy: A Theory Relating Self and Affect," *Psychological Review 94* (1987): 319–340. For a more theoretical discussion of discrepancy, see R. Schafer, "Ideals, The Ego Ideal, and the Ideal Self," *Psychological Issues 5* (1967): 131–174.

Chapter 7

Shame Like
Nobody Could Know:
William Leominster;
Aaron Donane; and Jack Blum

They forget when they give you a job they're giving a job to a person with eyes and ears, heart and muscle. They think we take anything that comes along and feel grateful. But they forget the heart and the muscle.

More than fifty years ago, in what has become a classic sociological study, Louis Wirth published a provocative article entitled "Urbanism as a Way of Life." The richness of this significant work cannot be briefly summarized, except to say that Wirth was highly pessimistic about the nature of social life as it had developed in densely populated cities. Although Wirth had much to say about the effect of city dwelling on the emergence of individual and family life, at least one notion in his work now is beginning to receive serious investigation.

It was Wirth's contention that crowded cities, which obliged city residents to treat each other impersonally, usually in terms of the roles people performed for one another, would eventually cut into kinship systems and eat away at the quality of human bonds. If air pollution and inadequate sewage systems ultimately could cause illness, then Wirth argued that broken kinship relations also could weaken people physically as well as spiritually. Said simply, loneliness can destroy people, and if one reads

James Lynch's book, *The Broken Heart*, one begins to find scientific evidence to support this saddening notion.[1]

Cities, of course, need not be the reason for kinship networks and family relations being severed. A simple death of natural causes making one a widow or widower may be all that a survivor need experience to feel that his or her life cannot go on.[2] What follows is an account of a man, recently a widower, who, simply put, chose not to live after his wife passed away. One is tempted to call his report a message of the spirit or will. But if this renders it too melodramatic, then one may call it a document testifying to the life giving strength that human bonds provide those persons who choose to be defined in part by these bonds. In thinking about this story, I always wonder what its conclusion might have been had there been a bond established not with another person necessarily, but with some valuable effort that would have qualified as work.

In more conceptual terms, the psychologist Mihaly Csikszentmihalyi wrote of this very notion in an essay on creativity:

> In the last years of the twentieth century, among sophisticated people of supremely high achievement, one may have expected a greater variety and more esoteric topics on which to build a life's narrative. It certainly appears to vindicate Freud's deceptively simple answer to an inquiry about the secret for a happy life: "Love and work," he said, and with those two words he may have run out of all the options.[3]

I.

Sixty-eight-year-old William Leominster and I had been friends for almost nine years. Tall, strong, a man who looked years younger than his age, William never knew or thought much about illness until his wife Helen died some two months before. Whereas he had always joked with me how he needed no one, he never could disguise his deep involvement with his wife of almost forty years. After joking about her, he would conclude by saying, "Well, I ain't got problems on that score 'cause I'm going to die way before her. My luck, she'll live to be a thousand!"

Helen Leominster died several weeks before her sixty-fourth birthday. A long period of hospitalization preceded the death, a period in which

William became depressed, but not so severely that he would reveal his mood to his wife. A childless couple, the Leominsters never had much money, and so William worried about hospital bills, insurance policies, and how he would manage when Helen recovered, as he always assumed she would. Worry, perhaps, is not the proper word. What troubled William Leominster most was a sense of powerlessness. He had nothing to say about Helen's care, nowhere to go to receive financial advice, no one to speak to, actually, about anything.

In listening to William describe the death of his wife—it was now months after Helen had passed away—one could not be certain whether he had known she would not recover, or merely assumed that after a few months of convalescing, everything would return to normal. Prepared or not for Helen's death, as if one were ever properly prepared, William indicated that Helen's end was like everything else in his life: out of his control. It was one of the first times anyone had heard him use that expression.

Typically, in telling about a matter they could not control, both Helen and William would say, "Well, it's in God's hands now." William uttered these words many times while Helen was confined to her hospital bed. Yet now, months after her death, new words came forth: "It's out of my control." The expression seemed to refer to everything about his life, and it seemed an apt description. At the time he was waiting to learn from a local housing commission whether he would be allowed to remain in the one bedroom project apartment in which he and Helen had lived since the building was opened nine years before. He was waiting to hear as well from insurance, welfare, and social security officers about money to which he might be entitled now that he had become a widower.

Then one night, as we sat together around a green Formica-covered table in his apartment, William Leominster made what he himself called a funeral speech. His words were more carefully chosen than I had ever before heard with this man, whose spirit was completely broken. The tone of the speech, however, was even, calm; there was an almost uncanny certitude in his style.

"You know, Tom, everything is out of my control. I am an unimportant person. If I live or I die matters to no one in the world. There are many people like me, too, so I don't worry that much about it. But right now, tomorrow to be exact, several people in this city will be looking over my folder. Insurance people, welfare people, social security people, they will all be making decisions about me. I will be on their minds for a few minutes.

It doesn't make me feel important, nothing in life has ever made me feel important. I have never made what anybody would call important decisions. I've made decisions for me, and for my wife, but nothing was anything I or you could call important. Anything that mattered to us was always out of my hands. Sometimes it was in God's hands, most of the time it was in the hands of people I never saw.

"Now, for the first time in my life that I can remember, I've made an important decision: I'm going to die. Simple as that. Death isn't so complicated as people make out. It's almost like actors on television. You fall over and you die. There is nothing wrong with me. I'm probably the healthiest sixty year old man I know. But I won't live out the year. Listen to what I'm telling you. I'm not making a prediction, I'm telling you what I'm going to make happen. For the first time I'm putting something important in my hands.

"I can see by your face you're thinking I'm going to commit suicide. That's what you're thinking. That isn't it. That would be missing the point. And I'm not going out to pay someone to murder me neither. Wouldn't have enough cash to do that even if I wanted to. No, I'm just going to make it happen by myself. It's the one little piece of strength I feel I have, and I'm going to put it to good use. I'd like to make a prediction, I'd like to tell you what's going to go wrong with me that's going to cause my death. My lungs or my heart. I can't say, of course, though I guess that in cases like mine it's usually the heart, isn't it? Well, you can tell them when they find me, check his heart first, that's where he would have put his money, if he was a betting man.

"I can't tell you when. Nobody can say that, not even the Devil. But I'll tell you if I had a calendar, I wouldn't need all those months. Won't take that long. Can't tell either how it will go: slow at first, slow at the end like Helen, fast at the end like my father and mother. I remember those deaths very well. Thought about them when my wife was so ill. Seems like all I've been doing over the last years is burying someone. Well, now someone else will have to bury me; I'll put that responsibility in someone's hands, just like all the other things around here. Someone will have to decide whether I get more money or less money, someone else will have to decide where they're going to put my body. Might even have to be you!

"I suppose I'm lonely. You know, you hear a word like that all your life, you're never really sure what it means, how it feels. If you were to ask me how do I feel, I'd say, and this is honest, don't feel anything at all. I'm not happy, but I don't feel all so much unhappy. I feel that I'm alone. I mean, I know that I'm alone, but I can't honestly say that makes me feel any one thing more than another. I am a healthy man with pretty strong hands, I think you'd have to admit, and not one worthwhile responsibility to put in them. Maybe I feel a little sad about that, although maybe not, I can't quite tell for sure. Anyway, I have my decision so I don't worry that much about not feeling anything. Well, that's not exactly what it is. What it is, see, is the feeling that nothing's inside. That may seem strange to you, maybe you'd even like to feel sorry for me. But you can save your strength because the not feeling inside is what I figure is going to be the weapon going to kill me.

"I figured it out in a way that sort of satisfies me. If you take any part of your body and cut off the blood going to it, that part is going to die. Suck the blood out and you suck the life out. Well, it came to me that maybe feelings work the same way. People say, 'how do you feel?' You say, 'I feel pretty good,' which means not too much more hurts than hurts you regular. Or you say, 'I feel bad,' which means a lot more than regular is hurting. But feeling good or feeling bad is much the same thing because either way all your body parts are working. They may not be doing their best, but they're working. But take a person like me, he answers, 'How do I feel? I feel nothing.' He's a person who's taking the blood out of his own body parts by himself. And that's about what I meant when I said having no feelings is the weapon, the murder weapon, only none of those detective types you see on television would be able to figure this one out. They wouldn't find the weapon, no finger prints, no clues. They couldn't even say for sure whether the man did himself in. No, I'm afraid this one's going to be a little bit more like one of those science fiction stories. They'll have the body, but they won't be able to figure out what in the hell caused the man to die.

"Now that I've told you, in this little funeral speach—I think that's an accurate name for it, too—you'll know. You're sort of the person hearing my last will and testament. It's the perfect crime: No weapon, no finger-prints, everything out of my hands. I have no feelings, don't you see. About everything. Or, I should say, about nothing. I have to die because I'm pulling the blood out of my own body parts. That's my last decent job, job with a payoff, too, I might say. You don't last all that long when you can't feel nothing. It's like you're freezing to death, freezing yourself out, only it isn't cold. Everything is without pain, the killing and the dying, the plan-ning and the doing it.

"I'm doing it now too, right now while I'm talking to you. Tell you the truth, I wanted to talk to you about it sort of to do a little experiment. I haven't talked to anyone about my plan, my mercy killing like I call it. So I thought, maybe I don't feel the way I think I do. Maybe it's a lot of words, because I'm a man who does his share of talking. So I decided, I'll talk it over with someone, tell him the whole thing and see for myself if I do or if I don't have feelings left in me. Feelings, mind you, about anything. That was the experiment: words or feelings? I have the answer now. Maybe I tried to get those feelings to come out, maybe I didn't try hard enough, but there's nothing there. I'm pulling the blood out right this minute. There's no more experiments. I've proved it to myself. It's happening now, I can't feel it, so that sort of proves it. Wouldn't you say so too, that it sort of proves it? If I had a feeling somewhere in there, it would have to come out now, wouldn't it? I'll tell you too, while I like you coming to talk to me, or let me talk to you 'cause I didn't give you a chance to talk much tonight, I still feel alone. Even with you sitting here, I'm alone. I know that. I feel that. That is one thing I do feel. I am all by myself."

Ten months later, William Leominster died. There was nothing mystical about his death. The physician who examined him when he was brought into the hospital diagnosed a massive coronary infarction. Presumably he died within minutes of the first warnings of pain, possibly death came in his sleep. He may not even have felt the stabbing pressure in his chest. Then again, it is unlikely that he slept through intense discomfort. I choose to imagine that he woke, and despite the excruciating distress, felt relieved that the death he had willed was so close at hand. I imagine, too, he remembered how he would have bet that his heart would go first. I'm certain he would not have smiled, but he might have died content in the knowledge that he had brought forth the end precisely as he had desired. Perhaps, too, he felt he could now rejoin his beloved Helen. Strangely, in retrospect, the whole process of his death seemed almost scientific in its purpose and execution.

There was, however, one other matter, something William had mentioned months or perhaps even a year before. Helen was alive at the time, barely, and William and I had met in the lobby of the large Boston Hospital where she had been a patient for several weeks. Almost in passing, almost out of context, he had said, "I could get through this whole thing if I had something to do in my life, some sort of effort I had to make everyday. I'm alright without it now, but if that woman passes, and I don't have anything, I don't know what will happen. I'm even afraid to think about it."

II.

In March 1977, somewhere around the time my work on unemployment began, the *London Times* ran a brief account of four deaths. Printed on the front page, the entire report consisted of six lines. It read: "A father, aged 30, and his three children were found dead yesterday in a car parked on the sea front at . . . A tube led from the exhaust pipe into the car. The father was unemployed or . . . " There was nothing more, no details, no further information, not that one was required. Still, the word unemployed caught one's eye. As detailed in the introduction it is often there, an innocuous term in the accounts of domestic violence, murder, arson, assault, suicide. Granted, many people are able to endure their unemployed status. Indeed, many in England in those days claimed that the dole may have turned out to be a better financial proposition for them than steady work. But clearly, others, as we have observed, are beaten down by months of being out of work. They strike out, against themselves, against others, and they collapse.[4] In Tony Gould and Joe Kenyon's words, they represent more stories from the dole queue.[5]

In London, where some of the preliminary research for this book was undertaken, as in the United States, unemployment must be examined against a background of a degree of poverty many people often overlook or never even know about.[6] London, like many large cities, has its form of closet poverty. Behind the lace curtains, as it is said, one finds a family living on or below the governmentally determined poverty line. According to a report prepared during those years by a Policy and Resources Committee chaired by Mr. Illtyd Harrington, Deputy Labour Leader of the Greater London Council, more that 25 percent of Greater London's 2.5 million families live below the so-called poverty level. Here are some precise statistics presented by Harrington.

First, 650,600 households subsist on incomes of 49 pounds or below per week, and this is for a three person family. Second, 200,000 men over the age of twenty-one earn less than forty pounds a week. Third, 250,000 pensioners receive supplementary benefits. Fourth, more than 150,000 people, apart from pensioners, require supplementary benefits.

The figures, shocking in their magnitude, must also be considered underestimations. As indicated earlier, statistics on the poor are likely to be the least accurate of all census statistics. The number and percentages of unemployed people are at best approximations. Yet even the approximations of unemployment figures appear disastrously high. Particular regions of England have always known cycles of unemployment. But cycles is the wrong word; why else would a West Yorkshire report use the term, "*chronic male unemployment.*"[7]

The statistics and facts of unemployment congeal as elementary sociology. As always, one is self-conscious about going over the same problems. Yet the same problems remain, or they get worse, and elaborate theories and elegant fact-finding committees fail to conceal the fundamental illness of chronic unemployment. What they typically do conceal, however, are the people, the chronically unemployed men and women, some of whom might admit that their lives sound to them a bit like elementary sociology.[8] Chloré Donane told me, in so many words, that the story of her husband Aaron, the man everyone called Bull, had begun to sound all too familiar, even to herself. In her years, Chloré had known too many Aaron Donanes. Chlore's account of almost a quarter of a century ago, would eventually launch my own work on unemployment. She is alive today and needs not one single reminder of the material presented here. She has forgotten not one detail of the story.

For almost ten years, Aaron Donane told his wife that if no job turned up, he would kill himself. The talk of suicide began on his fifty-fifth birthday, almost ten years to the day of his arrival in England from the West Indies. During the period following his residence in London, Aaron worked various jobs and went through a period of being unemployed. Then more jobs, then more unemployment. By the time he was fifty, he and his brother Walter were almost always out of work. Both had become angry and depressed. They needed one another badly, but their conversations invariably ended in bitter quarreling. Each apparently reminded the other of his own sadness, frustration, and sense of failure. Yet they cared for one another and had no one closer, not even their wives and children. For those who knew them or heard them fighting, especially when they had drunk too much, it almost seemed better that both were out of work. If one had been able to find a job and not the other, there was no telling what might have happened to their friendship. Their wives argued this point, insisting that a job for either one would have been far better than no jobs. Competition, the women agreed, may well lead to death. But unemployment practically guaranteed it!

Chloré Donane and her sister-in-law, Iris, loved each other as if they were sisters, although it was hardly this way in the beginning. Each admitted liking her husband's brother, but not his wife. Each felt, moreover, that it was her husband who was supporting his brother and his family. In fact both women were more than anxious about the emigration to England, but rather than find comfort in friendship, they found themselves competing. It was as though the fright and uneasiness about the move had turned into a contest, with each woman trying to show the other how much better her family would adjust. Although the Donane brothers never openly felt this way, there was no denying that they too might have led their lives in England along the lines of a contest. Gradually, however, the families recognized the importance of staying close in order to sustain the inevitable problems encountered during immigration. Out of their discussions grew a closeness on which all four people came to depend. Not a week went by when the families were not together. Realizing how badly the families needed one another, Aaron moved his family into a flat six streets away from his brother. For a while, the men even found jobs with the same firms, and there were no happier people in all of Brixton.

Then, one of the Donane brothers would lose his job, or both would be out of work, and a pall would set in on the two households. The children seemed uneasy, and Chloré and Iris would meet less often, and rarely with their husbands around. For it was no secret that both men, and especially Bull, became depressed when jobs were scarce. First he would appear sad, then, when his strength returned, he would go into fits of uncontrolled fury. "Look at me," he would yell at Chloré. "Forty-eight years old and what have I got! I got nothing. It's a waste, all of it, coming here, the plans, working, living, everything, it's a waste! Nobody can say it ain't. It's the biggest human waste anybody has ever seen! I don't give a good damn if a job comes up or not. They'd have to beg me to take it anyway. I'm not going out there scraping around on my hands and knees just to make a few quid. No more. It's all for younger men. You want more money coming into this home, you can work. I've had it up to here. It's all done and finished!"

Chloré knew that the best thing to do was keep her mouth shut tight and hope that the storm, as she called it, would pass quickly. She knew, too, that the angry periods would be followed by days of sadness, when Bull would stay in bed reading the same newspapers over and over again. Then, usually on a weekend, his spirits would lift, and although he wouldn't reveal his old confidence, Chloré could tell he was making plans to look for work. The only problem now would be to find something before the sadness and anger returned. So back he would go to the unemployment offices, retrieve his cards, and make his jokes about how he wouldn't be drawing his fabulous wealth of ten shillings the next week. Fortunately, he was usually able to find a position; he was back in business. The people in the employment office remembered Bull Donane as a kind man, a man of humor and passion. It hurt them to see him involved in employment situations which at best could last for no more than two or three months. But to these people he never complained. He told everyone he would rather be dead than play the game unethically. He had respect for the law, and he had pride in his nationality, his blackness, and his ability to work as hard as any man on any job. He bemoaned the state of being underemployed almost as much as the state of unemployment. He would tell Walter: "They forget when they give you a job they're giving a job to a person with eyes and ears, heart and muscle. They think we take anything that comes along and feel grateful. But they forget the heart and the muscle. They forget I have a brain just like them. But worst of all, they want to make *me* forget I have a brain. But I'll do it, because I'm going to work for them at any price rather than sit around and sit around and sit around. But I sure wish someone would tell me when they might get smart enough to think of ways where they could really use me. They shouldn't forget the eyes, the ears, the heart, the muscle and brain. What you drinking, brother of mine?"

Walter heard the references to death the same time Chloré did. Both were struck with the change in Bull's reactions to being unemployed. Of course he wasn't young any more, but fifty-five was hardly old, and Bull Donane, his brother knew from working with him, was as strong as when he was thirty-five. He would tell Bull, "Nobody's hiring people at fifty-five when they get kids damn near forty years younger. Hell, your own boy might be the one to put you out of work one of these days." Bull would smile at the thought of being replaced by young Julius. But then his eyes would grow moist and he would confide in his brother: "Maybe that's what kills me more than anything else. What the hell kind of father am I that my own kid can replace me and I got almost forty years experience on him? What the hell kind of business is that! I got no skill, I got no experience, I got nothing he can look up to. I did one thing in my life, I brought him here, or I got him born here. Can anybody call that an accomplishment?

Hey, man, the whole thing's a super waste. *I'm* a super waste, and the person who knows it best is my own boy. What the hell kind of security do I give him with me out of a job, or working situations he wouldn't even consider? You think he respects me? The hell he does. He tells his friends, my Dad had it tough. He protects me, *maybe*, but what's he really thinking? He thinks, some great bloke, my old man. Fifty-five and *when* he works, when he works, he takes away a few of the jobs kids ought to be working. Couple of months more, man, and they can bury me. I got too much pain to keep on like this."

Chloré was frightened by Aaron's increasing talk of suicide. Walter told her it was just words. Men speak that way when they get older and see jobs dwindling, especially men who cannot stand the idea of living on the dole. But Walter had to admit he too was worried by his brother's intense moods. Bull could go into deep depressions and vent anger with the best of them, but he always pulled out of it. Not only that, Bull had pride. He wouldn't be beaten by a bunch of employers for whom he had not the slightest respect.

Chloré always felt better after speaking with her in-laws. She would try to pull herself together and face her husband with renewed hope, but two minutes after being with him, Bull would start up about how he was going to get a gun and blow his brains out and if that made life hard on her and the children, then they'd just have to live with it. Besides, it was better to have a dead father than a depressed, unemployed man hanging around the house all day. How many more years did he have to live anyway? None, if he couldn't work, so why try to carry on just to make it through to that wonderful world of the dole and pensions? Let the people who really deserved their pensions live off them, he would tell Chloré. They earned it with their hands all their life, they're entitled. Later Bull would tell her:

"They had the same thoughts all those years like me. No one showed any special interest in them, but they never complained. They knew they were just doing whatever the hell they did because they had to. Never bitched, so they got it coming, all thirty pounds a week. All they're doing is getting back one millionth of what they put in, which puts them so far behind where they ought to be it's funny. Me, I'm going to give a nice little present to my country. I'm going to give my body to the Queen. She's going to get a nice pine box, and I'll write her a letter saying here's one person you don't have to make a pensioner so you can save forty quid a week. That ought to help the country a little bit, don't you think. Hell, maybe I'll be a model for people after all. Maybe they'll set up a statue to old Bull, the guy who invented a way to save the country millions of pounds. After all, these men go in and out of work all their lives, hey, kill themselves before they turn sixty and save the country all the money. Tell you something it would do: it would set me up as a nice model for my children. Don't you think, Chloré? Maybe I'd have a big statue of myself somewhere? Maybe in Battersea. All the people coming there on Saturdays and Sundays, walking around, looking up at this beautiful statue. 'Oh, yeah, that's the guy who killed himself and gave his body to the Queen and saved the country forty pounds a week. Great man, that Donane fellow. Must have wonderful children. Hey, the man was fifty-five. That's long enough for anybody to live, especially when you don't work for a living. Man had a bit of two lives: West Indies, England, man of the world. Must have led a beautiful life. Why else would they put a statue up to him. Must be like the King of Unemployment, you could say.'"

Then, surprisingly, this most frightening of moods dissipated, and Bull Donane found a part-time job with the local government office. It was one of the better situations he had ever known, and all talk of bleakness, hopelessness, and suicide vanished. Chloré, Walter, and Iris felt relieved, although none could forget the threats that had sounded so real only a few weeks before. The couples were again close, enjoying one another's company instead of merely needing one another for support. And spring was coming, which pleased them, as they had never adjusted well to the cold dampness of England's winters. About those few months, Chloré would say:

"We were all born again. Like everything bad was behind us. No one talked about mistakes, or how it could have been better. Everything was mellow like it's sort of supposed to be when you get to be our age. Best of all, nobody spoke about jobs, whether they were too hard or too easy, or whether people respected simple every day kind of work. We just ate a lot and drank a little bit too much too, and jabbered on about nothing, not that we didn't have a lot to talk about. We were sort of celebrating together. Like, we had all grown up. If things were going to be bad again, if Bull was going to lose his job again, it wasn't going to be any new kind of experience that we hadn't gone through a hundred times before. It was like we were all through feeling ashamed about what we were. From now on, the children could worry about what we'd worried about all our lives. We'd make do. A bit more money, a bit less money, we'd make do. Just being together's all that mattered, not having a job, or the right job according to the way you want to judge these things. Just being together mattered, because it meant we were all alive, and healthy, and even working has to come second to that. We took a lot of walks in Battersea at that time, too. I remember Bull didn't say nothing about that horrible statue idea of his. He didn't have to. I almost never thought about anything else when we went there. It got so I almost saw it standing there in one of the gardens. Bull saw it there too, he must have, even though I swear he was enjoying our celebrating as much as any of the rest of us."

According to Walter, Bull did indeed enjoy the celebrating. He wouldn't have said Bull was in the best of health during those days, but the man seemed happy. Walter, of course, could not forget the mention of suicide. He certainly thought long and hard about it the night the four of them had walked through Battersea Park and Bull, for no apparent reason, had asked him whether he had ever shot a rifle. "Never did," Walter answered dutifully. "Now, what you have in mind?" "Not a damn thing in the world, brother of mine," Bull had answered, with a peculiar air.

That is all that was said on the matter. Three days later Aaron Donane killed himself with a shot gun. He had been advised that his part-time job might be in jeopardy, although his boss told him not to worry. If he was to be made redundant, he would be given sufficient notice. The night of his death he told Chloré about the possibility of redundancy. But he promised her there would be no scenes, no bad moods, no talk of statues in Battersea. They both grinned. Then they embraced. They ate spare ribs that evening and drank dark beer. Forty-eight hours later, Aaron Bull Donane lay in a casket in a funeral parlor. He left his wife a note, the contents of which she has revealed to no one. Chloré said only that working regular meant a great deal to her husband.

III.

If there is one theme spawned by unemployment, or its pernicious relative, underemployment, it is that of human failure, or more precisely, the feeling that one is a failure. In a culture like ours, moreover, where material and public success signify the essence of the so-called American dream, to be unemployed or underemployed often becomes more than a man can sustain. This matter of literally being broken down by a systematic and codified set of expectations to succeed, was captured for me in a conversation with a man I came to call Jack "The Bomb" Blum.

It had been five years into my research with poor Jewish families.[9] Not surprisingly, most all of the people I met spoke of personal failure and its complicated connection to their being Jewish. How bitter it is, they would tell me, to have people say, "Jews are supposed to be successful," when that's all they think about day and night. Lots of families, it is said, have children cutting school, fathers out of work, mothers struggling in the house with chores that overwhelm the strongest of people, or working out of the home trying to earn money with their barely developed skills. They told of their depression, how they resented the fact that they always had to rely on others because reliance was a sign that they hadn't learned to manage life properly. They offered up elaborate sociological, political, and economic arguments for the existence of poverty, for the reasons really, that people like them struggled as they did. They advanced theories of how society forms, how poverty develops, but repeatedly I heard that ultimate determination about one's own personal sense of failure: It is *my* fault, *my* doing. "The culture forgets us, the society works against us, yet some of us make it through, and I should have been one of the ones who made it, not necessarily to the top, but certainly a long way from the bottom! Maybe the guy upstairs didn't have what it takes, but I did. Okay, not to be rich, but there's still a middle road, a place between making it big and ending up where I am."

These last words could very well represent the feelings of a great many people with whom I spoke, but in fact were uttered by Jack Blum, a man who looks considerably older than his forty-seven years. We spoke one evening in the hallway of his Boston apartment. It was dark in the hall, but not so dark that I couldn't see his face. There was no one who, in seeing what I saw, could have missed the bitterness and the hurt. Jack Blum looked like a man who had just lost a fight, and, in speaking about what he would do if he could manage a rematch, recognized he would do no better the second time. The thought of revenge only sickened him and added to his deep frustration:

"Now you add to all I've said the little gold star I got hanging 'round my neck. You just add that little bit of a reminder, and you know what you got? You got shame, man, like anybody could know it. I'm telling you this like I would talk in temple. When you're a Jew, man, you don't sit good with this sort of life position. A wife, a couple of kids, in and out of jobs. I'm not talking professions, I'm talking day-to-day survival. It's survival, baby. I can make the biggest federal case you're ever seen that survival is all there is, okay? What else is there but surviving, going to bed every night hoping, not even being assured, just hoping you'll get up healthy the next day. Survival's the game, but it don't wash. The Jews can preach all they want how their battle is just to survive, but there's not a Jew alive who's settling for survival. None of 'em!

"All right, you take your Nazi Germany period, you've got people teaching survival, that already makes sense. People going into death camps, they don't have much else on their minds. But today? Here? In this country a Jew talks survival, he's either got to be kidding or he's very, very, poor. We're supposed to have survival behind us, right? That's past stuff. We're supposed to be in the center of the society, economically fixed, set up so nobody can touch us. That's the way we muscled in, man, by being successful. If the game was money we out dealed them. If it took brain power, we came up with the brain power. If it took muscle, we gave 'em muscle. But that was what we needed, okay? But I ain't supposed to be where I am. We aren't supposed to be talking in this hall after finishing a couple beers. It isn't refined, it isn't Jewish. The whole scene here, the welfare clients, the unemployment, sick old people, that ain't supposed to be the Jewish scene. We're supposed to be the persecuted ones. Chosen and persecuted, right? That's us. People are supposed to know how bad we've got it and how we've been taking the short end of the stick for so long, but like this? You got to be kidding. This isn't for us. There's no *real* Jew lives like this.

"So what do you get when you add it up? I see a guy like myself, Jack Blum, average guy, average height, average build, average brain power, but no average Jew. I'm at the bottom and nobody likes it at the bottom. But okay, somebody's got to be at the bottom. You got a capitalistic system, somebody's going to the bottom. Poor people, all walks of life, ethnic types, Black, White, you don't make money, down to the bottom. Here's the real melting pot of this country. Look, look over here, if you can see anything in this goddamn light, the names on the buzzers. Greek, Italian, Jewish, Jewish, 'nother Italian. Used to be a Black guy here living with a Japanese chick. That's melting pot, everyone sloshing around at the bottom. But Jews aren't supposed to be here. Jewish people, non-Jewish people, they're all giving us the same look, You're a Jew, ain't ya? So what the hell you doing here? I thought all you guys were rich, okay?

"I'll go upstairs now, I don't know whether I got hot water. I don't know if I got heat. I got a kid ten years old, a kid thirteen years old, kids haven't slept one day of their lives in their own rooms. Melting pot. They don't sleep alone, and neither do any of their Greek, Italian, Irish, Black friends, and they got all kinds. What the hell kind of life is this for a man, a Jewish man, a non-Jewish man? This isn't living, it's dying. I ain't even at the level of *surviving*. I'm alive sure, you see me here, but the system's killing me off, okay? You say surviving, you mean *making* it. Somehow you got enough of whatever it takes to make it. But I don't. You can see that. You surely can *hear* it.

"All right, call me a conceited big shot, but I'll tell you, this is no position for a Jew. We've always had it tough, but how long's *that* supposed to go on! And suppose it goes on forever, why do I have it tough just because my father and grandfather had it tough? Couple thousand years of persecution isn't enough? My generation and my kid's generation has to have more of it? Another item: Jews are too smart to live like this. Other people, they're less exposed to things, less educated. Jews get a better education because they learn in the house. It's no wonder they put the pressure on their kids to grow up and be successful, because all their lives they're taught to be special, smarter. I'm smarter than the next guy I meet on the street. Okay? You want to call me conceited, fine, but I know, I talk to these guys. At work, in the employment lines, I talk, and I listen. These people don't think like I think. You ask them about their history, or what they got planned for the future, or what they'd plan if they got a break, it's thinner than what I think. You know what I mean by that, thinner? They don't have the depth or the detail. You hear it in the words they use. It's not *their* fault. They don't have our backgrounds, the experience that gets passed on.

"The way I see it, I pay an extra price over these guys. We all deserve better, but I'm prepared for things in a way they aren't. Everybody feels they're owed more than they got, but Jews deserve a little more because they've proved what they can do. You see what I'm driving at? I'm not content to be treated like I am because of my being a Jew. It makes me feel I can't be content living this kind of a life. All the Jews who made it big in this country no matter how they started out, they make me feel rotten. I'm talking about everybody, everybody Jewish who made it. It's like they're telling me, 'Hey, you down there, what's the matter with you? How come you're down there? You aren't supposed to be there. You're supposed to be up here.'

"So you tell me, how do I live with that? I don't. That's all, I don't survive. Okay? I'm alive, but I'm not living. I'm going nowhere so fast you can't even see me move. But I'm moving, to nowhere. And all these successful people are saying, 'Didn't I see you in temple?' I did, didn't I? So that means you're a Jew, yes? So what are you doing down there? You lost or something? Hey, you're sure you're Jewish? You didn't make a mistake or nothing?' Who do I blame? Myself? My wife? My parents? The country? The Nazis? Look at my situation and tell me, who do I blame? I blame myself, right? Who else do you blame? Who else does it make sense to blame? Maybe I should blame my kids? I blame me, right? What's the difference what anybody says? *I'm* the captain of the ship, right? I drown, it's my fault. That woman and those two kids upstairs in that cold apartment where I can't take a warm bath when I want to, they drown, that's also my fault. So maybe I'm also a murderer. Huh? You want to think about this thing that way? I kill me, my wife, and kids and they don't even know they're being murdered. They don't know where they're headed.

"Maybe one of the boys makes it when he grows up, and what does he say, 'Hey, dad, thanks for everything you did?' You think he's going to say that to me? He's going to say 'Hey, you, dad, what are you doing down there with all the other scum bums? You're supposed to be up here. Hey, if I made it you sure could make it.' Huh? Isn't that what he's going to say? You ask him now, he'll say he'll support me the rest of his life if he has to, but you catch him in twenty years. You'll see how he talks, like all the successful people of the world talk. And why shouldn't he talk that way? He's no different from all the rest of them. Listen, if he didn't talk that way, how would the rest of them know he was different? He keeps his mouth shut they might think he's just another bummy Jew boy. There aren't supposed to be murderers in our religion? They should only know.

"Go forget everything else I told you tonight; just remember this: I'm existing. That's what people say when they know they're living but they know they're not really alive. It ain't going to get any better. And the day I worry about is the day I lose all this anger. People say, Blum, you could make bombs with all the anger you got. They could call you Jack Bomb. That's fine, I *am* angry. I don't have the right? But the day that anger stops, like a motor, I'm dead. Kaput. Good-bye, Jack the Bomb Blum. That's the last day in temple for the Blum kid, the kid who was going to make it so big. No one had any special hopes for him, you understand, it was just that he was Jewish and Jewish guys aren't supposed to be just existing, they're supposed to be *living*!

"It's a sick joke. The anger shuts off, I see the world as it really is, they say *kadish* for me, the three people I got in the world, one of who probably won't make it to temple on time, my son Jessie, the younger one, he's always late, and they lower me six feet into the ground, and before they close the coffin, the rabbi leans over the grave, you know, and looks down at me, and he says, 'Hey Blum, what the hell you doing down there? That's for bums down there. You're supposed to be up here. Hey, maybe the *mensch* isn't Jewish. Maybe we just said *kadish* over some goddamn stranger.' I tell you the way I'm going, my own mother wouldn't like the idea of coming to the grave to identify me!"

NOTES

1. James Lynch, *The Broken Heart: The Medical Consequences of Loneliness* (New York: Basic Books, 1977).

2. On this point, see R. O. Hansson, M. S. Stroebe, and W. Stroebe, Eds., "Bereavement and Widowhood," *Journal of Social Issues 44* (1988): 3; and I. O. Glick, R. S. Weiss, and C. M. Parkes, *The First Year of Bereavement* (New York: Wiley, 1974).

3. Mihaly Csikszentmihalyi, *Creativity: Flow and the Psychology of Discovery and Invention* (New York: HarperCollins, 1996). See also R. L. Silver and C. B. Wortman, "Coping with Undesireable Life Events," in J. Garber and M. E. P. Seligman, Eds., *Human Helplessness: Theory and Applications* (New York: Academic Press, 1980).

4. On this point, see M. Bartley, "Research on Unemployment and Health in Great Britain," in D. Schwefel, P-G. Svensson, and H. Zollner, Eds., *Unemployment, Social Vulnerabilty, and Health in Europe* (New York: Spring 1987); J. Hayes and P. Nutman, *Understanding the Unemployed* (London: Tavistock, 1981); J. M. M. Hill, "The Psychological Impact of Unemployment" (New Society, January 1978), 118–20; P. R. Jackson and P. B. Warr, "Mental Health of Unemployed Men in Different Parts of England and Wales," *British Medical Journal 295* (1987): 525. In more general terms, see S. V. Kasl and S. Cobb, "Variability of Stress Effects Among Men Experiencing Job Loss," in L. Goldberger and S. Breznitz, Eds., *Handbook of Stress: Theoretical and Clinical Aspects.* (New York: The Free Press, 1982): 445–65.

5. T. Gould and J. Kenyon, *Stories from the Dole Queue* (London: Temple Smith, 1972).

6. On this point, see See D. Marsden and E. Duff, *Workless* (London: Pelican, 1975). See also P. B. Warr, "Reported Behavior Changes after Job Loss," *British Journal of Social Psychology 23* (1984): 271–75.

7. See D. Marsden and E. Duff, *op. cit.*

8. G. M. Breakwell, A. Collie, B. Harrison, and C. Popper, "Attitudes Toward the Unemployed: Effects of Threatened Identity," *British Journal of Social Psychology 23* (1984): 87–88.

9. Thomas J. Cottle, *Hidden Survivors: Portraits of Poor Jews in America* (Englewood Cliffs, NJ: Prentice Hall, 1980).

Chapter 8

After Unraveling, a Better Outcome: Gabriel Forman

No one teaches you how to handle the feeling of unraveling. Maybe that's insecurity taking hold of you, I don't know. Maybe that's the way all of us would feel if you take away the casing, which is work.

WORK AND IDENTIFICATION

The title of this book is intended to direct the focus on the worst-case scenarios of long-term unemployment. The purpose in these pages has been to focus attention on the lethal aspects of terminal unemployment. Clearly, the overwhelming majority of long-term unemployed people who struggle in the ways witnessed in the preceding chapters neither abandon their families nor end their lives. Yet the fact is that long-term unemployment has the potential literally to destroy people. Although this phrase may seem exaggerated, melodramatic even, we cannot forget that the premise of a man's mental representation of his own being is predicated on his work and career, and that this representation commences its formation early in childhood when he is asked the question: "What are you going to be when you grow up?" The dynamic conjoining work, the definition of self, with the formation of a worldview is part of the complex development of a child's life.[1]

Accordingly, we begin this chapter, one that focuses on a man whose life was altered, surely, but not permanently destroyed by long-term unemployment, by attempting to answer the question of how work and career come to be prominent components of a man's sense of self. Our discussion of this matter is continued in the following chapters.

Traditionally, the psychoanalytic argument has held that little boys begin to identify with their fathers after learning that their initial and seemingly natural identification with their mothers must somehow cease. Theoretically, it was argued that if this first and primary identification with the mother were perpetuated, it would lead the boy in the direction of culturally defined feminine identifications and enterprises.[2] In this regard, some theorists have suggested that girls may have it a mite easier developmentally, inasmuch as their original identifications may be pursued for a life time, whereas early in childhood, boys learn that they must break off their special psychological attachment to their mothers and reattach themselves to fathers who, again traditionally, were hardly available, much less emotionally accessible characters.[3] Psychoanalyst Ralph Greenson referred to this process of breaking away from the mother as "dis-identification."[4]

The "new" identification the boy made with his father was normally viewed as being complex and somewhat abstract not only because of the father's considerable absence from the home, but because the identification implied an incorporation into the outside (external) society. In contrast, an identification with the mother normally meant an attachment to family and hence (internal) activities of the home.[5] When a boy identified with his father (which in part means unconsciously believing he *is* his father, or at least identical to him), the boy necessarily is becoming indoctrinated into the ways of the world, ways that again find work and career at their center. When the boy proclaims, "I want to be like Daddy," he of course means big and strong, but even more, he means go to work like Daddy and have a career like Daddy,[6] and eventually develop mental representations of self and the world like Daddy.

From an early age, the boy is being socialized to fill the adult male or paternal roles that essentially involves the acts of procreation, providing for and protecting one's family. Together, these represent the cornerstones of the traditional father's role. But notice that only protection represents an activity a son might directly observe. Procreation and provision are implied, deduced. What the son does perceive, in traditional thinking anyway, is an ability to solve problems, think abstractly, get things done, take on others' problems as if they were one's own, rely on oneself, and take calculated risks, all qualities usually deriving directly from one's work. Traditionally, the emotions a boy witnessed in his father, typically anger and aloofness, if this does not sound stereotypical, stood in sharp contrast to the broader array of emotions observed in his mother who, significantly, revealed little self consciousness about her emotional displays. Care and vulnerability, cornerstones of the maternal role, typically were not observable in the traditional father's behavior.

In the end, much of a boy's identification with his father was partly abstract or imagined inasmuch as the boy had little idea of what it was precisely his father did when he went away to work. All he knew was that his father was somewhere in the world and that the reason for his absence was work. Without work, there would be no reason for a man to go in to the world; every boy knows this.[7] And many boys, like the young Frank McCourt, learned that if there were no work to be found, a father might not return home at all.[8]

Said differently, again in traditional psychological terms, a boy's identification with his father was essentially predicated neither on connection nor relationship, if by relationship we mean a psychological attachment to another person. Rather, it was more of a philosophical attachment to values, norms, principles, problems and solutions, activities, behaviors, status, and perhaps most important, moral constructs. In his seminal theory of the personality, Freud postulated that it was the father, not the mother, who represented the source of the superego, that part of the mind's structure devoted to the sense of conscience and ideal standards, the so-called ego ideal.[9] The harsher the father, the more well- (or over-) developed the superego. Significantly, morality seemed to emerge from the action of father as model rather than the daily involvements constituting the connection between or mutuality of father and son. Morality, moreover, meant (masculine) justice, not (feminine) care, hard-earned instrumental activity, not expressive or emotional mutuality.[10]

To repeat, making for the abstract nature of the son's identification with his father, was the father's extended absence from the family, and hence the son's inability to cognitively and psychologically comprehend the nature of work, when it was work that appeared to constitute father's identity. Society, in other words, characteristically assigned the task of solving abstract and typically impersonal problems to fathers, whereas mothers were meant to solve immediately real and highly personal ones. And so, not fully understanding this aspect of identity, the boy began to comprehend that problems and their solutions ineluctably take on somewhat abstract or remote qualities, not unlike the traditional father himself.

In traditional society, the remnants of which we continue to experience, a boy, it might be alleged, maintained a genuine relationship with his mother, but only an abstract conception of a relationship with his father. When the boy felt sad, he went to his mother who comforted him, but rarely to his father who presumably was less tolerant of emotional displays.[11] This differentiation reveals that the boy's feelings constituted part of the identification with his mother, but not, perhaps, an identification with his father. These particular feelings were part of (maternal) attachment and relationship, not (paternal) modeling and performance.[12] It was not only that the expression of emotions, like crying, was deemed feminine and hence inappropriate for boys, it was in addition that feelings do not belong in the context of the relationship with fathers; they simply were not part of the appropriate behavioral repertoire, nor acceptable as a component of the mature masculine personality. For a man to give into feelings was not only to reveal weakness, his feminine side as some still say, it was to admit to his need for or dependence on his mother, or on any relationship for that matter. In traditional terms, after all, men were taught not to seek ultimate solutions to problems in relationships. The traditional man did not speak to his wife about fright, insecurity, terror, anxiety, or any other emotion that might be associated, for example, with unemployment. Ultimate solutions to problems like not working were to be found outside of relationships. They were essentially impersonal problems to be resolved through (seemingly) impersonal measures.

A word about fright. In speaking with people generally, the issue of fright is frequently mentioned. Clearly, there are people who seem afraid of one part of their world or another, or afraid perhaps of merely being in the world. Something about their representations of the world, or of themselves more likely, causes them to feel afraid. It is not necessarily that they fear death lurking around every corner. Nor do they feel they will fail at opportunities offered them. Rather, it is their approach to living, their overall outlook, their worldview, that appears bathed in a fright born, perhaps, in the insecurity they carry with them from childhood.[13]

John Bowlby's work on attachment theory provides at least one perspective on these matters of insecurity and fright.[14] Studying the relationship, really the bonding between mothers and children, Bowlby theorized that attachment could take the form of security, ambivalence, or avoidance. In ambivalent attachment, a child is bonded to his mother, to be sure, but the quality of the bond yields an insecurity expressed in various forms of anxiety, unsuredness or lack of confidence. In avoidance attachment, one finds the insecurity or anxiety inherent in the bond emerging in the form of anger or what some have called narcissistic rage. On this point, Ernest Wolf wrote: Competitive or "mature aggression" is "directed at objects that stand in the way of cherished goals. Narcissistic rage, on the other hand, [is] directed at self-objects who threaten or have damaged the self."[15] One often observes this phenomenon, this typology of attachment, really, in adolescents who may convince others that they are "angrily self sufficient" or "stridently independent" when in truth they may be depressed, frightened, and insecure.

One antidote to fright is, of course, the job or career. Although normally we expect fright to surface in job interviews or confrontations with bosses, some of it is neutralized by job security. It is the job, typically, that causes other insecurities to recede, although presumably they will re-emerge if the job disappears, although this notion suggests the degree to which a man is able to compartmentalize features of his world and the emotions associated with them. Long-term unemployment brings forth a form of insecurity, especially in those people who have grown up in families where, in Bowlby's vernacular, the original attachments were ambivalent at best if not openly avoidant. One suspects, however, that terminal unemployment begins to attack even the securities formed in part by healthy attachments early in life. Surely, it begins to erode a man's ability to undertake the aforementioned compartmentalizing of activities and emotions.

It might be further alleged that emotional intelligence, said to involve the ability to identify as well as express emotions, develops in great measure through the identification with mother, an identification, it is further alleged, that must conclude somewhere between three and five years of age. We know that if one cannot express emotions and thereby feel comfortable in intimate circumstances, one inevitably lives in isolation, a theme found in many contemporary writings on masculinity.[16] Men are taught, after all, to be self sufficient—as if this were truly possible—again a trait, or at least an ideal, made possible in great measure through work. Without work, men are thrown back on to their feelings of helplessness and fright, emotions that can be neither felt nor expressed if one is to remain true to one's (traditional) masculine identifications.[17] Expressing anxiety about unemployment would be "unmanly." Even worse, women, theoretically the teachers of emotional expression and intimacy, would see through the anger and detect what the man hides beneath the surface: namely, help-lessness, insecurity, neediness, and fright. Interestingly, Jean Baker Miller pointed out that although men in Western culture are encouraged to deny feelings of weakness and helplessness, women actually are encouraged to cultivate this state.[18]

A boy reared in traditional society, therefore, pays a painful price for not being "allowed" to remain attached to his mother. The trauma—and some properly call it this—of detaching from her is felt by the child yet presumably mollified throughout the life cycle by the achievements gener-ated from work.[19] Here again, the notion of a man's capacity to compart-mentalize ostensibly works to quiet the anxieties and insecurities he may feel. Yet when he is unable to maintain the center of his existence, notably work, then theoretically, the original pain and fright are once again evoked, and the original narcissistic insult brought back his conscious world.

In many ways, this second (or secondary) narcissistic injury, unem-ployment, becomes almost too painful to bear, primarily because the fun-damental protection against it has been dismantled in the form of terminal unemployment. Making matters worse, men like George Wilkinson believed they had failed not only their fathers' teachings, but their fathers as well. They had failed, in other words, in the quintessential component of the original identification with their fathers. Yet there is something else to be observed here: namely, the inability to express the profound sadness that they felt not only from the loss of jobs, but from the reawakening of the original pain associated with the break from the mother, what Greenson called dis-identification. Unemployment hurls a man back on the very themes with which he felt uncomfortable as a child: dependency, sadness, fright, the need to be cared for, only now he is unable to express any of these sentiments and needs. To do so would be to once again become the boy. The primary protection, moreover, against such over-whelming feelings, namely, the capacity to compartmentalize, is dimin-ished if not wholly lost when work and career vanish.

What then does the unemployed man do? Exactly what we have discovered over these last chapters. To begin, he cannot allow himself to be perceived as a victim, although many would label him precisely this (and treat him as if he were), for this too, would be "unmanly." He finds himself lost, literally in a *no man's* land. Joblessness means he cannot consider himself a man; his desires for boyhood expressions of emotion and intimacy leave him perplexed, self-hating, and frightened. He becomes (to himself) almost a caricature of a man, exhibiting many of the stereotypic features of maleness and masculinity modern woman has come to dislike. Yet ironically, as William Pollock pointed out, these symptoms that so exasperate women may well be perceived as classical symptoms of post-traumatic stress. Surely, the terminally unemployed man reveals these symptoms, a matter explored in greater detail in the concluding chapter. For the moment, let us hold in mind that in the case of trauma, the feelings *and* the meanings associated with the event—long-term unemployment—become unbearable if not unspeakable.[20]

If Pollock's reasoning about masculine development is correct, the long-term unemployed man cannot express his fright to his wife essentially because he fears he will lose her. To understand this, we think again of the psychoanalytic model and the original identification of the boy with his mother. As a child, he did express every manner of emotion and feeling to her and look what *that* got him! So he grieves the loss of his job as well as the loss of his once idyllic attachment to his mother, barely able to live with the reality that for the first time in his life there has been no activity or work to substitute or compensate for feelings of sadness, fright, and loss, or perhaps just feelings.[21] Work, he learns—and we have heard this sentiment often in the previous chapters—was his primary protection, the basis of his ability to compartmentalize activities and emotions, his armor against wounds of all sorts, physical, spiritual, emotional. Until now, work had always healed what D. H. Lawrence called "the wounds to the soul."

The terminally unemployed man struggles because he believes that his legitimate place on the earth has been eclipsed, his one and only connection to life, albeit an apersonal one, has been shattered. He struggles, too, because in his mind he has lost any reason for being alive, and because long ago, through the normal evolution of identification, he lost "the right" to express to anyone the emotions he now feels so intensely. Finally, he struggles, as several of the men in this book have revealed, because he has learned of life's great mistakes. Ultimately, the very definitions of men's roles and maleness have failed him; the insidious construct of masculinity in which he has lived all these years proves to have no built-in safeguard against this sort of eventuality, this sort of loss, this sort of trauma. A man makes it, as his society (i.e., his father) planned for him to, for a man sees no way out of the tunnel of these paternally instilled expectations. It was expected in traditional society that his father would not openly express love for him; this was the unstated male understanding, an unwritten clause in the masculine social contract. Yet his father did honor the fact that someday when the boy grew up and went to work, and thereby truly became a man, he would earn what men earn: respect. Love, we recall, was not meant to be central to the relationship between father and son as it was between mother and son. If a father procreated, protected, and provided for his family, why, in addition, did he have to love them? Were not these activities themselves the embodiment of love?

The son, in contrast, recognizing an absence of love from his father, as compared to the sort of intimacy he once experienced with his mother, was left either to lie about successes or lack of them in school or work, or pretend to himself that he was not only admirable but *lovable* by dint of his academic and employment accomplishments. As long as feelings of sadness, loneliness, and fright were compartmentalized and thereby held in check, everything worked reasonably well, until, that is, long-term unemployment took hold of him. At that point, he was obliged to live with the unbearable burden not only of societal failure, which explicitly meant failing his father, but the recognition that he was unlovable. If dis-identification theory teaches us anything, it is that success in work, and with it the ability to procreate, provide and protect, substitutes for or constitutes a sense not only of masculine identity, but of esteem as well.[22] Success in work actually spawns the belief that one is caring, worthy of respect, and lovable.

Taking the argument one step further is to suggest that loss of work means loss of self. It is a process built into the life cycle that began at the time of the original dis-identification. If action, like working, evokes feelings, so too do memories, which means that all variety of emotions will come forth when (work) action ceases and never resumes. It would be lovely to suggest that in their "idleness," unemployed men could simply transform their identities and turn to the work of caring and loving, the so-called social welfare components of esteem. Many in fact are able to do just this, as the work of Mary Lynn Pulley illustrates.[23] Yet as Baker Miller pointed out, the act of caring appears as a luxury afforded traditional man only after he has fulfilled his primary requirements of manhood.[24] To be without work, however, is to fail these requirements and hence fail as a man. It is not surprising then, that in the traditionally masculine orientation, so many long-term unemployed men would continue to call the world unfair or unjust[25] rather than (in feminine terms) insensitive and uncaring.[26] It is too painful and difficult to move oneself from a morality defined by justice into a world and morality defined by care, or the lack of it, for this truly is the woman's world, and perhaps more precisely, the mother's world.[27]

Identification with parents has yet another significant implication for students of unemployment. When, in traditional theory, a boy essentially is taught that his identification must somehow switch from mother to father, he simultaneously learns that dependency (on mother) must give way to an incipient sense of independence (from mother *and* father). Thus, the move in identification actually may cause him to feel a sense of loss. It's a lovely (although unattainable) ideal to be self-sufficient and independent, but a child feels considerably safer depending on his or her parents. The traditional family nonetheless had fathers urging mothers not to overprotect or coddle the boy for fear of infantilizing or emasculating him,[28] or even worse, allowing him to remain in an essentially dependent mode of existence. Early on in psychoanalytic theory, one even discovered a notion that the overprotective mother who prevented the "proper" identification with the father might even cause the child to become homosexual.

If independence, especially from mother, was a primary goal of a male's developing identity, what better way to demonstrate and affirm it than by work and a rock-solid career? Is not the quintessential ingredient of independence self-employment? The phrases "going into the world to seek fame and fortune" and "making it on one's own" refer to a marriage of work and independence, or at least the end of reliance on parents. In contrast, unemployment leads directly back to dependence on wives, friends, the state, welfare, someone. For a man, the journey, life itself, perhaps, is over when work fails. From the men in this book we learn that the dependence caused by the ongoing struggle of terminal unemployment is unmasculine, not to mention unbearable. That traditionally, little boys may have desired to remain dependent on their mothers is assuredly true, but wanting, admitting, and acting are hardly identical, and so the fright of independence is silenced, perhaps repressed, although one suspects it often emerges as anger, outrage, repudiation, and cynicism.

There is, of course, an adaptive feature of anger, one we have observed in several of the accounts. Without it, ambition is almost impossible. Driving ambition is stoked by aggressiveness. It not only keeps the engines of a career grinding, it wards off nagging feelings of loneliness, sadness, and fright, not to mention the sense of abandonment inherent in dis-identification. Aggressiveness keeps one active, performing, action oriented, agentic, which in part means being able to compartmentalize activities and emotions and thereby withstand the rather empty feelings associated with having to postpone gratification.

WORK AND COPING

One question that keeps resurfacing in research of the effects on people of cataclysmic events is this: "Why is it that some men would be able to withstand the terror of very long-term unemployment, even rise above it, whereas others would be unable to make successful adaptations and even decide to end their lives?"[29] In more general terms, why does it appear, as the work of Gina O'Connell Higgins suggests, that some people reveal a greater resilience than others?[30] Although a fuller response to this question is addressed in chapter 10, which explores the nature of chronic trauma, a partial answer is found in the notion of an inborn inner strength or resiliency.

As studies conducted by Anthony as well as Kobasa and his colleagues indicated, many people are born with characteristically strong and hardy temperaments.[31] From the outset, they emerge as resilient people who appear to enjoy risking something of themselves in order to attain some job, occupational position, or even momentary gratification. They are people, moreover, who rarely seem to be stirred too much by serious setbacks or life's ineluctable obstacles and hardships. As for change, they may tell you they never worry all that much about it. If work plans shift and marriages end, they will of course experience strong emotional reactions, although nothing of the sort Peter Maris described in his work on change[32]; ultimately they will adjust and make do. Paraphrasing the title of William Bridges' useful book, I might note that they seem to know how to make sense of life's changes.[33] Conversely, if things remain as they are, that's fine too. One suspects that this resilient, although not necessarily stoic, group of people contemplates alterations in life patterns and destinies. They may even listen to astrologers speak to them of their futures, but they won't be unsettled if the news isn't what they wish to hear. More likely, they will go out and make news for themselves.

Other people, however, emerge early in their lives as more vulnerable and sensitive, not necessarily more caring—although this often is a concomitant of sensitivity—but more easily affected by rejection, hurt, and setback. Characteristically, it takes these people longer to get back on their feet after some temporary defeat. These well may be people who take fewer achievement risks and tend to play life a bit more closely to the vest. They may even prefer knowing that tomorrow will bring about the same experiences as today. One imagines that they don't like change or surprise all that much, but prefer instead to believe they are always able to see the paths of their lives unfolding.

To a certain extent, as the work of Richard Lazarus and Susan Folkman posited,[34] how one responds to serious events like a job layoff depends in part on how one appraises the situation. So-called cognitive appraisals, according to Lazarus and Folkman, fall into one of three categories. First, the person feels the event to be irrelevant. Second, it is seen as benign or even somewhat positive. Third, and most appropriate for understanding reactions to unemployment, the event is perceived as stressful, which in a sense means the person recognizes that he or she cannot adequately manage or respond. Not surprisingly, as Norman Feather wrote,[35] stress, a reaction to both individual and situational variables, is typically associated with emotions like fear, anger, and anxiety. This, in contrast to perceiving the event as a positive challenge as is observed in the writings of such authors as David Noer, Mary Lynn Pulley, and William Bridges.[36]

In somewhat similar conceptual terms, psychologist George Albee developed a model that helps one understand who might be resilient and who is at risk should an event such as long-term unemployment.[37] Risk, Albee postulated, can be seen as the final product of an equation. In the numerator of this equation are two components: *stress*, defined here as unemployment, plus *constitutional vulnerability*, or what has been referred to as inherent character. So the top line of the equation is represented by the components potentially causing trouble for a person: unemployment, coupled with the person's predisposition, generally, to deal with hardship.

The denominator, in contrast, is composed of four components that theoretically are meant to counteract or compensate for the pressures found in the numerator. The first component is what Albee called *competencies*, which can mean several things, including how good a person is at what he does and how good he is at finding work, for example, as well as his ability to deal with others in social situations. (Interestingly, it almost sounds as if the criteria of successful employment underwrote the dictionary's definition of *competence:* "Sufficient means for one's needs or for a comfortable existence.[38])

The denominator's second component is constituted of *coping skills,* which in the present context refer to a man's ability to deal with threatening situations and discouraging prospects.[39] In some respects, coping skills relate to what Feather called expectancy-value theory,[40] which, oversimplified, involves the manner in which people feel they can handle a particular situation coupled, significantly, with what they expect to be the outcome of their efforts. Thus, individual motivation marries with perceptions and belief systems to produce a value of expectancy. One sees immediately how complex this matter becomes when one considers all of the variables that enter into a person's thinking as he or she attempts to assess the outcome of a particular act, like looking for a job.

The dictionary's definition of *coping* may surprise some readers, for it turns out that coping is precisely what unemployed men *act out* in reaction to facing their employment crises.[41] Derived from the French word *couper,* meaning "to slash or to strike," *cope* is defined as "fighting or contending with." Not uncommonly, a man's first reaction to unemployment is to fight specifically against the news of his impending unemployment. Then he may fight the realities of his early days without work. Soon he is fighting his wife and children; management and employers; other workers, many of them friends; who have retained their jobs; successful people anywhere; and then the government and its failure to help the very men who, as they themselves would say, keep the engines of the country running. Finally, he fights (for) life itself, and the forces, seen and unseen, that have brought him to his presently unbearable situation.

Let me pause for a moment on this coping component in the risk equation. I recall several occasions when, unable to know what to say to various unemployed men, I found myself urging them to keep fighting and to somehow use the energy of their rage as a life force. Perhaps I imagined that I was boosting their "coping" abilities or reawakening some languishing life force. Keep in mind that these were men who once held steady jobs, maybe were entitled to two weeks of vacation a year, men who went back to the job the day after Christmas and perhaps the Friday after Thanksgiving. They were men who once had brought home good pay checks, most of the money going to their families, some of it being used to support elderly parents or parents-in-law or even a friend who might be "down on his luck" (yet another euphemism for being out of work).

They were also men who saw me as successful. I may not have been rich in their eyes, but at least I continued to make a living. When we separated after our conversations, they, presumably, continued to hang around the house while I went back to work. Unlike them, I had never stood for hours in unemployment lines, nor sat at desks opposite exhausted state workers, afraid and ashamed to meet their eyes, filling out scads of forms. I had never dressed up to meet with bankers about loans that probably would never be approved, nor received written rejections from scores of potential employers, if in fact they even responded at all. And finally, I wasn't obliged to answer the sort of questions that must have felt to them like a knife to the ribs:

"Hey, Fred, how come you're home? What'd you do, take early retirement?"

"Petey, you don't have to work? Somebody in your house hit the lottery? What, you got the wife working again?"

"Sam, don't be insulted, let me give you a little something. Come on, take it, it's last year's money. It's burning a hole in my pocket. It's called charity. You'd do it for me."

"What are you going to do, Brian, sit there doing nothing? The worst thing, believe me, is just sit there not moving. I know. I had an uncle once, didn't work for a helluva lot longer than you've been out of commission. Believe me, you don't move, you'll die sitting right there in that chair."

Hearing this last remark, Brian McShane, fifty-one years old and out of work for thirty-nine months—and he never stopped keeping track—looked at me and grinned. It was as if he wanted to say, "You see, Doc, this is what I have to put up with every day." In fact he did reply:

"Toonie O'Neill, meet Dr. Tom Cottle." Brian looked at me. "I've known Toonie forty years if I've known him a day. I was working pretty regular in those days. Hell, I was twelve years old. Life was filled with possibilities. Dr. Tom's studying guys like me, out-of-work guys, you know what I mean? Not like you, Toones. And he's got something important to tell you." Brian McShane winked in my direction as if to let me know, I hoped, that he really didn't perceive me as "studying" him. At least I hoped that this was what that wink had meant.

I rose from my chair and shook Toonie O'Neill's hand, which was broad and rough. "Tell him what, Mac?" I asked.

"Come on, you know. Tell him." He still wore that grin. Brian McShane was neither an old nor a close friend, but I knew him well enough to know how furious he had been made to feel by the suggestion that he should just get up out of his chair.

I looked at him quizzically and held my hands up as if to say, "I'm stumped."

"You're the doctor, Doc, so tell him. Tell him he hit the nail right on the head. Tell him the reason I don't get out of this chair is because there isn't a reason in the world good enough to get out of this chair. And if he's worried that I might die sitting in this chair, tell him he ain't more worried about it than I am. I *know* I'm going to die in this chair. Tell him, Doc, I *wanna* die in this chair. Tell him that's the way I'm *coping* with being unemployed. Tell him, he'll listen to you."

The third component in Albee's risk equation denominator is represented by *social supports*. This is a critical component, for irrespective of how strong and self-possessed an unemployed man believes himself to be—and few men care to admit they are neither—he is going to require a host of social supports. He may reject the admonitions and counsel of his wife, or brother or father, but if he is to make it psychologically during the long months of unemployment, some sort of support, perhaps in the form of group meetings, may be essential.

To say the least, this is hardly the course of action most unemployed men prefer, and certainly the course for which few have prepared. To be a man, after all, is to stand on one's own two feet, fight one's own battles, and depend on no one, particularly women! Doesn't a boy hear his father admonishing his mother for coddling her son, thereby keeping him from becoming a man? Does he not know every bromide about how real men don't cry on someone's shoulders, or how when the going gets tough, the tough get going? If nothing else, a man knows it is patently unmanly to break down, even reveal fear, or quit altogether.[42]

To recommend that a long-term unemployed man join a group of other unemployed people who, as it is said, are in his same boat, is normally met with some resistance; the reaction is not surprising. Indeed, this may be the quintessential ache of unemployment, that the utterly self-sufficient model of man and masculinity may have to be rejected and a new model advocating dependencies and reliance on social supports for the purpose of learning new life strategies and venting feelings—all of them sounding suspiciously feminine—may have to be instituted.[43]

Albee's fourth, and final, component meant to counteract stress is the *sense of power or control*. One can see how the ability to effect action, to be able to think and behave *agentically*,[44] which means to employ elements of the here-and-now to construct some end state later on is a fundamental part of a man's approach to living. Merely to believe that one possesses the power to effect results has a palpably beneficial effect. None of us wishes to believe that life is totally in the hands of our bosses or political leaders, or even the Fates. No one wishes to believe that we are helpless in any situation.[45] Even acknowledging the implausibility of certain acts, we wish to tempt destiny and see whether we can't reshape so-called preordained events.

No, that is not completely correct. To believe in personal power, to work to empower oneself, is to imagine that much of the future can be shaped; it is to believe that we have a say in outcomes. All of this, however, goes out the window when a man is told he is laid off and discovers that months, if not years later, little has changed. He has worked hard to improve his lot, sought every opportunity, pursued every lead, and still nothing has changed. In these months he learns a bitter lesson: namely, that all the personal effort and hard work in the world may come to nothing. The promises disappear along with the assumptions of what diligent and responsible effort were supposed to yield. He has come up empty handed, which means that he has lost not only his dignity, but the belief that once upon a time he had a bit of power, a capacity to shape the future, at least in his limited domain of work. Little wonder, then that recognizing they possess no power whatsoever, so many long-term unemployed men might in frustration turn to violent behavior.[46] Loss and mourning often make men furious and cause them to seek violence almost as compensation for the loss. If nothing else, the rush of rage temporarily blots out the depressive sensation of sadness.[47]

Although advanced by Albee in a different context, the components of power and control seem essential for understanding the plight of unemployed men. Understand that a sense of power and control theoretically is supposed to counteract the assault of the stresses created by unemployment. When a man says, "I'll manage, I'll find a way," he is drawing on some built-in mechanism driven in part by (a belief in his) personal power.[48] In effect, this belief represents the manner in which he attributes reasons for events occuring.[49] Yet his belief, no matter how constructed, may well be little more than an allusion of possessing power. No matter, for it can be argued that what matters to people psychologically is what they *believe* to be possible. Long-term unemployment, in other words, threatens entire systems of belief.

So now one asks, "What fuels this belief, this allusion?" Is it an accumulation of experiences in which a man has watched himself overcome the proverbial odds? Is it his capacity to compartmentalize activities and emotions? Or is it that aforementioned constitutional predisposition, an inborn optimism that somehow sustains him even as he acknowledges the difficult circumstances in which he finds himself? Either way, does he not have to experience some victories? Does he not have to feel uplifting experiences once in a while if only to reinforce the belief in his own sense of empowerment? More to the point of the work in this volume, how long do the faith, the allusion, the sense of personal power or agency last in the face of unemployment?[50] Three months? Six months? Two years?

We are about to balance the books somewhat by presenting an account where luck changed, fortunes turned, as they say, and a man got back on track and resumed earning his living after a lengthy period of joblessness. Something to note, however, in the account of Gabriel Forman, is that even men with optimistic outlooks can get battered down by prolonged periods of unemployment. These men, too, can become consumed by every facet, rational and irrational, of being out of work. One can practically observe these men even psychologically imploding until at last the cure for their malaise arrives in the form of good and steady work.

The resilient ones, like Gabriel Forman, often find other jobs if not too much time elapses since their original layoff. In the meantime, their spirits appear to hold up. Finding succorance in their family, church, clubs, or informal friendship networks, they hold on. In this instance, the equation's denominator is sufficiently high to substantially reduce the risk factor.

Notice, however, that even in this one story, a fundamental discovery in unemployment research continues to hold true: Once people are out of work for a lengthy period of time, it is rare that they ever get back into job situations comparable to the ones they held at the time of their original layoff. In most cases, job satisfaction is less in the new job, and salaries normally fall below the level of the previous job. It is common, furthermore, even with new work in hand, for careers (and lives) to be permanently altered, if not scarred. New jobs may be obtained, but the damage to career progression and status may be irreparable, although, as David Noer reported, many men do survive the initial trauma of being layed off, some of them even reporting a renewed strength of the sort they never before experienced.[51] In the clearly happier account we now encounter, we nonetheless hear the familiar themes of discouragement, despair, and fright that typically are associated with unemployment, and that social scientists have been examining for years.[52]

By all accounts, Gabriel Forman came from a complicated if not unhappy background. His parents were products of their time, both of them believing it was a woman's job to stay home and care for children, a responsibility Gabriel's mother, Margaret, believed in, but never fully enjoyed. It was clear to her three children that she would have preferred pursuing a career to staying home washing dishes, cleaning floors, and chauffeuring children. According to Gabriel and both his sisters, Margaret Forman resented parent–teacher conferences, which, with three children, seemed unrelenting. As a child, Gabriel dreaded these conferences, fearing they would result in his mother and teachers finding fault with him. As an adult, Gabriel was able to recognize that his mother's resentment derived mainly from her fear that teachers might see through her facade of happiness and discover her dissatisfactions, even her depression.

In contrast, by all descriptions, Gabriel's father, Howard, was a kindly if not submissive man. He accepted his wife's anger, tried to soothe her as best he could, but recognized that the most efficient solution for him, although not necessarily for the children, was to spend more time at work and in his basement wood-working shop. As a result of this avoidant behavior, Gabriel learned, albeit unconsciously, that work not only is a man's preeminent responsibility but carries with it the additional value of removing people from painful circumstances, like unhappy spouses.

Never one to enjoy school, Gabriel nevertheless did his best to succeed in the classroom, not that his best was ever outstanding. His father urged him to do better. Every semester the same admonishments from his father, the same promises to turn over new leaves from the son. Margaret appeared to be quitting on the boy. By his junior year of high school, she seemed reconciled to the idea that Gabriel would never be the scholar she hoped for and even began to doubt that he would gain admission to college. Gabriel's acceptance two years later to the local city college did little to change her assessments of her son. Hopefully he would earn a diploma, but then what?

In fact, the "then what?" turned out to be far better than anyone in the Forman family ever imagined, although Howard never lost faith in any of his children. After graduation, Gabriel found a job in a local department store and within a few years moved up to an assistant and then a senior buyer. Although he never loved the business, his progress was steady and his position sufficiently significant that his mother began seeing him in a new light. As the years went on, it was Gabriel's steady career advancement that seemed to lift her long-standing depression and what Gabriel called her self-absorption.

By the time he reached his early thirties, Gabriel had switched positions several times and now was one of the computer experts in the corporation that had purchased the store in which he had worked since graduation. By taking courses, he had attained a proficiency in computers and was quickly placed in computer research, a relatively new division for the corporation. This, in turn, led to positions in three different computer companies, where his expertise in sales always put him near the head of the pack.

By the time he reached his forties, Gabriel Forman was married with two children, lived in a lovely home in a suburban community, and surprisingly, had grown close to both his parents, Margaret having lost much of the bitterness that always accompanied full-time parenting. With almost no parental responsibilities, her anxiety lessened and she looked forward to visits with her children and grandchildren, of which there were many.

And so it would go, Gabriel assumed, for the rest of his life. He had pledged to father better than he had been fathered, which meant spending more time with his children, but he knew that he could never be more generous than his father had been. He also had avoided the mistake his father had made: namely, marrying a bitter and unhappy woman. Gabriel's wife, Helen, was a gem. Upbeat, optimistic, secure, she made the Forman house a happy one, something one could detect in the behavior of her children.

Then suddenly, although not without warning, because the signs were everywhere, the corporation began to fail. Businesses it owned were losing money, people were being laid off, first in distant departments that would not affect Gabriel's division, and then ominously closer. In time, Gabriel received the infamous phone call to report to his senior manager. He was convinced she would be firing him. To his amazement, the meeting was held merely to announce that she had been released from the firm and that all those under her, some fifteen men and women, had better prepare themselves, whatever that meant. The company would provide counseling and advice, but they best begin pulling in whatever outstanding chits they had accumulated.

"In that moment," Gabriel would say years later, "I saw everything in my life crumbling. I had felt secure in that job, secure in myself, but in the beat of a heart I saw it flying away like it was never there in the first place. It's like a string that holds a motor together, and the man says, 'I know it looks flimsy but it'll hold beyond the life of your car.' You know that line? Well, it broke and the motor blew up in my face."

"What made it all the more difficult was that the job held me together. I never would have said that before. I would have said my father had always believed in me. My mother was a bit of a case for a shrink, what with her anger and depression all the time, but everything was going to be made perfect by Helen. And I don't say that without recognizing that I was a good father. I went to games, I went to parent–teacher conferences, and you know my feelings about *them*. Helen was much better at it; she had more time, but I made that possible so that counts in the good-father ledger, right? But when the job went, it all began to unravel."

Unravel, it turns out, is the appropriate word. There was some switching from one department to another in an effort to hold onto this valued employee. Gabriel, after all, had been associated with the parent company and the original department store for almost twenty-five years. But eventually there was nothing, and on that fatal Friday in May, Gabriel packed up his few belongings and left his office for the last time. His secretary, Mindy Rainer, watched with horror and fright. Tears rolled down her cheeks and she practically fell apart when he presented her a wicker basket of flowers, a token of appreciation. Mindy herself had been fired two months earlier, but she insisted on being with Gabriel on his last day. Neither of them could believe it was happening.

"Irreal, unreal, I wouldn't know what to call it. I believed with all of my heart that one of the two hundred or so calls I made would bring me back into something before the benefits ran out. Had to be. I wasn't dumb, I knew the economic problems in the country, especially this region, but no one could convince me there were no jobs. Take a little cut in pay? I can live with that. Take a little cut in status? I can live with that too. One college tuition on the table and another coming up in a couple of years, we'll make it. I even sat there at the dining room table running numbers, figuring out how the mortgage payments were going to go, and about refinancing this and that. I took the bills for the last five or six years and tried to figure how inflation was going to factor into the whole thing. I was dead certain we could make it. Brother was I wrong!"

Among the factors Gabriel never calculated at his dining room table were the feelings of self-esteem, or more likely the drop in it, and the sensation he described as mourning that took hold of him over the next two and a half years. For it took that long before he achieved a position offering him some security. The feelings he recounted during this period fall close to the notions of self-esteem and mourning offered by the psychoanalyst Peter Blos, although Blos offered these words in the context of adolescent development: "The ego develops the capacity to secure on the basis of realistic achievement that amount of narcissistic supply which is essential for the maintenance of self esteem."[53]

Said simply, Blos suggested that for a person to feel the so-called proper amount of energy or healthy self-love, realistic achievement is required. Your mother and father can make you feel good about yourself merely by loving you and allowing you to take their love into yourself and transform it into the felt sense of self-love. But without realistic achievement and competence, the process is made difficult, to say the least.[54] If teenagers experience this, then so too do terminally unemployed people. The energy of self-love is hard to fetch or secure when realistic achievement, defined as steady work and periodic accomplishment, remain unattainable. Gabriel described the experience this way:

"I hated myself during that period. Not so much in the beginning when there was money coming in. Helen said little. She kept encouraging me, even when I went through this somewhat manic phase where I decided I would set up my own business. For two months we rearranged the house so I could have an office. I was going to be another one of the world's great computer consultants. I even talked about the idea of getting into high schools and teaching kids computers. Fat chance, getting a teaching job without my own *real* job. I could have advised the kids about unemployment. What's the expression, people who can, do, and those who can't, teach. Because they can't find a job!

"I had it all in that office. Phones, fax, the latest equipment, three different desks and matching lamps. Helen redid the curtains. No more guest room, hello, another one of America's consultants. You know what it takes to make all of those calls? 'Jimbo, if you hear of anything please call. Yeah, we can do lunch and golf and tennis and horseback riding.' What the hell. I can't afford any of those things, so why the hell not! Can anyone imagine what it's like selling yourself to people when you haven't got the credentials and everyone knows you're out of work and barely clawing your way back. You go days not making one call. You can't find the strength to pick up the phone and dial the number. Do you believe that! The act of making a phone call, the fright of it, that someone is about to see right through you and offer up these kindly words and probably tell himself how lucky he is not to be in your shoes, you can't imagine it. Or standing in line at the employment office and seeing the same people week after week, month after month, telling yourself you deserve it, you earned it, or you don't deserve it but you dread the day when the benefits run out. Then you think about all the benefits that are going down the tubes, like health insurance. You know how degrading that is? I lived my life a million miles from that stuff. But I was there for the handout, smiling at the people, making them think none of this was getting to me, and inside, I tell you, I was unraveling."

Gabriel Forman was experiencing the feeling of mourning. Several days a week he drove around the communities beyond his suburban town looking for little cemeteries where he could do stone rubbings, something to which his oldest sister had introduced him when they were teenagers. It was an activity he once found utterly foolish. Now, he might start out in the morning to pay a visit to a former colleague or potential employer, but more often than not he made his way to the cemeteries, finding them comforting spots and occasionally doing his rubbings, which he rarely showed anyone.

"That wasn't a hobby," he explained, "that was a sickness, a preparation for feelings I never wanted to admit I could ever conjure up. I figured, keep on rubbing, it beats the alternative. Can you imagine if Helen or the kids had ever found out about it! I was in love with Helen, but I knew that I'd lost something just as valuable, and if I couldn't replace Helen, if God forbid it ever came to that, I couldn't believe that I was unable to replace work. I couldn't believe this was going on. It was totally unreal."

Adding to the sensation of unemployment as something unreal was Gabriel's nagging feeling of his life unraveling. Years later he could look back and see that whatever he had used to construct a sense of identity had become hopelessly irrelevant. It had always been his career that anchored his sense of self. He hadn't recognized the feeling early in his work history, but without a career, without genuine responsibility, he lost his sense of identity and with it, not ironically, a sense of freedom.

This notion too is familiar to students of psychology and once again finds some of its roots in theories of adolescent development.[55] Along with other psychologists, David Elkind has described teenagers constructing a sense of self through a series of acts that find their meaning in the various contracts adolescents make with their parents or the society at large.[56] If the adolescent behaves responsibly, then freedom may be achieved. But responsibility itself requires a consistent sense of self as well as a notion of how relations with peers must develop. Without the freedom–responsibility contract, Elkind has alleged, adolescents achieve essentially false freedoms inasmuch as they are not properly earned through acts of genuine responsibility.

Thus it went for Gabriel Forman as well. During his hardest times, he expressed sentiments about not deserving to have anything, be anything, hold any role like husband or father. He found the concept of a responsibility–freedom contract perfectly logical:

"How can you be free when you haven't got a single responsibility to your name! I'm worse than a prisoner. I couldn't give advice away. Like the old expression, I couldn't get arrested if I tried. Maybe I had an arrested development, someone with three desks going nowhere. Amazingly, you always think people are totally aware of your circumstances. I'd imagine people looking at me the same way they did when I was in high school. See that guy over there all dressed up, you know damn well he's out looking for a job. That's a once-rich guy out of work! Then you start imagining audiences; they're there even when they're not there. Invisible people are looking at you, wondering why you even have the right to walk around. Aren't you supposed to be locked up somewhere? In a jail, or in an office?"

From Elkind's work we derive another notion applicable to men like Gabriel Forman. During the identity crisis of the adolescent years, it is likely, Elkind suggested, that one reacts to the anxiety caused by not yet having achieved a settled identity by making premature choices or merely drifting about aimlessly. The image of the proverbial aimless teenager unable to make a single good or responsible choice is hardly uncommon. Now a man approaching his fifties, Gabriel laughs at the choices he made during the hardest times. When the money had just about run out, he was looking for dishwashing, delivery, or sales jobs, any port in a tumultuous storm. When these jobs fell away or he couldn't take the humiliation of them anymore, he retreated back to the cemeteries, even in the middle of winter. We actually met once sitting in a snow bank in a small New Hampshire cemetery, where Gabriel spoke of his intolerance of everything and everyone:

"I hate everything: myself, this country, the idea that corporations screw people, that they call it downsizing or reduction in force rather than 'Buster, you're fired!' I hate them all and can't seem to gain control over it. I know I'm stereotyping. Helen, bless her, listens, but I can't take her tolerance much more either. Even as I'm doing it I know it's a defense against my sense of failure, this fat face of failure. I know I feel these things to protect myself, but I don't know how else to do it. I tell myself, they weren't loyal to me so how can I be loyal to anyone! Then I wonder, what the hell has loyalty got to do with it? It's like I'm a teenager joining a club and everything's based on who's loyal to who. Once they let you out of the club, you unravel and you stereotype and cry poor, and then become poor. I don't know anymore what to do with any of the feelings. I don't know what in God's name is the purpose of telling anyone anything. It makes them feel lousy, it makes me feel lousy, but I can't get on top of it. It's like my immune system has failed. I've got work AIDS, you know what I mean? I just know I'd rather be out here freezing than sitting someplace warm where I have to pretend I'm in good shape, all warm and fuzzy inside. Can you get any of this?"

Because of my research, I occasionally attended conferences devoted to issues of work as well as job fairs, where people come to seek employment. Put on by well-meaning and helpful people, job fairs offer a podium for professionals offering all sorts of advice and even better, leads to workers whose eyes tell the story of their discouragement. Normally attended by corporate types, job fairs are a constant reminder that the illness of long-term unemployment, what David Noer and others refer to as a survivors' syndrome,[57] is found in all sectors of the culture. At every event, one hears the sentiment that losing jobs often means never plugging back in.

At one such job fair held outside Boston in a rather swanky suburban lodge, actually, I spotted Gabriel working the room, as they say, taking business cards from people and generously offering his own. The exchange of business cards at job fairs almost replaces the ritual of shaking hands. An exchange of name and address, after all, might garner one a coveted position.

Gabriel always felt uncomfortable at these affairs. He claimed lectures by experts were helpful in maintaining his spirits, but one could see his mood decline within hours of leaving a conference. In one moment he might feel comforted by having spoken with someone who, irrespective of the bravura and optimism, clearly was in the same discouraged boat as he. He even drew strength, albeit perversely, from the fact that others hid their pain so poorly. What sickened him was the pathetic sort of competition he felt among the men, all of them making efforts to present (or package) themselves as psychologically together, and acting as if they attended job fairs merely to pick up an interesting tidbit here or there.

"Why the hell don't they just say it flat out? They're desperate. *I'm* desperate. It'd be better if someone stood up there and said, 'Would the people in this room who aren't at the end of their rope please leave! But before you go, why don't you just admit to the rest of us that you don't have the guts to admit it!'"

I often imagined the men attending these fairs as former athletes convening to celebrate a championship season years before, but none ready to admit they had lost most of their skills, and certainly unwilling to acknowledge that today's athletes are superior to their predecessors. The parallel, of course, is completely unfounded, for the men convening at job fairs have lost none of their skills and may actually be superior to the new crop of workers. Gabriel saw the fairs as high school reunions where no one was willing to admit he had become the failure everyone predicted he would become thirty or forty years before. "No, that's not right," he corrected himself. "They can't admit that the predictions that they would be great successes hadn't panned out. So they lie and pass themselves off as people who just happened to be in the neighborhood and heard there was an interesting program going on, so, hey, why not? Fact is, there isn't much to lose in these meetings. You've already experienced the big loss. So, maybe one of those fancy business cards with the letters embossed, never printed, mind you, because that's a total giveaway, will land you the lottery."

And then, surprise of all surprises, one business card did exactly that for Gabriel, although it took almost eight months for the job to materialize. The details were not all that dramatic. A man gave Gabriel a card and wrote a note on the back for Gabriel to give to the man's former college roommate who, with colleagues, was starting a small computer company. The financing was precarious at best, and Gabriel at the outset would work strictly on commission. It was hardly an offer sent from heaven; Gabriel could barely tolerate the insult of commission work, but he took the card, just as knew he would take the work if offered. After a series of telephone calls, he made a lunch date, not with the man whose name appeared on the card but a considerably younger man.

"A *considerably* younger man. I won't say I saw myself as a kid when we sat down," Gabriel reported several days after the meeting. "But there was a rippling of feelings sitting down with a guy, a kid, who saw through the whole thing. You could feel it like you could feel the silverware. All right, he's got to be thinking, this guy Forman has some experience, some knowledge, hey, he may even have some talent. But why's he out of work so long? Three months, I can understand that. But what's behind this two-years business? What's the line on this guy that nobody wants him? Guys have been laid off, but two years? Guy must have been in prison or something."

The commission job did materialize and, with it, some ancillary consulting work, because one of the new accounts, fortuitously, was with a moderate-size department store, which in time allowed Gabriel to become associated with the directors of a shopping mall. The work was hardly what he might have wished for, but he knew better than to complain. Although he daily uttered that phrase "beggars can't be choosers," Gabriel was back in business. "Well, just about," he would always say. "I'm just not in the business I thought was my business. I'm not back on what anyone would call a promising *career* path. But I've got places to go every morning. I'm not up all night at the dining room table. I'm not doing stone rubbings. That's got to tell you something, right? I've just got to keep going and hope that those two and half years don't come back, and then reevaluate nothing short of everything in my life."

The physical adjustment to once again getting up and going to work was pleasurable enough for this man now edging toward his fifty-third birthday. Long ago he had shed all vestiges of pride. "You take what you can get" was his motto, although occasionally it was said with a bitterness he recognized as sounding like his mother, for Gabriel continued to come upon less talented people in far more secure positions. Still, he knew better now, he claimed, than to construct his identity around a career. "Take the easy route," he cautioned. "Find a way to keep money in your pocket and let the big boys deal with real careers." It was evident that he never totally recovered from the loss of his original career identity. The new work was not able to help him fashion an acceptable sense of himself at middle age as the old work had. Feeling like a man wearing someone else's clothes, he sought to explain the difficulty of adjusting to new people, new strategies for work, but it was the discontinuity, the hiatus from work, that continued to trouble him. We both recognized his fear of jinxing himself by saying anything negative about any work, any career.

Now, some three years after assuming his new responsibilities, Gabriel seems happy enough and works hard convincing himself that employment is merely a process by which a man puts food on the table and gets the monthly bills paid. The old house is gone; the Formans now live in a pleasant, two-bedroom sunlit apartment, their daughters sharing a room. It's a far cry, he invariably says, from the old three-bedroom house with the cozy room off the kitchen leading to the deck and stone patio beyond, the patio that Gabriel and his father built one summer. Now it's barbecuing on a little balcony, but that's all right. It's all right, too, that private colleges are no longer in the running for his children, unless of course admissions officers take a charitable view of his income. Then again, he dreads the infamous financial forms that potential scholarship students must complete. Every number, he feels, would be a reminder of the hard times and the better but not best times that followed. Still, it could be worse. It already has been worse, he reminds himself. It could be worse again, which he dreads, and he knows the numbers are against him. Once out, hard to get back in to the same cushy seat as before. Out a second time and you may go without a seat altogether.

"The musical chairs of work still have me in the game. The music plays, we run around, the music stops and I dive for a chair. Took me two and half years to find this last one, I don't want the music to stop again. I'm only fifty-two, but pretty soon they'll take all the chairs away. Then what? That's the part I don't want to think about. Hover over me? Somedays. I worked on a wonderful project a few months back and truthfully never even thought about the old days. Never thought about my parents, Helen, the kids in those ways, you know . . ."

Interestingly, the return to work frequently caused this kindly man to think again of his childhood and the early days of launching a career. To be sure, there were hundreds of hours spent in the refashioned home office, where there wasn't much to do but think of such things. It surprised him that he reflected so often on his mother and what he called her "anti-maternal ways." He once had reached a point of blaming her for his failure. Of course she had nothing to do with downward turns in the economy and ill-advised decisions by the managers of his old corporation, but it was her being, he concluded, that caused him to be so frightened in the face of job loss. Had she genuinely believed in and loved her children, and made them feel secure, he could have come through the ordeal much more easily and perhaps have found employment sooner.

This became a constant image for him during the years of his own hardest times. Security, in work and in one's mind, was the critical concept, that and not being afraid to go look for work, make the phone calls, tell people the truth of everything that had happened, and not feel humiliated or self blaming, as Katherine Newman and Kathryn Marie Dudley described in their remarkable research,[58] particularly in the face of conversations with people twenty years one's junior who didn't have the faintest idea of what lies out there in their own futures. "Should the process begin all over again," Gabriel confided not that long ago actually, "I think I'd do it better. I think I could sustain the blows, you know, like a seasoned boxer. Take 'em on the arms and shoulders instead of the chin."

"But what about the connection with your mother?" I wondered, as we drove around his old neighborhood. With a newfound hopefulness, Gabriel had begun to contemplate purchasing another house.

"You liked that notion, didn't you, doctor? The shrink in you gets excited with that stuff. I'm not sure I need that idea anymore. My mother has changed. She was frightened as a mother of young children. She did a terrible number on one of my sisters; we all recognize that. Whenever Joannie tells my mother a problem she's having, my mother always says, 'It's my fault. I didn't do a good job when you guys were little.' I'm not sure that does Joannie much good, but it's better than it was in the old days. She did make us all scared, and sons don't know how to be scared and still be men. You know what I mean? She made me scared, not of my own shadow, but scared sometimes just to go out and do business.

"But when I look back on it from the standpoint of being back at work, I don't think it holds true. I think the knife cut to my security was all due to the job loss. You don't like to admit you see it in the mirror. You tell yourself you've never looked better. But you see it like a doctor in everyone else's face. You've been to those job fairs. People look pale, tired. But tired from what? From making three calls on Wednesday and two more on Friday, since you have to rest on Thursday from all the phone calls from Wednesday. My manager that fatal Friday, when she told us she was leaving, she looked like she had three days to live. You see it in the lines at the unemployment center. Pale people. Now *they're* scared, as if I wasn't when I stood with them. I think sometime I ought to go back there and tell those guys, I made it, stick with it, you'll make it too. I'd never do it, it'd kill me. I think very truly it would kill me.

"So, no, it wasn't my mother, who, incidentally, wasn't all that bad during those years when I had nothing. She didn't exactly radiate faith, mind you; it was probably better that I didn't see all that much of her because she was frightened for me, justifiably, but it was never her. It was me. No, it wasn't me either, it was being out of work. No one teaches you how to handle the feeling of unraveling. Maybe that's insecurity taking hold of you, I don't know. Maybe that's the way all of us would feel if you take away the casing, which is work. You rip open my body and the guts come out. That's not insecurity on the part of my insides, that's proof that all the delicate stuff inside needs protection, and maintenance.

"Cars don't fall apart from insecurity. They fall apart because they aren't being maintained. My maintenance, and I suspect a lot of other men's maintenance, is a good career. You don't have to love it, you just have to know it's there, like a car in the garage. It's there, night or day, ready to go. Career is regular lube jobs, oil changes, tire alignments, proper gas levels. That's what they call security twenty-four seven. You don't need a mother to run your car. And you sure as hell don't need her to run your life when you reach the age of thirty or forty or fifty. Nice work will do it for you every time. Just get up in the morning and it starts. And you start right along with it."

NOTES

1. For a discussion of so-called normal family development, see F. Walsh, "Conceptualizations of Normal Family Functionin," in F. Walsh, Ed., *Normal Family Process* (New York: Guilford, 1982); and K. Kreppner and R. M. Lerner, *Family Systems and Life Span Development* (Hillsdale, NJ: Lawrence Erlbaum Associates, 1989). See as well M. Rosenberg, *Conceiving the Self* (New York: Basic Books, 1979); and "The Self-Concept: Social Pruduct and Social Force" in M. Rosenberg and R. H. Turner, Eds., *Social Psychology: Sociological Perspectives* (New York: Basic Books, 1981).

2. On this and related points, see E. Goldstein, "The Ego and Its Functions," in *Ego Psychology and Social Work* (New York: The Free Press,

1984); A. J. Horner, "The Unconscious and the Archeology of Human Relationships" in R. Stern, Ed., *Theories of the Unconscious and the Self* (Hillsdale, NJ: The Analytic Press, 1987); M. H. Erdelyi, *Psychoanalysis: Freud's Cognitive Psychology* (New York: W. H. Freeman, 1985); and Peter Blos, *On Adolescence: A Psychoanalytic Interpretation* (New York: The Free Press, 1962).

3. See W. Pollack, *Real Boys: Rescuing Our Sons from the Myths of Boyhood* (New York: Random House, 1998); and W. Pollock and R. Levant, Eds., *A New Psychology of Men* (New York: Basic Books, 1995).

4. See R. R. Greenson, *Explorations in Psychoanalysis* (New York: International Universities Press, 1978). Traditional psychoanalysis founded much of its theory about male development on notions of separation (from mother), identification (presumably with father), and then ultimate individuation.

5. On this point, see C. L. Shannon, *The Politics of the Family* (New York: Peter Lang, 1989); S. A. Beebe and J. T. Masterson, *Family Talk* (New York: Random House, 1986); and M. Walters, B. Carter, P. Papp, and O. Silverstein, "Toward a Feminist Perspective in Family Therapy," in *The Invisible Web: Gender Patterns in Family Relationships* (New York: Guilford Press, 1988).

6. On this point, see M. A. Fitzpatrick and A. L. Vangelisti, *Explaining Family Interactions* (Thousand Oaks, CA: Sage Publications, 1995); H. D. Grotevant and C.R. Cooper, "Patterns of Interaction in Family Relationships and the Development of Identity Exploration," *Child Development* 56 (1985): 415–28.

7. On this and related points, see A. E. Gottfried and A. W. Gottfried, Eds., *Redefining Families: Implications for Children's Development* (New York: Plenum Press, 1994); and K. Owens, *The World of the Child* (New York: Macmillan, 1993) (See especially parts I and IV.).

8. See F. McCourt, *Angela's Ashes* (New York: Scribner, 1996).

9. See S. Freud, *The Complete Introductory Lectures on Psychoanalysis* (New York: W. W. Norton, 1966); S. Freud, *The Ego and the Id* (London: Hogarth Press, 1949); and Anna Freud, *The Ego and the Mechanisms of Defense* (New York: International Universities Press, 1946).

10. On this point, see Carol Gilligan, *In a Different Voice* (Cambridge, MA: Harvard University Press, 1982).

11. On this and related points, see W. W. Hartup and R. Zubin, *Relationships and Development* (Hillsdale, NJ: Lawrence Erlbaum, 1986);

and P. Marris, *Attachment Across the Life Cycle* (London: Tavistock/ Routledge, 1991).

12. On this point, see Jean Baker Miller, *Toward A New Psychology of Women* (Boston: Beacon Press, 1976). See also J. B. Miller and I. P. Stiver, *The Healing Connection: How Women form Relationships in Therapy and in Life* (Boston: Beacon Press, 1997).

13. On this point of security, see F. Earls and M. Carlson, "Towards Sustainable Development for American Families," in *America's Childhood, Daedalus* (1993): 93–121.

14. J. Bowlby, *Attachment and Loss* (New York: Basic Books, 1980); *A Secure Base: Parent–Child Attachment and Healthy Human Development* (New York: Basic Books, 1989.); M. Ainsworth, "Attachment: Retrospect and Prospect," in C. Parkes and J. Stevenson-Hinde, Eds., *The Place of Attachment in Human Behavior* (New York: Basic Books, 1982).

15. From *Treating the Self: Elements of Clinical Self Psychology* (New York: Guilford, 1988). See also, H. Kohut, "Thoughts on Narcissism and Narcissistic Rage," in P. H. Ornstein, Ed., *Search for the Self: Selected Writings of Heinz Kohut* (New York: International Universities Press, 1978): Vol. 2, 615–58; and L. Layton and B. A. Schapiro, Eds., *Narcissism and the Text: Studies in Literature and the Psychology of Self* (New York: New York University Press, 1986). I am grateful to Donald Paladino for these references.

16. See, for example, S. Osherson, *Finding Our Fathers* (New York: Free Press, 1986); and R. Bly, *Iron John* (Reading, MA: Addison-Wesley, 1991).

17. This notion of being thrown back on one's feelings is reminiscent of Rollo May's work on the three modes of being, the *Mitwelt*, the *Umwelt*, and especially the *Eigenwelt*. See his *The Discovery of Being* (New York: W. W. Norton, 1983).

18. *op. cit.*

19. Pollock, *op. cit.* See also B. A. van der Kolk, Ed., *Psychological Trauma* (Washington, DC: American Psychiatric Press, 1982.). See especially chapter 1; S. Eth. and R. Pynoos, Eds., *Post-Traumatic Stress Disorder in Children* (Washington, DC: American Psychiatric Press, 1985); and M. E. Wolf and A. D. Mosnaim, Ed., *Post-Traumatic Stress Disorder: Etiology, Phenomenology, and Treatment* (Washington, DC: American Psychiatric Press, 1990).

20. See A. Young, "Suffering and the Origins of Traumatic Memory," *Daedalus 125* (1996): 245–60. See also his *The Harmony of Illusions: Inventing Posttraumatic Stress Disorder* (Princeton, NJ: Princeton University Press, 1995).

21. On the subject of loss see Fred Weinstein, *Freud, Psychoanalysis, Social Theory: The Unredeemed Promise* (Albany, NY: State University of New York Press, in press).

22. On this point, see J. G. Bachman and P. M. O'Malley, "Self Esteem in Young Men: A Longitudinal Analysis of the Impact of Educational and Occupational Attainment," *Journal of Personality and Social Psychology 35* (1977): 365–80; and L. E. Wells and G. Marwell, *Self Esteem: Its Conceptualization and Measurement* (Beverly Hills, CA: Sage Publishing, 1976).

23. M. L. Pulley, *Losing Your Job—Reclaiming Your Soul* (San Francisco: Jossey-Bass, 1997).

24. *op. cit.*

25. See L. Kohlberg, *Essays on Moral Development* (San Francisco: Harper & Row, 1981). See also L. Kohlberg and C. Gilligan, "The Adolescent as a Philosopher," in J. Kagan and K. Coles, Eds., *Early Adolescence* (New York: Norton, 1972): 144–79.

26. See C. Gilligan, *In A Different Voice. op. cit.*; see also C. Gilligan, et al., *Making Connections* (Cambridge, MA: Harvard University Press, 1990).

27. On these points, see N. Chodorow and S. Contratto, "The Fantasy of the Perfect Mother," in B. Thorne, Ed., *Rethinking the Family* (New York: Longman, 1981); R. Schaffer, "Mothering as Interlocution," in *Mothering* (Cambridge, MA: Harvard University Press, 1977); and S. Freud, *My Three Mothers and Other Passions* (New York: New York University Press, 1988).

28. On this and related points, see H. Kohut, *The Kohut Seminars: On Self Psychology and Psychotherapy with Adolescents and Young Adults* (New York: Norton, 1987). See also A. Goldberg, *Advances in Self Psychology* (New York: International Universities Press, 1980.)

29. On this question, see R. L. Silver and C. B. Wortman, "Coping with Undesireable Life Events," in J. Garber and M. E. P. Seligman, Eds., *Human Helplessness: Theory and Applications* (New York: Academic Press, 1980).

30. G. O. Higgins, *Resilient Adults: Overcoming a Cruel Past* (San Francisco: Jossey-Bass, 1994).

31. E. J. Anthony, "Risk, Vulnerability, and Resilience: An Overview," in E. J. Anthony and B. J. Cohler, Eds., *The Invulnerable Child* (New York: Guilford Press, 1987); and S. C. Kobasa, S. Maddi, and S. Kahn, "Hardiness and Health: A Prospective Study," *Journal of Personality and Social Psychology 42* (1982): 168–77.

32. P. Marris, *Loss and Change* (New York: Routledge, 1986).

33. W. Bridges, *Transitions: Making Sense of Life's Changes* (Reading, MA: Addison-Wesley, 1980).

34. R. S. Lazarus and S. Folkman, *Stress, Appraisal and Coping* (New York: Springer-Verlag, 1984).

35. N. T. Feather, *The Psychological Impact of Unemployment* (New York: Springer-Verlag, 1989).

36. M. L. Pulley, *Losing Your Job—Reclaiming Your Soul* (San Francisco: Jossey-Bass, 1997); D. M. Noer, *Healing the Wounds* (San Francisco: Jossey-Bass, 1993); and W. Bridges, *Job-Shift: How to Prosper in a Workplace Without Jobs* (Reading, MA: Addison-Wesley, 1994).

37. See, for example, John Morgan et. al., "Primary Prevention of Child Maladjustment: Real-World Efforts in a Community Mental Health Setting," *The Child, Youth, and Family Services Quarterly 14* (1991): 7.

38. *Webster's New World Dictionary of the American Language* (New York: The World Publishing Co., 1957).

39. Two books relevant to the coping process are *Losing Your Job—Reclaiming Your Soul* by M. L. Pulley, *op. cit.*; and D. M. Noer, *Healing the Wounds op cit.* Three additional studies relevant to the topic of coping and unemployment are R. C. Kessler, R. H. Price, and C. B. Wortman, "Social Factors in Psychopathology: Stress, Social Support and Coping Process," *Annual Review of Psychology 36* (1985): 531–72; L. J. Pearlin and C. Schooler, "The Structure of Coping" *Journal of Health and Social Behavior 21* (1978): 2–21; and R. S. Lazarus, *Psychological Stress and the Coping Process* (New York: McGraw-Hill, 1966).

40. N. T. Feather, *op. cit.*, 1989.

41. On this point, see M. Armstrong-Stasses, "Coping with Transition: a Study of Lay-off Survivors," *Journal of Organizational Behavior 15* (1944): 597–621.

42. During the Persian Gulf War, one heard a great deal of comment about the soldiers who admitted to being frightened. Either it came as a surprise to some that soldiers actually do feel fear, or more likely—and this is the point—that they would admit to it publicly. It must have confused some people to witness the peculiar combination of events: soldiers expressing fear and a resounding 100-hour victory in Iraq.

43. On this point, see R. Bly, *op. cit.*, and S. Osherson, *op. cit.*

44. D. Bakan, *The Duality of Human Existence* (Chicago: Rand McNally, 1966).

45. On this point, see L. Y. Abramson, M. E. P. Seligman, and J. D. Teasdale, "Learned Helplessness in Humans: Critique and Reformulation," *Journal of Abnormal Psychology 87* (1978): 49–74; and R. A. Dupue and S. M. Monroe, "Learned Helplessness in the Perspective of the Depressive Disorders: Conceptual and Definitional Issues," *Journal of Abnormal Psychology 87* (1978): 3–20.

46. On this point, see M. A. Strauss and R. J. Gelles, *Behind Closed Doors* (Garden City, NY: Anchor Books, 1981); and R. J. Gelles, *Family Violence* (Newbury Park, CA: Sage Publications, 1987).

47. On this and related points, see A. Young, "Suffering and the Origins of Traumatic Memory," *Daedalus 125* (1996): 245–60.

48. On this point, see S. E. Taylor, "Adjustment to Threatening Events: A Theory of Cognitive Adaptation," *American Psychologist 11* (1983): 1161–73.

49. Feather, 1989, *op. cit.*

50. On this point, see A. Bandura, "Self Efficacy Mechanism in Human Agency," *American Psychologist 37* (1982): 122–47.

51. D. M. Noer, *Healing the Wounds op. cit.*

52. See, for example, B. Zawadski and P. F. Lazarsfeld, "The Psychological Consequences of Unemployment" *Journal of Social Psychology 6* (1935): 224–51; *The Pilgrim Trust, Men Without Work.* (Cambridge, MA: Cambridge University Press, 1938); N. Israeli, "Distress in the Outlook of Lancashire and Scottish Unemployed," *Journal of Applied Psychology 19* (1935): 67–9; P. Eisenberg and P. F. Lazarsfeld, "The Psychological Effects of Unemployment," *Psychological Bulletin 35* (1938): 358–90; E. W. Bakke, *The Unemployed Man* (London: Nisbet, 1933); H. L. Beales and R. S. Lambert, *Memoirs of the Unemployed* (London: Gollanz, 1934); M. Komarovsky, *The Unemployed Man and His Family: The Effect of Unemployment Upon the Status of the Man in 59 Families* (New York: Dryden, 1940); and E. W. Bakke, *The Unemployed Worker* (New Haven: Yale University Press, 1940).

53. P. Blos, *op. cit.*, 91.

54. On this point, see B. Shamir, "Self-Esteem and the Psychological Impact of Unemployment," *Social Psychological Quarterly, 49* (1986): 61–72.

55. See, for example, E. H. Erikson, *Childhood and Society* (New York: W. W. Norton, 1950).

56. See D. Elkind, "Egocentrism in Children and Adolescents," in *Children and Adolescents: Interpretive Essays on Jean Piaget* (New York:

Oxford University Press, 1974); and *The Hurried Child* (Reading, MA: Addison Wesley, 1981).

57. D. M. Noer, *op. cit.*, see especially chapter 3; see also E. M. Fowler, "Survivors' Syndrome in Layoffs," *New York Times*, 3 June 1986, D23.

58. See K. Newman, *Falling from Grace: The Experience of Downward Mobility in the American Middle Class* (New York: The Free Press, 1988); and K. M. Dudley, *The End of the Line: Lost Jobs, New Lives in Post-Industrial America* (Chicago: University of Chicago Press, 1994).

Chapter 9

The Shame
of Unemployment

Working is breathing. It's something you don't think about; you just do it and it keeps you alive. When you stop you die.

LIVES OF SHAME AND GUILT

One day, driving home from a visit with Charlie Petronelli, an out-of-work construction worker who had used his injured leg as an excuse for not being able to find work over the past four and a half years, I found myself thinking about the death of my father. I recalled that a family friend had visited him in the hospital, weeks actually, before my father died. A psychiatrist, the friend was visibly shaken by my father's weakening condition. My mother was eager to speak with him and get a psychological reading on my father. "He's very depressed, isn't he?" she asked rhetorically. "Not at all," the psychiatrist answered with uncharacteristic sternness, as if he were protecting my father's reputation. "He's not depressed at all, he's dying!"

Suddenly, the visits with Cy Mullen, Ken Hawkins, Peter Rosenbloom, Ollie Sindon, and George Wilkinson were coalescing in my mind around that single theme. Steady and rewarding work allows a man to feel he has personal as well as social value. Underemployment means he has low, even minimal value. Unemployment means the absence of value, again, personal as well as social, and no promise of any sort of reward in the immediate future. It wasn't simply that these men were feeling sorry for themselves; technically, perhaps, they all could have been diagnosed as depressed or anxious. More precisely, they saw themselves as struggling to remain alive, or perhaps feeling guilty that indeed they were alive after so long a period of idleness. Then again, some felt that they were in fact dying.[1] George Wilkinson said it this way: "There's only two worlds for me: Either you work every day in a normal nine-to-five job with a couple weeks' vacation, or you're dead! There's no in-between. . . . Working is breathing. It's something you don't think about; you just do it and it keeps you alive. When you stop you die."

They all knew it, as clearly as a man knows it when a doctor tells him he has only a few months to live. Some of the ones who disappeared, I imagined, went away to die, like weary elephants looking for the burial ground they believe is out there somewhere. In almost atavistic fashion, they knew it was not meant for them to die at home near their families. No one ever discussed this lugubrious matter with them, but they knew. Death was something their wives and children were not meant to witness.

In time, it became apparent that these were not merely discouraged workers, nor survivors of layoffs, they were people describing an illness, or even worse, mourning their deaths, and lives. Almost surreal in nature, inquiries into their personal and work histories, remembrances of parents, descriptions of early career aspirations, and evaluations of their lives, became an opportunity for them to compose their obituaries. Their accounts were part of a final self-assessment, a final remembrance.

Aware of it or not, the men were offering their memoirs. The longer our visits went on, the more they believed their lives might have had some merit. Not ironically, the same formula applies to a newspaper's obituary page where the esteemed of the society earn long columns, even front page stories. The rung of people beneath them earn four to five inches on the obit page, the special among them meriting photographs, often ones in which they appear youthful. The rest of the world receives brief mention in the small type lists. No accomplishments, no life histories, no educational experiences, no description of work or charitable activities, just a list of names in alphabetical order, like grade school class lists, and some information regarding religious services and burials.

A palpable sadness lived in the homes of these men. The happy talk and politeness were a charade, devices meant to lessen the sadness. In time, the meetings came to resemble hospital visits with terminally ill people. Patients know why we have come, but it seems it is always *they* who have to comfort *us* during the ordeal of conversing. "You want to know how far my cancer's spread? You want to know how much time they're giving me?" And I want to respond, I do, and I don't. I don't know what we should be talking about. And they're saying, "We should be talking about you and me and about cancer and dying and living." Many of the men were describing this same thing: We should be talking about working and not working, about living and dying.

Once, when he was trying to reconstruct his father's life, Johnnie Nobles remarked: "There are things that make you an expert. No one would have called my father an expert, but every man's an expert on what not working does to him. The priest tells you about death but he doesn't know. He's just heard about death. He gives last rights, but that's as close as he'll come. He hasn't touched anything there, he's just present at the dying, doing his job. My father and a bunch of his friends, they can tell you about death. They can tell you about the last bits of life seeping out your body when you don't have a job. Because you know how you know if a man's an expert? You listen to him, and you watch him, and something inside you says, this guy knows what he's talking about. He hasn't just *heard* about this, he's *lived* this!"

Perhaps the men were indeed experts on death and dying. What else would one say in the face of these words spoken by Gerry Murphy, a man made ill from his experiences on a nuclear test sight? "I would like to work. I don't think I'm unable to do anything. . . . I'm told I'm unemployable. I can't really do anything. I don't seem to have any concentration. . . . I couldn't sit in one place for an hour. I'm sort of lost in the general scheme of things. I don't even know what I'm doing, you know? I'm what they call 'free falling.' There's no plans or anything. I feel like I'm in a fog. I don't read the newspaper. I try. It's just I can't really concentrate. I used to be able to."[2]

Perhaps feeling embarrassed, many unemployed men didn't wish to be seen. Months before, these same men had spoken with a characteristic toughness. The reader will recall Jack Blum saying: "I'm at the bottom and nobody likes it at the bottom. But okay, somebody's got to be at the bottom. Poor people, all walks of life, ethnic types, Black, White, you don't make money, down to the bottom! *Here's* the real melting pot of this country." Many men spewed vitriol at state and federal governments for letting them down or outright abandoning them.[3] One frequently heard comments about the government "taking my taxes for thirty years, and now they claim they've run out of benefits!" "The government bails the S and L boys out of trouble with *our* money, but don't bail *us* out when we didn't break a single law, how do you explain *that* one?"[4]

In time, their anger receded, as though their bodies could no longer sustain it. Once upon a time George Wilkinson, Amos Payton, and Jack Blum rode the energy of anger as though life itself drew electricity from it. Amos had said: "'Fraid of getting angry, and getting angry 'cause I get afraid. Hell, man, afraid of *not* being angry no more. Anger and fear, they're gonna keep you alert, like an animal. Got to keep on the prowl." During one of his angry moods, Jack had cautioned: "The day that anger stops, like a motor, I'm dead. Kaput. Good-bye, Jack the Bomb Blum."

Whereas once their anger clearly provided a life force, once-strong men had now grown weary from this very same anger. A profound transformation had occurred during the tenure of their unemployment. With the anger receding, one recognized the sounds of shame and guilt.[5] As it dawned on the men that re-employment was unlikely, they retreated from earlier perspectives. Their masculinity assaulted, their strength sapped, they appeared shameful, childlike, as if they deserved to be the invisible, reclusive people they in fact had become. Thus, they acted out the parts of men ashamed of the mess they had made of their lives.[6] Jack Blum constantly joked that shame and guilt were his middle names: "I drown, it's my fault. That woman and those kids upstairs in that cold apartment where I can't take a warm bath when I want to, they drown, that's also my fault. So maybe I'm also a murderer, huh? I kill me, my wife and kids, and they don't even know they're being murdered."

Similarly, no one could assault Ollie Sindon as he himself did; Ollie was a master of self-blame, a characteristic closely aligned with depression.[7] No matter what the topic, Ollie could bring it back on himself in the most searing forms of self-indictment: "Even if they have 20 percent unemployed, they still have 80 percent employed, and a lot of that 80 percent is Black, ain't they? So lots of men living right in this community may be in the same boat I am, but most of 'em ain't! . . . Man like me wants to yell out, 'It's somebody else's fault.' But it's *my* fault. I could have done it so it would have come out better." One wonders whether Ollie's words depict what psychoanalysts call a form of narcissistic rage, or in Heinz Kohut's words, "mature aggression."[8] Or is it perhaps that the rage masks the pain and guilt of being out of work as Robert Jay Lifton and Eric Olson suggested in an essay on trauma survivors?[9] Work, after all, becomes part of the self, and hence the loss of steady work represents more than the loss of a significant piece of the self. In the world of some men, it may represent the entire loss of self.

Early in their days of being out of work, one observed brazen defiance, even rage. On line at local unemployment offices—the men often convened at five thirty in the morning in order to get a place near the head of the line–one heard strong protestations: They were innocent victims, they had worked regular shifts, rarely taken days off, rarely arrived late. It was the government, the corporations, the economy that was at fault. Like a chorus, the others nodded in agreement shouting out, "Damn straight," "You got that right!" Somewhere around the one-year anniversary of their unemployment, the themes shifted. Now the men portrayed themselves as wrongdoers, transgressors, people guilty of grievous offenses. Suddenly, they were hiding, running away from it all, unable to face anyone, and particularly themselves.

An observation on incest survivors, actually, by Judith Wilbur-Albertson helps in understanding this pattern of breaking away: "Shame and humiliation can make it difficult to seek out connection unless you create a false front, someone who isn't quite you."[10] Underlying this notion, perhaps, is a statement offered by Pulley: "The death of job security leaves us with a gaping void where once there was a path. Culturally we are in need of a new myth that informs our daily life."[11] For men who haven't worked in years, the idea of a false front was unthinkable, a new myth inconceivable, the days of masquerading as successful workers and good fathers long past.

The origin of the guilt expressed by the men seems obvious. Culture teaches that a man is meant to hold a steady job. In traditional terms, men believe this is *all* they are meant to do. Ken Hawkins described it this way: "Men leave in the morning and come back at night with a pay check in their hand. That make me old fashioned? Then I'm old fashioned!" In the worker's mind there is nothing wrong with the idea of returning home at the end of a day expecting dinner to be on the table and the children ready for a little play before their nightly bedtime routines. Chauvinistic or not, for centuries men have been taught that full-time employment entitles them to this form of human recompense. Although the values of the culture clearly have shifted, one recognizes these same traditional strains as the scene of men returning from war. Having done their noble service, they feel entitled to the amenities of home life that, again traditionally, women are "meant" to provide them.

When a man loses his job, therefore, the one and only obligation earning him not merely his wage, but his status in his home as well, is lost, along with his right merely to be there. Without a job, he cannot face his wife. He hasn't earned his keep, or his place. Without a job, moreover, he forfeits his rights to any form of recognition. How can a child feel proud of his or her father when all he does is mope around the house, or drink! Exasperated, his wife finally erupts: "You want the truth?" she shouts. "I'm sick of looking at you, sitting there all day. Fact is I don't want to come home anymore and have you be the first thing I see!" Rosemary Mullen's frustration with her husband was especially painful: "He should have taken me somewhere, threw me down, slapped me if that was the only thing that would have quieted me, and made love to me. I mean, pull my clothes off and rape me. . . . Anything to show me he was alive. I mean it. I wanted to be roughed up that night, and feel he was really a man. But he was dead."

Granted, at times the men fought back, hardly valiantly, for their shame, guilt, and overriding self-blame precluded much of a contest. "If you can't stand the sight of me," they argued, "you can always leave." Hardly original, their expressions could not have been more disingenuous, for above all they feared being abandoned by their families, despite believing they deserved no less a punishment. The anger derived from the shame was often directed at their children who heard this sort of outburst: "What the hell you looking at? If you want a show, go watch television!"

If the children learned anything, it was to stay away from Dad when he was in "one of his moods." But the duration of "the moods" was lengthening, until eventually all of Dad's life was one dark mood, no matter how everyone tried to pretend otherwise.[12] Early on, the children were ordered not to speak publicly about their father's unemployment, and never to question him about it, for raising the subject would only cause further hurt. Indeed, anyone speaking even obliquely about unemployment in these households ran the risk of causing the man and his family to experience shame.[13]

Several times in our conversations, and especially toward the end, George Wilkinson spoke about unemployment in terms not merely of shame, but of the stigma of it as well. He had come to the conclusion that he was like a mental patient, branded and unwanted. In many of his accounts he spoke of society's undesirables, often using the word *stigma*.[14] "See if you can understand this," he had said, standing erect, almost proudly, before his living room windows, peering out at the street in that characteristic pose of his. "I'm more affected by being unemployed than by the fact that I can't find work." Then he turned to look at me. "Think I'm nuts?"

George barely ventured outside his home during his last months. He simply could not let himself be seen, an action that calls to mind Erikson's telling observations on shame: "He who is ashamed," Erikson wrote, "would like to force the world not to look at him, not to notice his exposure. . . . He who is ashamed would like to destroy the eyes of the world."[15] In the past, George could pass among the unemployed, wearing his tweed sport jacket, freshly pressed slacks and polished shoes, pretending not to be one of them. Standing on line waiting for his unemployment check, he almost had himself believing he wasn't one of them. When he no longer could pass—this was his word—and the pain of the stigma became too intense, he remained at home.

"You've become a shut-in," I unnecessarily reminded him one morning, more out of concern than anything else.

"I'm a shut out," he corrected me.

Other men too, had spoken of stigmatization, although few of them had used the word as George had done. Robert Barnes, a forty-eight-year-old man who, for fifteen years, had been vice president of a small manufacturing company, was someone never able to make a successful adjustment to unemployment, as if anyone truly does. He, too, contemplated the notion of stigma when he recalled the simple act of going to a hospital emergency room. When employed, he would have gone directly to his doctor's office. Now he went, as he said, "like all the rest," to take his chances in the emergency room. Out of work for twenty-six months, which meant that it had been over a year and a half since his last unemployment benefits, his narratives revealed a man watching himself watching himself.

"The second I walked into that emergency room I felt those eyes looking at me. People might just as well been screaming when they looked at my records and saw how I used to go to the better part of the hospital. And that fatal question, as if they even had to ask it. You think my pain went away? I wish, 'cause I was so embarrassed standing there answering 'no' to practically every question this woman was asking. I told myself, the hell with my lousy pain. I don't need a doctor, I don't even deserve one. You think my gut stopped hurting? Filling out those forms made my whole body ache, every rotting inch of it. I was trying to disappear, that's the only thought on my mind. Come to think of it, maybe my body was trying to do the same thing. Maybe that's what was causing all the pain."

The themes of stigmatization can be summarized by reviewing Peter Rosenbloom's often humorous but mainly bitter account of the fateful restaurant meeting with his brother Marcus. The stigmatization that George Wilkinsin and Bob Barnes had described emerged within minutes of the Rosenbloom brothers getting together. Marcus' suggestion that Peter leave the city points up again the image of the terminally unemployed as contagious, undesirable, leperous: "No one in his neighborhood should see him with me," Peter had said: "You also don't throw people away or hide them because a serious problem has got them. What am I, a crook that's making trouble for people?"

Peter was also disturbed by his brother's preoccupation with status. "It doesn't look so good that he's got a brother who, in his heyday, was a taxi driver." If Marcus had his way, Peter would never be seen again. Only later did I fully recognize what Peter had offered as a solution to his own and Marcus' problem: start time all over again. One may recall his ironic reference to reclaiming the family's original Hungarian name, followed by the image of commencing life anew: "This is my brother speaking to me. Like I'm a little baby."

As noted, men come early to the conclusion that life requires them to work. When a woman works outside the home, we unthinkingly ask, "Does she have to or does she want to?" We never ask this of a man. Like it or not, he works. If he doesn't, it is because he is rich, retired, or disabled. Or he has been fired, and at that point, he loses his position in society.[16] From that moment to the moment he is re-employed, he is stigmatized, no matter how sensitive and understanding society claims to be. If a man can't find work after exhausting his full complement of unemployment benefits, then he alone assumes the blame, not the society, even though in his mind he believes that society, in the form of employment opportunities, no longer provides a source of life.[17]

These issues surely play out the same way for women; no one knows this better than the men and women of America's workforce who live every day with the reality or threat of long-term unemployment.[18] Although many in the culture complain of the dehumanizing elements of their work, occasionally bringing their grievances to authorities, the unemployed worker experiences the ultimate act of dehumanization. There is no authority to whom he may turn, just as there is no one to oversee his elemental grievance, namely, that he has lost his humanity. But a "real man," it is said, learns how to live with unemployment, just as he learns how to live with pain; tolerance of heartache is a cornerstone of the so-called macho perspective.

Interestingly, when a woman loses her job, and perhaps her home as well, she draws our sympathies, but not so much the unemployed man, not so much the man living in the streets. Somehow we assume that he has brought these circumstances on himself. There must be a part of his story people aren't telling us.[19] We grieve for the homeless woman and child but question how it is possible for a man to have reached this point. He must be schizophrenic, or an alcoholic, just as he must also be responsible in some way for the homeless woman and her child.

If wrongly we blame the victim of rape, then, perhaps too, we blame the victims of unemployment.[20] If a man can lift his arms or use his brain, we insist, there is no reason for him not to be working. It's amazing his wife hasn't kicked him out, we remark. It's incredible that he wouldn't set aside his damnable pride and take some menial job. Let him flip hamburgers, we grumble, reading about the number of unemployed people in America and the drain they continue to be on benefit and insurance programs.

Or maybe he's just lazy, the buzzword once reserved to describe certain minority groups. It is easier, after all, to attribute a psychological deficit for the high rate of African American unemployment than explore the complicated economic and sociological underpinnings of this problem.[21] Nowadays, laziness is attributed to the terminally unemployed, Black and White; better to make the unemployed and not unemployment the problem, a strategy unemployed men know only too well. How often have they heard this sentiment: "You couldn't hold a job if they tied it to your neck. There are always jobs. You just don't *want* to work!"

That theorists, some employed by the government, continue to assert that long-term unemployed workers are psychologically equipped and eager to use their newly found "free time" for devotion to community efforts reveals how removed are some of these authorities from the psychological realities of long-term unemployment. When an air force base in Maine closed down, for example, several government reports were issued, one of which contained this purportedly helpful recommendation:

"It is anticipated that the contract curtailment [the base closing] could serve as a motivating factor for increased community participation and provide an outlet for the large numbers of affected secondary workers who will now have substantially more available time to devote to the community."[22]

BROTHERHOOD, BOUNDARIES, AND FAMILY ROLES

Like all families, those with an unemployed member learn their roles in an unfolding drama, a phenomenon regularly observed in therapeutic work with all families.[23] The notion of a drama is not insignificant, for it reveals how shame is learned by family members, how it is to be responded to, and more generally how families learn to deal with the severe problems or circumstances of anyone of its members. In a sense, this orientation suggests that the society and the family teach shame as well as reactions to it. In time, these teachings become ritualized patterns of family interactions as well as individual psychologies.[24] A brief account of a family whose story has not been told in these pages may serve as illustration of these points.

Tessie Blake, the thirteen-year-old daughter of Artie Blake, who had not worked in almost two years, suddenly began to reveal uncharacteristically violent behavior in school. Psychological testing and a series of interviews with her guidance counselor yielded little insight into the problem. Interviews with her parents yielded even less information. No one could come up with an explanation of her outbreaks other than that they were due to biochemical transformations, or drug abuse, which she adamantly denied. After her being suspended from school on three occasions, the school reluctantly suspended Tessie for an indefinite period. As the principal told the Blakes at the final hearing, Tessie had damaged school property and seriously injured two students, one of them her best girlfriend, Lisa Monan. She simply could not be forgiven these acts.

For the first two weeks at home, everything appeared calm. Tessie stayed away from her father, who had constructed a lifestyle in which he stayed away from his wife. When the family ate dinner together, Artie emotionally removed himself. The couple was never in the kitchen at the same time for breakfast and lunch. Then suddenly, Tessie experienced what a social worker later diagnosed as an acute anxiety disorder. For several minutes she revealed an aphasia, she could not utter coherent sounds. At the same time, she became violently uncontrollable, her mother described her as demonic. The social worker diagnosed the outbreak as possibly homicidal, not suicidal. Witnessing the explosion made Artie more guilty and self-destructive.

Because of the intensity and acuteness of Tessie's episode, Artie Blake's two-year history of unemployment no longer could be concealed from medical authorities. The attending psychiatrist was struck with the fact that Artie's unemployment and subsequent depression predated Tessie's original violent outbursts in school. When asked by the psychiatrist whether she perceived a connection between her father's unemployment and her own personal difficulties, Tessie became panic stricken and broke down in tears. After a few minutes, however, as everyone waited for her to compose herself, her body relaxed and she began to giggle. Softly, she repeated the words: "The secret is out, the secret is out."

Tessie's story became clear to everyone. She had been warned not to tell anyone of her father's unemployment as public knowledge of it might damage the family and "destroy any opportunity" for him to find work. These were precisely the words her mother had used. Tessie was to think of her father's unemployment, moreover, as society's fault, not her father's. All she had to do was look at Daddy to see how badly society had treated him.

This was the significant message. Daddy was unhappy; everyone could see that. He wasn't really Daddy anymore, even Mommy acknowledged this much. And because he was not to blame he could not be punished, no matter how angry one felt about him sitting in his chair all day, or how frightened one felt when he began yelling. But Mommy now had designated the culprit: It was society, whatever that meant to this thirteen-year-old, and so she set about to punish society in order to avenge her father's honor. How to define society? Anything close to her, which meant her school and best friends.

Tessie did her best, everyone assured her, to preserve the family's dreaded secret, but it proved impossible to live this lie and perpetuate the family's shame. In her own words, it was an "unfair secret" her parents had demanded that she keep. She did her best to avenge her father, but she never released the anger she felt at both her parents, her father for not working and changing as he had, and her mother for insisting that she lie. If only she could have told one friend, she said one afternoon over hot chocolate. "Was it Lisa you wanted to tell?" I asked. She nodded yes, Lisa being the child she had hurt in one of school fights.

In the end, Tessie Blake had more than felt her parents' shame. She felt her own shame too, although she never understood its meaning or source. The weight of the distress overwhelmed her, literally made her "go crazy" that one afternoon before the eyes of her despairing father. When the secret finally was made public, a palpable weight was removed from the child, and in a matter of weeks most of her symptoms dissipated. In time, her school reinstated her and she reconciled with Lisa, something that deeply pleased her parents, for the family had come to depend on this valuable relationship. No amount of time, however, brought Artie Blake closer to full-time work.

Kenneth Hawkins' story represents one of the more complex aspects of men's unemployment: namely, the exchange with one's wife of traditional male and female roles. Most visitors to the Hawkins home viewed the establishment of a "new life" as an adequate adjustment to Ken's work circumstances. They remarked on how well he tolerated the provocative comments of neighbors and withstood the stares and looks of confusion on the faces of former colleagues. By the end, he had everyone convinced that he had "worked it out."

Nothing hit him harder, however, than the pain of his financial dependence on his wife. It was not only that she worked regular hours, or even out-earned him, it was that matter of his depending on her in ways that, in his mind, men aren't supposed to do. Inequality in a relationship was one thing, but dependence on a woman was infantilizing. It brought him back to childhood, and it became intolerable, as it had for Peter Rosenbloom as well.

Ken didn't feel guilty, exactly, that his wife worked while he remained idle. Surely he never felt guilt when he supported his parents after his father lost his job. While he never said much about his father's guilt, it nonetheless lay in the seams of his own marriage. Something about becoming the economic provider for his family during his own adolescence troubled him. Perhaps the role reversal with his wife evoked the shameful feelings he had hidden for years involving his father's unemployment. Perhaps he never admitted to himself how deeply his family had felt the shame of that unemployment experience. Perhaps he never could face the fact that he had followed in his father's footsteps, as perverse as this thought seemed to him.

And something else. Kenneth and his mother had enjoyed their earlier household partnership. Although never openly admitted, they enjoyed the exclusion of his father from this partnership. Ken's steady job meant that for the first time in years good money was coming into the family; it would have been impossible for him and his mother not to rejoice over their newly found material pleasures. But Kenneth's success only made his father feel more incompetent and act more sickly in his wife's eyes, but these matters, too were never mentioned.

In his mind, Ken had become his father; what better definition after all, is there of father than he who provides money for a family? As a result, too many of the boundaries that properly differentiate family member had all but disappeared, although no one ever recognized this. In the end, Kenneth's employment had pushed his father out of the immediate family circle. Now, however, as his own unemployment persisted, he had to acknowledge how superfluous this drama had been. No one needs to push a father out of the family circle; he automatically forfeits this position when he loses his job. As Ollie Sindon put it: "Because I don't work I'm only his father by title. I carry the title, like I carry a card saying 'I got a right to work.' Neither of them does no good."

Years later, when once again unemployment meant that he would be switching family roles, Ken Hawkins' feelings of guilt resurfaced, and despite his protestations and even eloquent disquisition on gender role equity, he never could silence them. Just as he yearned for love and support,[25] he rejected offers made to him. His wife and closest friends were totally convinced of his new adjustment, but everyone misjudged him. Everyone missed the deeper message buried in Ken's words: "The trouble is that the rotten nine-to-five boredom routine we've invented called work, *that* affects who you are, what you are, how much you can love." Clearly, people play out distinctive family dramas, and some of the participants turn out to be rather spectacular actors.[26]

Still on the subject of fathers and sons, I ask the reader to recall the portion of George Wilkinson's narrative in which he spoke about his father teaching him about the rich. The elder Wilkinson always insisted that the country's highest standards were established and maintained by the rich, powerful, and influential people whose actions and decisions move the country. On the surface, George's accounts convey a common sentiment and hardly appear unusual coming from someone in the throes of reconciling dreams of success and wealth with an anxiety about whether he would ever work again. His is the classic case of a man who did exactly as his culture and family admonished him: out-earn your father. Presumably there is little shame associated with earning more than one's father, it is said to be the very embodiment of success. Indeed, it may be the only thing a son is "permitted" to do better than his father. But to earn less than one's father, particularly a father who believes so vehemently in the power and influence of rich families, is to transgress. About this, there can be no hiding one's shamefulness.

If George was a failure—and surely he believed himself to be—then it was more in his (imagined) father's eyes than in the eyes of society. Unemployment crushed him economically, lowered his status, and caused him to believe that his father considered him a failure. Whereas years before he may have had to resolve the competitive feelings with his father that he brought to the labor market, feelings based in part on a fear that he might do the very thing he was meant to do, namely out achieve his father, he now realized he had lost the most important competition of his life. Clearly, he questioned whether his father could still love and respect him.

To digress for a moment, I find that it is not uncommon to observe men asking their wives to evaluate them. Not unlike the elderly Private Ryan in Steven Spielberg's movie *Private Ryan*, they hunt for confirmation of whether they have led good lives, or whether long-term unemployment has forever destroyed this possibility. Probably they want to know as well, whether they are still admired and loved. The answers proffered by their wives mean little, however, as clearly the men have already decided that love is something one earns through one's labors. Without a job, one forfeits all rights to be loved, along with a confirmation of having led a useful and productive life, once again essentially defined through work. So no matter how their wives respond, the men seemed unsatisfied, unblessed. If a woman says she still loves her husband, he questions it: "How could you when I don't work?" If she dares to admit she has lost her love and respect for him, he responds: "Of course you have. How could anybody love a failure?"

In some cases, George being one of them, the men asked questions of their wives that they once may have wished to ask their parents, and especially their fathers. "Am I worthwhile? Am I lovable?" Love is what they desired, a blessing for life, and confirmation that they were good people, not merely because they went to work Monday through Friday, but because something about them personally made them lovable. It was their fathers, moreover, they hoped would sanctify this unconditional regard. It seemed as if they hoped their fathers would proclaim that the standards of a man are underwritten by his goodness and decency, not by the size of his pay check or work history.

George Wilkinson knew where his father stood on these matters. The rich were the winners, everyone else an also ran. The unemployed were unlovable. It may be fine to comfort a crying child when he fails at something, although one does risk coddling the boy, but one never embraces the failed man. George's father had made it abundantly clear of what his son's life was to consist. The other people in the unemployment line may not have thought about these matters, but George pondered them again and again, which raises another issue.

In the early days of being out of work, when benefits still come in and hope continues to run fairly high, a brotherhood is often forged among unemployed men. Birds of a feather, men in the same boat, they refer to themselves, as they connect to one another, however tenuously, as part of a life support network.[27] On the unemployment line, in the bars, in the meeting halls, they appear as fellow protesters, witnesses, sufferers, victims. Over time, when these networks begin to crumble, various professionals may intervene to reestablish some of the connections once uniting these men, both collectively and psychologically. Whereas earlier they drew strength from one another, now there are good reasons for not hanging out with the others.

At this point in their unemployment, a certain competition appears to develop, which, coupled with the shame of their circumstances, often leads the men in to more reclusive lifestyles. The reader may recall Ethel Wilkinson's words to her husband about Joel Epstein: "I mean, how come he didn't tell you what he was doing all along? Because he's in competition with you as much as you are with him. He doesn't want you to know what he's planning because if he doesn't get the job he goes down a few notches in *your* eyes, right?"

Ostensibly, a fellow unemployed man represents competition for the few jobs that might come one's way. Over time, the competitive stance gives way to more irrational fears of other men, if not overt animosity. The competitiveness or envy often leads to a man seeming especially touchy, a characteristic Lifton and Olson found as well among the traumatized survivors of the Buffalo Creek flood disaster.[28] No longer does the discouraged worker feel uplifted by his colleagues' circumstances, now he is driven even further downward by the recognition of and association with them. Unemployment suddenly emerges as a contagious disease. Men proclaim an ungenerous society to be a virus while in their minds they may blame other unemployed workers for "spreading the illness."

Notions of contagion and competition notwithstanding, unemployed people join together. Occasionally, these meetings are successful, but they require enormous psychological effort on the part of each participant. Men may well find support and encouragement in speaking with those "in the same boat," but all too frequently competitive issues intervene. The meetings frequently revealed the sort of ranking Alfred Syre called "the least successful men on earth," as if the men had to determine once and for all who was the greatest failure among them. On the surface, one might have imagined these meetings to be little more than self pity contests, "pity parties" some called them, but on reflecting further on George Wilkinson's statement regarding his father's observations on society's standards, we find that a different dynamic emerges. "George," I asked him once, "do you ever wonder which of the guys I talk to I like the most, or think is the most likely candidate for unemployment?"[29] George listened intently but said nothing. "Let me ask another question: Do you ever hate me for being the success, at least in your eyes, that your father wanted *you* to be?" He just continued to stare at me. "Do I sound like a shrink?" "Yup," he answered finally, with a trace of a smile starting to form. "Yup to everyone of your damn questions!"

Later in that same conversation he made it clear that he dreaded his association with the world of the unemployed. It was not that he imagined himself a snob, nor was he undergoing the characteristic forms of denial often heard among the unemployed. It was simply that unemployment was a world meant for others. He elaborated this point with a wide-ranging discussion about society meting out rewards, recognition, and status, and although imperfect, remaining the powerful and central governing force of our lives. His reflections were sociological in nature, but clearly he was addressing a far more personal matter: In George's mind, society was the embodiment of the concept of father. It's hardly an unusual notion as many children grow up believing their fathers represent their own connection to society. Increasingly, women, too, represent this connection for the child, but traditionally it has been the father who went into the world and "brought home" the values and standards practiced "out there," along with their pay checks. If, in the traditional paradigm, mothers organized and looked over the (internal) emotional world of the family, then fathers prepared their children for careers and all varieties of circumstances to be met in the world external to the family.

Because of his father's teachings, George viewed society as organizing and governing life, yielding social integrity as well as causing conflict for people, and in the end, rendering determinations about each man's successes and failures, all of them predicated on status and income. If society established standards, then it was the father who imparted and underwrote them, exactly as Freud described in his concept of the superego. If society permitted the rich and powerful to make significant decisions, then, by dint of the power and richness accorded him by his family, it was the father who made significant decisions, like letting millions of men go without work and eventually infecting one another.

Here again was that same catch: One doesn't reach the status of father merely by siring a child; one reaches it by maintaining steady work, providing and protecting, which in turn legitimates and defines one's status and authority. When a man loses his job, he loses not only the foundation of the father's role and once again becomes the boy, he loses "fatherness," which is to say, the father's legitimate position in society. Ollie Sindon's son, Davey, offered confirming evidence of this notion: "Man's got a job so he thinks he's got the right to order us around. Nobody's told him you got to earn your place in the house. You don't just get it for free. I might have thought he was pretty cute when I was small, but I don't see nothing cute about him now."

As his father (or in Ollie's case, his son) throws him out, so, too, do social institutions castigate him, leaving him bereft of work, purpose, and status. At this point, the man has lost his position within the society. In his mind he has become a leper, sentenced to lead an isolated existence. There will be no satisfaction, for his father (society) has expelled him, and because his father lives forever in his mind, there can be no sanctuary.

George Wilkinson died believing his father despised him for what had occurred. Yet he, too, despised the failure he saw in the mirror, the "complete bust of a man," as he said. One wonders whether this kindly man believed he had to kill himself for failing so miserably in the eyes of society, or whether, given his circumstances, he performed the one act he imagined society, his father really, would deem appropriate.

"You know what they call people like me?" he asked one afternoon returning from a meeting with several other unemployed men.

"Long-term unemployed? Discouraged worker?"

"You're not even close."

"Depressed?"

"Well, that too? "

"Suicidal?"

"Who isn't?"

"Am I getting closer?"

"You're thinking too much like a psychologist. Think like a man."

"They call men like you bums."

"Now you're hot. They call us undesirables. You hear that? They don't want us around. They don't want us seen. They don't even want us seeing one another, or ourselves. They don't want *us*. We clog up their systems. We're no good to anyone, especially our families. We're undesirables."

All those close to George Wilkinson blamed themselves for not doing something before it was too late. Then again, they had all told him he was loved, but this only prompted him to mumble something about people becoming too preoccupied with popular psychology. His wife repeatedly told him of her love and respect and that didn't save him. One continues to wonder what might have happened if that keenly intelligent man had known in his heart of hearts that his father loved him, believed in him, and would not alter these sentiments one iota in the face of his son not being able to secure a job.

At this juncture, a caveat seems in order. The purpose of this book has been to make the reader aware of the stories of long-term unemployed men living at a time when the U. S. economy is seen to be flourishing. Simply put, it was hoped that the men might be known to people other than the few who surround them, or more likely, walk on egg shells around them.

Importantly, the unemployed have no argument with women. They don't blame women for their predicaments and destinies, although at times there is no one but women on whom to vent their frustrations and despair. Surely they hold no one in their families responsible for their circumstances. To the contrary: Reeking with self-reproach and barely able to face their families, knowing the failure their lives have become, they could not be more disappointed with anyone than they are with themselves.

The purpose, therefore, in offering suggestive male–female differences in time orientations, styles of thought, philosophical outlooks, varying capacities to compartmentalize one's life and identity, as we do in this and the following chapter, is to indicate why it is that on occasion, a man might descend to chauvinistic thoughts and actions. It is too simple to claim that long-term unemployed men demanded their wives serve them dinner, or asked to be relieved from parenting responsibilities on the grounds that this was women's work. In fact, research indicates that working-class men, those with steady jobs anyway, spend more time with their children than do affluent men, who tend to use their free time working around the house but not necessarily interacting with their children.

Without employment, a man finds it difficult to function within the natural boundaries of his family. He observes the charade of his children being careful never to sit in his seat at the head of the table, even though he no longer earns this seat, perhaps any seat, for that matter. Attempting to see the world through his son's eyes, Ollie Sindon observed: "If you're old enough to see your old man ain't working, and you're old enough to understand when he don't work it means he ain't bringing home a fuckin' dime, then you're old enough to get away from that man as soon as you can 'cause he *ain't* no man. He *ain't* no father."

Rarely did the men demand that their wives perform duties out of some traditional sense of women maintaining subservient roles. In truth, many of the men felt as uncomfortable asking for anything as they did not asking. As a result, they just sat in their favorite chairs saying little to anyone. The manifestly sexist language uttered by some men was not necessarily heard in pejorative ways by their wives who felt their husband's guilt and shame as well as their own. They, too, had to offer explanations of and excuses for their husband's unemployment. Every other day, moreover, someone admonished them to find new things to occupy their "free" time, or new ways of relating to people, or perhaps just thinking about unemployment.

WORK AND THE MEANING OF TIME

Our discussion of work and the meaning of time, hardly a new association in the literature of unemployment, commences with the theme of starting over, something heard in numerous accounts.[30] Perhaps the feeling that one has returned to the beginning of life is ignited by the helplessness, the babylike sentiment of being out of work and thus dependent on others, even children. Ed Zegler had used the word *baby* when describing his tortured neighbors Peter and Stacy Bennett, Peter having been out of work for many months: "What she was doing, see, was trying to convince him he was no better than a baby. She said it right to his face: 'A fucking baby girl can do more than you.'" Later he added, "The Bennetts were riding other people's living, and it made them into babies." In this same vein, we recall Victoria Sindon yelling at her husband: "You act like you were his *baby* brother 'stead of his father. 'Bout time you started acting like his father!"

The theme of starting anew was noted as well in a characteristically male-oriented perception of time.[31] Years ago in a study having nothing to do, actually, with unemployment, I asked men and women to play a game of fantasy. I instructed them to pretend that they had all the money in the world and I had all the time. Now, I inquired, how much of their money would they offer to know the future in advance and regain the past? What would they do, furthermore, should they actually regain past time?

The results shed some light on the matter of long-term unemployment. Essentially, women disliked the idea of knowing the future, whereas men suggested that although mystery was important to them, knowing at least a few things about the future might prove especially enlightening. More about this in a moment.

As for the fantasy of regaining past time, women and men alike jumped at the opportunity to play the game of time retrieval. Where the genders differed, however, was in the use to which they would put this retrieved time. Women typically claimed they would return to good past times and *relive* them. Men, in contrast, wished to return to certain troubling times, more precisely, times of failure, and *re-do* them, this time making everything come out right.

The data generated in that earlier research are suggestive at best, but they do point to something significant. Men are raised, as David Bakan suggested, to engage life in terms of *agentic* thinking and acting.[32] They are instructed, in other words, to conceive of the present moment essentially in terms of how it may be employed to transport one to, as well as shape future moments. It goes without saying that one can only live or tell one's story from the perspective of the here and now. On this point, Polkinghorne, referring to Roland Barthes, wrote, "At the individual level, people have a narrative of their own lives which enables them to construe what they are and where they are headed."[33] Yet according to Bakan, the man's here-and-now is not necessarily meant to be enjoyed or perhaps even experienced in and of itself, but rather employed to make some future moment possible. Women, in contrast, appear to enjoy the here-and-now in and of itself, or at least embrace it as the only time they possess and can directly experience. Bakan called the feminine orientation *communal*, inasmuch as women seek connection with the immediacy of the here-and-now for whatever it offers, and not necessarily for what it portends.[34]

One sees in these orientations a potentially dangerous strain for men: namely, that one is never permitted to fully experience the immediacy of the moment. If a man constantly prepares for the future, if his present signifies little more than the origin of the future, then, in a sense, he is constantly alienated from time. It's a bit like asking children why they attend first grade. The girl's answer is that it's important for her to be learning reading, writing, and arithmetic, whereas the boy responds that he has to if he wants to get to second grade.

Women, moreover, appear content to let the future arrive in due course, whereas men seem less able to reconcile the natural flow of time. Men prefer to use the present in order to construct the future, sculpt it according to their present as well as anticipated needs and desires. Rarely do they appear content merely to let the future come to pass. Men become more preoccupied than women with predicting, prognosticating, and projecting, and will seek to employ historical information not just to explain present circumstances, but to provide them insight into the imagined structure and content of the future.[35] Then again, in the most elementary terms, there was Ed Zegler's terse comment about the Bennetts, who at the time were living through their unemployment months: "When you have a situation like theirs, deep-rooted unemployment which gets worse every day, you begin to see the future very clearly."

Quite possibly, men and women engage in verbal and philosophical conflicts that they are unable to recognize as deriving from fundamental differences in perceptions of time. A man claims, for example, that his wife's argument lacks logic. "But you said something totally different two minutes ago," he challenges her in utter frustration. His claim may or may not be philosophically valid, but his need to have the past, present, and future flow together in what he perceives to be logical and continuous fashion remains paramount in his thinking.[36] Illogical reasoning for him, implies not only psychological or cognitive deficiency, but a break in the continuity and connection of time zones, to which men's entire rational and calculable life is devoted, and on which it rests.

To repeat, a man prefers to use the immediate moment and therefore (believe he can) know the next moment, which in turn makes it possible for him to understand the meaning of the prior moment. Taking this point to its logical conclusion, it follows that a man reads history in order to understand not only the present, but to foresee the future as well, whereas a woman may be freer to read history not only for these same purposes, but also to enjoy history for its own sake. What possible enjoyment, women may ask, could a man derive from reading the history of wars. Having witnessed General Norman Schwarzkopf's victory in the Persian Gulf, the answer men would offer is simple: One reads the history of past wars in order to learn how to win future ones.

It is not merely the utilitarian nature of a particular enterprise that makes a difference, it is the fundamental orientation to temporality that influences men and women as they undertake a particular venture. One sees it in art as well. How often does one hear boys question the purpose of painting or sculpting. What will it get them (in the future, that is)? In the minds of some young men, if there is not future financial or career payoff to an activity like painting, then there is little point to becoming involved in it. Oscar Wilde's assertion of art for art's sake must strike many men as an anathema.

From one perspective, the question of knowing the future is preposterous, although many of us are attracted to those people claiming psychic or prescient powers. Men and women have forever argued with one another over the validity of claiming to know the future. But if men doubt women's investment in astrology, then quite a few women have questioned men's efforts to "know" the future by imagining that one's plans or predictions are tantamount to constructing it.

Seeking to shape and thereby know the future stands at the center of a man's most significant work, or so he has been taught. Early in his life, parents and teachers pointed him toward the future. Barely was he able to talk when adults began inquiring what he wanted to be when he grew up. Irrespective of his answer, at least he was learning to give serious thought not only to the idea of career, but to the idea of the future and his eventual (and agentic) role in it.

How then, does a boy grab on to the future—a time that by definition can never arrive, for when it does it is properly described as the present—and still maintain himself on a rational course? The answer is that society provides it for him in the name of work. It is his job and commitment to a career that carry him nonstop from the present to the future. It is not by accident that a man maps out his life as early as adolescence, nor that he lays out for himself a reasonable time table of prospective career steps, or makes the claim that he will be married or have made his first million by the time he is thirty. Nor is it accidental that he thinks of investment strategies and pension programs decades before his retirement. He reasons these matters out, even as others may label his endeavors premature. Yet always it is through work that he makes these connections with the future.

Other aspects of his life may be predicated on this same temporal orientation. Betting, financial speculating and planning, investing, purchasing items on time, preparation of all kinds, provide the man direct links with the future. He cannot take seriously the advice of astrologers, for purposeful activity refutes the notion of fate, that the future merely lies in the stars. He has been taught to believe (and hope) that one can personally control much of what the future yields.[37] A man's life must not be viewed as some grand mystery, each day delivering something new and different. Tomorrow takes form, the man imagines, because of what he accomplishes today, and the plans he has worked hard to design. Indeed, establishing plans represents the essential purpose and reward of today. A day is wasted not only if concrete efforts cannot be observed and measured, but if the content of tomorrow has not been established or outlined.

It emerges as a master plan for work, finance, and living, and every man contemplates it. He makes his infamous daily to-do list—a list containing a bit of magic—and has it completed before permitting himself to leave his office or the plant. In his quiet hours, he dreams about finances: This year I make so much, next year I figure to get a raise, by the time I'm sixty-five I should be able to retire earning so much per month. Quite probably, he calculates the figures to the penny. George Wilkinson described it this way: "Oh, I'll think about Friday afternoons a lot on Monday mornings, but just as often I'll think about Monday morning on Saturday night when I'm supposed to put work out of my mind. But most men are like that."

The sociologist Max Weber noted that action becomes rational and purposeful when one (believes he) can calculate it.[38] And what better way to calculate life than by planning one's career, earning capacity and estate? Calculation is one of the grand dividends of steady work and a life in which one's lot annually improves, and employment remains the cornerstone of rational, calculable masculine action. It may well be the essence of what Weber called the Protestant ethic and the spirit of capitalism.[39] It also may well be, as noted earlier, the cornerstone of (masculine) physical and mental health. What other activity could better prepare a man to take on life? And death? As Ollie Sindon put it: "I may not love what I'm doing, but I'm working, and working is the act we're put on earth to do."

When a man asks, "What's the point of all this?" or, "Why go on when nothing makes sense?" he receives one response: It is in the work and in working that one's consciousness takes shape, and life reveals its meaning, if only because in working a man believes he has made some sense of life's mysteries and found some reasonable method of avoiding metaphysical questions. In work, the irrational becomes rational, the incalculable becomes calculable, the meaningless assumes meaning. And so, when a man has lost something profoundly valuable, when he feels battered down by the unfairness of political systems or the capriciousness of fate, he can always say, "Thank God, at least I have my job."

When, however, after months of hunting for work, he is left without benefits, income, or hope, the entire plan, the entire orientation to time and destiny falls away, and he is left with nothing. He finds little within himself, minimal strength at best, and certainly no philosophical or psychological foundation to carry him beyond the immediate circumstances of unemployment. Time, somehow, is stripped away from him; the present, future, and past must now be totally redefined. And, as the one hold he has maintained on life gives way, he well may pray for death to take him. Or perhaps he feels it already has.

"Beware the man who tells you he lives day to day," Albert Syre warned me. "That is a man who's either recovering from alcohol, unemployed, or a man planning to die. No healthy man with a job lives that way. He lives with an eye to the present and an eye to the future. When there's no future, he only looks at the present because now he's lost sight in one eye. And you don't have to know much to know when you lose one eye you're bound to lose the other. This man knows he's going blind."

Men seem fascinated looking down long stretches of road and viewing the horizon, the mountains in the distance, the endless space beyond the clouds. These characteristically masculine visions develop in part not from spatial orientations, but from temporal ones.[40] When he looks down the road, he sees endpoints, goals, results. Men live with the Greek notion of *telos*, goal, or endpoint, embedded in their minds. They hunt for action and work because in work there are means and ends, origins and conclusions, and above all, designated purpose no matter how frivolous it appears to others. This is what Weber meant when he spoke of the rational, calculable worldview that we now see married to the concept and reality of working.

Ken Hawkins took this notion one step further: "Society says there's only one kind of work. You leave your home to do work in the morning, and you travel to your place of work, and you travel home before dinner. You do this five days a week, and you get paid, and then what you do is called work."

NOTES

1. On this point, see M. H. Finley and L. A. Terence, "The Terminated Executive: It's Like Dying," *Personnel and Guidance Journal* 59 (1981): 382–84.

2. Cited in T. J. Cottle, "Men with No Answers," in *At Peril: Stories of Injustice* (Amherst, MA: University of Massachusetts Press, in press).

3. See D. M. Noer, *Healing the Wounds* (San Francisco, Jossey-Bass, 1993).

4. For a discussion of this point, see K. L. Schlozman, *Injury to Insult: Unemployment, Class and Political Response* (Cambridge, MA: Harvard University Press, 1979); and C. R. Leana, *Coping with Job Loss: How Individuals, Organizations, and Communities Respond to Layoffs* (New York: Lexington Books, 1992).

5. On these topics, see G. Piers and M. B. Singer, *Shame and Guilt* (New York: Norton, 1971); G. Kaufman, *Shame: The Power of Caring* (Cambridge, MA: Schenkman, 1980); G. Kaufman, *The Psychology of Shame* (New York: Springer, 1989); A. P. Morrison, *The Culture of Shame* (New York: Ballantine, 1996); and D. L. Nathanson, *The Many Faces of Shame* (New York: Guilford, 1987).

6. On a related point, see G. Valliant, *Adaptation to Life* (Boston: Little Brown, 1977).

7. On this point, see C. Peterson, S. M. Schwartz, and M. E. P. Seigman, "Self-Blame and Depressive Symptoms," *Journal of Personality and Social Psychology 41* (1981): 253–59.

8. H. Kohut, *Search for the Self. Selected Writings of Heinz Kohut, Vol. 2* (New York: International Universities Press, 1978).

9. R. J. Lifton and E. Olson, "The Human Meaning of Total Disaster: The Buffalo Creek Experience," *Psychiatry 39* (1976): 1–18.

10. Quoted in J. Hawkins, "Rowers on the River Styx," *Harvard Magazine*, March/April (1991): 51.

11. Mary Lynn Pulley, *op. cit.*, 21.

12. On the subject of unemployment and depression, see N. T. Feather and J. G. Barber, "Depressive Reactions and Unemployment," *Journal of Abnormal Behavior 92* (1983): 185–95.

13. I have written elsewhere about unemployment as a family secret. See T. J. Cottle, *Children's Secrets* (Reading, MA: Addison Wesley, 1980).

14. On this point, see E. Goffman, *Stigma: Notes on the Management of Spoiled Identity* (Englewood Cliffs, NJ: Prentice Hall, 1963). Then again, having certain types of jobs actually stigmatize a worker. On this point, see K. M. Dudley, *The End of the Line* (Chicago: University of Chicago Press, 1994).

15. E. H. Erikson, *Childhood and Society* (New York: Norton, 1963).

16. On this and related points, see J. Hayes and P. Nugman, *Understanding the Unemployed* (London: Tavistock, 1981).

17. For an interesting discussion of the role of social situations in self-blame, see R. Janoff-Bulman, "Characterological Versus Behavioral Self-Blame," *Journal of Personality and Social Psychology 37* (1979): 1798–1809.

18. On this and related points, see S. Aronowitz, *False Promises: The Shaping of American Working Class Consciousness* (New York: McGraw-Hill, 1973); and L. Mischel and D. M. Frankel, *"The State of Working America, 1990–1991 Edition."* (Armonk, NY: Economic Policy Institute, 1991). This work is cited in Dudley, *The End of the Line, op. cit.*

19. See J. Kozol, *Rachel and Her Children: Homeless Families in America* (New York: Crown, 1988).

20. For a discussion of this point, see W. Ryan, *Blaming the Victim* (New York: Random House, 1972).

21. On a related point, see J. D. Owen, *Reduced Working Hours: Cure for Unemployment or Economic Burden* (Baltimore, MD: Johns Hopkins University Press, 1989).

22. Prepared by the Office of Economic Adjustment, Office of the Assistant Secretary of Defense (Installations and Logistics), The Pentagon, Washington, DC. I am grateful to Peter J. Ezzy for bringing this material to my attention.

23. On a related point, see P. Minuchin, J. Colapinto, and S. Minuchin, *Working with Families of the Poor* (New York: Guilford, 1998).

24. On this point, see M. Komarovsky, 1940, *op. cit.*; R. Liem and J. H. Liem, "Psychological Effects of Unemployment on Workers and Their Families," *Journal of Social Issues 44* (1988): 87–105; and L. McKee and C. Bell, "His Unemployment, Her Problem: The Domestic and Marital Consequences of Male Unemployment." In C. Allen, A. Waton, K. Purcell, and S. Woods, Eds., *The Experience of Unemployment* (London: Macmillan, 1986).

25. On this point, see P. Ullah, M. H. Banks, and P. B. Warr, "Social Support, Social Pressures, and Psychological Distress During Unemployment," *Psychological Medicine 15* (1985): 283–95.

26. See S. Minuchin, *Families and Family Therapy* (Cambridge, MA: Harvard University Press, 1974).

27. See Noer, *op. cit.*; and Dudley, *op. cit.*

28. R. J. Lifton and E. Olson, *op. cit.*

29. See Noer, *op. cit.*

30. On this rich topic, see M. J. Bond and N. T. Feather, "Some Correlates of Structure and Purpose in the Use of Time," *Journal of Personality and Social Psychology 55* (1988): 321–29; M. L. De Volder and W. Lens, "Academic Achievement and Future Time Perspective as a Cognitive-Motivational Concept," *Journal of Personality and Social Psychology 42* (1982): 566–71; N. T. Feather and M. J. Bond, "Time Structure and Purposeful Activity Among Employed and Unemployed University Graduates," *Journal of Occupational Psychology 56* (1983): 241–54; W. Lens, "Future Time Perspective: A Cognitive-Motivational Concept," in D. R. Brown and J. Veroff, Eds., *Frontiers of Motivational Psychology: Essays in Honor of John W. Atkinson* (New York: Springer-Verlag, 1986); T. J. Cottle, *Perceiving Time: An Investigation with Men and Women* (New York: Wiley, 1976); D. M. Fryer and S. P. McKenna, "The Laying Off of Hands: Unemployment and the Experience of Time," in S. Fineman, Ed., *Unemployment: Personal and Social Consequences* (London: Tavistock, 1987); J. Nuttin, *Future Time Perspective and Motivation* (Hillsdale, NJ: Lawrence Erlbaum, 1985).

31. T. J. Cottle, *Perceiving Time, op. cit.*, see especially chapter 5.

32. See his *Duality of Human Existence* (Chicago: Rand McNally, 1966).

33. D. E. Polkinghorne, *Narrative Knowing and the Human Sciences* (Albany, NY: State University of New York, 1988).

34. These notions are familiar to readers of Henri Bergson. See, for example, *Matter and Memory* (New York: Humanities Press, 1970).

35. On this point, see J. B. Burg, *The Idea of Progress* (New York: Dover, 1955).

36. For a general discussion of this point, see R. Brumbaugh, "Logic and Time," *Review of Metaphysics 18* (1965): 656.

37. See, for example, J. T. Fraser, Ed., *The Voices of Time* (New York: Braziller, 1966).

38. See his *Economy and Society* (New York: Bedminster Press, 1968).

39. On this point, see A. Furnham, "The Protestant Work Ethic and Attitudes Toward Unemployment," *Journal of Occupational Psychology* 55 (1982): 277–286; H. L. Mirels and J. B. Garrett, "The Protestant Ethic as a Personality Variable," *Journal of Consulting and Clinical Psychology* 36 (1971): 40–44; N. T. Feather, "Protestant Ethic, Conservation, and Values," *Journal of Personality and Social Psychology* 46 (1984): 1132–41; J. R. Feagin, "Poverty: We Still Believe That God Helps Those Who Help Themselves," *Psychology Today* 6 (1972): 101–29.

40. On this point, see M. Merleau-Ponty, *The Structure of Behavior* (Boston: Beacon Press, 1963); and M. Heidegger, *Being and Time* (New York: Harper & Row, 1962).

Chapter 10

The Trauma
of Unemployment

The trouble is that the rotten nine-to-five boredom routine we've invented called work, that *affects who you are, what you are, how much you can love.*

THE ROLE OF WORK IN NORMAL DEVELOPMENT

It is essential to understand that work is not merely something a man does, nor even his reason for living. As William Julius Wilson and Katherine Newman[1] have pointed out, work provides the structure and substance of a man's life as well as his thinking. It is the activity causing him to feel sane and whole. It is the activity assuring him he is who he is, whatever his deficiencies, whatever his broken dreams and seemingly wasted efforts. It remains the centerpiece of his story. From Newman: "But for our more diverse and divided society, participation in the world of work is the most powerful force of social integration."[2]

Robert Kegan suggested that an event becomes an experience only when one gives it meaning.[3] While carrying certain predictable outcomes, the event of unemployment requires a man to give it meaning before he processes it as an experience. Much of the human life cycle is constituted of events that must assume meaning before we experience them as milestones, distinguishable moments, or stages. What, for example, is the special significance of turning thirty, forty, or fifty? It is merely that people decide these ages represent notable landmarks by which point accomplishments or levels of maturity are meant to be demonstrated.

Turning forty is an arbitrary non-event to which we impute meaning. For that matter, dying could be considered a non-event to which we give meaning. But let us be more precise. A man of seventy-five dies and one hears, "He led a long life. What more was left for him to do?" Or we say, "Surely he could have had ten more good years." The individual death at seventy-five exists as mere event, but our reactions to this death actually construct the experience of death at seventy-five, and hence the meaning of being seventy-five.

Similarly, we ask, "What is old age?" For some, it's a mere number. For others, it is defined in terms of changes in occupation, relationships, health, and levels of activity. For still others, old age is characterized by alterations, some subtle, some not so, in cognitive capacities, quality of life, or the successful or unsuccessful completion of roles, like parenting and grandparenting. And still others perceive old age as the commencement of discontinuities in the life cycle.

Examining the latter stages of the life cycle, Erikson theorized that the final years were characterized by dilemmas of *generativity versus self-absorption* and *integrity versus despair*.[4] The latter dilemma essentially means that people are experiencing what Erikson called a lack of ego integration. Either they are able to accept and incorporate with some satisfaction the prior years of their life, or they are doomed to lament their existence and ultimately judge their lives a failure. The dilemma points as well to the idea that people dread death, or imagine in some way that they cannot properly prepare for it, either because there is too little time left for them, or because they have been permanently damaged, somehow, by the prospect of it. If, on the other hand, these dilemmas are successfully resolved, that is, if the person feels the strengths of generativity and integrity, then a lasting outcome reveals itself in the person's ability to emerge productive, caring, and wise. The critical point for Erikson was that people come to terms with life, assess their lives as successful, and on reflection feel fulfilled. If they cannot achieve these tasks, it is likely that they lead lives of hopelessness and stagnation.

Kegan referred to the final stages of life as *institutional and inter-individual* (as opposed to the interpersonal period of adolescence). Paramount in Kegan's final stages are concerns about love, intimacy, and career. For both Kegan and Erikson, the culture guides people through profound self-definitions and personal assessments. Toward the end of life, people must assume for once and for all, genuine authorship of their lives, which implies authorship of intimacy and career. Kegan's ideas are not that distant, actually, from Freud's famous criteria of health, namely the capacity for love and work.

Kegan, moreover, is concerned with the role of ambition, personal enhancement, and career advancement in personal as well as culturally defined contexts. Ideology too, he noted, as did Erikson, plays a significant role in self-definition, and suggests that job loss is crucial during this time of measuring one's ultimate worth. In the end, independent and interdependent definitions of self arise, definitions influenced by the forces of one's culture and society. Accordingly, it seems almost impossible to reach a conclusion of a successful life (Erikson's integrity stage), when one's latter years are bereft of work.

Offering additional import for those concerned with unemployment, Kegan repeatedly made a distinction between "having a job," the focus typically of young people, and "having a career," something indicative of a more mature position on the life span. Having a job is fine for someone looking merely to make money. When one speaks of genuine satisfaction and the fulfillment of life goals, however, it is a career, as Newman[5] too pointed out, and not simply a job that one is addressing. (Indeed, it is the reality of career that defines certain work as underemployment.) Too regularly, the long-term unemployed never do regain their foothold in anything resembling a career.

Few make these points as well as the late Daniel Levinson.[6] Even a cursory examination of Levinson's stages of male development reveals the central role of career, not merely job history, in shaping a man's life as well as his self-image.

A key to understanding Levinson's theory is found in the concept of a developmental transition from one stage to the next. A man, Levinson wrote, is constantly building and transforming the structure of his life, a structure built in part on the successful completion of tasks. Consider, for example, the period of the late teens through the early thirties, the developmental period

Levinson labeled the *novice phase*. The paramount tasks of these years are first, forming a dream and providing it a place in the structure of one's life; second, forming mentor relationships, which essentially are oriented around career issues; third, forming an occupation—Levinson purposely eschewed the phrase "holding down jobs"—and fourth, forming love relationships, which, biased as this may seem, means marriage and family. Erikson too, had believed in these processes, suggesting that a man's occupation, and not merely his job became a major force in resisting the role confusions often found in adolescence. Like Levinson, Erikson before him believed that adulthood is marked in great measure by the necessity of creating projects and bringing them to life. Clearly, work lies at the center of these so-called projects.[7]

From this point until the age of about forty, a man is "settling down," Levinson alleged, which implies advancing on a ladder of personal enterprises, and establishing his niche in society. In a word, he is trying to "make it," although he may break out into new structures. Either way, career and work loom as the central focus of identity. They do as well during one's forties, Levinson theorized, when a man is less tyrannized by ambition and the illusions of youth. Through his perspective on the world, sculpted in part by career, a man asks, "What have I done with my life, and how can I use my career to reshape it?" There may even be what Levinson called significant marker events during this time, one of which, major job change or job loss, will permanently alter the course of his life.

Holding the realities of unemployment in mind, consider the structures and sentiments normally present in the lives of men going through what Levinson called *middle and later adulthood*. These are the years when men are expected to fulfill their dreams, feel happy with their accomplishments, and become heroes to themselves. It is anticipated that they will take pride in their competence and what it has earned them, and proceed to map out the next steps of the journey. Putting aside petty vanities, animosities, and moral teachings of early childhood, it is now time to plan the structures of a more creative life, ideally one filled with stimulation and purpose. Men must focus as well on contributing to their families and communities where, given their career histories, they represent a force for stability. More generally, they are meant to become content with the place they have created for themselves in the world (a notion not dissimilar to Erikson's concept of integrity). Need one even mention the role of career in this particularly masculine structure of identity?

There is at least one more significant element in these latter periods of development. As a man contemplates societal and cultural matters, religion, ethnicity, various ideologies, so too must he attempt to establish a new involvement with society. In part this means creating new links between the value of self and the values advanced by society. What, in other words, does the society desire and deem desirable, and how does a man incorporate these definitions into his own sense of self, an issue about which the playwright Arthur Miller spoke directly:

> Society is inside of man and man is inside of society, and you cannot even create a truthfully drawn psychological entity on the stage until you understand his social relations and their power to make him what he is and to prevent him from being what he is not. The fish is in the water and the water is in the fish.

Any point on the path of one's life emerges as a non-event ultimately to be appraised intellectually and emotionally, or perhaps overlooked by the maturing person. That I had three children means I am successful, but perhaps not as successful as four children would have made me. That I held a job means my life was successful, but not as successful as it might have been had I earned more money or derived greater satisfaction from my work.

More generally, all events are open to subjective definitions that change as a function of experience. Who is to say, for example, what point on the life cycle constitutes the conclusion of adolescence? Is it graduating high school? Obtaining a job? Attending college? The point is neither abstract nor whimsical. People derive their definitions of the life cycle from cultural norms and values. Employing these criteria, events are given meaning and thus are experienced by individuals as significant if not life altering. In the end, much of what we claim life offers we ourselves have constructed.

A man in his thirties is involved in an accident and left paralyzed. He now must decide whether it seems worthwhile to go on with his life. It is not that he contemplates suicide, rather, the event to which he must now assign meaning has brought him, in his mind, to contemplate the end of life. Surely it is not time for him to die, but an event has caused him to redefine his life cycle as well as his position on it. "It is over for me," he says in despair. "Why continue to live?" Unemployment is that paralyzing accident. In the mind of the unemployed man, the end of work and career only logically brings a man to the end of the life cycle; there is nothing more to do but die. Let me spell this out.

Beyond mere chronology, old age is defined in biological, psychological, social, and what psychologists call functional terms, that is, age based on cognitive capabilities and capacities. All of these terms are colored by cultural factors as well. In truth, the notion of development becomes a synonym for aging. Thus, there are physiological, psychological, and social contexts of aging of which we are all familiar. Intellectual changes involve variations in crystalline and fluid intelligence, the former being the product of experience and education. Personality, it is alleged, becomes less flexible, less adaptable with age. The adjective "crotchety" surely wouldn't apply to a toddler, whom we might rather call "cranky." Interesting too, gerontologists inform us that differences between men and women tend to recede as the years pass.

Then there is the matter of evaluating one's life, a process that although occurring throughout the life cycle, assumes greatest significance during the latter years when one commences evaluations of an entire career. Typically, the elderly assess their lives according to disabilities as well as to work histories. The critical concept in these evaluations is adaptation: How well do we adapt to the reality that our children no longer require us? How well do we adapt to our diminished physical abilities? How well do we adapt to what Erich Lindemann called the "loss of patterns of conduct,"[8] something so central to long-term unemployment? And how well do we adapt to terminal unemployment when we acknowledge that steady work and enduring careers cause us to conclude that our lives have been successful?

Sadly, accounts of the long-term unemployed reveal men occupying empty spaces in their families. More precisely, men perceive themselves as empty spaces, disabled, failures as providers, husbands, and fathers. Logically, these self-perceptions lead them to conclude that they are old despite the fact that chronologically they may occupy Levinson's middle or later adulthood stages. Successful aging, in other words, finds men adapting to later stage roles (Erikson's integrity stage).[9] The question then is not whether a person should retire, but how comfortable he imagines himself to be in retirement. But what contributes to a person's feeling of comfort? Gerontologists speak of five components potentially providing meaning or significance for a role.

First, biological *renewal and/or continuity* alert us to factors that are substantially inhibited if not altogether eliminated when one is unemployed. Second, *emotional self-fulfillment* also is diminished by long-term unemployment. Third is being used as a *resource person*, the village wise man or woman in the familiar example. Again, the unemployed hardly envision themselves as resource people, unless, of course, people wish to know firsthand the experience of being out of work. The reader will recall Gabriel Foreman, at a time when he was out of work, contemplating the possibility of teaching computer technology to high school students: "I even talked about the idea of getting into high schools and teaching kids computers. Fat chance, getting a teaching job without my own *real* job. I could have advised the kids about unemployment. What's the expression, people who can, do, and those who can't, teach. Because they can't find a job!"

The fourth criterion of so-called role meaning is the capacity to *accomplish vicariously*. Ideally, an aging man delights in the successes of his children and grandchildren. Yet here too, the inability to rise above one's own depression, what Lindemann observed as an agitated depression typically found in bereavement, or sense of a failed life, make it almost impossible for the long-term unemployed to enjoy the accomplishments of others, a fact often remarked on by relatives.

Fifth and finally, a man tends to enjoy old age more if he believes that he continues to have some *effect on people*, particularly family members, even though he may be physically remote from them. But as we have repeatedly observed, the unemployed perceive themselves more as lepers than positive influences. On what, they would ask, could their influence or status possibly be predicated?

Even styles of grandparenting offer clues as to why long-term unemployed men would define themselves as having reached the end of their lives. In studies performed decades ago, Bernice Neugarten and Karol Weinstein[10] classified grandparents as *formal*, which assumes that they derive a certain respect and status, *fun seeking*, which suggests the absence of depression and despair, *surrogate parents*, an almost impossible status for the terminally unemployed who years ago forfeited any belief in their ability to parent, the *reservoir of family wisdom*, another implausible category for someone who has lost confidence in himself, and finally, the *distant figure*, most definitely the style of the long-term unemployed. Discouraged workers are indeed distant figures, men believing they reside in the empty spaces of their own, their family's, and their culture's evolution.

As we age, three basic entities shape the way we undertake these afore-mentioned self-assessments. The first entity is represented by our *families of orientation*, our parents, siblings, grandparents, and so on. A man asks, for example, "Am I a good son?" The second entity is constituted by the families we have created, *families of procreation* they are called by anthro-pologists. Now we assess ourselves as fathers, mothers, grandparents. A man asks, "Am I more successful now than my father was at this same age?" The third entity influencing our assessments of ourselves is what might be called *societal roles*, or more precisely, the manner in which we manage soci-etal roles and obligations, the major one in contemporary American cul-ture being that of worker. Assessment of success in this category typically is defined in terms of ego involvement and life satisfaction.

The matter of assessing successful aging or development is further refined by noting six criteria of happiness that, in the present context, now might be applied to elder citizens as well as long-term unemployed men. According to researchers at the University of Wisconsin, happiness is predicated upon first, *self-acceptance*, feeling good, in other words, about one's past and present; second, *autonomy*, which implies being able to fol-low one's own convictions; third, *mastery*, which suggests having a sense of control over one's daily life; fourth, *positive relations*, which normally is thought of as sustaining trusting ties with others; fifth, *purpose*, or the pos-session of goals that give life its meaning; and sixth, *personal growth*, which refers to forms of self-realization. Once again, one wonders whether any of these criteria could be met in the wake of not having had satisfying work, not to mention a successful career, or for that matter not having worked in years![11]

In the late 1960s, a group of social scientists at the University of Chicago advanced two theories of aging. Looked at from one perspective, these researchers offered a lovely differentiation of successful and less suc-cessful approaches to the latter years of the life span, and hence ultimate happiness. Looked at from the perspective of the concerns in this book, the theories provide as well insight into the experience of long-term unem-ployment.

More precisely, Robert Havinghurst and his colleagues advanced what they titled an *Activity Theory of Aging*, a theory recognizing the inevitable biological changes in older people, but carrying the assumption that the elderly nurture many of the same psychological and social needs as middle-aged people.[12] Activity Theory acknowledged that decreased social interaction results not so much from elderly persons withdrawing from society, but rather society withdrawing from them. As we know, a decrease in social interaction is hardly what the elderly desire.

Activity Theory also argued for the now well established notion that active lives make for healthy lives, an adage implying that the elderly must maintain numerous activities as well as seek substitutes for former ones now forsaken. Similarly, they must maintain old friendships as well as establish substitutes for friends and family members who have died. Easier said than done perhaps, but if the pages of this book document anything, it is that long-term unemployed men struggle with everyone of these criteria.

In *Disengagement Theory*, Havinghurst and his associates perceived the disengagement of the elderly from society more as a natural process of aging than one imposed by the society on the individual. Disengagement Theory argued that decreased social interaction is caused by the individual and society mutually withdrawing from one another, resulting in the individual reaching a greater psychological distance from society. This in turn yields altered relationships with friends and families, and usually decreased social interaction with everyone else. An essential point of disengagement theory is captured in the following passage by Laura Carstensen:

> Drawing on both structure, societal and intrapsychic processes, disengagement theory suggests that preconscious awareness of imminence of death instigates increased ideas about conflict, self awareness and social withdrawal. Grounded in psychodynamic ideas about conflict and defenses, this view represents social inactivity as a normal adaptive process. Thus, emotional quiescence, pensive self reflection, and a turning away from the social world are considered to be a natural part of aging.[13]

It is easy to see that the men in this book experienced disengagement of varying sorts, still another factor, perhaps, accounting for their failing physical health, depression, lack of energy, passive or passive-aggressive approaches to problems, moodiness, affectlessness, apathy, and overriding sense of disappointment. More than merely an interesting sociological variable, the concept of disengagement speaks directly to the question of why long-term unemployed men welcome the specter of death. At very least, it is something with which to become engaged.

If terminally unemployed men discover minimal ego involvement and satisfaction in a career and thereby rate themselves as failures as sons, husbands, fathers, and grandfathers, they experience as well what gerontologists describe as discontinuities in adapting to aging. One must adapt, after all, to reduced physical and cognitive capacities as well as to disruptions in status, social expectations, and responsibilities. Normally, these changes evolve gradually, almost imperceptibly, and in their way constitute a continuous flow of a lifetime. In sharp contrast, long-term unemployment constitutes a jolting discontinuity that makes the activity of planning the next stage or creating newer patterns of adaptation nearly impossible. Especially noticeable is the long-term unemployed man's inability to deal with discontinuities in independence. Harsh infantilizing dependencies overtake him and often prove unmanageable.

As several of the previous accounts indicate, some men never recover from the discontinuities of their work lives. For the very concept of personality development too, is predicated on a man's ability to work and find not only ego involvement in that work, but enjoy the ego that is formed and informed by work. We should not forget this point: A man works and thus builds something—an airplane, a business, a reputation. Simultaneously, he builds relationships with others as well as an ego, but it all goes to ruin when work is denied him. Daniel Bell[14] surely was correct when he alleged that postindustrial man is not only alienated from nature but no longer creates objects, or tangible products. But postindustrial man, involved as he is in service industries and the business of what Bell called "interpersonal consciousness," at least may find steady employment, which will sustain if not nurture him.

To summarize, definitions of normal development, aging, naturally occurring life-cycle changes, the quality of postparental life and grandparenting, and the criteria of happiness, all contribute to the meanings and assessments a man constructs for himself and his life. These are the elements on which he draws when attempting to give form to an experience, or transform an event like aging into the experience of aging. On making his assessments, the long-term unemployed person may reach the conclusion that irrespective of his age, or where he sits on the life line, he is old and ready for death. Unemployment thus looms as an insurmountable human discontinuity.

None of these notions should be thought of merely as theoretical constructs. They are the very themes one hears in speaking with long-term unemployed men. In my offering these observations of life stages, I hope that the reader comes to perceive the association between long-term unemployment and death in sociological and psychological terms, and not merely in metaphorical ones. Long-term unemployment is a social psychological process of (experiencing) aging, perhaps even instant aging. If the men are to be believed, when one's work is gone, one's time has come.

UNEMPLOYMENT, DYING, AND BEREAVEMENT

All of which brings us to Elisabeth Kübler-Ross' classical research on death and dying, and its possible connection to long-term unemployment.[15] Kübler-Ross' stages of coping mechanisms exhibited by people with terminal illnesses become particularly interesting to review when considering the lives of the long-term unemployed who, not so incidentally, are labeled terminally unemployed.

In Kübler-Ross' first stage of coping, people deny their situation and attempt to isolate themselves. Denial serves as a buffer against the pain first of the news and then the enduring reality of death or unemployment. The person is unable to collect himself, all the while attempting to employ useful defenses. Interestingly, in the context of unemployment, David Noer pointed out that "the higher a person resides in an organization, the more he or she will be invested in denying the symptoms or the sickness."[16] When the denial fades, however, a second stage of coping begins to emerge, this one characterized by the presence of anger.[17]

If one emotion dominates the accounts of long-term unemployed workers, it is anger. And accompanying anger are its familiar partners, envy, rage, and resentment, all of them forming what Noer called "feeling clusters."[18] "Why me?" men repeatedly ask. We have also observed anger being displaced on to anyone from the closest family member to unseen and remote legislators, and that ill-defined entity called society or "the system." Anger, Kübler-Ross suggested, may recede when the dying patient is accorded respect and understanding, something long-term unemployed men rarely experience. Eventually, their resentment of and dissatisfaction with long-term unemployment make their anger that much more intense and embedded. Human failure, after all, is difficult to understand, much less respect.

In Kübler-Ross' third stage, the terminally ill patient seeks to bargain. Perhaps an agreement with someone, God perhaps, might alter the course of the illness. Perhaps the right contract (or contact) will postpone the inevitable. Perhaps if one is less angry and more understanding, one's pleas will be heeded. Sentiments of this sort also are expressed by unemployed men, although none of them literally believe a bargain will be struck. Some refuse to surrender their anger, believing it either to be lifesaving or the sure fire guarantee of death. For others experiencing the hardest times, death would arrive as the logical conclusion to their grieving, if not relief.

Depression looms as the preeminent emotion of the fourth coping stage. With it comes numbness or stoicism, and perhaps too, an overriding sense of loss: loss of job, income, friends, loss of interest in being alive, loss of self-respect and dignity, loss even of one's self, or its vital components. Depression represents both a reaction to actual events, especially loss,[19] and a preparation for later eventualities. Like terminally ill patients, long-term unemployed men recognize there is no silver lining and that all finally is lost. Kübler-Ross found a growing stoicism among terminally ill patients, something observed as well in long-term unemployed men, although eventually rage, numbness, and stoicism will be replaced by a profound sense of loss.[20]

Then there is the matter of how one deals with the terminally ill and terminally unemployed. Although we encourage patients to give full rein to their emotions, we often find ourselves intolerant of the emotional expressions of the unemployed. How much longer, we wonder, do we have to confront their depression and rage, their complaining, their bitterness, and hopelessness? Ironically, these are the very questions the unemployed ask themselves. They, too, have come to the end of their rope with their own depression, rage, and hopelessness.

In Kübler-Ross' fifth and final coping stage, the terminally ill patient allegedly achieves some form of acceptance. At this juncture, anger and depression recede, if not vanish completely, and one begins to accept one's fate. Acceptance of this sort, and with it the release of anger and depression, hardly guarantees happiness or serenity. In fact, Kübler-Ross was quick to assert that acceptance may be experienced as an absence of any feeling. The pain may have disappeared, the struggle is over, now it is time for rest. How appropriate these observations are for long-term unemployed people whose affect in the latter months of their lives seems so flat, and whose detachment from people so palpable. These are the signs, surely, that the fight is over, the strength is gone, the accomplishments of one's work history and career completed. Reflecting on past triumphs brings little comfort. The struggle is over, and there comes a time for "the final rest before a long journey."[21]

Faith during these last stages is tremendously important to the terminally ill person as it is as well for the unemployed man, if in fact he has not already lost it. Equally valuable to the patient is the belief that what he or she is experiencing may be valuable for others, but no comparable sentiment is found among the unemployed, who too regularly speak of begging for death to take them. Communication during these stages seems vital for Kübler-Ross, although it becomes an arduous task for visitors, especially those who have never lived through the death of a loved one (or through long-term unemployment). In contrast, family members and friends of the unemployed often lose interest in communication. The conversations become too draining, too angering. For their own well-being, visitors remove themselves from these men. If families of dying patients urge them to let go, families of long-term unemployed men are only too eager to let go, which in turn encourages the men to let go of life. If, after death, moreover, families must be encouraged to release their feelings of sadness, guilt, anger, and resentment, the families of the long-term unemployed have long ago expressed these feelings in one way or another directly to the man who they recognize has given up.

The parallels between the terminally ill and the terminally unemployed worker rest on a precarious foundation, namely, that long-term unemployed men are not necessarily dying. Surely, society does not perceive them as dying, even though this is what they may be feeling. The sentiment expressed to the terminally ill patient, "Take satisfaction in all that you have accomplished," will not suffice for the terminally unemployed man. There is no accomplishment, only humiliation, hence there can be no successful completion of the life cycle; it is necessary, fitting even, that the end be reached. It is for these reasons that abandonment, disappearance, and death occupy such prominent roles in the narratives of discouraged workers.

For solace, one thinks in this context of the Buddhist notion that because we all live with the dead, we must console them and undertake virtuous acts to return them to the human realm. One can just imagine Alfred Syre hearing these words. Alfred would look at me, smile and say, A steady job would be plenty virtuous enough. "Alfred would have felt more in tune with Malcolm Cowley's words: "More and more the older person is driven back into himself, more and more he is occupied with what goes on in his mind."[22]

If the stories heard in this book convey anything, it is that the loss of a job is felt by some men to be a loss of the self, a notion, actually, not unfamiliar to students of bereavement.[23] From the literature on bereavement, we learn that although men are meant to be adept at compartmentalizing the various experiences of their lives, their private lives from their work lives, for example, many clearly are not able to successfully navigate this difficult process, and especially during the period of unemployment. Also discovered in this literature is the notion that the longer one focuses on the lost object, one's job in this case, the longer the period of intense pain continues. Evidently, the men heard in this book were unable to focus their attention on anything other than their unemployment status, which only prolonged their expressions of pain. Said differently, they were perhaps unable to deal with the profound discrepancies between the actual event of long-term unemployment, and any internal model they might have conceived to explain or reconcile such an event.[24] The obvious result of this failure in mentation is the expression of emotions like anger, sadness, and anxiety.

What becomes obvious in people grieving the loss of something like a job, is the need to perceive and integrate some sense of the connection first, between their past and present, and then between their present and future. Yet the critical question is what constitutes these connections in the minds of men, especially those men raised to believe that employment, work, and human endeavor serve as the cement permanently sealing past, present, and future, something the psychiatrist Edward Hallowell spoke of in his study of human connection.[25]

If, as Martin Buber wrote, life fundamentally is predicated on encounters and the mutualities that these encounters provide, then what happens to the human mind and spirit when encounters cease, mutualities cease, and men are obliged to totally rearrange their conceptions of their identities, their life stories that derived from these encounters in the first place? If theorists like Carol Gilligan, Jean Baker Miller, and Irene Stiver are correct,[26] women are better able to sustain the discontinuities caused by unemployment inasmuch as their egos have developed primarily through human encounters, human mutualities. The female self, Baker Miller and Stiver argued,[27] emerges from the constant interaction of the self with other selves, whereas the so-called male ego emerges more in the interactions, as it were, with objects, ideas, ideals, concepts, and most notably work. Thus, the loss of work for a woman in ego terms need not sever established continuities between past and present, nor anticipated continuities between present and future. As long as the people in her life remain, her ego may not be as assaulted by job loss as is the ego of a man who has been taught literally to place his eggs in the basket of employment. Take things away from a man, his land, his possessions, his tools, his job, and he may never recover. They may be more important to him than people, for unlike people, he has created them through his work, thus in a sense, his identity is constituted of the single compartment containing his things. Angela Phillips said it this way: "A girl can . . . make herself important through relationships. A boy learns that relationships . . . depend on money and power."[28]

It must be understood that work, as we have seen, holds a variety of meanings for a man, and hence constitutes a variety of roles in his definition of self. The essential role would seem to be that of support; it is in the job that a man earns his living, which in turn allows him to support his family. But the accounts of long-term unemployed men make it evident that work, as Wilson and Newman described[29] becomes the centerpiece of the social structure in which men generally define themselves. Sadly, and more significantly, there are no collective patterns and no delineated rituals for mourning the loss of work as there are for mourning the death of loved ones. Although a man maintains a sense of continuity between himself and a dead parent by using an object like a photograph, a keepsake, or even through an inheritance, society offers him few guides for connecting with lost jobs. Surely, there are few tangible reminders of his employment tenure other than the sight of hundreds of people going off to (their) work every morning. It brings him little solace, apparently, to recall the years he has devoted to working.

In a word, a man knows that he is going to die and that inevitably during his lifetime, he will witness the deaths of loved ones. It is not, however, inevitable that he is going to lose his job or remain jobless for long stretches of time. He may contemplate unemployment, but the best that society offers is the concept of (forced or voluntary) retirement, a moment in life some men dread, fearing there is no life after work, there is no other compartment, in other words, from which to draw experiences to shape an identity. There is, moreover, no productive way to construct a meaning of

the self experiencing unemployment that allows one to retain some measure of personal significance. Those persons welcoming retirement know
they have earned it; they have already achieved personal significance.

In the absence not only of his job but of a ritual intended to sustain
him during his grieving, in the absence really of a social construction for
mourning job loss, a man turns to a biographical construction. He
retreats, in other words, to his own story, his own work history, which
publicly enhances his image as self-centered, self-preoccupied, and self-
pitying.[30] In the end, the genre of autobiographical constructions of long
term unemployed men is unique for it contains descriptions not only of
their own illness and death, their own being as death object, but of the
time that succeeds it. This is the genre of autobiographical constructions
we have encountered in the previous chapters, constructions of the sort
Anne Hunsaker Hawkins called pathographies.[31]

Whereas many people imagine that lost loved ones return to them as
transformed objects, such as the bird that suddenly appears at their window, a plant that inexplicably takes root, or more likely a ghost, narratives
of long-term unemployed workers reveal profound transformations of the
self. As the common expression goes, they reveal men holding mental representations of themselves as mere shadows of their former selves. More
precisely, the men themselves have turned into ghosts, something to which
their wives and children would attest. And if this sounds too much like
mere metaphor, let us be reminded of Judith Herman's descriptions of
post-trauma victims claiming that not only are they different people, they
are not people anymore.[32]

Bereavement researchers might describe the men studied here as
revealing a so-called illness model of grief.[33] It is a model, researchers note,
derived from a "loss-oriented process," of death rather than a "restoration
process," which is what many of the families of unemployed men experience. The restoration process implies the presence of social and personal
support systems and rituals allowing a man to reappraise himself in a more
positive light, what amounts to a positive social construct of long-term
unemployment. Surely, the illness model of grieving fails in this purpose.
As examples of this, we have encountered men who focus on their joblessness, indeed who appear obsessed with the loss of their jobs, while their
wives seek to restore normalcy, constancy, and optimism essentially by
attempting to shift this focus or dent the obsession. Surely, it is difficult for
these women to hear that their husbands have lost what is for them the

most important object of their lives, that work is not something their husbands have or do, but something that they *are*, which in turn means that the men are no more. Predictably, the wives claim they want the old Ken, the old George, the old Ollie back.

Together, husband and wife grieve the loss of his job, but they do so in somewhat different fashion, and often with different consequences. She wants the resurrection of her old relationship with her husband and the return of his "old" personality. Instead, she discovers that, as part of his grieving, she and her husband have become polarized. Where she seeks to uplift, he repeatedly reminds her of his distress. Where she seeks to restore, he insists his situation remains incurable. She argues that work is impersonal, mere activity, and that the equally significant personal and interpersonal elements of his life remain in tact. He barely can formulate an argument against this position, nor find the words to describe how work is both personal and interpersonal, that it is creative, alive, and ultimately that it is his life. He cannot properly describe perhaps, the confluence of his mental representations of self and work, and how it is that work defines and even more, serves almost as a surrogate parental figure, something especially salient, as we have observed in the case of George Wilkinson, when actual parental figures are deceased. For it is work that provides a man the ingredients normally thought to be furnished by one's family: security, nurturance, a sense of worth, esteem, competence, identity, even morality. He finds it difficult, moreover, to explain and justify the manner in which he is attached to work, for these matters involve ways that would seem to be reserved only for other human beings.

Plaintively, his wife urges him to "move on" or conceive of unemployment as temporary, a respite, a "time off. " In response, he insists that the end of work is a permanent condition, like the end of life. She accuses him of wallowing in his misery, something he grudgingly allows to be true, but this well may be a man's first encounter with the personal expressions of grief, something he allegedly finds more daunting than does his wife. For the first time perhaps, he must give voice to these expressions as he constructs his biography, or what he might envision to be his obituary. Even more, in the absence of a lost object, in the severing of significant attachments, as Bowlby[34] postulated, a person experiences a compulsion to preserve the lost object, work in this case, and in its absence, the feelings of sadness and grief, even despair, generated by the loss.[35] For it is the feelings alone that serve to connect the man with the lost job, and hence connect past and present to future. Whereas once he might have reflected on what he has accomplished on his job and all that is left to do, now he ruminates on his loss, his sadness, his aloneness, the fact that there is nothing to do and that there will be no further significant personal transformations or evolution. As Lifton and Olson observed, trauma can cause a person to lose faith in human continuity, the very continuity inherent in Levinson's formulation of the male life cycle.

Predictably, the unemployed man either psychologically or physically removes himself from his household, not simply because of his depression, but because the loss of work denies him his fundamental role as provider, protector, caretaker. In immediate grief, as observed in the case of George Wilkinson or delayed,[36] as in the case of Ken Hawkins, the man responds to what bereavement researchers speak of as the loss of a functional dependency. One depends on one's father or husband to be the family caretaker. When, however, he no longer is able to provide for his family, the dependence comes to a sudden if not traumatic end. Why even allow a man to sit at the dinner table, the children may wonder, if he no longer provides the meal! What the children may not understand is that like them, their father too has lived with a sense of functional dependence, but trained to depend on no one but himself, his dependent object has become his work. Without work, he necessarily is thrown back on himself, his days of feeling himself to be the head of the household long gone.

UNEMPLOYMENT AS TRAUMA

It goes without saying that losing a job causes mental stress. But the problem of long-term unemployment extends far deeper than stress. Work accomplished over the period of a life time provides the purpose, rationality, and calculability a man requires in order to stay sane. Surely, unemployment feels like mental illness. Without purpose, without the belief, however much it appears as illusion, that he is making time unfold through purposeful action, there can be no healthy means for a man to encounter the world and survive.

In response to a man losing his job, well-meaning people encourage him to join support groups and meetings of all varieties. The intentions are fine, for a while the activities seem beneficial, possibly even therapeutic. Yet the purpose of these gatherings is essentially to establish what Bakan[37] called a *communal orientation*, an orientation normally associated with femininity. It is not surprising, therefore, that many unemployed men feel themselves "feminized" by these meetings, just as they feel infantilized by unemployment.

It is also not surprising that Ken Hawkins' life would unfold as it did. It wasn't that he felt he had become a woman, the proverbial "Mr. Mom." The problem he barely could articulate was the experience of watching his world view eviscerated and replaced by circumstances foreign and alienating. Like the others, Ken saw his future vanish into the morass of unemployment, taking with it any sense of personal effort and purpose. Because explanations and assessments of life are based in part on one's mental representation of the future, when hope is denied, life reaches its conclusion, even though the human heart continues to beat strongly.

Long-term unemployed men often discover little relief in communing with others. Nor do they find that certain life force in their families, despite the love they hold for their wives and children. They know they are not engaging simply in feminine activities or dependent roles, but in activities and perspectives representing the end of their world outlooks, purposes, and intentions. Purpose, rationality, sanity, goal-oriented behavior, agency, instrumentality, intentionality, and personal integrity, all the ingredients of a man's worldview, vanish with the recognition that there will be no more work. That his funds have dried up is but a part of his dilemma; his very soul has begun to wither.

With his soul goes his humanity and physicality. "Human behavior above the level of reflex," Polkinghorne wrote, "is infected with the features of meaning."[38] Simply stated, when life loses its meaning, which it does on the recognition that there will be no more work, a man is left with little more than reflexive capacities. Conversing with a man, for example, about sexual matters, typically yields uncomfortable moments, to say the least. Yet when the topic at hand is unemployment, men and women alike speak of these matters and confront the question of why it is that a purely animal instinct would disappear, and so quickly, "merely" because one has lost one's job? Artie Blake's response went this way:

"What's the point. No one's trying to have a baby. How can you find joy in the sack when every part of you has died. I ain't got nothing to give anybody. You want to talk about a person drying up, you're looking into the eyes of a prune. We're talking Sahara Desert. 'Not tonight, honey, I got a headache.' I wish I *had* a good excuse. I never thought it would come to this, me crawling in *my* side, her crawling in *her* side. Me afraid to look at her for fear she's maybe wearing something provocative and I have to show I'm not interested. You want to talk about the tortures we go through, well, that's one. You know what they say, when one part goes, all parts go. Sound like a cliché? Unemployment's a damn cliché. Roll over and go to sleep, Artie, boy. Your days in the sun are gone. From now on there's nothing but the night and a couple of old people snoring."

Sexuality, the only act of communion left to these men, too often disappeared, or in Polkinghorne's words, lost its meaning when the man's source of health and manliness disappeared. Most every man spoke about it. Their sexual "deadness," as many called it, was now a fact of life, "right up there 'long side the birds and the bees," as Artie said.

It was more than feeling castrated or emasculated. It was again that matter of soul death, the cutting of the tether that binds a man to his community and family, and thus to his future, rendering him alone and obsolete. Tell a young, employed man he's worthless, and it may spur him on to perform great deeds if only to prove you wrong. Then again, he may lose his motivation and turn off the machine. Early in their history of unemployment, men turned to women to draw new life blood. Sexuality assured them they were whole, vital, alive. They may have failed in the workforce, but not in bed. But after months of unemployment, the flings and quiet embraces held little meaning; nothing anymore sustained these men. Truly, they had been traumatized, and quite possibly, the stories heard in this volume are nothing less than accounts of posttraumatic stress disorder. The literature on this subject supports such a position.

The early research on posttraumatic stress disorder (PTSD) focused primarily on the short- and long-term psychological affects of experiencing a particular trauma. Early in this research, the writings of Hans Seyle dominated much of the thinking about stress reactions as he asserted the notion that it was the trauma rather than any particular personal vulnerability that accounted for the presence of an extreme reaction.[39] Said differently, PTSD was precisely that: a reaction to trauma that appeared to extend beyond the so-called normal or appropriate range of stress reaction, typically considered to be about two years, irrespective of one's personality. Causing this alleged extreme reaction were the most conspicuous features of the reaction, notably the helplessness experienced in the face of possible death, or perhaps severe anxiety resulting from having barely escaped death.

Since the time of Seyle's groundbreaking theoretical work, research has indicated that personal vulnerability, and not just the nature of a particular trauma or stressor, must be taken into account if one is to understand the nature of such prolonged reactions to a stressor. Recent work, for example, has suggested that genetic predisposition may play a role in PTSD, along with family history factors such as traumatic experiences and various personality components. Unfortunately, and surely the men in this book confirm this notion, no one can predict whether exposure to a so-called traumatic stressor such as job loss will result in the sort of de-compensation, lack of initiative and planning, unstable sense of self, and inability to reconnect with the world, what Herman[40] called a "learned helplessness," that one regularly observes in trauma victims. Obviously, a host of people enduring long-term unemployment do not experience the same sorts of reactions as the men in this book have revealed, in the same way that not all war veterans experience symptoms of PTSD.

Theorizing a rather straightforward relationship between trauma and symptomatology,[41] Mardi Horowitz observed that the more powerful the trauma, the more severe and long lasting the emerging symptoms. Implicit in this idea is that any response to trauma may be adaptive or maladaptive, in which case symptoms remain for extended periods of time. The Horowitz theory, however, has been challenged by research indicating that personal vulnerability in the form of various psychiatric disorders may be the critical factor explaining both the intensity and unusual duration of posttraumatic reactions. More specifically, research has suggested that pre-existing depressive neurosis as well as anxiety neurosis may be what trigger the formation of PTSD symptoms. In fact, some research now suggests that a pure form of PTSD would be a rare occurrence, inasmuch as many studies of PTSD patients show comorbidity with certain disorders.

Complicating this picture and throwing a new light on the topic of PTSD is the seminal work on prolonged trauma undertaken by Judith Herman. It was Herman, working with child sex abuse victims and prisoners of war, who instructed for the first time that if symptoms can be chronic, so too can trauma. Long-term unemployment reveals the same characteristic of the stressor existing for long and still longer periods of time. Herman postulated that in these instances, in contrast to cases of acute or single-episode trauma, enduring personality changes often increase in intensity and character rather than diminish, a fact that causes a traumatized person to be criticized even more harshly by family and friends. The fact that the symptoms continue so long, even growing worse in some instances, causes the people close to the traumatized person to believe only a pre-existing characterological disorder could account for the prolonged reaction. No one reduced to the level of mere survival, as we have observed in the stories of unemployed men, could possibly represent evidence of mere trauma. They must be viewed as inappropriate dependent if not outrightly masochistic, two characteristics, not so incidentally, of trauma patients. And let us not forget in this context, that people close to trauma patients themselves may reveal symptoms of trauma, as I. Lisa McCann and Laurie Anne Pearlman demonstrated.[42]

Many professional therapists, Herman noted, may reach this same conclusion: Only character disorder and not long-term unemployment could account for the prolonged existence of symptoms, and this perspective represents only a small piece of the often callous behavior revealed in response to prolonged trauma. It is interesting, therefore, to recall Abram Kardiner's words of almost forty years ago:

> Traumatic neurosis is a disease very closely related to schizophrenia . . . both from the point of view of central dynamics and from the *ultimate withdrawal from the world* which is set in motion. The deteriorations undergone in both conditions have a striking resemblance to each other. (italics added)

In truth it is almost impossible to summarize the dynamics of long-term unemployment in terms of the traumatic affects it has on workers. Yet consider the following list of features noted in these workers: psychological numbness or the almost spaced-out manner of acting; the inability, on occasion, to associate the actual events with the feelings one is experiencing; an overriding anxiety and difficulty in self-nurturing; a sense that one is going mad; the perpetual feeling of being upset; a desire to become invisible or the belief that one is a fraud; a fright coupled with rage; moments of agitation mixed with moments of almost eerie calm; the inability to concentrate sufficiently well to even read a newspaper; and finally, the commitment one morning to battle unemployment with renewed intensity followed by a morning in which one appears to have succumbed to the status, or relinquished all personal struggles. In fact, these features point to at least one significant theoretical perspective: namely, posttraumatic stress,[44] or what psychologist Judith Pierson called nature's reaction to intense pain.[45]

In *Trauma and Recovery*, Herman pointed to at least six profound personal alterations that together constitute the reaction not merely to an acute trauma, but to the continuing experience of trauma.[46] Holding in mind that although we tend to think of unemployment as a single event, that being the moment one is laid off, it is the ongoing status of not working that exacerbates the original wound,[47] thereby rendering the condition chronic. Long-term unemployment, therefore, becomes a perfect example of what Urie Bronfenbrenner had in mind when he constructed an ecological scheme for describing the development of the human personality. Categorizing influential experiences, Bronfenbrenner postulated a realm he called the chronosystem,[48] theoretically meant to designate experiences occurring at one point in a person's life, but continuing to influence the personality, thereby leaving the person forever affected. Divorce of one's parents or the death of a parent typically are offered as examples of lingering chronosystem events, but long-term unemployment, the year-after-year experience of not working, is an equally good illustration.

Herman's theory of categories of trauma reaction begins with *alterations in affect regulation*. Writing about the experiences of prisoners of war and children who have been repeatedly abused, Herman described the person's persistent unhappiness, what psychologists label dysphoria, or a sense of emptiness. She described as well in this first alteration, explosive anger, sexual inhibition, and suicidal ideation, all familiar themes in the lives of the men we have come to know.

Second, is *alterations in consciousness*. Here too, the long-term unemployed reveal symptoms almost identical to those revealed by prisoners of war and victims of abuse. In this category we find people either unable to recall a great many details of the abuse, or, in contrast, living with intense almost overwhelming recollections of the abuse, although one cannot predict whether they will attach so-called appropriate feelings to the events in the manner of the classical dissociative disorder.[49] Struggling with their remembrances and everyday thoughts, they tend to relive the scenes of unemployment, ruminating on them, as we have noted, to the point of the activity becoming almost obsessive in nature.[50] Or perhaps they depersonalize the events, or *derealize* them, a term meant to convey a mental process in which events are conceived almost as if they never occurred in the first place.

Alterations in self-perception constitutes the third category of personal transformations. We are now more than familiar with the themes Herman offers of helplessness, shame, guilt, a desire to become invisible, self-blame, protracted self-punishment, and an inability to initiate any action that may be in one's best interest. Nothing the victim of continual abuse can tell himself, apparently, will assist him in overcoming the feeling that he is deficient, defective, inadequate, or worthless. And one thing more might be added to this category: stigma, a sense, as Erving Goffman[51] described, that one is profoundly different in the most negative of terms from others, as well as from one's own sense of what one always imagined one's identity to be.

Herman's fourth category speaks to *alterations in perceptions of the perpetrator*. It is hardly a theoretical stretch to liken society to the guards in prisoner of war camps or the people who perpetrate abuse of all sorts. More than the actual employer who originally pronounced their layoff, unemployed men, as we have repeatedly witnessed, continue to perceive the villain in their demise as society, and not surprisingly, for posttrauma theory would suggest this, remain preoccupied with this perpetrator to whom they ascribe almost complete and total power. Society, therefore, is seen as all powerful, unchangeable; one must accept its systems of beliefs, definitions of values, rewards and punishments, rational actions and definitions of human achievement, or the lack of it. Predictably, victims of trauma ascribe fault to themselves, and only themselves. In their minds they are the primary cause of their present circumstances. Inevitably, the long-term unemployed will compare themselves with others in the society who continue to hold jobs. Or perhaps they will insist that in the face of an all powerful society, they are small, weak, helpless, impotent. Only steady work, they conclude, can mediate between culture's power and the vulnerability of the single human life.

Alterations in relationships with others is Herman's fifth category of posttraumatic reaction, the same category, not so incidentally, Lindemann outlined in his essay on bereavement in which he noted the irritability of bereaved people and their proclivity to avoid social situations.[52] Herman speaks here of withdrawal from friends and family if not outright isolation,[53] one of the most common characteristics of traumatized people, actually, since eventually others move on with their lives, leaving the traumatized ones unable to reformulate structures that establish meaning, and what Lifton and Olson called "orderly rhythms" to their lives.[54] Intimacy patterns only naturally are disrupted, patterns bespeaking a person's inability to satisfy his or her most fundamental needs and desires.

Granted, the isolation mixes with a neediness of the sort that can become burdensome for others, as we have seen, even as the traumatized person continues to hope for a rescuer, someone to remedy their situation, and make the pain, and probably too, the original traumatizing events, go away. On the one hand, the victim of trauma remains open and vulnerable, the wound has never properly healed. On the other hand, the humiliation ignited by the trauma causes the person to feel self-protective to the extent that he appears permanently armored, or outrightly hostile, even to his closest family members, and of course himself as well. It is interesting to note that many men who regain full employment after long periods of idleness continue to reveal these same posttraumatic symptoms.

Finally, Herman's sixth category refers to the *alterations in the system of meaning*. These symptoms, too, have been exhibited by long-term unemployed men who long ago lost any sense of a sustaining faith or spiritual fortitude. Living with what Herman called their "terrible knowledge," their hopeless and despairing outlook, destroys any belief or ideology that the world could be conceived as predictable or controllable, meaningful or merciful. The endless period of unemployment yields a conception of the world without sense, without rationality, and a God, perhaps, who is perceived as anything but beneficent.

To summarize the connection between long-term unemployment and PTSD, we turn to the work of McCann and her associates.[55] According to these authors, five fundamental needs must be met in order for a person to successfully adapt to trauma, needs that are anticipated in the work of Herman, Lifton and Olson and others: safety, dependency, and/or trust, power, esteem, and the capacity for intimacy. We have seen all of these needs at work in the narratives of long-term unemployed men. It goes without saying that these men trust few people, feel totally powerless, utterly unsafe, and unable to allow people to get close to them.

Beyond causing physical symptoms, trauma destroys a man's sense of how the world operates. Self-conceptions, conceptions about the world, and a vital sense of personal vulnerability are profoundly challenged if not distorted by trauma.[56] As noted earlier, if nothing else, steady work convinces people that life operates according to some ultimately rational, calculable dynamics. At least it appears that certain outcomes are possible; if I work long enough I will receive financial benefits on retiring. Or perhaps rational and calculable features allow a man to believe in certain causalities. The proverbial food on the table and roof overhead bespeak the very nature of steady employment. And if some would charge that these are mere allusions, then apparently they are allusions making possible successful adaptation to everyday stress. At very least, they keep a man's mood positive and optimistic.

Then comes chronic trauma, not a single acute event, as is the case of long-term unemployment, and a man's understanding of himself and the world, his fundamental frames of reference as McCann and Pearlman and Erich Fromm called them,[57] generated in greatest measure by work, are challenged. Trauma, in other words, has altered long-standing mental representations of the self and the world. As Richard Epstein noted,[58] once benign and meaningful, the world now appears malignant, anarchic even, or utterly meaningless.

Human beings constantly struggle with the realities of death, freedom, isolation, and meaninglessness. If there is no preordained design in life, we must construct our own meaning. Similarly, the self, once deserving of respect, esteem, trust, and an assessment of worth, now is viewed by the man himself and the world as well, he imagines, as worthless, powerless, untrustworthy, alienated,[59] and lacking in any value that might earn him respect. In the end, it is the chronic trauma and his inability to successfully adapt to it, that leads him not only along the path of bereavement, but convinces him that either he must die, or he already has died.

If the men whose stories appear in these pages are to be believed, their very perceptions and sensations, the moment by moment working of their conscious minds, their mental representations, their personal and social frames of reference, grew out of their employment, or at least out of their anticipation of working. This is the essence of what scholars like William Julius Wilson and Katherine Newman meant when they spoke of the social structural value of work. But then having been unemployed for months beyond any compensation—the period clearly of hopelessness—the men were left with little more than their reflections on, and remembrances of work. As a result, their minds, now chronically traumatized, shut down, or found no reason for being. Every ingredient of calculability and causality had diminished, if not vanished altogether. So they too, or many of them, shut down, or vanished, like a giant plant that once had 10,000 employees working day and night shuts down, and eventually disappears.

In time, a man, like the plant, begins to rot. Everybody watches, everybody wonders, everybody comments on the unnecessary waste of it all. In the meantime, the rotting continues, and no one is able to find new uses for the plant, or the man. No one is able to convert the plant or the worker into something valuable or beautiful. And although the plant and the man continue to stand, everyone recognizes they are moribund. At last there is nothing to do but raze the plant and bury the man.

NOTES

1. William Julius Wilson, *When Work Disappears: The World of the Urban Poor* (New York: Knopf, 1996); and Katherine Newman, *No Shame in My Game: The Working Poor in the Inner City* (New York: Knopf, 1999).

2. Newman, *ibid.*, 88.

3. *The Evolving Self* (Cambridge, MA: Harvard University Press, 1982).

4. Erik Erikson, *Childhood and Society* (New York: W. W. Norton, 1963). See also his *Adulthood* (New York: W. W. Norton, 1978).

5. Newman, *op. cit.*

6. See his *Seasons of a Man's Life* (New York: Knopf, 1978).

7. See Lawrence J. Friedman, *Identity's Architect: A Biography of Erik H. Erikson* (New York: Scribner, 1999).

8. "Symptomatology and Management of Acute Grief," *American Journal of Psychiatry 101* (1944): 141–48.

9. On this point, see M. Baum and R. Baum, *Growing Old: A Societal Perspective* (Englewood, NJ: Prentice Hall, 1980). See also B. L. Neugarten, Ed., *Middle Age and Aging* (Chicago: University of Chicago Press, 1968); and S. de Beauvoir, *Coming of Age* (New York: Putnam and Sons, 1972).

10. B. L. Neugarten and K. K. Weinstein, "The Changing American Grandparent," *Journal of Marriage and the Family 26* (1964): 199–206.

11. A recent study indicates that as people become older they become happier! Essentially, the authors of the study allege that this is because older people are better able than younger ones to regulate their emotions in the face of external events. Interestingly, the study suggested that young people reported higher levels of sadness, nervousness, and even hopelessness. The most happy group in the sample was married, extroverted men. One wonders how these results might be altered had the population under study contained a sample of long-term unemployed men. See D. K. Mroczek and C. M. Kolarz, "The Effect of Age on Positive and Negative Affect," *Journal of Personality and Social Psychology 75* (1998): 1333–49.

12. R. Havinghurst, "Disengagement and Patterns of Aging," in B. L. Neugarten *Middle Age and Aging* (Chicago: University of Chicago Press, 1968). See also, H. Z. Lopata, *Widowhood in an American City* (Cambridge, MA: Schenkman, 1973); and M. Sarton, *As We Are Now* (New York: W. W. Norton, 1973).

13. L. L. Carstensen, "Evidence for a Life Span Theory of Socioemotional Selectivity," *Current Directions 4* (1995): 151. On this point, see as well E. Cumming and W. E. Henry, *Growing Old: The Process of Disengagement* (New York: Basis Books, 1961).

14. D. Bell, *The Coming of Post-Industrial Society* (New York: Basic Books, 1999).

15. E. Kübler-Ross, *On Death and Dying* (New York: Macmillan, 1969).

16. Noer, *op. cit.,* 6.

17. On this point, see E. Becker, *The Denial of Death* (New York: The Free Press, 1973).

18. Noer, *op. cit.,* 6.

19. For an exceptional discussion of the meaning of loss, see F. Weinstein, *Freud, Psychoanalysis, Social Theory: The Unredeemed Promise* (Albany, NY: State University of New York Press, in press).

20. This is a paraphrasing of Kübler-Ross, *op. cit.,* 85.

21. Kübler-Ross, *op. cit.,* 113.

22. M. Cowley, *The View from 80* (New York: Penguin, 1980).

23. Many of the thoughts in this section were stimulated by a symposium entitled "What's New in Bereavement Research?" American Psychological Association Meetings, Boston, MA, August 22, 1999. The papers presented included, Susan Folkman, "Characterizing Bereavement Response: Form Matters"; Phyllis R. Silverman, "Children's Construction of a Relationship With Their Deceased Parent: Developmental Perspectives"; Kathrin Boerner, "How Gender Roles Affect Family Dynamics Following Parental Loss"; and Margaret Stroebe, "Social Context of Grieving: A Theoretical and Empirical Analysis." The symposium was chaired by Robert S. Weiss. In addition, see C. M. Parkes and R. S. Weiss, *Recovery From Bereavement* (New York: Basic Books, 1983).

24. On this point, see M. Horowitz, N. Wilner, N. Katreider, and W. Alvarez, "Signs and Symptoms of Posttraumatic Stress Disorder," *Archives of General Psychiatry 37* (1980): 85–92.

25. E. M. Hallowell, *Connect* (New York: Pantheon, 1999).

26. C. Gilligan, in *A Different Voice: Psychological Theory and Women's Development* (Cambridge, MA: Harvard University Press, 1982); J. Miller, *Toward a New Psychology of Women* (Boston: Beacon Press, 1976); and J. Miller and I. P. Stiver, *The Healing Connection: How Women Form Relationships in Therapy and in Life* (Boston: Beacon Press, 1997).

27. *Ibid.*

28. A. Phillips, *The Trouble with Boys* (New York: Basic Books, 1994).

29. Wilson, *When Work Disappears, op. cit.*; Newman, *No Shame in My Game, op. cit.*

30. This point is reminiscent of the descriptions offered in *Tally's Corner, op. cit.*

31. A. H. Hawkins, *Reconstructing Illness: Studies in Pathography* (West Lafayette, IN: Purdue University Press, 1993). I am grateful to Donald Paladino for this reference.

32. J. Herman, "Complex PTSD: A Syndrome of Survivors of Prolonged and Repeated Trauma," *Journal of Traumatic Stress 3* (1992): 377–91.

33. On this point, see R. A. Kalish, *Death, Grief, and Caring Relationships* (Monterey, CA: Brooks-Cole, 1985).

34. J. Bowlby, *Attachment and Loss* (New York: Basic Books, 1980). See also P. Marris, *Attachment Across the Life Cycle* (London: Tavistock/ Routledge, 1991).

35. On this point, see J. Archer and V. Rhodes, "The Grief Process and Job Loss: A Cross-Sectional Study," *British Journal of Psychology 84* (1993): August, 395–410.

36. R. S. Weiss and C. M. Parkes, *Recovery from Bereavement* (New York: Basic Books, 1983); and E. Lindemann, *op. cit.*

37. D. Bakan, *The Duality of Human Existence* (Chicago: Rand McNally, 1966).

38. *Op. cit.*, 17.

39. On this and related points, see R. Yehuda and A. C. McFarlane, "Conflict Between Current Knowledge about Posttraumatic Stress Disorder and its Original Conceptual Basis," *American Journal of Psychiatry 152* (1995): 1705–13.

40. J. Herman, "Complex PTSD," *op. cit.*

41. M. J. Horowitz, *Stress Response Syndromes* (New York: Jason Aronson, 1976).

42. L. McCann and L. A. Pearlman, "Vicarious Traumatization: A Framework for Understanding the Psychological Effects of Working with Victims," *Journal of Traumatic Stress 3* (1989): 131–149.

43. A. Kardiner, "Traumatic Neuroses of War," in S. Arieti, Ed., *American Handbook of Psychiatry*, Volume 1 (New York: Basic Books, 1959).

44. See B. A. van der Kolk, *Psychological Trauma* (Washington, DC: American Psychiatric Press, 1987).

45. In lecture, Boston University, April 1999.

46. J. Herman, *Trauma and Recovery* (New York: Basic Books, 1992).

47. On this and related points, see J. S. March, L. Amaya-Jackson, and R. S. Pynoos, "Pediatric Stress Disorder," in J. M. Wiener, Ed., *Textbook of Child and Adolescent Psychiatry*, 2nd ed. (Washington, DC: American Psychiatric Press, 1997).

48. U. Bronfenbrenner, *The Ecology of Human Development: Experiements by Nature and Design* (Cambridge, MA: Harvard University Press, 1979).

49. D. Finkelhor, "The Victimization of Children: A Developmental Perspective," *American Journal of Orthopsychiatry 65* (1995): 177–193.

50. A. Young, "Suffering and the Origins of Traumatic Memory," *Daedalus 125* (1996): 245–60.

51. Goffman, *Stigma, op. cit.*

52. E. Lindemann, *op. cit.*

53. On this point, see R. S. Weiss, *Loneliness: The Experience of Emotional and Social Isolation* (Cambridge, MA: MIT Press, 1975).

54. Lifton and Olson, *op. cit.*

55. L. McCann, D. K. Sakheim, and D. J. Abrahamson, "Trauma and Victimization: A Model of Psychological Adaptation," *Counseling Psychologist 16* (1988): 531–94.

56. On this point, see R. Janoff-Bulman, "The Aftermath of Victimization: Rebuilding Shattered Assumptions," in C. R. Figley, Ed., *Trauma and Its Wake: The Study and Treatment of Posstraumatic Stress Disorder* (New York: Brunner/Mazel, 1985), 15–35.

57. E. Fromm, *The Sane Society* (New York: Rinehart, 1955).

58. R. S. Epstein, "The Self-Concept, the Traumatic Neurosis, and the Structure of Personality," in D. Ozer, J. M. Healy Jr., and A. J. Stewart, Eds., *Perspectives on Personality, Volume 3* (Greenwich, CT: JAI Press, 1989).

59. On this point, see R. J. Lifton, *Home from the War* (New York: Simon and Schuster, 1973).

Epilogue

Beware the man who tells you he lives day to day. That is a man who's either recovering from alcohol, unemployed, or a man planning to die.

THE INEVITABILITY OF UNEMPLOYMENT

In reflecting on the nature of work, sociologist Kai Erikson remarked: "High rates of unemployment are thought to be not only inevitable but natural" (italics added).[1] In a similar vein, after examining a long-standing perspective on unemployment to which, importantly, they do not prescribe, Seymour Bellin and S. M. Miller commented, "high levels of unemployment are *economically necessary and morally acceptable*" (italics added).[2] Replete in the literature of economic theory, Bellin and Miller pointed out, are discussions of natural rates of unemployment and noninflationary full employment rates, terms meant to disguise an ideological bias, namely, that for our culture to "work," a certain number of people must be out of work.

Although to some economists this position seem understandable, there may be a more pernicious aspect to this conclusion, one that Charles Reich addressed when he commented: "When a person in our centrally managed economy is denied an opportunity to earn a living despite being fully qualified and ready to work, this guarantee [of life, liberty and property] has been violated. . . . Requiring work when there is no work is . . . cruel and hypocritical."[3] Max Frankel couched the same point in the form of a question: "Does our economic stability *require* that some fraction of the population be kept in poverty?"[4] And might that fraction, again, accurately be described by André Gorz's phrase the "nonclass of nonworkers."[5]

Ultimately, this is the tragedy of unemployed workers experiencing the hardest times. More than anything, they despised the idea that they would be thought of as numbers, if in fact anyone outside their immediate family even thought of them, and that no one saw fit to mend their lives. Finding it difficult, perhaps, to learn firsthand the personal consequences of long-term unemployment, some people prefer to conceive of it strictly in statistical terms. Little hurt workers like Ollie Sindon, Ken Hawkins, or Amos Payton as much as experts arguing for the necessity of a certain base unemployment rate. Nothing disturbed them more than experts celebrating the down turn of unemployment rates when they knew that even 3 percent or 4 percent unemployment—surely "promising" numbers—meant that hundreds of thousands of human beings were suffering as they had.

Nothing hurt as much as hearing reports that their inability to locate jobs was due to psychological or personal shortcomings, or that affluent people, far removed from the everyday circumstances of unemployment debated the pros and cons of unemployment proposals and policies while they and their families went another month without work. Bellin and Miller spoke for a host of men when they concluded: "Our assumption is that unemployment is an issue of policy, not of the structure of the labor market alone."[5]

The government, Erikson noted, always possesses "the power to balance unemployment and employment in ways they see fit."[6] And this is the point: Who will see fit to alter the histories of these millions of Americans? Who will see fit to locate suitable and rewarding work for them? The cure to the "illness," after all, lies right before us, if not in immediately practical terms, then in ideological ones. As Boston schoolteacher Ellen Welch remarked years ago: "Our part of the city, and other poorer parts of the city, have a very serious common problem of unemployment. Instead of throwing crumbs and letting everyone scramble for the same crumbs, the politicians should be working to get everyone a job, fed and housed."[7]

In the end, as much as the men in this book struggled to maintain control over their lives, economic and market forces along with human decisions combined to break them down, if not ultimately destroy them. Of course, the men recognized this; it was the topic of hundreds of conversations. How many times did strong, articulate, eloquent men, people who believed fiercely in the goodness of America, offer their lamentations and expressions of incredulity? They could neither fathom nor reconcile the idea of their country forsaking them, given the dues—in all meanings of that word—they had paid all these years. All would have agreed with Randy Albelda's statement: "We need policies that help workers take care of their families and let families take care of their workers."[8]

Like the social scientists quoted in these pages, very long-term unemployed workers understood the power of government as well as the implications of policies, or lack of them, on employment and unemployment. They read the statistics, labor reports, and newspaper accounts. They read as well transcripts of their own words, hunting, perhaps, for the humanity that regularly gets lost in discussions of unemployment. Even more, they hunted for themselves, and for something they long ago had lost and now were convinced would never regain. In the end, they hunted for a single reason to keep going, and despaired over the fact that the existence of the wives and children they so adored no longer sufficed as that reason.[9] Still, they were aware of the group to which they belonged, and despite the expected competitive feelings and collective shame, they found this network of unemployed men, seen and unseen, to be a sacred congregation. "Lost sheep," Jack Blum once called them. And all of them, Alfred Syre used to say, shaking his head so that his silvery yellow hair fell over his forehead, could be saved.

To be sure, some of the men in these chapters represent the end of the line, their lives depicting worse case scenarios. Northrop Frye might have called their narratives ironic, inasmuch as the events and circumstances coalesced to overwhelm them.[10] Their accounts illustrate what happens when society rebuffs the very people who have led their lives decently and anonymously, and want only to work in order to earn their living, in all meanings of that word. The accounts depict what happens to people who forever remain loyal to laws and moral order, and who, when they knew steady employment, complained little about things having to do with life, liberty, and the pursuit of happiness. Yet, some of the accounts describe the final hours of one of America's most ironic and egregious tragedies. In the end, the hardest times are characterized by a lack of respect, the very same respect provided a man by his work. More generally, how people feel about themselves and others, how they treat themselves and others, becomes, as S. M. Miller and Karen Marie Ferroggiaro suggested, "standards of a society" "Respect and self-respect are now burning questions of inequality, policy and politics. They share the public spotlight with the distribution of income and wealth as our society's central stratification worries."[11]

The same point is made by the philosopher Charles Larmore, who, while not focusing on unemployment per se, surely has our concerns in mind in his examination of the larger political context in which employment and unemployment occupy prominent positions: "I am certain . . . that our commitment to democracy or political self-determination cannot be understood except by appeal to a higher moral authority, which is the obligation to respect one another as persons."[12]

Not so long ago I received a telephone call from a Massachusetts man. Unaware of my research on unemployment, he sought some information. Our conversation lasted no more than a few minutes."

How long you been out of work?" I asked him.

"Seven months" came the reply in a voice that sounded vaguely reminiscent of the other voices, filled as it was with heaviness, and that barely perceptible timbre of hopelessness."

Benefits gone," I stated flatly.

"Long gone."

"What kind of work you do?"

"I'm glad you said 'do' and not 'did,'" came the response. Years ago, before I trained with Ken, Cy, Ollie, and the others, I would have said 'did.' "I was a computer salesmen and consultant."

"Bad time for that, huh?"

"The worst."

"Feeling lousy?"

"Real."

"Depressed?"

"No doubt."

I didn't pause for a second. "Suicidal?"

"I may be, I'm not sure. I mean, I don't think I'd ever do it. I mean, I can't see myself doing it, for the kids."

"How many you got?"

"Three."

"How old are you?"

"Forty-nine. I did call the Samaritan hotline a few weeks ago. They asked the same things."

"What'd you say?"

"That I couldn't see myself doing it. I don't have the guts."

"You think about it though." Again my words came forth as a statement, not a question.

"I guess all the time now."

Sitting in my office, staring at the shelves of books, I envisioned the rooms where I had sat with those special men. "Look," I began, "I won't ask your name. Don't give it to me unless you want to. Here's my address, you have my phone. Call me if you want to. You don't have to say anything now." Assiduously, I was following the procedure Alfred and Jack had taught me. "Don't come at these guys too strong," Alfred had advised. "Tell them where you are and let them come to you. They're frightened. Treat them like cats. Stay still, and they'll come to you. They want to, 'cept they don't know how to do it."

After a pause, he said, "That would be great. I mean it. I really appreciate it."

"I will await word from you," I responded. "Thanks a lot for calling."

"Yeah." And that was that.

Alfred, I thought, I think I did it right, but the man is approaching the hardest times. He'll get there too, if someone doesn't see fit to do something about it.

NOTES

1. In K. Erikson & S. P. Callas, (Eds.), *The Nature of Work: Sociological Perspectives* (New Haven, CT: Yale University Press, 1990).

2. "The Split Society," in Erikson and Vallas, *ibid.*, 18.

3. From "Opposing the System" by Charles Reich, quoted in *The Boston Globe*, 9 November 1995, 75.

4. Max Frankel, "What The Poor Deserve," *New York Times Magazine*, 22 October 1995, 46.

5. Bellin and Miller, *op. cit.*, 177.

6. Erikson, *op. cit.*, 11.

7. Cited in Mike Prokosch, "Summer Jobs Unequally Distributed," *Bay State Banner*, 6 July 1978, 18.

8. Randy Albelda, "Now We Know: 'Work First' Hasn't Worked," *The Boston Globe*, 24 May 1999, 103.

9. R. Weiss, *Staying the Course* (New York: Free Press, 1990.)

10. See his *Fables of Identity* (New York: Harcourt, Brace, and World, 1963). Kenneth and Gergen would call these narratives regressive inasmuch as the heroes end up far removed from the goal of employment they

always had set for themselves. See his "The Social Constructionist Movement in Modern Psychology," *American Psychologist 40* (1985): 266–75.

11. S. M. Miller & K. M. Ferroggiaro, "Respect," *Poverty & Race 5* (1996): 1.

12. C. Larmore, "Moral Basis of Political Liberalism," *The Journal of Philosophy*, XCVI (1999): 599–625.

Bibliography

Abramson, L. Y., Seligman, M. E. P., & Teasdale, J. D. (1978). Learned helplessness in humans: Critique and reformulation. *Journal of Abnormal Psychology*, *87*, 49–74.

Ainsworth, M. (1982). Attachment: Retrospect and prospect. In C. Parkes & J. Stevenson-Hinde (Eds.), *The place of attachment in human behavior*. New York: Basic Books.

Albelda, R. (1999, May 24). Now we know: "Work first" hasn't worked. *The Boston Globe*, 103.

American Management Association (1996). *1995 AMA Survey: Corporate downsizing, job elimination, and job creation*. New York: Author.

Anderson, A. (1990). Racial tension, cultural conflicts, and problems of employment training programs. In K. Erikson & S. P. Vallas (Eds.), *The nature of work: Sociological perspectives* (pp. 214–234). New Haven, CT: Yale University Press.

Anderson, E. (1999). *Code of the street: Decency, violence and the moral life of the inner city*. New York: Norton.

Anthony, E. J. (1987). Risk, vulnerability, and resilience: An overview. In E. J. Anthony & B. J. Cohler (Eds.). *The invulnerable child*. New York: Guilford Press.

Applebaum, H. (1998). *The American work ethic and the changing workforce: An historical perspective*. Westport, CT: Quorum Books.

Applebaum, H., Simpson, R., & Shapiro, B. T. (1987). The tough test of downsizing. *Organizational Dynamics*, *16* (2), 68–79.

Archer, J. & Rhodes, V. (1993). The grief process and job loss: A cross-sectional study. *British Journal of Psychology*, *84* (3), 395–410.

Armstrong-Stasses, M. (1944). Coping with transition: A study of lay-off survivors. *Journal of Organizational Behavior*, *15* (7), 597–621.

Aronowitz, S. (1973). *False promises: The shaping of American working class consciousness*. New York: McGraw-Hill.

Aronowitz, S. (1994). *The jobless future: Science-tech and the dogma of work*. Minneapolis: University of Minnesota Press.

Bachman, J. G. & O'Malley, P. M. (1977). Self-esteem in young men: A longitudinal analysis of the impact of educational and occupational attainment. *Journal of Personality and Social Psychology*, *35*, 365–380.

Bakan, D. (1966). *The duality of human existence*. Chicago: Rand McNally.

Baker Miller, J. & Stiver, I. P. (1997). *The healing connection: How women form relationships in therapy and in life*. Boston: Beacon Press.

Baker Miller, J. (1976). *Toward a new psychology of women*. Boston: Beacon Press.

Bakke, E. W. (1933). *The unemployed man*. London: Nisbet.

Bakke, E. W. (1940). *The unemployed worker*. New Haven, CT: Yale University Press.

Bandura, A. (1982). Self-efficacy mechanism in human agency. *American Psychologist, 37*, 122–147.

Bartley, M. (1987). Research on unemployment and health in Great Britain. In D. Schwefel, P. G. Svensson, & H. Zollner (Eds.). *Unemployment, social vulnerabilty, and health in Europe*. New York: Spring.

Baum, M. & Baum, R. (1980). *Growing old: A societal perspective*. Englewood, NJ: Prentice-Hall.

Beales, H. L. & Lambert, R. S. (1934). *Memoirs of the unemployed*. London: Gollanz.

Beane, A. (1999). *The supervision of student teachers: An emphasis on self-reflection*. Unpublished manuscript, Boston University, Boston, MA.

Becker, E. (1973). *The denial of death*. New York: The Free Press.

Becker, H. S. (1958). Problems of inference and proof in participant observation. *American Sociological Review, 23 6*, 652–660.

Becker, J. (Ed.), (1965). *In aid of the unemployed*. Baltimore: Johns Hopkins University Press.

Beebe, S. A. & Masterson, J. T. (1986). *Family talk*. New York: Random House.

Bell, D. (1999). *The coming of post-industrial society*. New York: Basic Books.

Bergson, H. (1970). *Matter and memory*. New York: Humanities Press.

Berkell, D. E. (1991). Working toward integration. *The Forum, 17 2*, 3.

Blau, J. (1999). *Illusions of prosperity: America's working families in an age of economic insecurity*. New York: Oxford University Press.

Blos, P. (1962). *On adolescence: A psychoanalytic interpretation*. New York: The Free Press.

Bly, R. (1991). *Iron John*. Reading, MA: Addison-Wesley.

Bond, M. J. & Feather, N. T. (1988). Some correlates of structure and purpose in the use of time. *Journal of Personality and Social Psychology, 55*, 321–329.

Borman, K. & Reisman, J. (Eds.), (1986). *Becoming a worker*. Norwood, NJ: Ablex.

Bowlby, J. (1980). *Attachment and loss*. New York: Basic Books.

Bowlby, J. (1989). *A secure base: Parent–child attachment and healthy human development,*. New York: Basic Books.

Braddock, II, J. H. & McPartland, J. M. (1987). How minorities continue to be excluded from equal employment opportunities: Research on labor market and institutional barriers. *Journal of Social Issues, 43* (1), 5–39.

Breakwell, G. M., Collie, A., Harrison, B., & Popper, C. (1984). Attitudes toward the unemployed: Effects of threatened identity. *British Journal of Social Psychology, 23*, 87–88.

Brenner, M. H. (1980). Importance of the economy to the nation's health. In L. Eisenberg & A. Kleinman (Eds.). *The relevance of social science for medicine* (pp. 371–395). New York: Reidel.

Brenner, M. H. (1973). *Mental illness and the economy*. Cambridge, MA: Harvard University Press.

Brenner, M. H. (1987). Relation of economic change to Swedish health and social well-being. *Social Science Medicine, 25*, 183–195.

Bridges, W. (1994). *Job-shift: How to prosper in a workplace without jobs*. Reading, MA: Addison-Wesley.

Bridges, W. (1980). *Transitions: Making sense of life's changes*. Reading, MA: Addison-Wesley.

Bronfenbrenner, U. (1979). *The ecology of human development: Experiments by nature and design*. Cambridge, MA: Harvard University Press.

Brumbaugh, R. (1965, June 18). Logic and time. *Review of metaphysics*, 656.

Bruner, J. (1986). *Actual minds, possible worlds*. Cambridge, MA: Harvard University Press.

Burg, J. B. (1955). *The idea of progress*. New York: Dover.

Buss, T. F. & Stevens Redburn, F. (1988). *Hidden unemployment: Discouraged workers and public policy*.

Caminiti, S. (1994a, March 11). From coast to coast, from affluent to poor, poll shows anxiety over jobs. *New York Times*, A1.

Caminiti, S. (1994b, June 13). What happens to laid-off managers. *Fortune*.

Caplan, R. D., Vinokur, A. D., Price, R. H., & Van-Ryn, M., (1989). Job seeking, re-employment, and mental health: A randomized field experiment in coping with job loss. *Journal of Applied Psychology, 74* (5), 759–769.

Carstensen, L. L. (1995). Evidence for a life span theory of socioemotional selectivity. *Current Directions, 4* (5), 151.

Chinoy, E (1955). *Automobile workers and the American dream*. Garden City, NY: Doubleday.

Chodorow, N. & Contratto, C. (1981). The fantasy of the perfect mother. In B. Thorne (Ed.). *Rethinking the family*. New York: Longman.

Cobb, S. (1995). Social support as a moderator of life stress. In A. M. Edward & J. E. Dimsdale (Eds.). *Classics from psychosomatic medicine*, 1959–1979. Washington, DC: American Psychiatric Press.

Cohen, M. (1980). Job training: A Boston bust. *The Boston Globe*.

Coons, P. (1980). Job training plans for young people. *The Boston Globe*.

Cottle, T. J. (1976). *Barred from school*. Washington, DC: New Republic Book.

Cottle, T. J. (1976). *Perceiving time: An investigation with men and women*. New York: Wiley.

Cottle, T. J. (1977). *Private lives and public accounts*. Amherst: University of Massachusetts Press.

Cottle, T. J. (1980). *Children's secrets*. Reading, MA: Addison Wesley.

Cottle, T. J. (1980). *Hidden survivors: Portraits of poor Jews in America*. Englewood Cliffs, NJ: Prentice-Hall.

Cottle, T. J. (1993). Witness of joy. *Daedalus, 122* (1), 123–150.

Cottle, T. J. (1998). *Drawing life: Portraits of adults and children*. Unpublished manuscript.

Cottle, T. J. (in press). *At peril: Stories of injustice*. Amherst: University of Massachusetts Press.

Cowley, M. (1980). *The view from 80*. New York: Penguin.

Craypo, C. & Nissen, B. (Eds.), (1993). *Grand designs: The impact of corporate strategies on workers, unions, and communities*. Ithaca, NY: ILR Press.

Crimmins, J. (1980, March 2). Opening job door for hard core. *The Chicago Tribune*, 10.

Crittenden, A. (1977, April 21). U. S. scientists report effect of economy on mental health. *International Herald Tribune*, 4.

Croddon-Tower, C. (1998). *Exploring child welfare*. Boston: Allyn & Bacon.

Csikszentmihalyi, M. (1996). *Creativity: Flow and the psychology of discovery and invention*. New York: HarperCollins.

Cumming, E. & Henry, W. E. (1961). *Growing old: The process of disengagement*. New York: Basic Books.

de Beauvoir, S. (1972). *Coming of age*. New York: Putnam.

De Volder, M. L. & Lens, W. (1982). Academic achievement and future time perspective as a cognitive-motivational concept. *Journal of Personality and Social Psychology, 42*, 566–571.

Delattre, E. J. (1989). Character and cops-ethics in policing. Washington, DC: American Enterprise Institute for Public Policy Research.

Dew, M., Bromet, E. J., & Penkower, L. (1992). Mental health effects of job loss in women. *Psychological Medicine, 22* (3), 751–764.

Diggs, A. D. (1999). Barrier-breaking resumes and interviews: Jumping the hurdle of unemployment and getting a job. New York: Times Books.

Dionne, E. J., Jr. (1999, June 8). Proof arrives that low unemployment doesn't have to mean inflation. *The Boston Globe*, A15.

Dubin, R. (1973). Work and non-work: Institutional perspectives. In M. D. Dunnette (Ed.), *Work and non-work in the year 2001*. Monterey, CA: Brooks-Cole.

Dudley, K. M. (1994). *The end of the line: Lost jobs, new lives in post industrial America*. Chicago: University of Chicago Press.

Dumanoski, D. (1981, January 11). Youth unemployment: Who's to blame? *The Boston Globe*, C2.

Dupue, R. A. & Monroe, S. M. (1978). Learned helplessness in the perspective of the depressive disorders: Conceptual and definitional issues. *Journal of Abnormal Psychology, 87*, 3–20.

Earle, W. (1972). *The autobiographical consciousness*. Chicago: Quadrangle Books.

Earls, F. & Carlson, C. (1993). Towards sustainable development for American families. In *Daedalus*, 93–121.

Eisner, E. (1991). *The enlightened eye*. New York: MacMillan Publishing Company.

Elder, G. H. (1978). *Children of the great depression*. Chicago: University of Chicago Press.

Elder, G. H. & Caspi, A. (1988). Economic stress in lives: Developmental perspectives. *Journal of Social Issues, 44,* 25–45.

Elkind, D. (1974). Egocentrism in children and adolescents. In *Children and adolescents: Interpretive essays on Jean Piaget.* New York: Oxford University Press.

Elkind, D. (1981). *The hurried child: Growing up too fast too soon.* Reading, MA: Addison Wesley.

Epstein, S. (1989). The self-concept, the traumatic neurosis, and the structure of personality. In D. Ozer, J. M. Healy Jr., & A. J. Stewart (Eds.). *Perspectives on personality.* Greenwich, CT: JAI Press.

Erdelyi, M. H. (1985). *Psychoanalysis: Freud's cognitive psychology.* New York: W. H. Freeman.

Erikson, E. (1978). *Adulthood.* New York: W. W. Norton.

Erikson, E. H. (1950). *Childhood and society.* New York: W. W. Norton.

Erikson, E. H. (1968). *Identity, youth and crisis.* New York: W. W. Norton.

Erikson, K. & Callas, S. P. (Eds.), (1990). *The nature of work: Sociological perspectives.* New Haven: Yale University Press.

Estes, C. P. (1992). *Women who run with the wolves: Myths and stories of the wild woman archtype.* New York: Ballantine Books.

Feagin, J. R. (1972). Poverty: We still believe that God helps those who help themselves. *Psychology Today, 6,* 101–129.

Feather, N. T. (1980). Values in adolescence. In J. Adelson (Ed.), *Handbook of adolescent psychology* (pp. 247–294). New York: Wiley.

Feather, N. T. (1984). Protestant ethic, conservatism, and values. *Journal of Personality and Social Psychology, 46,* 1132–1141.

Feather, N. T. (1989). *The psychological impact of unemployment.* New York: Springer-Verlag.

Feather, N. T. & Barber, J. G. (1983). Depressive reactions and unemployment. *Journal of Abnormal Behavior, 92,* 185–195.

Feather, N. T. & Bond, M. J. (1983). Time structure and purposeful activity among employed and unemployed university graduates. *Journal of Occupational Psychology, 56,* 241–254.

Feather, N. T. & O'Brien, G. E. (1987). Looking for employment: An expectancy-valence analysis of job-seeking behavior among young people. *Journal of Occupational Psychology, 78,* 251–272.

Fine, M. (1991). *Framing dropouts.* Albany: State University of New York Press.

Finkelhor, D. (1995). The victimization of children: A developmental perspective. *American Journal of Orthopsychiatry, 65* (2), 177–193.

Finley, M. H. & Terence, L. A. (1981). The terminated executive: It's like dying. *Personnel and Guidance Journal, 59* (6), 382–384.

Fitzpatrick, M. A. & Vangelisti, A. L. (1995). *Explaining family interactions.* Thousand Oaks, CA: Sage Publications.

Folger, R. (Ed.), (1984). *The sense of injustice: Social psychological perspectives.* New York: Plenum Press.

Fowler, E. M. (1986). Survivors' syndrome in layoffs. *New York Times,* D23.

Frankel, M. (1995, October 22). What the poor deserve. *New York Times Magazine*.

Fraser, J. T. (Ed.), (1966). *The voices of time*. New York: Braziller.

Fraser, R. (1969). *Work: Twenty personal accounts*. London: Penguin.

Freeman, R. R. & Holzer, H. J. (Eds.), (1986). *The Black youth unemployment crisis*. Chicago: University of Chicago Press.

French, J. (1963). The social environment and mental health. *Journal of Social Issues, 19* (4), 39–56.

French, J. & Caplan, R. (1970). Psychological factors in coronary heart disease. *Industrial Medicine, 39* (9).

French, J. R. P., Caplan, R. D., & Van Harrison, R. (1982). *The mechanisms of job stress and strain*. New York: Wiley.

Freud, A. (1946). *The ego and the mechanisms of defense*. New York: International Universities Press.

Freud, S. (1949). *The ego and the id*. London: Hogarth Press.

Freud, S. (1966). *The complete introductory lectures on psychoanalysis*. New York: W. W. Norton.

Freud, S. (1988). *My three mothers and other passions*. New York: New York University Press.

Fried, M. (1973). *The world of the urban working class*. Cambridge, MA: Harvard University Press.

Friedman, L. J. (1999). *Identity's architect: A biography of Erik H. Erikson*. New York: Scribner.

Fritz, M. (1998, December 25). Steelworkers say Clinton's campaign promises have rusted. *The Boston Globe*, A21.

Fromm, E. (1955). *The sane society*. New York: Rinehart.

Frye, N. (1963). *Fables of identity*. New York: Harcourt, Brace and World.

Fryer, D. M. & McKenna, S. P. (1987). The laying off of hands: Unemployment and the experience of time. In S. Fineman (Ed.), *Unemployment: Personal and social consequences*. London: Tavistock.

Furnham, A. (1985). Youth unemployment: A review of the literature. *Journal of Adolescence, 8*, 109–124.

Furnham, A. (1992). The protestant work ethic and attitudes toward unemployment. *Journal of Occupational Psychology, 55*, 277–286.

Galbraith, J. K. (1992). *The culture of contentment*. Boston: Houghton Mifflin.

Garraty, J. A. (1978). *Unemployment in history: Economic thought and public policy*. New York: Harper & Row.

Geertz, C. (1973). *The interpretation of cultures*. New York: Basic Books.

Gelles, R. J. (1987). *Family violence*. Newbury Park, CA: Sage Publications.

Gergen, K. J. (1985). The social constructionist movement in modern psychology. *American Psychologist, 40*, 266–275.

Gilligan, C. (1982). *In a different voice: Psychological theory and women's development*. Cambridge, MA: Harvard University Press.

Gilligan, C., Lyons, N. P., & Hanmer, T. J. (1990). *Making connections: The relational world of adolescent girls at Emma Willard School*. Cambridge, MA: Harvard University Press.

Gitlin, T. & Hollander, N. (1970). *Uptown: Poor Whites in Chicago*. New York: Harper Colophon.

Glasgow, D. C. (1981). *The black underclass: Poverty, unemployment, and the entrapment of ghetto youth*. New York: Vintage Books.

Glassman, J. K. (1997, December 22). Lonely unemployment line. *US News*.

Glick, I. O., Weiss, R. S., & Parkes, C. M. (1974). *The first year of bereavement*. New York: Wiley.

Goffman, E. (1963). *Stigma: Notes on the management of spoiled identity*. Englewood Cliffs, NJ: Prentice-Hall.

Goldberg, A. (1980). *Advances in self-psychology*. New York: International Universities Press.

Goldstein, E. (1984). The ego and its functions. In *Ego psychology and social work practice*. New York: The Free Press.

Gorz, A. (1982). *Farewell to the working class: An essay on post-industrial socialism*. Boston: South End Press.

Gottfredson, D. C. (1985). Youth employment, crime and schooling: A longitudinal study of a national sample. *Developmental Psychology, 21*, 419–432.

Gottfried, A. E. & Gottfried, A. W. (Eds.), (1994). *Redefining families: Implications for children's development*. New York: Plenum Press.

Gould, T. & Kenyon, J. (1972). *Stories from the Dole queue*. London: Temple Smith.

Gowland, G. (1992). *Money, inflation and unemployment: The role of money in the economy*. New York: St. Martin's Press.

Granovetter, M. (1995). *Getting a job*. Chicago: University of Chicago Press.

Greenberger, E. & Steinberg, L. (1986). *When teenagers work*. New York: Basic Books.

Greenson, R. R. (1978). *Explorations in psychoanalysis*. New York: International Universtities Press.

Greve, F. (1977, November 20). Vietnam vets-lost generation. *The Boston Globe*.

Grotevant, H. D. & Cooper, C. R. (1985). Patterns of interaction in family relationships and the development of identity exploration. *Child Development, 56*, 415–428.

Gurney, R. M. (1981). Leaving school, facing unemployment, and making attributions about the causes of unemployment. *Journal of Vocational Behavior, 18*, 79–91.

Hacker, A. (1997). *Money: Who has how much and why*. New York: Scribner.

Hakim, C. (1993). *When you lose your job: Laid off, fired, early retired*. San Francisco: Barrett-Koehler.

Halle, D. (1984). *America's working man*. Chicago: University of Chicago Press.

Hallowell, E. M. (1999). *Connect*. New York: Pantheon.

Halverson, G. (1991, March 28). Professionals join ranks of nation's unemployed. The *Christian Science Monitor*, 1.

Hamilton, V. L., Broman, C. L., Hoffman W. S., & Renner, D. S. (1990). Hard times and vulnerable people: Initial effects of plant closing on auto workers' mental health. *Journal of Health and Social Behavior, 31* (2), 123–140.

Handlin, O. (1951). *The uprooted*. Boston: Little, Brown.

Handelsman, J. (1996). Growing myself. New York: Dutton.

Hansson, R. O., Stroebe, M. S., & Stroebe, W. (Eds.), (1988). Bereavement and widowhood. *Journal of Social Issues*, 44, 3.

Hartup, W. W. & Zubin, R. (1986). *Relationships and development*. Hillsdale, NJ: Lawrence Erlbaum.

Havinghurst, R. (1968). Disengagement and patterns of aging. In B. L. Neugarten (Ed.), *Middle age and aging*. Chicago: University of Chicago Press.

Hawkins, J. (1991, March/April). Rowers on the River Styx. *Harvard Magazine*, 51.

Hayes, J. (1981). *Understanding the unemployed: The psychological effects of unemployment*. New York: Methuen.

Hayes, J. & Nugman, P. (1981). *Understanding the unemployed*. London: Tavistock.

Health, Education, & Welfare Department, (1971). *Work in America* (report of Special Task Force to the Secretary of Health, Education and Welfare). Cambridge, MA: M. I. T. Press.

Heidegger, M. (1962). *Being and time*. New York: Harper & Row.

Heilbroner, R. (1980). *The making of economic society*. Englewood Cliffs, NJ: Prentice-Hall.

Herman, J. (1992). Complex PTSD: A syndrome of survivors of prolonged and repeated trauma. *Journal of Traumatic Stress*, 3 (1), 377–391.

Herman, J. (1992). *Trauma and recovery*. New York: Basic Books.

Hernandez, R. (1998, March 23). Most dropped from welfare don't get jobs. *New York Times*, A1.

Higgens, E. T. (1987). Self-discrepancy: A theory relating self and affect. *Psychological Review*, *94*, 319–340.

Higgins, G. O. (1944). *Resilient adults: Overcoming a cruel past*. San Francisco: Jossey-Bass.

Hildreth, J. (1980, June 5). Stark facts of recession: A bad dream for workers. *Philadelphia Bulletin*.

Hill, J. M. M. (1978, January). The psychological impact of unemployment. *New Society*, 118–120.

Horner, A. J. (1987). The unconscious and the archeology of human relationships. In R. Stern (Ed.), *Theories of the unconscious and the self*. Hillsdale, NY: Analytic Press.

Horowitz, M. J. (1976). *Stress response syndromes*. Northvale, NJ: Jason Aronson.

Horowitz, M. J., Wilner, N., Kaltreider, N., & Alvarez, W. (1980). Signs and symptoms of posttraumatic stress disorder. *Archives of General Psychiatry*, *37*, 85–92.

Howard, G. S. (1991). Culture tales: A narrative approach to thinking, cross-cultural psychology, and psychotherapy. *American Psychologist*, *46* (3), 187–197.

Hunsaker Hawkins, A. (1993). *Reconstructing illness: Studies in pathography*. West Lafayette, IN: Purdue University Press.

Israeli, N. (1935). Distress in the outlook of Lancashire and Scottish unemployed. *Journal of Applied Psychology*, *19*, 67–69.

Jackson, D. Z. (1999, January 20). Creating, not curbing, poverty. *The Boston Globe*, A15.

Jackson, M. P. (1985). *Youth unemployment*. London: Croom Helm.

Jackson, P. R. & Warr, P. B. (1987). Mental health of unemployed men in different parts of England and Wales. *British Medical Journal, 295*, 525.

Jackson, P. R., Stafford, E. M., Banks, M. H., & Warr, P. B. (1983). Unemployment and psychological distress in young people: The moderating role of employment commitment. *Journal of Applied Psychology, 68*, 525–535.

Jahoda, M, (1981). Work, employment and unemployment: Values, theories and approaches in social research. *American Psychologist, 36*, 184–191.

Jahoda, M. (1982). *Employment and unemployment: A social psychological analysis.* New York: Cambridge University Press.

Jahoda, M. (1988). Economic recession and mental health: Some conceptual issues. *Journal of Social Issues, 4*, 13–23.

Janoff-Bulman, R. (1979). Characterological versus behavioral self-blame. *Journal of Personality and Social Psychology, 37*, 1798–1809.

Janoff-Bulman, R. (1985). The aftermath of victimization: Rebuilding shattered assumptions. In C. R. Figley (Ed.), *Trauma and its wake: The study and treatment of posttraumatic stress disorder* (pp. 15–35). New York: Brunner/Mazel.

Jencks, C. & Peterson, P. E. (Eds.), (1991). *The urban underclass.* Washington, DC: Brookings Institute.

Judis, J. B. (1993, March 15). The jobless recovery. *The New Republic*, 20–23.

Kalish, R. A. (1985). *Death, grief, and caring relationships.* Monterey, CA: Brooks-Cole.

Karasek, R & Tores T. T. (1990). *Healthy work.* New York: Basic Books.

Kardiner, A. (1959). Traumatic neuroses of war. In S. Arieti (Ed.), *American handbook of psychiatry* (Vol. 1, p. 256). New York: Basic Books.

Kasl, S. & Cooper, C. (Eds.), (1987). *Stress and health: Issues in research methodology.* New York: Wiley.

Kasl, S. V. (1982). Strategies of research on economic instability and health. *Psychological Medicine, 12*, 637–649.

Kasl, S. V. & Cobb, S. (1982). Variability of stress effects among men experiencing job loss. In L. Goldberger & S. Breznitz (Eds.), *Handbook of stress: Theoretical and clinical aspects.* New York: The Free Press.

Katz, M. (Ed.), (1993). *The underclass debate: Views from history.* Princeton, NJ: Princeton University Press.

Kaufman, G. (1989). *The psychology of shame.* New York: Springer.

Kaufman, H. (1980). *Shame: The power of caring.* Cambridge, MA: Schenkman.

Kegan, R. (1982). *The evolving self.* Cambridge, MA: Harvard University Press.

Keil, C. (1966). *Urban blues.* Chicago: University of Chicago Press.

Kelvin, P. & Jarrett, J. E. (1985). *Unemployment: Its social psychological effects.* Cambridge, MA: Cambridge University Press.

Keniston, K. (1977). *All our children: The American family under pressure.* New York: Harcourt Brace and Jovanovich.

Kessler, R. C., Price, R. H., & Wortman, C. B. (1985). Social factors in psychopathology: Stress, social support, and coping process. *Annual Review of Psychology, 36*, 531–572.

Kessler, R. C., Turner, J. B., & House, J. S. (1987). Unemployment and health in a community sample. *Journal of Health and Social Behavior, 58*, 51–59.

Kessler, R. C., Turner, J. B., & House, J. S. (1987). Intervening processes in the relationship between unemployment and health. *Psychological Medicine, 17,* 949–961.

Kline Hunnicutt, B. (1996). *Kellogg's six-hour day.* Philadelphia: Temple University Press.

Kobasa, S. C., Maddi, S., & Kahn, S. (1982). Hardiness and health: A prospective study. *Journal of Personality and Social Psychology, 42,* 168–177.

Kohlberg, L. (1981). *Essays on moral development.* San Francisco: Harper and Row.

Kohlberg, L. & Gilligan, C. (1971). The adolescent as a philosopher. The discovery of the self in a post-conventional world. In J. Kagar & R. Coles, 12–16: Early adolescence. New York: W. W. Norton, 1972, 144–179.

Kohut, H. (1978). Thoughts on narcissism and narcissistic rage. In *Search for the self: Selected writings of Heinz Kohut Vol. 2,* 615–658. New York: International Universities Press.

Kohut, H. (1978). *Search for the self. Selected writings of Heinz Kohut,Vol. 2.* New York: International Universities Press.

Kohut, H. (1987). *The Kohut seminars: On self-psychology and psychotherapy with adolescents and young adults.* New York: Norton.

Komarovsky, M. (1971). *The unemployed man and his family. The effect of unemployment upon the status of the man in 59 families.* New York: Arno Press.

Kornhauser, A. (1965). *Mental health and the industrial worker.* New York: Wiley.

Kotre, J. (1995). *White gloves: How we create ourselves through memory.* New York: The Free Press.

Kozol, J. (1988). *Rachel and her children: Homeless families in America.* New York: Crown.

Kreppner, K. & Lerner, R. M. (1989). *Family systems and life span development.* Hillsdale, NJ: Lawrence Erlbaum.

Kubler-Ross, E. (1969). *On death and dying.* New York: MacMillan.

Kunzier, T. (1998). *Revealing the mystic cipher.* Unpublished manuscript, Boston University, Boston.

Langner, T. S. & Michael, S. T. (1963). *Life stress and mental health.* New York: The Free Press.

Larmore, C. (1999). Moral basis of political liberalism. *The Journal of Philosophy, XCVI* (12), 599–625.

Lawrence-Lightfoot, S. (1989). *Balm in Gilead.* Reading, MA: Addison Wesley.

Lawrence-Lightfoot, S. & Hoffman Davis, J. (1997). *The art and science of portraiture.* San Francisco: Jossey Bass.

Layton, L. & Schapiro, B.A. (Eds.), (1986). *Narcissisism and the text: Studies in literature and the psychology of self.* New York: New York University Press.

Lazarus, R. S. (1966). *Psychological stress and the coping process.* New York: McGraw-Hill.

Lazarus, R. S. & Folkman, S. (1984). *Stress, appraisal, and coping.* New York: Springer-Verlag.

Leana, C. R. (1992). Coping with job loss: *How individuals, organizations and communities respond to layoffs.* New York: Lexington Books.

Lecht, L. A. (1969). *Manpower needs for national goals in the 1970's*. New York: Praeger.

Lemann, N. (1992). The promised land: *The great Black migration and how it changed America*. New York: Vintage Books.

Lens, W. (1986). Future time perspective: A cognitive-motivational concept. In D. R. Brown & J. Veroff (Eds.). *Frontiers of motivational psychology: Essays in honor of John W. Atkinson* (pp. 173–190). New York: Springer-Verlag.

Lerner, M. J. (1980). The belief in a just world. New York: Plenum Press.

Leventman, P. G. (1976). Nonrational foundations of professional rationality: Employment instability among scientists and technologists. *Sociological Symposium, 16*, 83–112.

Leventman, P. G. (1981). *Professionals out of work*. New York: The Free Press.

Levine, S. & Scotch, N. (1971). *Social stress*. Chicago: Aldine.

Levinson, D. (1978). *Seasons of a man's life*. New York: Knopf.

Lewis, O. (1959). *Five families*. New York: Basic Books.

Liebow, E. (1967). *Tally's corner*. Boston: Little Brown.

Liem, R. & Liem, J. H. (1988). Psychological effects of unemployment on workers and their families. *Journal of Social Issues, 44*, 87–105.

Lifton, R. J. (1973). *Home from the war*. New York: Simon & Schuster.

Lifton, R. J. & Olson, E. (1976). The human meaning of total disaster: The Buffalo Creek experience. *Psychiatry, 39*, 1–18.

Lindemann, E. (1944). Symptomatology and management of acute grief. *American Journal of Psychiatry, 101*, 141–148.

Linn, M. W., Sandifer, R., & Stein, S. (1985). Effects of unemployment on mental and physical health. *American Journal of Public Health, 75*, 502–506.

Lowry, L. (1998). Interview. The Boston Globe, 11ff.

Lopata, H. Z. (1973). *Widowhood in an American city*. Cambridge, MA: Schenkman.

Loth, R. (1991, March 24). A jobless pool that's different. *The Boston Globe*, A17.

Lynch, J. (1977). *The Broken Heart: The medical consequences of loneliness*. New York: Basic Books.

Lynch, M. C. (1981, December 7). As recession deepens, white-collar workers join the jobless ranks. *The Wall Street Journal*, 1.

Mallinckrodt, B. & Fretz, B. R. (1988). Social support and the impact of job loss on older professionals. *Journal of Counseling Psychology, 35* (3), 281–286.

March, J. S., Amaya-Jackson, L., & Pynoos, R. S. (1997). Pediatric stress disorder. In *Textbook of child and adolescent psychiatry*, (2nd ed.). Washington, DC: American Psychiatric Press.

Mariotti, M. (1971). Working conditions and manner of aging. Paris: International center of social gerontology.

Markus, H. & Nurius, P. (1986). Possible selves. *American Psychologist, 41*, 954–969.

Marris, P. (1986). *Loss and change*. New York: Routledge.

Marris, P. (1991). *Attachment across the life cycle*. London: Tavistock/ Routledge.

Marsden, D. & Euan Duff, E. (1975). *Workless*. London: Pelican.

May, R. (1983). *The discovery of being*. New York: W. W. Norton.

McCann, I. L. & Pearlman, L. A. (1989). Vicarious traumatization: A framework for understanding the psychological effects of working with victims. *Journal of Traumatic Stress, 3* (1), 131–149.

McCann, I. L., Sakheim, D. K., & Abrahamson, D. J. (1988). Trauma and victimization: A model of psychological adaptation. *Counseling Psychologist, 16,* 531–594.

McCourt, F. (1996). *Angela's ashes.* New York: Scribner.

McKee, L. & Bell, C. (1986). His unemployment, her problem: The domestic and marital consequences of male unemployment. In C. Allen, A. Waton, K. Purcell, & S. Woods (Eds.), *The experience of unemployment.* London: Macmillan, 134–149.

McKenna, S. P. & Fryer, D. M. (1984). Perceived health during lay-off and early unemployment. *Occupational Health, 36,* 201–206.

McLean, A. (1970). *Mental health and work organizations.* Indianapolis: Rand McNally.

Mead, L. (1981). *The new politics of poverty: The non-working poor in America.* New York: Basic Books.

Merleau-Ponty, M. (1963). *The structure of behavior.* Boston: Beacon Press.

Miller, R. C. (1999). *Matthew's story: The reintegration of a child with emotional and behavioral disabilities from a private to public school.* Unpublished doctoral dissertation, Boston University, School of Education, Boston.

Miller, S. M. & Ferroggiaro, K. M. (1996). Respect. *Poverty & Race, 5* (1), 1.

Minuchin, P., Colapinto, J., & Minuchin, S. (1998). *Working with families of the poor.* New York: Guilford.

Minuchin, S. (1974). *Families and family therapy.* Cambridge, MA: Harvard University Press.

Minuchin, S. (1984). *Family kaleidoscope.* Cambridge, MA: Harvard University Press.

Mirels, H. L. & Garrett, J. B. (1971). The protestant ethic as a personality variable. *Journal of Consulting and Clinical Psychology, 36,* 40–44.

Mischel, L. & Frankel, D. M. (1991). *The state of working America, 1990–1991 Edition.* Armonk, NY: Economic Policy Institute.

Mishel, L., Schmitt, J., & Bernstein, J. (1993). *The state of working America.* Armonk, NY: ME Sharpe.

Moberg, D. (1999, October 16). Most young workers have missed out on the boom. *The Boston Globe,* A21.

Morgan, J. (1991). Primary prevention of child maladjustment: Real-world efforts in a community mental health setting. *The Child, Youth, and Family Services Quarterly, 14* (1), 7.

Morrison, A. P. (1996). *The culture of shame.* New York: Ballantine.

Moustakas, C. (1961). *Loneliness.* New York: Prentice Hall.

Mroczek, D. K. & Kolarz, C. M. (1998). The effect of age on positive and negative affect: A developmental perspective on happiness. *Journal of Personality and Social Psychology, 75* (5), 1333–49.

Nathanson, D. L. (1987). *The many faces of shame.* New York: Guilford.

Neugarten, B. L. (Ed.), (1968). *Middle age and aging.* Chicago: University of Chicago Press.

Neugarten, B. L. & Weinstein, K. K. (1964). The changing American grandparent. *Journal of Marriage and the Family, 26* (2), 199–206.

Newman, K. (1988). *Falling from grace: The experience of downward mobility in the American middle class.* New York: The Free Press.

Newman, K. (1999). *No shame in my game: The working poor in the inner city.* New York: Knopf.

Nissen, B. (1995). *Case studies of labor-community coalitions confronting plant closings.* Albany: State University of New York Press.

Noer, D. M. (1993). *Healing the wounds.* San Francisco: Jossey-Bass.

Nolan, T. W. (1999). *Character education for police officers: Station house as moral milieu.* Unpublished manuscript, Boston University, Boston.

Nuttin, J. (1985). *Future time perspective and motivation.* Hillsdale, NJ: Lawrence Erlbaum.

Orwell, G. (1958). *The road to wigan pier.* New York: Harcourt, Brace, Jovanovich.

Osherson, S. (1986). *Finding our fathers.* New York: The Free Press.

Osterman, P. (1980). *Getting started: The youth labor market.* Cambridge, MA: MIT Press.

Owen, J. D. (1989). *Reduced working hours: Cure for unemployment or economic burden.* Baltimore, MD: Johns Hopkins Press.

Owens, K. (1993). *The world of the child.* New York: Macmillan.

Eisenberg, P. & Lazarsfeld, P. F. (1938). The psychological effects of unemployment. *Psychological Bulletin, 35*, 358–390.

Palmore, E. (1969). Physical, mental, and social factors in predicting longevity. *Gerontology, 9* (2), 103–108.

Palmore, E. (1969). Predicting longevity: A follow-up controlling for age. *Gerontology, 9* (4), 247–250.

Palmore, E. (1981). *The perceptions and attitudes of some urban, unemployed Black youth regarding the extrinsic/intrinsic utility of a world of work.* Unpublished doctoral thesis, Boston University, Boston.

Pappas, G. (1989). *The magic city: Unemployment in a working class community.* Ithaca, NY: Cornell University Press.

Parkes, C. M. & Weiss, R. S. (1983). *Recovery from bereavement.* New York: Basic Books.

Payne, R. L., Warr, P. B., & Hartley, J. (1984). Social class and psychological ill-health during unemployment. *Sociology of Health and Illness, 6*, 152–174.

Pearlin, L. J. & Schooler, C. (1978). The structure of coping. *Journal of Health and Social Behavior, 19*, 2–21.

Pepitone, A. (1967). Self, social environment, and stress. In M. H. Appley & D. Trumbull (Eds.), *Psychological stress.* New York: Appleton-Century-Crofts.

Peterson, C., Schwartz, S. M., & Seligman, M. E. P. (1981). Self-blame and depressive symptoms. *Journal of Personality and Social Psychology, 41*, 253–259.

Peterson, W. (1994). *Silent depression: The fate of the American dream.* New York: Norton.

Phillips, A. (1994). *The trouble with boys.* New York: Basic Books.

Piers, G. & Singer, M. B. (1971). *Shame and guilt.* New York: Norton.

Podgursky, M. (1984, July). Sources of secular increases in the unemployment rate. *Monthly Labor Review,* 1969–1982.

Polkinghorne, D. E. (1988). *Narrative knowing and the human sciences.* Albany: State University of New York Press.

Pollack, W. (1998). *Real boys: Rescuing our sons from the myths of boyhood.* New York: Random House.

Pollock, W. & Levant, R. (Eds.), (1995). *A new psychology of men.* New York: Basic Books.

Polner, R. (1996a, January 23). Cuts vex young workers, *New York Newsday,* A5.

Polner, R. (1996b, June 11). Youth suicide said to rise in Europe. *New York Times,* A6.

Price, R. H. (1992). Psychosocial impact of job loss on individuals and families. *Current Directions in Psychological Science, 1* (1), 9–11.

Prokosch, M. (1978, July 6). Summer jobs unequally distributed. Bay State Banner, 11ff.

Pulley, M. L. (1997). *Losing your job-reclaiming your soul.* San Francisco: Jossey-Bass.

Eth, S. & Pynoos, R. (Eds.), (1985). Post-traumatic stress disorder in children. Washington, DC: American Psychiatric Press.

Rifkin, J. (1995). *The end of work: The decline of the global labor force and the dawn of the post-market era.* New York: Jeremy P. Tarcher/Putnam Book.

Roediger, D. & Philip Foner, F. (1989). *Our own time: A history of American labor and the working day.* Westport: Greenwood Press.

Rosenberg, M. (1979). *Conceiving the self.* New York: Basic Books.

Rosenberg, M. (1981). The self-concept: Social product and social force. In M. Rosenberg & R. H. Turner, (Eds.), *Social psychology: Sociological perspectives.* New York: Basic Books.

Roy, H. (1998). *Inclusion: Voices from the inside.* Unpublished manuscript, Boston University, Boston.

Ryan, W. (1972). *Blaming the victim.* New York: Random House.

Sales, S. M. (1969). Organizational roles as a risk factor in coronary heart disease. *Administrative Science Quarterly 14* (3).

Sanger, D. E. & Lohr, S. (1996, March 9). A search for answers to avoid the lay-offs. *New York Times,* 11.

Sarton, M. (1973). *As we are now.* New York: W. W. Norton.

Schafer, R. (1967). Ideals, the ego ideal, and the ideal self. *Psychological Issues, 5,* 131–174.

Schaffer, R. (1977). Mothering as interlocution. From *Mothering* (pp. 61–77). Cambridge, MA: Harvard University Press.

Schlozman, K. L. (1979). *Injury to insult: Unemployment, class, and political response.* Cambridge, MA: Harvard University Press.

Schor, J. (1991). *The overworked American: The unexpected decline of leisure.* New York: Basic Books.

Schwarz, J. E. & Volgy, T. J. (1995). *The forgotten Americans*. New York: Norton, 1992.

Seib, G. F. (1980). Recessions cause death rates to rise, as pressures of coping take hold. *The Wall Street Journal*, 13.

Shamir, B. (1986). Self-esteem and the psychological impact of unemployment. *Social Psychological Quarterly, 49*, 61–72.

Shannon, C. L. (1989). *The politics of the family*. New York: Peter Lang.

Sifford, D. (1980, March 25). The right job: A life saver. *The Boston Globe*.

Silver, R. L. & Wortman, C. B. (1980). Coping with undesirable life events. In J. Garber and M. E. P. Seligman (Eds.), *Human helplessness: Theory and applications*. New York: Academic Press.

Slater, P. E. (1970). *The pursuit of loneliness*. Boston: Beacon Press.

Solow, R. M. & Taylor, J. B. with an introduction by B. M. Friedman, (1998). *Inflation, unemployment, and monetary policy*. Cambridge, MA: MIT Press.

Stafford, E. M., Jackson, P. R., & Banks, M. H. (1980). Employment, work involvement and mental health in less qualified young people. *Journal of Occupational Psychology, 53*, 291–304.

Stake, R. E. (1995). *The art of case study research*. Thousand Oaks, CA: Sage.

Stern, D. & Eichorn, D. (Eds.), (1989). *Adolescence and work*. Hillsdale, NJ: Lawrence Erlbaum.

Stevenson, R. W. (1999, November 21). For the jobless rate, the forecast is hazy. *The New York Times*.

Straus, M. (1999). *No talk therapy*. New York: Norton.

Strauss, M. A. & Gelles, R. J. (1981). *Behind closed doors*. Garden City, NY: Anchor Books.

Swartz, T. R. & K. Maas (Eds.), *America's Working Poor*. South Bend, IN: University of Notre Dame Press.

Summers, L. (1990). *Understanding unemployment*. Cambridge, MA: MIT Press.

Taylor, S. E. (1983). Adjustment to threatening events: A theory of cognitive adaptation. *American Psychologist*. 1161–1173.

The New York Times, (1996). *The downsizing of America*. New York: Times Book.

The Pilgrim Trust, (1938). *Men without work*. Cambridge, MA: Cambridge University Press.

Thernstrom, S. (1968). Urbanization, migration, and social mobility in late nineteenth-century America. In J. Barton (Ed.) (pp. 158–175). *Towards a new past: Dissenting essays in American history*. New York: Pantheon, 158–175.

Thomas, K. (Ed.), (1999). *The oxford book of work*. New York: Oxford University Press.

Thomas, P. (1967). *Down these mean streets*. New York: Knopf.

Thurow, L. C. (1999, April 20). Jobless figures deceptive. *The Boston Globe*, C4.

Tiffany, D. W., Cowan, J. R., & Tiffany, P. M. (1971). *Unemployed: A social psychological portrait*. New York: Prentice-Hall.

Tiggemann, M. & Winefield, A. H. (1984). The effects of employment on the mood, self-esteem, locus of control, and depressive affect of school-leavers. *Journal of Occupational Psychology, 57*, 33–42.

Tilgher, A. (1930). *Work: What it has meant to men thorough the ages*. New York: Harcourt Brace.

Uchitelle L. & Kleinfield, N. R. (1996, March 3). On the battlefields of business, millions of casualties. *The New York Times*, 1ff.

Ullah, P., Banks, M. H., & Warr, P. B. (1985). Social support, social pressures and psychological distress during unemployment. *Psychological Medicine*, *15*, 283–295.

Valliant, G. (1977). *Adaptation to life*. Boston: Little Brown.

van der Kolk, B. A. (Ed.), (1987). *Psychological trauma*. Washington, DC: American Psychiatric Press.

Voydanoff P. & Donnelly, B. W. (Eds.), (1988). *Families and economic distress: Coping strategies and social policy*. Beverly Hills, CA: Sage.

Wagner, M. (1989). Youth and disabilities during transition: An overview and description of findings from the National Longitudinal Transition Study. In J. Chadsey-Rusch (Ed.), *Transition Institute at Illinois: Project Director's Fourth Annual Meeting* (pp. 24–52). Champaign: University of Illinois.

Walsh, F. (1982). Conceptualizations of normal family functioning. In F. Walsh (Ed.), *Normal family process*. New York: Guilford.

Walters, M., Carter, W., Pap P., & Silverstein, O. (1988). *The invisible web: Gender patterns in family relationships*. New York: Guilford Press.

Warr, P. B. (1984a). Job loss, unemployment and psychological well-being. In V. Allen & E. van de Vliert (Eds.), *Role transitions* (pp. 263–285). New York: Plenum.

Warr, P. B. (1984b). Reported behavior changes after job loss. *British Journal of Social Psychology*, *23*, 271–275.

Warr, P. B., Banks, M. H., & Ullah, P. (1985). The experience of unemployment among Black and White urban teenagers. *British Journal of Psychology*, *76*, 75–87.

Warr, P. B., Jackson, P. R., & Banks, M. H. (1982). Duration of unemployment and psychological well-being in young men and women. *Current Psychological Research*, *2*, 207–214.

Weber, M. (1968). *Economy and society*. New York: Bedminster Press.

Websters New World Dictionary of the American Language, (1957). New York: The World Publishing Company.

Weinstein, F. (In press). *Freud, psychoanalysis, social theory: The unredeemed promise*. Albany: State University of New York Press.

Weiss, R. S. (1975). *Loneliness: The experience of emotional and social isolation*. Cambridge, MA: MIT Press.

Weiss, R. S. (1990). *Staying the course: The emotional and social lives of men who do well at work*. New York: The Free Press.

Weiss, R. S. (1996). Responding to the mental health implications of downsizing. Unpublished manuscript.

Wells, L. E. & Marwell, G. (1976). *Self-esteem: Its conceptualization and measurement*. Beverly Hills, CA: Sage.

Weiss, R. S. & Parkes, C. M. (1983). *Recovery from bereavement.* New York: Basic Books.

Wells, M. (1980). To your good health. *Labor News, 35* (40).

Westin, S. (1990). The structure of a factory closure: Individual responses to job loss and unemployment in a ten-year controlled follow-up study. *Social Science and Medicine, 31* (12), 1301–1311

Wilson, W. J. (1987). *The truly disadvantaged: The inner city, the underclass, and public policy.* Chicago: University of Chicago Press.

Wilson, W. J. (1996). *When work disappears: The world of the urban poor.* New York: Knopf.

Wolf, E. S. (1978). *Treating the self: Elements of clinical self-psychology.* New York: Guilford.

Wolf, M. E. & Mosnaim, A. D. (Eds.), (1990). *Post-traumatic stress disorder: etiology, phenomenology, and treatment.* Washington, DC: American Psychiatric Press.

Yehuda, R. (1999). *Risk factors for posttraumatic stress.* Washington, DC: American Psychiatric Press.

Yehuda, R. & McFarlane, A. C. (1995). Conflict between current knowledge about posttraumatic stress disorder and its original conceptual basis. *American Journal of Psychiatry, 152* (12), 1705–1713.

York-Barr, J., Schultz, T., Doyle, M. B., Kronberg, R., & Crossett, S. (1996). Inclusive schooling in St. Cloud: Perspectives on the process and people. *Remedial and Special Education, 17* (2), 92–105.

Young, A. (1966). Suffering and the origins of traumatic memory. *Daedalus, 125* (1), 245–260.

Young, A. (1995). *The harmony of illusions: Inventing posttraumatic stress disorder.* Princeton, NJ: Princeton University Press.

Zawadski, B. & Lazarsfeld, P. F. (1935). The psychological consequences of unemployment. *Journal of Social Psychology, 6,* 224–251.

Zippay, A. (1991). *From middle income to poor: Downward mobility among displaced steel workers.* New York: Praeger.

Index

acceptance, as coping state, 264
accomplish vicariously, in role
  satisfaction, 259–60
"Activity Theory of Aging," 260–61
African-Americans, 4, 16–17, 145–46,
  150–51, 155
Agee, James, x
agentic thinking and acting, 205, 223,
  244
Albee, George, 201
Albelda, Randy, 284
alterations
  in affect regulation, 275
  in perceptions of the perpetrator,
    276
  in relationships with others, 276
  in self-perception, 275
  in system of meaning, 277
American dream, so-called, 25–26, 183
American Psychological Association
  (APA), 28–29
Anderson, Elijah, 4, 150
anger, as coping stage, 263
Applebaum, Herbert, 25
attachment theory, 194–95
autobiographical memory system, 6
autonomy, as element of happiness,
  260

Bakan, David, 244, 273–74
bargaining, as coping stage, 264
Barthes, Roland, 244
Beane, Arthur, 32
Becker, Joseph, 17
Bell, Daniel, 262
Bellin, Seymour, 283–84

bereavement, 263–70
Berkell, Dianne, 146
biological renewal or continuity, in
  role significance, 259
Blake, Artie, 271
Blau, Joel, 3
blue-collar workers, 18
Blum, Jack, 285
Boston Globe, The, 4–5
Boston University of Medicine,
  21
Bowlby, John, 195, 269
Brenner, Dr., Harvey, 20
Bridges, William, 200–01
Brill, Dr., Peter L., 29
British Labour Party, Greater London
  Council, 177
"Broken Heart, The," 172
Bronfenbrenner, Urie, 275
Bruner, Jerome, 31
Buber, Martin, 266
Buddhism, 265

cancer. See, Unemployment, physical
  and psychological effects.
Carstensen, Laura, 261
Carter, Jimmy, 17
CEO salaries, 13
Chinoy, Ely, 25
chronosystem, 275
communal orientation, 274
competencies, 201–02
Comprehensive Employment and
  Training Act (CETA), 147
constitutional vulnerability, 201
continuity, in role satisfaction, 259–60

ABOUT THE AUTHOR

THOMAS J. COTTLE is Professor of Education at Boston University. He was written over twenty-five books, including *Private Lives and Public Accounts, A Family Album, Children in Jail, Children's Secrets, Hidden Survivors, Time's Children, Like Fathers, Like Sons, Barred from School, Perceiving Time, Black Children-White Dreams*, and *Black Testimony*. His work has appeared in many scholarly journals as well as mainstream media.